American
state political parties
and elections

The Dorsey Series in Political Science

Consulting Editor   SAMUEL C. PATTERSON   *University of Iowa*

# American
# state political parties
# and elections ☆☆☆

MALCOLM E. JEWELL
*University of Kentucky*

DAVID M. OLSON
*University of North Carolina
at Greensboro*

1978

**The Dorsey Press**

Homewood, Illinois 60430

Irwin-Dorsey Limited   Georgetown, Ontario   L7G 4B3

ISBN 0-256-02053-1
Library of Congress Catalog Card No. 77–085796
*Printed in the United States of America*

1 2 3 4 5 6 7 8 9 0 ML 5 4 3 2 1 0 9 8

# Preface

The purpose of this book is to compare the political party and elections systems in the 50 states. Most of us who study or teach state politics or who practice it know much more about the operation of the political system in our own state than in any other. We have discovered that students who have learned something about their own state's political system usually make one of two incorrect assumptions about the politics of other states: either that the patterns and style of politics throughout the United States are just about the same as they are in their own state, or else that their state's political system is somehow unique. Practitioners are usually so wrapped up in the political practices that have become familiar to them that it does not occur to them that other approaches might be feasible or even work better. Even those scholars who study, teach, and write about state politics often seem to be oblivious to its comparative dimensions. Too often studies of politics in a state seem to have been written in a vacuum, without any understanding of whether the practices they describe are typical, unique to that state, or perhaps are ones that fit into one of several patterns of politics found among the states.

Our purpose is to enable those who are familiar with politics in one state to place it in perspective, and so to better understand it. Compared to other states, how competitive are the parties, how strong and effective are the party organizations, how broadly based is political competition in the state? More broadly speaking, our purpose is to identify the most important dimensions of political systems on which the states differ and to classify the states along these dimensions. The next step is to try to determine why these differences have arisen and to identify significant trends in political systems among the states.

In a sense, of course, the political system in each U.S. state is unique. It has a history all its own, from the earliest days of its settlement to its most recent elections. Each state has its own folk heroes and famous political leaders, from Henry Clay to "Happy" Chandler in Kentucky, from Sam Houston to Lyndon Johnson in Texas, from John Adams to John Kennedy in Massachusetts. When we talk about the politics of our own state, we tend to talk in terms of personalities and recent events such as crucial elections. There are differences in geography, economic characteristics, and ethnic and religious variables that we take for granted, but that make each state different from all the others. When we try to explain the reasons for political practices and norms in our state, we are likely to speak in very particularistic terms and to ignore political patterns that may be common to other states. The job of the student of comparative state politics is not to ignore these particularistic characteristics but to try to find patterns in them when comparisons are made with other states. The legacy of Huey Long is unique to Louisiana, but there may be other states in which the factional structure of a dominant party has been shaped for many years by one leader.

There are political and social trends at work that have effects on all of the states, and some of these trends are having a nationalizing effect on our politics, making the contrasts among the states less sharp than they were a generation ago. But these trends have not obliterated the differences among the states nor made it less important to understand what these differences are. If anything, it may be more important to understand why these differences persist in the face of nationalizing trends.

Students taking courses that cover state politics have greater opportunities for research than are found in many political science courses. They have access to state and local election data and census figures; they can rely on state newspapers for description and analysis of politics; and they have opportunities for interviewing and observing political practitioners. We believe that this book can facilitate such research in at least two ways. We provide a number of examples of research, based on various kinds of data from one or a few individual states; these studies can be replicated in other states or brought up to date in the same states. We also provide a number of tables comparing the states on a variety of dimensions: levels of party competition, divided control of government, primary competition and turnout, and presidential primaries, for example. This enables students to compare their state with others, to try to explain the differences, and to compile further data along the same lines: for local levels of government, other elected offices, or other years. This volume should be useful not only because it helps students put the politics of their own state into comparative perspective, but because it suggests productive lines of first-hand exploration into state parties and elections.

## ACKNOWLEDGMENTS

We are indebted to a number of persons and organizations for assistance in preparing this book. The *Western Political Quarterly* has permitted us to use in Chapter 4 some of the tables and text from an article by Professor Jewell in its June 1977 issue. For making available various kinds of unpublished electoral data, we are indebted to the Inter-University Consortium for Political Research, the Congressional Quarterly, and the secretaries of state or electoral commissions in a number of states.

Acknowledgment is due to Charles Bell for his contribution of patronage data to Chapter 3, and to James Seroka for a critical review of the same chapter. Professor Olson wishes to thank the students in his "Workshop in Practical Politics" course for their knowledge and enthusiasm about campaign politics. Thanks are due to numerous colleagues in the field of political science who have answered our queries about political practices in their states, as well as to countless anonymous practicing politicians who have provided insight and information about the conduct and organization of state politics around the nation.

We are particularly indebted to Samuel C. Patterson for reading the manuscript and providing helpful comments.

December 1977 **Malcolm E. Jewell**
**David M. Olson**

# Contents

# 1 ★ ★ ★

# State political systems in a national setting ★ ★ ★

Each of the 50 states has a political system that is unique and distinctive. At the same time, state political systems are affected by national political forces and by many of the characteristics of the U.S. political system. Our job in this chapter is to untangle the state and national political systems, to show in what respects the states are different, and to show how they are influenced by national trends and traditions.

## DISTINCTIVE CHARACTERISTICS OF STATE POLITICAL SYSTEMS

### Constitutional and legal factors

Anyone who undertook the arduous task of reading the 50 state constitutions would find many similarities, but would also find some important differences. Some of the constitutions are relatively brief, and others are so detailed that large numbers of amendments must be

1

adopted every year or two. Some were originally drafted in the early
19th century, many were drafted or thoroughly revised in the late 19th
century, and a few have been completely rewritten within recent years.
Although all of them establish three branches of government in very
similar forms, there are some important differences. Some give governors a four-year term, and a few only two years; some place restrictions on consecutive gubernatorial terms. The amount of authority
over the executive branch granted to the governor varies significantly.
Legislatures vary in size, the upper house from 19 to 58, and the lower
house from 39 to 400. Some constitutions restrict the length of legislative sessions or the frequency of such sessions, while an increasing
number let the legislature meet whenever it wants. Some states limit
the scope of legislative power by providing for the initiative and/or
the referendum. Such constitutional provisions establish the framework for the distribution of political power in a state and help to explain some of the differences in the operation of political systems.

Statutory law has a less enduring effect on the political system because it can be more easily changed, but its impact can be just as great.
Such laws, of course, even more than the constitution, reflect the
preferences of the dominant political forces in the state. If state law,
for example, makes it difficult for third-party or independent candidates to get on the ballot, we may assume that this law results from—
while it helps to perpetuate—two-party domination of state politics.
Some states impose rather detailed control over the structure and
activities of party organizations, while others have a minimum of regulatory legislation. As we shall explain more fully in chapter 4, the
operation of state primaries and nominating conventions is very much
affected by laws concerning who can vote in the primaries and how
much of a voice the party can have in nominations. The timing of elections is, of course, a matter of law. It makes a difference whether the
governor is elected in a presidential election year, in a congressional
election year, or at some other time, and whether local officials are
elected when state officers are. Constitutional and statutory laws on
legislative apportionment and districting determine how popular votes
are translated into seats and may significantly affect the balance of
legislative power between and within parties. Although the Supreme
Court's decisions on apportionment have severely limited the states'
freedom of choice in this field, districting legislation still has an effect
on political power. The use of nonpartisan elections in many local
governments weakens the local power base of the parties. In the past,
before the Supreme Court intervened to protect voting rights, the

shape of the political system was very much affected by laws in many states that restricted the franchise or made it difficult to register and vote. Even today, differences in registration requirements can affect the size and makeup of the electorate.

This list is not exhaustive, but it is long enough to demonstrate that the states have reached a variety of decisions on such questions as who can vote, when they can vote, whether primaries are open or closed, how long officials can serve, which candidates are chosen on a partisan ballot, how many elected officials there are, and what kinds of issues are submitted to the voters for a decision. Although many of these political ground rules take the form of statutes rather than constitutional provisions, they are not frequently changed. Although the national government (usually through the judiciary) has imposed certain standards—generally to broaden participation and prevent discrimination—there are many areas in which the states are free to make their own choices. Even when there has been a strong national trend to adopt legislation, such as the direct primary movement early in the 20th century, the states have usually responded to the trend in somewhat different ways. The constitutional and statutory ground rules have the effect of perpetuating a certain kind of political system in each state. Although they result from political traditions and practices, they have a continuing impact on the political system and the culture within which it operates.

## Patterns of party competition

One of the fundamental differences among the states is in the character and intensity of two-party competition. Some states have had close competition between the Democratic and Republican parties with hardly any interruption since the Civil War. In other states such competition has been interrupted for long periods of time or has only recently developed. There are a few states in which there is only a low level of competition today, despite national trends toward greater competition. The level of competition can be measured by several criteria: turnover in control of the governorship, legislature, and other offices; closeness of elections for major offices; number of voters who register with the two parties or turn out to vote in the two primaries; the frequency with which both parties run candidates for office; or the proportion of voters who (in surveys) indicate that they identify with each of the parties. The differences among the states in several of these measures of competition are described in several of the following chapters (particularly chaps. 2 and 4). The factors that explain differences in levels of two-party competition are described in chapter 2. National political trends and partisan realignments have an effect on state two-party competition, but, for a variety of reasons, the states react differently to these national trends. The pattern of party competition in each state is rooted in the state's political history and in traditional partisan loyalties and habits that are not easily changed. For these reasons many of the states that had been dominated by a single party for all or most of the time since the Civil War were slow to change in the period after the 1932 election, when the national political realignment undermined the sectional base of politics and a new, more competitive national pattern of politics began to emerge.

## Geographic, economic, social, and historical factors

At the risk of appearing to state the obvious, we should point out the enormous variety in American states. They differ in natural resources, urbanization, extent and types of agriculture, industrialization, size and density of population, patterns of migration, ethnic and religious character of the population, and many other important respects, each of which has some effect on the political system that has evolved. The types of interests that are organized and influential, the form of partisan alignment, and the major issues that have arisen in a state are all shaped by these factors. The political history of each state is different, and some states have a political history much longer than others; Massachusetts and Alaska illustrate this obvious difference. Whether a state belonged to the Union or the Confederacy during the Civil War, or whether it had not yet then been settled, are factors that affect state politics during the 1970s. The history of migrations in and out of a state is equally important. Conflicts between regions of a state or between urban and rural areas may have historical roots that are at least 200 years old. In several of the border states the deep divisions that arose over the issue of slavery and the question of secession in 1861 are reflected in partisan divisions that exist today.

## Differences in the political culture of states

Anyone who studies or observes several states carefully is likely to come to the conclusion that there are differences in the styles and customs of politics that cannot simply be explained by such tangible characteristics as laws, elections, or economic realities. Sometimes we are tempted to explain some aspects of politics in a state by saying, "That's just the way they do it." As political scientists, we resist an explanation that appears to be so unscientific and unsystematic, and we grope for something better. The best answer may be to borrow a term, "political culture," that has been used frequently by scholars who are interested in cross-national comparisons of political systems. Verba has defined political culture as "the system of empirical beliefs, expressive symbols, and values which defines the situation in which political action takes place" (Verba, 1965: 513). We might clarify the concept further if we specified that these beliefs, symbols, and values are widely shared in a society and have an enduring quality that is based on history and tradition. Elazar has described political culture as "the historical source of such differences in habits, concerns, and attitudes that exist to influence political life in the various states" (Elazar, 1972: 85).

If it is possible to define and identify national political cultures, does that necessarily mean that there is a distinct political culture in each of the 50 states? We recognize that there are cultural differences between the North and the South, but are there—for example—significant differences among the southern states? Is it not likely that cultural differences within a state, between its black and white citizens, or between its urban and rural residents, would be more important than cultural characteristics that distinguish a state from its neighbors? In suggesting that the state political culture is a meaningful concept, we are not arguing that the most significant differences in political culture that exist are necessarily those that follow state lines or that the beliefs and attitudes of Texans or of Hawaiians are homogeneous. We are suggesting that the political system of any state is affected by what the citizens of that state think and believe. The viewpoints on some questions that are widely shared by the people of one state may be quite different from those that predominate in another state. Moreover, each state has a history and traditions that are unique and that will help to shape the dominant beliefs and attitudes in that state. In that sense it is useful to talk about, and to study, state political culture. (See Patterson, 1968.)

The first step in understanding the political culture of a state is to identify the kinds of persons who inhabit that state. Scholars have been able to trace patterns of immigration to this country and patterns of migration from one state to another. We can identify the most important national, racial, and religious elements in a state's population and analyze the effects of the differences that are found on state political culture. Not only are the attitudes of whites and blacks different on many politically salient questions, but their attitudes may vary depending on the distribution of whites and blacks in a state. Similarly, the viewpoints of Catholics, Protestants, and Jews may differ depending on the degree of religious homogeneity in a state. Differences among nationalities remain important, at least in a number of eastern states, and in states like Texas, California, and Hawaii. No one would undertake to explain Massachusetts politics without understanding the influence of Irish Catholics, nor would they seek to explain New York politics without understanding Jewish influences, or analyze Alabama politics without studying the conflicting views of black and white citizens. In some states the importance of national, racial, or religious factors may be less obvious, but these factors need to be examined if the roots of political culture are to be understood.

Economic and social developments within a state also affect its political culture. We often talk about the differences in attitudes and life styles of urban and rural residents. Some of these differences may have ethnic roots, but others may be inherent in the contrasts between urban and rural living. Urban residents, for example, may have different viewpoints concerning the necessity of government playing an active role because they recognize the need for government services that are not so important in rural areas. Historians have emphasized the effects of the frontier on American political culture, and we would expect to find differences in attitudes toward the role of government or the importance of law and order, for example, in some of the western states that, until recently, were on the frontier. Economic factors can affect political culture. States in which the land was suitable for growing cotton were the ones in which there was most support in the early 1800s for the institution of slavery. The Populist and Free Silver movements of the late 1800s were strongest in states where the soil was relatively poor and agriculture somewhat marginal and in states where silver mining was important.

The ethnic, economic, and social forces that we have been discussing help to explain differences in the political histories of the states, which in turn affect their political culture. The political culture of southern states has been shaped not only by the cotton economy existing in the 1850s and the high proportion of blacks in these states but also by the fact that these states seceded, lost the Civil War, and were occupied by Union troops during the period of Reconstruction. The Populist movement had a lasting effect on the political culture of western states, extending beyond anything that can be explained by the quality of the soil or the number of silver mines in the state. The strength of the Progressive movement in the early 20th century in such states as Wisconsin, Minnesota, and the Dakotas can be explained in part by the ethnic makeup of those states, specifically the large proportion of Scandinavian and German voters, but the Progressive movement has affected voters of all nationality backgrounds in those states.

In other words, the political culture of a state today is a product of its entire history. National political developments, such as the Civil War, Reconstruction, Populism, the Progressive movement, and the New Deal, have left different imprints on each state, depending on the geography, economy, and characteristics of population in that state. Moreover, particularly important political leaders, controversies, and crises within individual states have left an impact on state political culture. It would be impossible to understand the political culture of Louisiana today without some knowledge of the dynasty of Huey and Earl Long, or to understand Michigan politics without some recollection of how the labor union movement developed in the auto industry during the 1930s and 1940s.

Daniel Elazar (1972) has made the most extensive attempt to identify and describe political culture in the American states. He has identified three major types of political culture, the individualistic, moralistic, and traditionalistic, and has—in a series of maps—identified the states, and the sections of states, in which one or more of these cultures is dominant. It is an ambitious effort, but because the designation of state and sub-state cultures is more impressionistic than systematic, it is open to criticism. Actually anyone who is fully acquainted with several states can play the game of describing their dominant political cultures.

The first step in such a description must be to identify those dimensions of political culture that are particularly salient for state politics and along which the states can be expected to differ significantly. We suggest the following as dimensions that deserve study:

1. The attitude toward the role of government in society.
2. The attitude toward broad public participation in the political process, and the degree of deference toward political authority that exists.
3. Willingness to change society, or a preference for the status quo.
4. Attitudes toward the party system, and the extent of identification with and loyalties to political parties.
5. Styles of political activity.

6. Attitudes on major social questions, particularly views concerning racial and other minorities and tolerance of dissent.
7. A sense of state identity and pride.

Although these dimensions of culture are distinct, they are not necessarily independent of each other, and it is likely that certain patterns of political culture, representing several parallel dimensions, will be common in the states. The three types of political culture that Elazar has identified in the states are based on the dimensions pertaining to the role of government, public participation in politics, and attitudes toward the party system.

According to Elazar (1972: 93–110), the *individualistic* political culture is characterized by a belief that the role of government should be limited; a perception of politics as a specialized process that is largely left to professionals; and an acceptance of party organization, discipline, and two-party competition. Elazar believes that this is the dominant political culture in southern New England, the Northeast, Ohio, Indiana, and Illinois. The *moralistic* culture is one in which there is a willingness to use government to solve social problems and regulate individuals and business; a belief in the necessity for all citizens to participate in politics; and a distrust of political parties and professional politicians. This is predominant in northern New England, the upper Midwest (Michigan, Wisconsin, and Minnesota), the northern plains states, and the Northwest. In the *traditional* culture, which is elitist and paternalistic, there is a reluctance to use the power of government except to maintain the existing social order; a belief that the mass public should play a minimum role in politics; and a distrust of party competition and parties because they encourage broader participation in politics. The southern states, and to a lesser extent the border and southwestern states, are characterized as traditional.

In recent years it has been more difficult to recognize differences in state attitudes toward the role of government because the federal government has encouraged and almost forced states to undertake a wide variety of programs by providing matching funds. At an earlier period in history, such differences were more obvious. Much of the state regulatory legislation arose in the states where the Progressive movement was strong. The eastern and midwestern states established systems of public education before southern states did. Jack Walker (1969) has devised an "index of innovation," designed to measure which states were quickest to adopt legislative innovations that eventually spread to most of the states. In the absence of state-level survey data, this may be the best available measure of state attitudes toward the role of government. According to the Walker index, the most innovative states are New York, Massachusetts, California, New Jersey, Michigan, Connecticut, and Pennsylvania; close behind are a number of midwestern, northwestern, and northeastern states. The least innovative states include many of those in the South, along with several in the West and Southwest. Among southern states, Louisiana, Virginia, and North Carolina are most innovative, and Mississippi, South Carolina, and Texas are least innovative.

In some states, as we will note in later chapters, there is a much higher rate of participation in general elections than there is in other states. We will also measure differences in participation levels in primary elections, which are not exactly the same. Some states have adopted laws that make it particularly difficult to register and vote, although in recent years the decisions of Congress and the Supreme Court have invalidated some of those restrictions. (Such restrictions were motivated only in part and only in some states by the desire to prevent blacks from voting.) These laws and practices are the consequences of different norms and attitudes regarding the breadth of public participation in the political process, differences of fundamental importance in understanding state political culture. Where there is a widespread acceptance of the idea that everyone has a right and a responsibility to participate in politics, individuals are likely to have a higher sense of civic duty and political efficacy. At the other extreme would be states in which most citizens do not believe that it is either possible or desirable for them to have much impact on the decisions of government, a situation that is sometimes described as "deference politics."

In 1968 a national survey (Black, Kovenock, and Reynolds, 1974) was conducted, which also included surveys of 13 states in various parts of the country. The sampling procedure makes it possible to compare these states and also six regions of the country. Table 1–1 shows the differences among the states in public responses to questions measuring a sense of citizen duty and political efficacy (both being indexes based on several questions). There are substantial differences among the states; Minnesota, California, and South Dakota rank highest on both measures, and Alabama, Louisiana, and Texas rank lowest. Moreover, these are not merely the consequences of regional differences. There are sharp contrasts between states within a region, Minnesota and Illinois, for example, or Florida and North Carolina.

Questions such as these, however, are an imperfect and incomplete

# Table 1-1
## Political culture: State and regional variations in public attitudes toward government and politics, based on 1968 survey (in percentages)

| State | Cynicism about state government | | | Index of citizen duty | | | Political efficacy | | | Favorable to change | Identify as independent | Favor neighborhood integration | Pride: Agree state best place to live |
|---|---|---|---|---|---|---|---|---|---|---|---|---|---|
| | Low | Med. | High | High | Med. | Low | High | Med. | Low | | | | |
| U.S. ....... | 32 | 45 | 23 | 47 | 35 | 18 | 30 | 49 | 19 | 25 | 27 | 46 | 63 |
| N.E. ....... | 29 | 46 | 25 | 52 | 31 | 17 | 32 | 49 | 19 | 27 | 27 | 58 | 53 |
| Midwest .... | 31 | 47 | 21 | 53 | 32 | 15 | 35 | 51 | 15 | 27 | 32 | 43 | 56 |
| Mount. ..... | 43 | 39 | 19 | 52 | 37 | 11 | 40 | 43 | 17 | 28 | 34 | 38 | 69 |
| W. Coast ... | 30 | 42 | 28 | 51 | 39 | 11 | 39 | 51 | 11 | 35 | 24 | 63 | 70 |
| Border ..... | 34 | 45 | 23 | 39 | 37 | 23 | 22 | 50 | 27 | 17 | 23 | 33 | 70 |
| South ...... | 38 | 46 | 17 | 29 | 44 | 27 | 18 | 57 | 24 | 17 | 22 | 28 | 73 |
| Mass. ...... | 18 | 48 | 34 | 54 | 31 | 16 | 32 | 50 | 19 | 29 | 35 | 69 | 43 |
| N.Y. ....... | 28 | 49 | 23 | 52 | 29 | 19 | 33 | 46 | 21 | 30 | 29 | 59 | 47 |
| Pa. ........ | 30 | 44 | 26 | 50 | 35 | 15 | 31 | 49 | 21 | 23 | 15 | 53 | 63 |
| Ill. ....... | 23 | 54 | 23 | 50 | 31 | 19 | 33 | 51 | 17 | 30 | 32 | 44 | 49 |
| Minn. ...... | 47 | 41 | 13 | 56 | 34 | 10 | 46 | 43 | 11 | 31 | 30 | 50 | 67 |
| Ohio ....... | 41 | 41 | 18 | 50 | 34 | 16 | 35 | 50 | 15 | 25 | 33 | 44 | 62 |
| S. Dak. .... | 54 | 32 | 13 | 53 | 35 | 13 | 37 | 48 | 15 | 28 | 19 | 40 | 62 |
| Calif. ..... | 26 | 43 | 30 | 52 | 40 | 9 | 40 | 48 | 12 | 35 | 24 | 63 | 62 |
| Fla. ....... | 22 | 42 | 36 | 39 | 43 | 18 | 30 | 47 | 23 | 24 | 28 | 34 | 72 |
| N.C. ....... | 44 | 41 | 15 | 29 | 43 | 28 | 19 | 48 | 33 | 11 | 17 | 26 | 82 |
| Tex. ....... | 35 | 45 | 20 | 38 | 36 | 26 | 25 | 51 | 24 | 22 | 24 | 38 | 75 |
| Ala. ....... | 52 | 38 | 10 | 27 | 40 | 33 | 17 | 52 | 31 | 8 | 22 | 21 | 79 |
| La. ........ | 36 | 43 | 22 | 30 | 38 | 32 | 15 | 56 | 30 | 18 | 16 | 33 | 68 |

Source: Merle Black, D. M. Kovenock, and W. C. Reynolds, *Political Attitudes in the Nation and the States* (Chapel Hill: Institute for Research in Social Science, University of North Carolina at Chapel Hill, 1974), pp. 50, 171–205.

way of measuring underlying norms and attitudes concerning participation. It would be preferable to examine a wide range of attitudes and
behavioral manifestations of attitudes in order to evaluate and understand differences in culture. In his classic study of *Southern Politics,*
V. O. Key (1949:36) described the differences in the political culture
of two southern states, with particular reference to participation and
deference:

The political distance from Virginia to Alabama must be measured in light
years. Virginian deference to the upper orders and the Byrd machine's re-
straint of popular aberrations give Virginia politics a tone and a reality
radically different from the tumult of Alabama. There a wholesome contempt for authority and a spirit of rebellion akin to that of the Populist days
resist the efforts of the big farmers and the "big mules"—the local term for
Birmingham industrialists and financiers—to control the state. Alabamians
retain a sort of frontier independence, with an inclination to defend liberty
and to bait the interests.

Attitudes toward change and the status quo may be an important
dimension of a state's political culture even though they may be difficult to measure or to distinguish from attitudes toward particular issues, such as the role of government. Table 1–1 shows that there were
some differences among the states in the answers to a question on
whether "too many people are trying to change things too fast in this
country," although the differences were not dramatic.

There appear to be differences among the states in attitudes toward
the political parties and party organizations. Party loyalties appear to
be stronger in the East than in the West. In some states voters appear
more likely to vote consistently (over time and at one election) for a
party, and more willing to follow the advice of the party organization
on the nomination of candidates. In states where the Progressive
movement was strongest, there seems to be the greatest distrust of organizational leadership. Where the primary has been established long-
est, is used for the largest number of offices, and has the highest
turnout, we may assume that there is not only a high sense of citizen
participation but an unwillingness to leave nominating decisions to the
party professionals. We have very little evidence about interstate differences in attitudes toward party. One clue may be found in the proportion of citizens who say that they are independent and do not
identify with either state party. Table 1–1 shows that the largest proportion of independents is found in Massachusetts, Ohio, Illinois, and
Minnesota, the smallest proportion in Pennsylvania, Louisiana, North
Carolina, and South Dakota. Impressionistically, we would expect

somewhat different findings: higher party loyalty than the poll indicates in Ohio and Illinois, greater independence in South Dakota and California.

Attitudes toward political parties presumably are a product of recent experience as well as history and tradition. In states with strong, disciplined party organizations, voters may become accustomed to and at least tacitly approve of strong parties. Because voters are usually not very familiar with political practices in other states, it is hard to tell what perceptions they have of their state party system and what evaluations they are likely to make about it.

The styles of politics differ from state to state in ways that are more difficult to measure. Certain norms exist, based on habit and tradition, about how politics is carried on. Citizens may not be conscious of these norms unless they move from one state to another. In some states ethnic differences—racial, national or religious—seem to permeate every aspect of politics: the way factions arise, slates are balanced, and party allegiances are structured. In some states political oratory is unusually flamboyant, and politicians particularly colorful. Political conflict seems to have a much stronger ideological base in some states than it does in others. In certain states corruption appears to be a way of life, a norm that is accepted by the politicians and tolerated by the voters. There are differences in norms concerning whether there should be much continuity or high turnover in political office, and how essential patronage is to the operation of political organizations. Some of these characteristics that are described as "style" are rooted in other dimensions of culture. Others seem to be rooted simply in tradition, and can be explained only by saying, "That's just the way we do it here."

It is reasonable to expect that attitudes on a variety of social issues will differ from region to region and state to state. Those attitudes that are particularly pertinent for state politics are ones that concern relationships among groups in a state. In any state that has one or more substantial racial or national minorities, the attitudes of both majority and minority groups of citizens toward each other are important ingredients in political culture. These attitudes are affected not only by the size of the minority groups, but the past history of conflict or harmony among the groups. Table 1–1 shows that on questions involving racial relations (blacks moving into white neighborhoods) there are substantial differences not only between regions but between states in a region.

V. O. Key (1949) and others have argued that the persistence of one-party control of southern states resulted in part from the unwillingness of white political leaders to permit open competition that might encourage parties to seek the votes of blacks. The differences in the proportion of blacks voting in various southern states prior to the mid 1960s resulted from differences in the attitudes of whites toward black political participation. In more recent years, the attitudes of both blacks and whites have affected their ability to form political alliances in both southern and northern states. In many of the northern industrial states the intensity of party factionalism along ethnic lines has depended on the attitudes of ethnic groups toward each other. There may be differences in public attitudes toward minorities that are based on more than racial and ethnic factors. Several studies have suggested that public opinion in the South is less tolerant of various kinds of nonconformity and minority rights than is true in the North.

We have suggested that conflicts within a state may follow a number of lines, regional, urban-rural, class, racial, ethnic, and others. The more heterogeneous a state, the greater the potential for conflict. But what is important is not just the numerical distribution of various groups in the state, but the patterns of attitudes shared by members of these groups that have developed as a result of historical experience in the past.

One dimension of political culture that might be pertinent to state politics is a sense of pride in one's state. Commentators frequently mention examples of state pride, with Texas being a notable case, but it is not so obvious why the intensity of pride should differ from state to state. Perhaps differences in the makeup of population or geographic barriers such as mountains undermine the sense of state identity that may be a prerequisite for pride. The rivalries and conflicting interests between New York City and upstate New York or between Chicago and downstate Illinois may undermine both state unity and pride. Similar rivalries are evident between northern and southern sections of California. If in fact Texans are unusually proud of their state, it is not because of either ethnic or geographic homogeneity. Pride in a state is not easily measured. The question summarized in Table 1–1 about whether respondents consider their state the best place to live shows the highest favorable response in southern states, but this may refer more to climate and living conditions. Pride in a state is not necessarily transferred to its political institutions, and it is not obvious what might be the political consequences of state pride.

## NATIONAL FACTORS INFLUENCING
## STATE POLITICS

### Constitutional, statutory, and judicial factors

The similarities in state constitutional structures are more obvious than their differences. The structures of the executive and legislative branches of government in most states are very similar, with office-holders elected for fixed terms of two or four years on partisan ballots, and with bicameral legislatures (Nebraska being an exception, with its unicameral, nonpartisan legislature). The states are similar partly because as new states entered the Union they adopted constitutions that were modeled on those of the existing states and to some extent the national government. Moreover, throughout our history, major changes in state constitutional structure have spread relatively quickly from state to state. For example, from the Revolution to the Jackson Administration, there was a rapid expansion in the franchise to include all adult males in almost all states. In the early 20th century the direct primary election spread quite rapidly throughout the states. Other changes, such as the reorganization of state government and the executive budget, were adopted rapidly in many states after being pioneered by a few. Other changes resulted from amendments to the United States Constitution, such as women's suffrage, the 18-year old vote, and popular election of U.S. senators.

Since the start of the New Deal, the actions of the federal government have had a profound effect on state governments. Congress has passed a large number of laws designed to encourage the states to adopt particular programs by providing federal funds on a matching basis. As a result, the policy outputs of the states have become increasingly similar in areas ranging from welfare and education to highway construction and environmental protection. Obviously the states have differed in their levels of spending for various programs, but there has been a great similarity in the agendas of the legislatures and in their policy outputs. Federal tax programs have had the effect of shaping state tax programs as well. Almost all of the states have come to place major reliance on the general sales tax because it is the only major source of tax revenue left untouched by Washington (other than local property taxes). Some federal legislation has had a direct effect on the structure of state government. One example would be legislation banning the use of political patronage in agencies receiving federal funding, and another would be federal laws and regulations that have forced the states to establish planning agencies capable of developing plans that will meet federal standards. Federal programs of aid to urban governments have also affected the relationships between state and local governments. An indirect effect of federal activities has been to encourage the development of stronger governors because of the massive increase in the activities and programs of state government. In general we can conclude that the administrative structure, legislative agenda, and policies and programs of the states have grown more similar in the last 40 years as a result of decisions made by Congress and the federal executive.

Decisions of the Supreme Court have also had a major impact on the states, for the most part resulting in smaller differences among the states. Perhaps the most obvious example is the series of Supreme Court decisions on school desegregation and busing, which have forced the states to make major changes in their school systems. The Court's decisions on the rights of defendants in trials have reduced the variations in state judicial systems. The policies adopted by the Supreme Court as well as by Congress have eliminated the obstacles to voting by blacks, thereby ending one of the most important differences in state electoral practices. There have also been recent judicial decisions preventing states from imposing long residence requirements as a prerequisite to voting and from establishing long waiting periods for persons who shift party registration.

The judicial decisions with the more significant impact on state politics have been those affecting legislative reapportionment. Before 1962 the constitutional or statutory base of apportionment in some states grossly discriminated against urban residents, and in states where the party alignment had an urban-rural base this often had the effect of guaranteeing one-party (usually Republican) control of the legislature, whatever the electoral trends in the state. A series of judicial decisions in the mid 1960s required substantial population equality for legislative districts. As a consequence, urban areas are no longer seriously underrepresented in any state, and no party is barred from a legislative majority by the apportionment system, even though a particular districting plan may have a short-term effect of favoring one party at the expense of the other.

## Partisan trends

State political party systems do not exist in isolation from national political trends. National party alignments determine the approximate proportion of Democrats and Republicans in a state and establish the bases for (or virtually prohibit) two-party competition in a state. The

actual development of two-party competition at the state level, however, depends on a number of state variables as well as on national
alignments. Much of Chapter 2 is devoted to an explanation of how
national and state factors combine to determine the level of state
party competition. Major national party realignments, such as occurred in 1896 and in the early 1930s and in the South in the 1950s and
1960s, have a profound effect on state party systems. The effect of
realignments that have occurred since the start of the New Deal has
been to increase the level of party competition in most states to the
highest point in more than a century, even though competition continues to lag behind in many parts of the South.

In addition to these major party realignments, in almost every national election there are political trends that favor one or the other
political party (or occasionally contradictory trends in different regions). These trends have some effect on state gubernatorial and legislative races. Changes in the length of gubernatorial terms and the timing of gubernatorial elections have resulted in a larger proportion of
gubernatorial races being held in congressional than in presidential
election years. Although this has isolated gubernatorial elections from
presidential races, it has not isolated them from national trends that
are sometimes very strong in congressional election years, for example
in 1958 and 1974. Most legislators in lower houses are elected for two-
year terms and most state senators are elected for staggered four-year
terms (or sometimes two-year terms). This means that a large proportion of state legislative seats are contested in presidential years, often
in the middle of a governor's four-year term. A careful examination of
year-to-year partisan changes in legislative seats shows that state legislative races in most states are significantly affected by national trends
as well as by developments at the state level. It often happens that a
state party which has long been in the minority makes a breakthrough
in an election that coincides with a strong national trend in favor of
that party. There are only four states—New Jersey, Kentucky, Virginia, and Mississippi—in which gubernatorial and legislative races
are held in odd-numbered years, when neither presidential nor congressional races are scheduled. (Louisiana elects a governor in February of presidential election years.)

## National political culture

It is probably unnecessary to point out that there are trends in the
national political culture, in the attitudes and beliefs of Americans

generally, that have an effect on state political culture. Just as no state is isolated from national partisan trends, none is isolated from the national media and from events that are national in scope. A more important point is that there appear to be nationalizing trends in this country that may be reducing the importance of differences in regional and state political cultures. These differences are so obvious that they need only be mentioned. At the same time, we must admit that there is little hard evidence to show how strong these nationalizing forces are. We know that regional and state differences in public attitudes remain, but we do not know exactly how much they have been eroded in the last generation or so.

One factor that may erode the distinctiveness of state cultures is the growing population mobility, particularly in those states, such as Florida, Nevada, Arizona, Colorado, and California, that have had proportionately large influxes of residents. The migration of blacks from South to North during and after World War II as well as the influx of Northerners into many southern states made the South somewhat less distinctive. The decline of agriculture and the expansion of industry and commerce have somewhat eroded the distinction between urban and rural states. The growing importance of mass media, national magazines and press services, as well as television and radio networks, clearly contributes to the development of national public perceptions and attitudes. The Great Depression, World War II, the Korean and Vietnam Wars were events that obviously had a nationwide impact and that overshadowed events taking place at the state level. Since the death of Huey Long, it is hard to think of a state political figure who has had an impact on his state that is comparable to the impact on citizens of all states of national figures such as Roosevelt, Eisenhower, Kennedy, Johnson, or Nixon.

National influences on political culture are so obvious and so powerful that they tend to overshadow the more subtle, underlying, traditional forces that continue to distinguish state political cultures. It seems undeniable that the differences in state political cultures, and consequently differences in state political systems, are becoming less important. That very fact makes it important to conclude this chapter by emphasizing that the process of nationalization has not been completed and that significant differences remain in the political culture of the states and in many aspects of state political systems. Our purpose in the chapters that follow is to examine and explain the many variations in American state political systems.

# 2 ★ ★ ★

# Two-party competition ★ ★ ★

In a book on state parties and elections, high priority must go to the study of patterns of party competition in the states, and the causes and consequences of variations in that pattern. It is the most important dimension along which we measure the states. It is important largely because there are major variations, with some states dominated by one party and some highly competitive, and because significant trends in competition have occurred in many of the states in recent years. In the period since World War II more of the states have become more competitive, and we need to understand why.

The pages of political science journals are strewn with a variety of indexes of party competition, varying in complexity and utility. No single one can be described as the "best"; the choice of an index depends on what aspects of competition one is most interested in measuring. Specifically, one must decide what time period and offices to include and what criteria of competition are most meaningful. The calculation of average competition over a long time period may obscure recent trends, but a focus on the most recent years may be misleading because it exaggerates the influence of short-term forces. We are interested in showing trends in competition, and we have organized the election data in the tables and maps into four time periods: 1900–30, 1932–44, 1946–58, 1960–76. The divisions appear to be logical in terms of political trends and realignments. We are principally concerned with gubernatorial elections as the focal point of state politics. Legislative elections are also important because they measure the breadth of party competition and because the legislature plays a crucial role in state policy making. Elections to the U.S. Senate and House are less important to the state political system, although data on such elections may be symptomatic of levels of two-party competition.

There is no single criterion or measure that will accurately and fully describe party competition, and therefore we must use several:

1. The percentage of elections with two-party competition might be considered a measure of the minimum level of competition. We will use it in southern states, where both parties have not consistently contested elections.

2. The closeness of races for an individual office is a useful measure. The closer the race, the greater the likelihood that the voters had a realistic choice among serious candidates and the more promising the minority party's chances in the next election.

3. The size of the majority party membership in a multimember body such as the legislature is an indirect measure of the breadth of party competition in the state and also suggests how much legislative conflicts are likely to follow party lines. (The number of contested legislative elections is also a good measure of the breadth of party competition, but such data are difficult to obtain in a comprehensive fashion over a long time period.)

4. The division of partisan control of the governorship and the legislature over a period of years is obviously important. In the long run it is difficult for a state party to maintain its competitive position unless it at least occasionally wins control of state government.

5. The proportion of voters registered in each party is a useful measure of competition in those states where party registration is required throughout the state and statewide data are reported, but inconsistencies among the states make this an imperfect and incomplete measure for comparisons among the 50 states.

6. The percentage of voters who identify as Democrats and Republicans constitutes a useful measure of competition, but such data are available over a number of years in only a few states.

7. The proportion of voters who participate in the primaries of each of the two parties may be a useful measure in some cases, but it is less useful in states where contested primaries are infrequent or organiza-

tional influence on primaries is great. This measure is analyzed further in Chapter 4.

If we are interested in finding trends in party competition, we should recognize that voters are often slow to change their registration from one party to another, and similarly slow to shift from voting in one primary to the other. Therefore, partisan trends are likely to appear first in general elections, and later in primaries and registration. We do not have enough data at the state level to determine how quickly shifts in party identification appear.

We have used several of these measures in an effort to provide a concise picture of trends in two-party competition. Tables A–1, A–2, and A–3 in the Appendix show, for each time period, the length of time that each party controlled the governorship, the average margin of the winning party, the partisan division of each state legislature over time, and the average percentage of seats held by the winning party. Data for southern states include the proportion of contested gubernatorial elections. We have used the data in these tables to provide a classification of each state according to its level of competition in the various time periods, and these categories are summarized in the maps later in the chapter. Data for the most recent period are also summarized in Table 2–2.

The more closely we examine data on party competition, the more obvious it becomes that each state is different—in the level of competition and in the timing of trends toward greater competition. We cannot account for all of the differences, but can only look for explanations that are pertinent to a number of states. The character of party competition in each state is a product of national political forces as well as factors unique to that state. The differences among the states result from the personalities and events of today, but also from historical factors that are often ancient enough to have been forgotten by persons whose behavior is influenced by them. It is this blend of national and state historical and contemporary influences that makes state party systems complicated and also fascinating.

One way of illustrating the different effects of national and state forces on state party competition is to examine the interstate differences in party identification of various groups. We know that certain categories of voters are more likely to be Democrats and others more likely to be Republicans, partly because of national political developments and trends. One reason why the Democrats are stronger in certain states is that those states contain a larger proportion of the types of persons who are more likely to be Democrats. Table 2–1 contains

**Table 2–1**

**National party identification (Democrats and Republicans) in 13 states in 1968 for various population categories (in percentages)**

| State | Total | | Catholics | | Union members | | Central city residents | | Rural residents | |
|---|---|---|---|---|---|---|---|---|---|---|
| | D | R | D | R | D | R | D | R | D | R |
| U.S. .......... | 45 | 26 | 48 | 17 | | | 54 | 19 | 44 | 33 |
| S. Dak. ....... | 41 | 43 | 65 | 18 | 66 | 19 | 42 | 38 | 42 | 42 |
| Pa. ........... | 45 | 39 | 60 | 24 | 67 | 21 | 50 | 27 | 38 | 50 |
| Ohio ......... | 41 | 31 | 50 | 13 | 51 | 20 | 50 | 18 | 40 | 41 |
| Ill. ........... | 40 | 29 | 45 | 18 | 53 | 11 | 51 | 19 | 35 | 38 |
| N.Y. .......... | 43 | 31 | 47 | 25 | 45 | 25 | 54 | 18 | 15 | 64 |
| Minn. ......... | 41 | 27 | 48 | 16 | 65 | 6 | 45 | 26 | 40 | 25 |
| Calif. ......... | 50 | 27 | 59 | 13 | 61 | 12 | 51 | 28 | 47 | 32 |
| Mass. ......... | 45 | 19 | 59 | 6 | 50 | 8 | 63 | 7 | 14 | 35 |
| Fla. ........... | 49 | 22 | 58 | 19 | 75 | 2 | 58 | 19 | 54 | 11 |
| N.C. ......... | 60 | 21 | — | — | 59 | 12 | 58 | 20 | 61 | 21 |
| Ala. ......... | 53 | 11 | — | — | 52 | 9 | 53 | 6 | 51 | 17 |
| Tex. .......... | 58 | 10 | 64 | 17 | 69 | 5 | 64 | 13 | 57 | 10 |
| La. ........... | 69 | 9 | 58 | 9 | 52 | 9 | 59 | 16 | 77 | 5 |

Source: David M. Kovenock, and J. W. Protho et al., *Explaining the Vote* (Chapel Hill: Institute for Research in Social Science, University of North Carolina at Chapel Hill, 1973), common table 1.

data from a 13-state opinion survey conducted in 1968 and shows the percentage of persons identifying with each party (eliminating the independents). It includes three categories of persons who are inclined to be more Democratic: Catholics, members of union blue-collar households, and residents of central cities (not suburbs). It also includes one group, rural residents, who (at least outside the South) are inclined to be more Republican than residents of other areas.

It is obvious at a glance that the proportion of each of these groups that is Democratic or Republican varies greatly from state to state. In other words, Massachusetts is more Democratic than Illinois not merely because it contains more Catholics but because its Catholics are more likely to be Democrats than are those in Illinois. South Dakota is more Republican than Minnesota not only because it has a larger proportion of rural voters but also because they are more inclined to be Republican. The table also shows a number of interesting variations in patterns of party identification from state to state. Union members are more heavily Democratic in Florida and Minnesota than in New York. Catholics are more heavily Democratic in South Dakota and California than in New York or Pennsylvania. One reason for Pennsylvania's Republican strength is that its rural voters are more

Republican than in states like Minnesota. The table also shows that in southern states there are smaller differences between residents of the central cities and the rural areas than there are in most northern states. The differences from state to state in patterns of party allegiance result not only from socioeconomic and urban-rural variations but also from historical developments that are unique to each state. Moreover, the relative success of the two parties in a state depends on several other factors besides the distribution of party allegiances.

A full understanding of the political party system in any state requires knowledge about patterns of migration into the state from the early 19th century to the present time; economic trends such as the growth of industry and urbanization; the impact that national political developments such as the Civil War and Reconstruction or the Populist movement had in the state; and the history of politics in the state. Some awareness of these factors is necessary to make comparisons among the states.

## HISTORICAL PATTERNS OF NATIONAL PARTY COMPETITION

The Civil War and Reconstruction had a massive and enduring effect on national and state politics, establishing Democratic domination in southern states and Republican domination in most northern states. From the end of Reconstruction until the start of the New Deal most political trends and developments had the effect of strengthening and reinforcing this one-party dominance in most, though not all, states, as well as one-party control of county and city government even in states where there was stronger competition at the state level. V. O. Key (1964: 232) has defined sectional politics as "a sharing of interests and attitudes by people of all sorts in a major geographical region against a similar clustering of interests and attitudes of the people of another region." The sectional division grew out of the loyalties and antagonisms generated by the Civil War and persisted largely because of regional economic differences. As long as it persisted, new partisan alignments based on class or urban-rural differences failed to develop. Moreover, each of the national parties was dominated by the political leadership located in the section of the country where that party held a dominant position.

The New Deal signaled the end of sectional politics and the nationalization of political issues. In the realignment that followed, class occupation, and economic interest became more important than re-

gion as determinants of party identification, although ethnic and religious loyalties did not entirely lose their impact. The realignment
produced a massive shift of party loyalties, particularly among
younger voters, with the net advantage going to the Democratic party,
and Republican control over the northern states began to break down.
More recently the loyalty of southerners to the Democratic party has
begun to erode, and Democratic dominance of southern politics has
become less absolute. Increasing migration from state to state has
helped to undermine one-party domination, particularly in the South,
and intrastate migration from rural to metropolitan areas has increased
the percentages of voters living in counties of relatively strong party
competition. Most recently it has become clear that party loyalties are
fading, that more voters are professing independence and/or crossing
party lines in their voting; and as a consequence state political party
systems are growing more fluid. In the face of all the pressures for
change, however, state political systems have lagged behind the national system, and the evolution of competitive party systems has pro-
gressed more slowly in many states than we might expect—given the
national forces at work. Our task is to understand how these national
trends have actually affected the states and what obstacles have existed to delay such effects.

## Sectional politics

Because the pattern of politics in individual American states today
has been shaped so much by history, it is important to understand the
main outlines of American political history, at least since the Civil
War. In Key's (1964: 232) words, "The Civil War made the Democratic
party the party of the South and the Republican party, the party of the
North." The most complete and enduring pattern of one-party control
was found in the 11 states of the old Confederacy—the Solid South.
Between 1880 (following the end of Reconstruction) and 1944, Democratic presidential candidates carried every one of these states in every
election, except in 1928 when Al Smith failed to carry five of them (and
in 1920 when Tennessee voted Republican). From 1916 (when they
were first elected) to 1944, every U.S. senator from the South was a
Democrat. From 1880 to 1944 every southern governor was a Democrat (or, rarely, an independent), except for several Republicans in
Tennessee and one in North Carolina. The only centers of Republican
strength during this period were found in the Appalachian mountain
areas (western North Carolina, southwestern Virginia, eastern Tennes-

see). These were areas where there had been very little slavery (because you could not grow cotton on hillsides) and very much opposition to secession. Consequently, they became Republican, and have remained Republican to the present, providing the Republican party a head start in recent years that it has lacked in other southern states.

The North was never as solidly Republican as the South was Democratic, and Republican control gradually eroded between the end of the Civil War and the 1896 election, for a variety of reasons. Counties in the southern half of both Indiana and Illinois were populated largely by southerners, a migration pattern that produced Democratic majorities in those areas. The waves of migration from Europe also had an important impact on the political patterns of northern states. The earlier immigrants were from northern Europe, often German or Irish; in later years a larger proportion came from southern and eastern Europe. As each new wave entered the country, a large proportion of them settled in the major urban and industrial centers of the Northeast and Midwest. For a variety of reasons many of the immigrants, when they achieved citizenship and the right to vote, became Democrats. The Republican party was largely Protestant, middle class, and nativist in its orientation, and the Republican organizations did not very often seek to recruit the new immigrants. The Democratic party was more Catholic and working class in composition, and the Democratic organizations in the cities actively recruited new voters. The urban organizations provided a variety of services for these new citizens, and in return it got their votes, which were mobilized with considerable efficiency.

In most northern states the Republican party was the majority party, but the Catholic, ethnic, and urban base of the Democratic party was extensive enough in a number of northern states to constitute an increasingly serious challenge in the late 19th century. Democratic presidential candidates were particularly successful in New Jersey, Connecticut, New York, and Indiana, and they made enough inroads into northern states so that the elections of 1876, 1880, 1884, and 1888 were all very close.

The patterns of one-party dominance in state politics were much less evident in the western states. There were a few states, like Oklahoma, in which the migration patterns from northern and southern states coincided with sections of Republican and Democratic control. In some western states the ethnic and religious loyalties to parties that new immigrants had developed in the East persisted as these immigrants moved further west. Because the western states had Protestant, rural majorities and had been settled primarily by northerners, they usually produced a majority of votes for Republican candidates at the state and national level (Key, 1956: 218–27). But, beginning in the 1870s, the citizens of many western states—and particularly the farmers—were becoming increasingly dissatisfied with both of the national parties, which appeared to be under the domination of eastern business interests. A series of economic setbacks for farmers led to demands for a variety of reforms, including cheap money and various forms of regulation of business, particularly the railroads. When the two major parties largely ignored these demands, the farmers began to give serious attention—and some of their votes—to a series of minor parties, in both state and national elections. The third-party movement reached the height of its electoral success in the 1892 presidential elections when the Populist party polled over one million votes (more than 8 percent), won a plurality in five western states, and relegated the Democratic party to third place in three other western states. That year the Populist party elected governors in three western states. (See Sundquist, 1973: chap. 6.)

The success of the Populist party and the depression of 1893 led the Democratic party in 1896 to repudiate the conservative economic policies of its President, Grover Cleveland, and to nominate as its presidential candidate William Jennings Bryan. The stage was set for a major party realignment in the 1896 election. By adopting the Populist economic platform, particularly the inflationary free silver plank, the Democratic party won the support of Populist voters in the western states, but it failed to make significant inroads among Republican voters in those states. In 1896 Bryan carried some, though not all, of the western and plains states, but the gain was short-lived; in subsequent presidential elections most of these states slipped back into the Republican column. In state elections most of the western states remained competitive from 1900 through 1930, with control over the governorship alternating between the parties and with neither party winning state elections by large margins. During this period the West was the only competitive region in the country (figure 2–1).[1]

The short-run Democratic gains in the West were more than offset by long-run losses in the major urban states. The Republican party made a vigorous and largely successful effort to win the votes of the urban working class, who were dismayed by the inflationary policies

---

[1] For a description of the criteria used to classify states according to competition and tables showing the number of years each party controlled the governorship and legislature, see the Appendix.

Figure 2–1
Levels of party competition in states, 1900–1930 elections (governorship only)

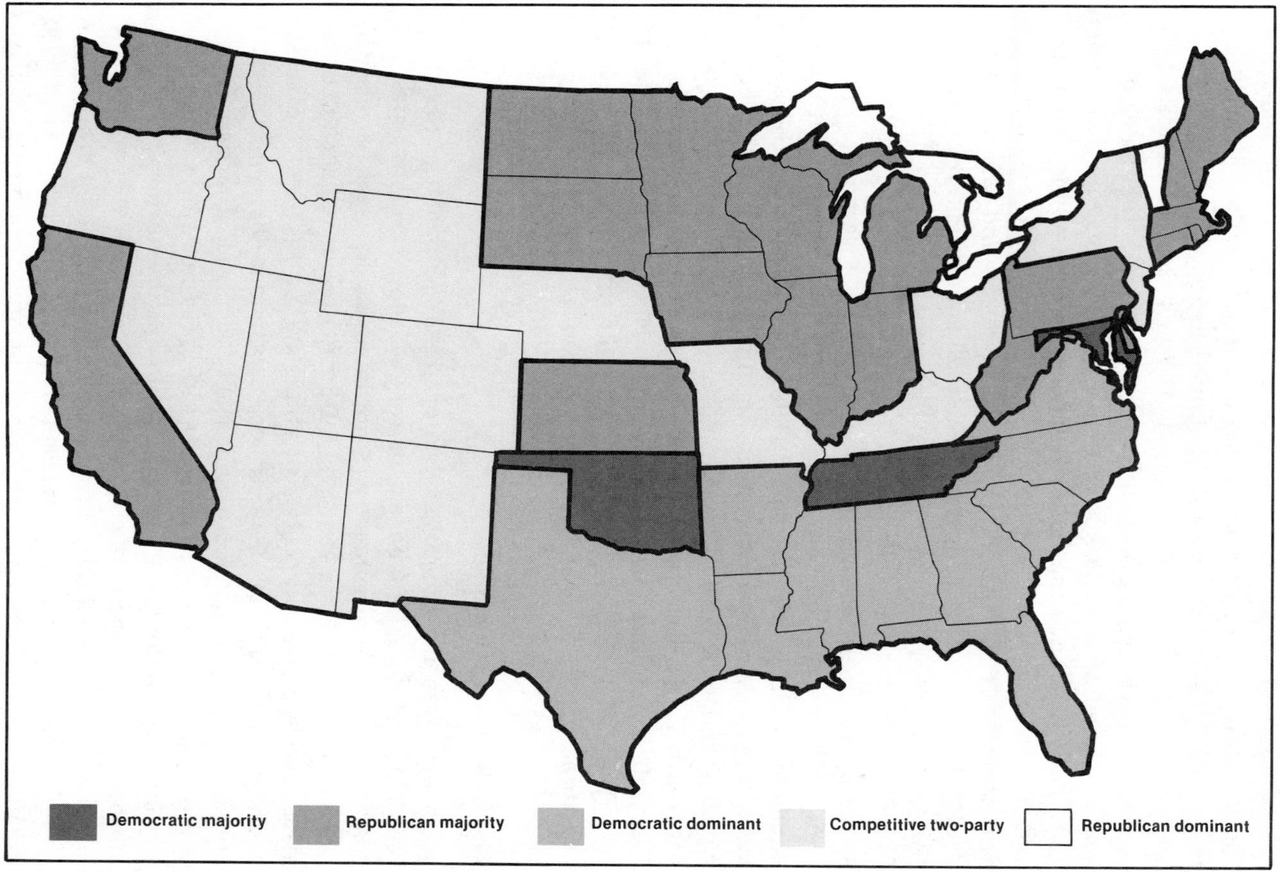

Democratic majority | Republican majority | Democratic dominant | Competitive two-party | Republican dominant

espoused by the Democratic party and were attracted by the Republican protective tariff policies. The result was that a large number of urban voters shifted to the Republican party in the 1896 election, and many of them continued to vote Republican in the elections that followed. The Democratic party continued to keep many of the Catholic and recent immigrant voters, but it had lost its broad, urban, working-class base. Consequently, the major industrial states of the Northeast and Midwest, some of which had been leaning Democratic and all of which had been closely balanced, became solidly Republican and remained so until the New Deal. The Democrats even lost their firm control over border states such as Kentucky and Missouri. Only the South remained unchanged by the realignment, and it became the only solid base of Democratic strength (figure 2–1).

From 1896 to 1930 there were ten northeastern and midwestern states in which the Democrats never won the governorship, or else won it for no more than four years and with less than a majority vote: Maine, New Hampshire, Vermont, Delaware, Pennsylvania, West Virginia, Illinois, Michigan, Wisconsin, and Iowa. There were 8 others in which Democratic governors held power no more than 8 out of 32 years, often with less than a majority: Massachusetts, Rhode Island, Connecticut, Indiana, Minnesota, Kansas, North and South Dakota. New York, New Jersey, and Ohio were the only really competitive industrial states.

## The New Deal realignment

The realignment of the 1930s destroyed the sectional base of American politics and the Republican control over most northern states. The character of that realignment was not immediately clear because the Democratic party in the 1932 and 1936 elections made such massive gains among almost all classes of voters. When the Democratic tide began to recede in the 1940s, it became obvious that the American political landscape had been irrevocably changed. The new Democratic coalition in the northern states included not only Catholic and ethnic group voters but a large proportion of the lower- and middle-income voters in the urban and metropolitan areas. The working-class voters were mobilized by labor unions that established a firm alliance with the Democratic party. Because the metropolitan centers had been growing rapidly in population, large Democratic majorities in these centers usually resulted in Democratic majorities in the state. (See Sundquist, 1973: chap. 10.)

In the years since the New Deal, the metropolitan base of the Democratic coalition has changed, but it has not disappeared. One change has been the increasing importance of the black voters, who have identified overwhelmingly with the Democratic party. A second change has been the growth of suburban sections of metropolitan areas, sections where the Democratic party has been weaker than the central city. Finally, in some elections in which social issues have overshadowed economic issues, the Democratic party has lost votes among white, working-class voters. As a result of these developments, the pattern of voting within metropolitan areas has become more variable and complex, but these areas remain the key to success for the Democratic party.

In the early years of the New Deal, the farm vote was heavily Democratic, but since that time the farm vote has been less predictable and has varied with changing farm prices and other economic conditions. There has also been a class division among rural voters paralleling that among urban voters, with the lower-income farmers more likely to vote Democratic. Democratic success in agricultural states such as Iowa, Kansas, Nebraska, and the Dakotas has varied with economic conditions in the farm belt, but in recent years—as these states have become more industrial—the outcome of elections has depended less on the farm vote.

At the outset, it appeared that the New Deal had destroyed the sectional base of politics in the North without disturbing Democratic domination of the Solid South. From 1932 to 1944 every southern state voted Democratic in every presidential, senatorial, and gubernatorial election, and all but a few House districts remained Democratic. But the South was no longer the essential base of the Democratic coalition; in all four of his elections Franklin Roosevelt would have won if he had carried none of the southern states. The policies of the national Democratic party on economic and social issues, and particularly on questions of civil rights and desegregation, alienated a large proportion of southern voters. Four southern states voted for a third-party southern candidate in the 1948 presidential election. In the presidential elections of 1952, 1956, and 1960, Republican candidates Eisenhower and Nixon actively sought southern votes and succeeded in carrying five southern states one or more times (Florida, Virginia, and Tennessee three times; Texas, twice; Louisiana, once). In 1964 Barry Goldwater was the first Republican to win four states in the Deep South: Alabama, Georgia, South Carolina, and Mississippi, in addition to Louisiana. The collapse of the Solid South became complete in 1972, when

Richard Nixon became the first Republican presidential candidate to win the votes of every southern state. During this period since 1952 the Republican party has won gubernatorial or senatorial seats at one time or another in seven southern states (all except Alabama, Georgia, Louisiana, and Mississippi) and has won an increasing proportion of House seats. (See Sundquist, 1973: chap. 12; and Seagull, 1975.)

In the years since 1932 the sectional pattern of American politics has been eroded. In all parts of the country similar groups of voters support the Democratic party, and other groups support the Republican party. Although certain states tend to be more Democratic and others tend to be more Republican in presidential politics, both national parties compete vigorously and with some success throughout the country. Since 1932 every state has voted at least once for a Democrat and at least once for a Republican in presidential races. In 1964 the Democratic presidential candidate, Lyndon Johnson, carried 44 states. Only 8 years later, in 1972, the Republican presidential candidate, Richard Nixon, carried 49 states. In the 1976 presidential election there was a very close balance between the two parties. Although Jimmy Carter carried every southern state except Virginia, his margin was narrow in some southern states and was often dependent on the black vote. He also won many of the industrial states of the Northeast and Midwest, while losing every western state.

## PATTERNS OF STATE PARTY COMPETITION

The political realignment that has made every state competitive in presidential elections has had an equally important, but more gradual, effect on state political systems. In most of the Republican-dominated northern states the Democrats were able to win one or more gubernatorial elections during the Roosevelt years, but in most of these states they made only limited or temporary inroads into the Republican-controlled legislatures. The development of strong Democratic state parties, able to compete on even or better than even terms, occurred more gradually in the postwar period and in some states not until the late 1950s, or early 1960s. In many of the most urbanized states the malapportionment of state legislatures made it difficult or impossible for the Democrats to win a majority in one or both legislative houses until the mid 1960s. In the states that had been the most heavily Republican, the Democratic party sometimes found it difficult to run enough candidates to win legislative majorities even when the party was able to win the governorship.

**Figure 2–2**
**Levels of party competition in states, 1932–1944 elections**

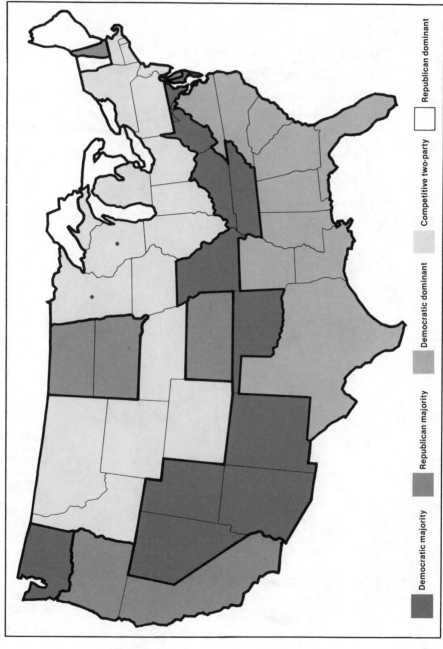

| | | |
|---|---|---|
| Democratic majority | Republican majority | Democratic dominant | Competitive two-party | Republican dominant |

* States that had three-party systems during the period or a minor party providing the competition with one major party.

Figure 2–3
Levels of party competition in states, 1946–1958 elections

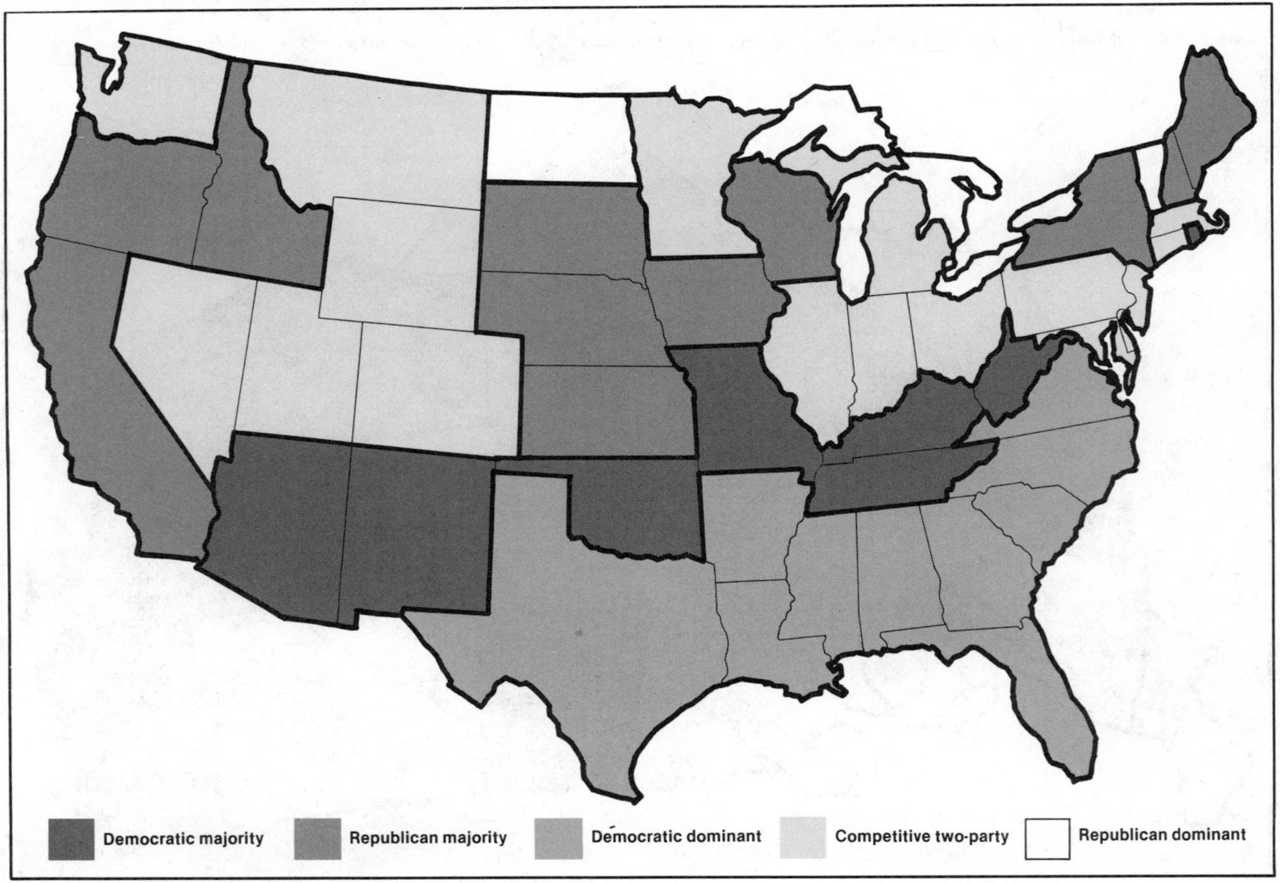

Democratic majority ■ Republican majority ■ Democratic dominant ■ Competitive two-party □ Republican dominant

**Figure 2–4**
Levels of party competition in states, 1960–1976 elections

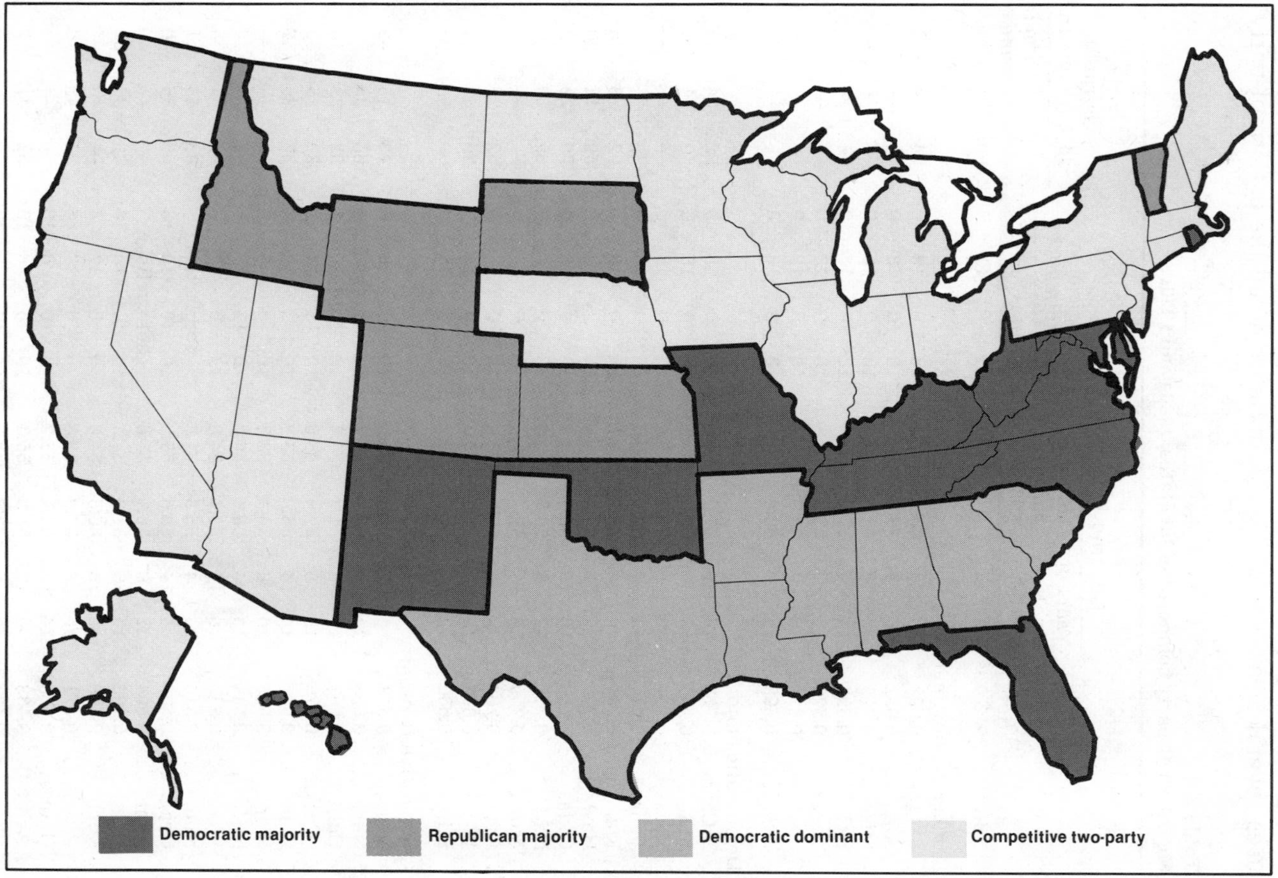

Democratic majority    Democratic dominant

Republican majority    Competitive two-party

The maps in figures 2–2, 2–3, and 2–4 show the changing patterns of state party competition since the start of the New Deal, and table 2–2 uses several measures to describe in more detail the pattern of party

**Table 2–2**
**Measures of party competition for states, 1960s and 1970s**

| State | Ranney index of competition 1962–73 | Governorship Years of control 1961–78 D | R | Majority margin 1960–76 D | R | Legislative control 1961–78 Senate D | R | House D | R | Party registration 1976 (percent) Dem | Rep | None and other |
|---|---|---|---|---|---|---|---|---|---|---|---|---|
| **Democratic dominant** | | | | | | | | | | | | |
| La. .... | 0.993 | 18 | 0 | 66.1 | — | 18 | 0 | 18 | 0 | 94 | 4 | 2 |
| Ala. .... | 0.952 | 18 | 0 | 79.8 | — | 18 | 0 | 18 | 0 | — | — | — |
| Miss. ... | 0.915 | 18 | 0 | 61.3 | — | 18 | 0 | 18 | 0 | — | — | — |
| S.C. .... | 0.894 | 14 | 4 | 55.0 | 52.0 | 18 | 0 | 18 | 0 | — | — | — |
| Texas ... | 0.878 | 18 | 0 | 62.2 | — | 18 | 0 | 18 | 0 | — | — | — |
| Ga. ..... | 0.871 | 18 | 0 | 58.6 | — | 18 | 0 | 18 | 0 | — | — | — |
| Ark. .... | 0.865 | 14 | 4 | 69.4 | 53.4 | 18 | 0 | 18 | 0 | — | — | — |
| **Democratic majority** | | | | | | | | | | | | |
| N.C. .... | 0.775 | 14 | 4 | 57.2 | 51.4 | 18 | 0 | 18 | 0 | 72 | 24 | 4 |
| Md. .... | 0.765 | 16 | 2 | 61.6 | 49.5 | 18 | 0 | 18 | 0 | 70 | 24 | 6 |
| Va. ..... | 0.754 | 9 | 8 | 55.8 | 51.6 | 18 | 0 | 18 | 0 | — | — | — |
| Tenn. ... | 0.744 | 14 | 4 | 62.6 | 52.0 | 18 | 0 | 16 | 0 | — | — | — |
| Fla. .... | 0.741 | 14 | 4 | 58.5 | 55.1 | 18 | 0 | 18 | 0 | 67 | 28 | 5 |
| Hawaii .. | 0.731 | 16 | 2 | 55.4 | — | 16 | 2 | 18 | 0 | 59 | 12 | 29 |
| Okla. ... | 0.730 | 10 | 8 | 56.1 | 55.5 | 18 | 0 | 18 | 0 | 76 | 22 | 2 |
| N.M. .... | 0.711 | 12 | 6 | 53.8 | 50.8 | 18 | 0 | 18 | 0 | 65 | 29 | 6 |
| Mo. .... | 0.709 | 14 | 4 | 57.7 | 55.2 | 18 | 0 | 18 | 0 | — | — | — |
| Ky. ..... | 0.704 | 14 | 4 | 55.1 | 51.2 | 18 | 0 | 18 | 0 | 67 | 29 | 4 |
| W.Va. .. | 0.695 | 10 | 8 | 58.3 | 52.8 | 18 | 0 | 18 | 0 | 66 | 32 | 2 |
| R.I. ..... | 0.686 | 12 | 6 | 57.3 | 58.2 | 18 | 0 | 18 | 0 | — | — | — |
| **Competitive two-party** | | | | | | | | | | | | |
| Mass. ... | 0.673 | 6 | 12 | 52.9 | 55.5 | 18 | 0 | 18 | 0 | 43 | 15 | 42 |
| Nev. .... | 0.606 | 14 | 4 | 65.1 | 52.2 | 12 | 4 | 14 | 4 | 60 | 33 | 7 |
| Calif. ... | 0.602 | 10 | 8 | 51.7 | 55.2 | 16 | 0 | 16 | 2 | 52 | 32 | 16 |
| Alaska .. | 0.576 | 10 | 8 | 52.4 | 48.9 | 10 | 6 | 14 | 2 | 29 | 15 | 56 |
| Conn. ... | 0.567 | 14 | 4 | 56.3 | 53.8 | 16 | 2 | 10 | 8 | 37 | 26 | 37 |
| Mont. ... | 0.555 | 10 | 8 | 54.1 | 53.2 | 16 | 0 | 8 | 10 | — | — | — |
| N.J. ..... | 0.544 | 13 | 4 | 58.1 | 59.7 | 6 | 12 | 12 | 6 | — | — | — |
| Wash. .. | 0.542 | 6 | 12 | 52.1 | 54.6 | 18 | 0 | 12 | 6 | — | — | — |
| Neb. .... | 0.513 | 14 | 4 | 55.5 | 61.5 | nonpartisan | | | | 43 | 46 | 11 |
| Oreg. ... | 0.508 | 4 | 14 | 58.5 | 55.0 | 18 | 0 | 10 | 8 | 56 | 36 | 8 |
| Minn. ... | 0.504 | 12 | 6 | 56.1 | 51.6 | nonpartisan | | | | — | — | — |
| Del. .... | 0.495 | 12 | 6 | 51.6 | 54.3 | 10 | 6 | 10 | 8 | 43 | 33 | 24 |
| Mich. ... | 0.490 | 2 | 16 | 50.5 | 54.0 | 6 | 8 | 12 | 4 | — | — | — |
| Pa. ..... | 0.471 | 10 | 8 | 54.9 | 53.8 | 8 | 8 | 12 | 6 | 54 | 43 | 3 |
| Utah .... | 0.465 | 14 | 4 | 62.1 | 52.7 | 8 | 10 | 8 | 10 | — | — | — |
| Ariz. ... | 0.438 | 6 | 12 | 51.8 | 55.3 | 10 | 8 | 8 | 10 | 52 | 41 | 7 |
| Ill. ...... | 0.425 | 12 | 6 | 52.7 | 58.1 | 4 | 12 | 6 | 12 | — | — | — |
| Wis. .... | 0.425 | 12 | 6 | 53.0 | 52.3 | 4 | 14 | 10 | 8 | — | — | — |
| Ind. ..... | 0.416 | 8 | 10 | 53.3 | 55.7 | 8 | 10 | 4 | 14 | — | — | — |
| Iowa .... | 0.411 | 6 | 12 | 58.6 | 55.0 | 8 | 10 | 6 | 12 | 35 | 31 | 34 |

**Table 2–2 (continued)**

| State | Ranney index of competi-tion 1962–73 | Governorship | | | | Legislative control 1961–78 | | | | Party registration 1976 (percent) | | |
|---|---|---|---|---|---|---|---|---|---|---|---|---|
| | | Years of control 1961–78 | | Majority margin 1960–76 | | Senate | | House | | None and | | |
| | | D | R | D | R | D | R | D | R | Dem | Rep | other |
| Competitive two-party (continued) | | | | | | | | | | | | |
| N.Y. .... | 0.405 | 4 | 14 | 58.6 | 50.1 | 2 | 16 | 8 | 10 | 41 | 32 | 27 |
| Maine .. | 0.405 | 8 | 6 | 51.6 | 51.4 | 2 | 16 | 6 | 12 | 36 | 36 | 28 |
| Ohio .... | 0.369 | 6 | 12 | 54.2 | 57.1 | 4 | 12 | 6 | 12 | — | — | — |
| N.H. .... | 0.360 | 6 | 12 | 59.9 | 52.4 | 0 | 14 | 0 | 18 | 33 | 40 | 27 |
| N.Dak. ... | 0.346 | 18 | 0 | 52.1 | — | 0 | 18 | 4 | 14 | — | — | — |
| Republican majority | | | | | | | | | | | | |
| Idaho .. | 0.345 | 8 | 10 | 62.6 | 51.2 | 0 | 18 | 0 | 18 | — | — | — |
| Color. ... | 0.339 | 6 | 12 | 53.8 | 54.4 | 2 | 16 | 6 | 12 | 36 | 26 | 38 |
| Kans. ... | 0.338 | 10 | 8 | 54.8 | 53.2 | 0 | 18 | 2 | 16 | — | — | — |
| S.Dak. . | 0.337 | 8 | 10 | 56.1 | 54.8 | 4 | 14 | 0 | 16 | 44 | 47 | 9 |
| Vt. ..... | 0.331 | 8 | 10 | 58.8 | 54.3 | 0 | 18 | 2 | 16 | — | — | — |
| Wyo. ... | 0.320 | 6 | 12 | 55.8 | 57.2 | 0 | 16 | 2 | 16 | 40 | 45 | 15 |

Note: When the years of Democratic and Republican control of the legislature add up to less than 18 years, it means that control of a legislative chamber was divided for one or more sessions. Maine had an independent governor for 4 years. States for which no registration data are listed either do not have partisan registration or do not have statewide registration requirements.

Source: The Ranney Index of Party Competition is found in Austin Ranney, "Parties in State Politics," in Herbert Jacob and Kenneth N. Vines (eds.), *Politics in the American States,* 3d ed. (Boston: Little, Brown, 1976), p. 61.

competition since. (The states in the table are listed according to their ranking on Austin Ranney's index of party competition, which gives equal weight to four factors: the average Democratic percentage of the gubernatorial votes, the average Democratic share of seats in the state Senate, and in the House, and the percentage of terms the Democrats controlled the governorship and each legislative branch.)[2]

We can summarize the data on the growth of two-party competition in the northern states formerly dominated by the Republican party as follows:

In Rhode Island, Massachusetts, and West Virginia, the Democratic party became competitive at the start of the New Deal and soon became the dominant party. In recent years the legislatures of these states have been heavily Democratic while gubernatorial races have been more competitive.

---

[2] The Ranney index is found in Ranney (1976: 61). Another useful index of party competition, along with a valuable collection of voting data over time, is found in David (1972).

Connecticut, Indiana, and Illinois became competitive at the start of the New Deal and have remained competitive since that time.

Delaware, Michigan, and Minnesota became competitive soon after World War II, although Democrats remained underrepresented in the Michigan legislature until the 1960s, and the Minnesota legislature was nonpartisan until 1975.

Pennsylvania, California, Iowa, Wisconsin, and Maine are all states in which the Democratic party, despite some victories during the New Deal, did not attain a strongly competitive position until the 1950s. There are some important differences among these states. In Pennsylvania the Democrats gained a strong minority position in gubernatorial races and in the legislature during the New Deal, but were slow to translate this into gubernatorial victories. Gubernatorial elections began to be close in Iowa with the start of the New Deal, but the Democratic party, after victories in the early 1930s, did not regain power again until the mid 1950s, after which it remained highly competitive. During the New Deal years the Wisconsin Democrats were overshadowed by a third party, but they became competitive after the war and began to win gubernatorial and legislative victories in 1958. In Maine the Republicans continued to hold large legislative majorities until 1970 despite Democratic victories in the 1950s and 1960s.

Kansas, North Dakota, South Dakota, New Hampshire, and Vermont are all states in which the gubernatorial elections became competitive in the 1950s or early 1960s, but in which Republican legislative margins generally remained large until the mid 1970s. In all of these states the Democrats held gubernatorial office at least one third of the time from 1961 through 1978; the most extraordinary state was North Dakota, where the Democrats always held the governorship and rarely the legislature during this period. We have classified three of these states, Kansas, South Dakota, and Vermont, as Republican majority states for the 1961–78 period, but this majority position has been slipping in recent years, even at the legislative level.

Although most western states have remained relatively competitive throughout the 20th century, there are several states along the Border and in the Southwest in which elections became less competitive during the New Deal and have grown more competitive since that time. Utah, Nevada, Arizona, New Mexico, Kentucky, and Missouri were all competitive from 1900 to 1930 and all became solidly Democratic during the New Deal. They have had closer gubernatorial races, with some Republican victories, since World War II. In New Mexico, Kentucky, and (since 1958) in Missouri, the legislature has been solidly Democratic, often by large margins. Maryland and Oklahoma are states that have been predominantly Democratic since 1900 (but less so than the southern states). Since World War II the Republican party has held a strong minority position, with occasional victories, in gubernatorial races, but has consistently been badly outnumbered in the legislature.

It is obvious from the maps and table in this chapter that Republican parties in southern states have been slow to take advantage of the party's presidential victories that began in those states in 1952. It has taken a decade or more for the Republican party to win gubernatorial and senatorial victories, and in most states it has taken even longer for the party to win more than a small minority of legislative seats. In no southern state has the Republican party won a legislative majority in either house. The southern states can be divided into three categories, according to the extent of Republican gains.

In four states, which we have classified as "Democratic Majority"— Tennessee, North Carolina, Virginia, and Florida—the Republican party elected a governor at least once from 1960 to 1976, and in all four states there were significant Republican gains in the legislature. In the first three states the Republican party started with a small bloc of legislative seats that it had frequently won in the past and a bloc of 25 percent to 35 percent of the votes consistently won in past gubernatorial elections. In Florida the party started from scratch in the legislature and from a very weak gubernatorial position. In recent years it has seriously contested gubernatorial races, held about one third of the legislative seats, and sharply increased its share of the registered vote to more than one fourth.

Arkansas, South Carolina, Georgia, and Texas are classified as "Democratic Dominant" states, and in all four there have been spasmodic signs of Republican success. In Arkansas and South Carolina a Republican governor was elected, in both cases because of Democratic divisions, but Republican strength in the legislature has been negligible. The Georgia Republican party has made some significant legislative gains, beginning in 1964, but has failed to elect a governor— though in 1966 it won a plurality only to have the legislature choose a Democrat as governor. The Texas Republican party has made very slow and modest inroads into the legislature and has made several serious but unsuccessful gubernatorial challenges.

In the remaining states, Louisiana, Alabama, and Mississippi, there have been negligible Republican gains in the legislature and infrequent and usually ineffective efforts to win the governorship.

## SOURCES OF VOTING SUPPORT FOR
## TWO-PARTY COMPETITION

State political systems do not exist in isolation from national politics, but state political systems react slowly to national trends. A variety of factors have the effect of delaying and sometimes distorting the impact of national political trends on state politics. If we understand these factors, we can see why some states react more quickly than others to national trends. V. O. Key (1956: 229) has provided a useful definition of the two criteria that are needed for two reasonably strong parties to exist in a state: "First, within the electorate itself two major groups must exist with each possessed of the capacity to maintain a corps of political leaders. . . . Second, a substantial similarity should prevail between the divisions created among the people of a state by the issues of both national and state politics." If a state is relatively homogeneous (entirely rural, for example), it is unlikely that two parties will develop. If there are several major interests in the state but they all share a loyalty to one of the national parties, there is also no reason to expect two-party competition in the state.

In order to understand how national political trends affect states that have been dominated by one party for a long period, we need to examine more carefully the ingredients that are necessary to create a majority party at the state level. The minority party that is seeking majority status starts out with a bloc of voters who have been traditionally loyal to that party. Northern Democratic parties in the 1930s could count on the support of Catholic and ethnic minorities, particularly in the urban centers. In the 1950s some of the southern Republican parties, such as those in North Carolina and Tennessee, could count on strong support in the mountain areas. In the Deep South, however, the number of traditional Republican voters was very small. Obviously a minority party that starts out with the dependable, traditional support of 35 percent or 40 percent of the electorate is much better off than one that begins with only 10 percent or 15 percent of the voters. Moreover, if these traditional minority party voters are geographically clustered, the party will control a number of counties—an obvious source of patronage and statewide candidates.

The second source of support for the minority party is that group of voters who have become supporters of the party's presidential candidates as a result of national party realignments. These are potential supporters of the party's candidates for governor, senator, and other state and local offices. Obviously, the larger this group, the greater the minority party's opportunity. The potential impact of the New Deal realignment in the 1930s was obviously greater in the northern states that were heavily urbanized and industrialized than it was in the pre-dominantly agricultural states. As presidential candidates in the 1950s and 1960, Eisenhower and Nixon made their greatest southern gains among the middle- and upper-income voters in metropolitan areas. Consequently, the potential gain for Republican state parties was greatest in the more urbanized states, such as Florida, Texas, and Virginia.

The formula for calculating the potential vote for a minority-state party during a period of realignment appears to be rather simple. You add the party's traditional voters in state elections to the new voters who are supporting the party's presidential candidates. Rhode Island is an example of a state where both the traditional vote and the new vote for the Democratic party were high at the start of the New Deal. The state had a high proportion of Catholics and ethnic minorities, pro-viding the Democratic party with a strong base. Although the Demo-cratic party had won the governorship for only 6 years from 1900 to 1930, it averaged 46 percent of the gubernatorial vote in the years that it lost. Moreover, it was a heavily urban-industrial–labor union state in which the New Deal policies would have an obvious appeal. Almost immediately after 1932 the Democratic party gained a majority posi-tion in state politics, which it has maintained to the present time. At the other extreme is the state of Vermont, a heavily rural, Protestant, Yankee state. The Democratic party never won the governorship from 1900 to 1930 and averaged only 34 percent of the vote. The New Deal had a very limited appeal in Vermont—it was one of two states voting Republican in 1936, and the Democratic party did not succeed in gain-ing a competitive position in the state until the 1960s.

In reality, the formula for calculating the potential minority party vote is a little more complicated; it may involve subtraction as well as addition. The same partisan realignment that brings new voters to the party may cause some of the traditional voters to desert the party. Some of the Democratic voters in northern states whose loyalty was based on religious or ethnic ties but whose views or interests conflicted with New Deal policies gradually drifted away from the Democratic party. There were also defections among Democratic isolationists during World War II.

## OBSTACLES TO TWO-PARTY COMPETITION

### Conflicts between new and old leaders

There are a number of reasons why minority parties have been slow to realize their potential for winning a majority of votes in state elections. The first reason is that there may be difficulties in combining traditional and new voters in a single state party. In a state where one party has long been in the minority, the leadership of the party may be in the hands of persons who have grown complacent and even satisfied with the party's status. They may benefit from patronage arrangements made with the national party, or even with the leadership of the opposite party that holds state power. They may be reluctant to share their power with new leaders. Even if the leadership is more aggressive, it usually represents the traditional voters in the party. It is likely to recruit candidates and support policies and political strategies that suit the needs and wishes of these voters rather than those of the newer supporters of the party. The likely result will be that the new group of voters who have begun to support the party's national candidates will not be attracted to the state party and its candidates.

A crucial stage in the regeneration of a minority party may come when there is a struggle for control between the established leaders and a new group representing the new voters. In a number of the northern states the new group of Democratic politicians did not succeed in winning control of the party until the years after World War II. An example was in Michigan, where the Democratic party was dominated by conservative, patronage-oriented politicians until after the war. During the 1930s and the war years the United Auto Workers (UAW) developed into one of the strongest, most issue-oriented, and most liberal unions in the country, with a powerful base of support in Michigan. In 1948 the leaders of the UAW and other unions formed an alliance with a group of liberals in the business and professional communities. They won control of the Democratic party at a state convention and succeeded in nominating and electing G. Mennen Williams as governor. Labor union members have continued to play an active part in the state Democratic party, and the union has worked effectively for state and national Democratic candidates, helping Williams to win reelection repeatedly for a total of 12 years.

In several southern states in the early 1950s the new Eisenhower Republicans found that the state parties were run by a small group of leaders who were content with the status quo. In Texas, for example, "from 1923 to 1950 the organization of the party was under the control of its long-time national committeeman, R. B. Creager of Brownsville, who looked upon the party in Texas as mainly a national patronage dispenser for Republican presidents. He allowed incomplete state Republican tickets to be nominated, but he took little or no interest in working for their election." (Weeks, 1972: 209). The struggle for leadership began over the choice of delegates to the 1952 national convention. In Texas large numbers of Eisenhower supporters were denied admission to county Republican caucuses on the grounds that they were instant converts from the Democratic party. The Eisenhower supporters help rump conventions, sent their own delegation to the national convention, and were seated. In the aftermath of Eisenhower's nomination and election, this new breed of Republicans won control of the Texas party and other southern parties where similar conflicts had occurred.

Obviously any struggle for power in the minority party may be costly because the supporters of the losing side may be unwilling to support the party's candidate in state elections. In many of the northern states there have been continuing struggles for power between union and liberal leaders, representing the voters brought into the party by the New Deal realignment, and established but waning political organizations, representing the old Catholic and ethnic base of the party. More recently, as new groups of voters—the blacks and the young, for example—have become important parts of the Democratic coalition, state Democratic parties in some states have gone through recurring crises of division that have sometimes damaged their electoral prospects.

The Republican parties in southern and border states have not been immune to such conflicts. In Kentucky the Republican party has been damaged by personal rivalries that have been rooted in the differences between the traditional Republicans in the mountains and the new Republicans emerging in the metropolitan areas, particularly Louisville. In Florida in the 1950s a new group of Republican leaders emerged who were seriously interested in building an organization and running candidates for state and local office. In the 1960s and 1970s, however, a factional rivalry developed after a newcomer, Claude Kirk, won the governorship in 1966. A bitter primary over his renomination in 1970 divided the party and contributed to his defeat for reelection, and the same year a divisive primary destroyed the party's chances of winning a Senate seat (Dauer, 1972: 144–46).

## Entrenched southern Democratic parties

Republican parties in the South have been handicapped by another factor, one that did not affect northern Democratic parties earlier. Some of the new supporters of national Republican candidates in southern states have been transplanted northerners, but most of them have been native southern Democrats. Their votes for Republicans in presidential elections have reflected disillusionment with the program and candidates of the national Democratic party. As long as the southern Democratic parties have remained in conservative hands and Democratic governors have pursued conservative policies, these voters have had no strong incentive to vote for Republican candidates at the state level. A conservative Texas Democrat who had supported Republican presidential candidates was asked a few years ago why he had not joined the state Republican party. He pointed out, with excellent logic, that Texas politics was dominated by the Democratic party and that that party was dominated by the conservatives. Why should he, and fellow conservatives, abandon this position of power?

The position of southern Republican parties is frustrating because, however skillful and aggressive their organizational efforts, and however attractive their candidates for state office, their success largely depends on the failure of conservatives within the Democratic party. Texas is a good example of a state in which the Republican potential is considerable, but the governor's office has been consistently under the control of conservative Democrats. The growing power of black voters and other liberal groups within state Democratic parties—and the defection of some conservatives to the Republican party—have led to occasional victories of more liberal Democrats in southern primaries for governor and other statewide offces. Sometimes the Republican party has been able to capitalize on this development and to defeat the more liberal Democrat in the general election. The election of Republicans to the governorship and a Senate seat in Florida in 1966 and 1968 resulted from the voting support of conservative Democrats after liberal candidates had won the Democratic primaries. (We have noted, however, that subsequently Republican disunity led to defeats.) Other examples of liberal Democratic candidates for governor or senator being defeated by Republicans after divisive primaries can be found in North Carolina, Tennessee, and Virginia.[3]

---

[3] For an analysis of the problems faced by southern Republican parties, see the individual state chapters in Havard (1972), and also Seagull (1975), Bartley and Graham (1975), and Bass and DeVries (1976).

In some southern states during the 1950s and 1960s racial issues such as desegregation and busing dominated state politics. Democratic governors and gubernatorial candidates who took strong stands in favor of segregation were often able to command the support of a large majority of white Democratic voters. In Virginia the Byrd machine announced a policy of "massive resistance" to the 1954 school desegregation decision of the U.S. Supreme Court. The Republican candidate for governor in 1957, who attacked this policy of resistance, went down to defeat by a lopsided margin—partly because the Eisenhower administration had just sent troops to Little Rock, Arkansas, to enforce school desegregation. In Alabama, Governor George Wallace's policies on segregation and related issues were so popular that the Republican party ran no opponent against him in 1962 and in 1970 and offered only token opposition in 1974. When Mississippi Republicans began running gubernatorial candidates in the 1960s, they faced opponents who had won the Democratic primary by convincing voters that they had the best record or prospects of defending segregation, and they found it impossible to stake out an even more segregationist position that might attract voters. One exception to this pattern can be found in Arkansas, where Republican governor Winthrop Rockefeller won election for the first of two two-year terms by defeating a candidate whose segregationist views were extreme enough to alienate a number of Democratic voters. The election demonstrated that it is possible for liberal or antisegregationist Democrats to help elect a Republican candidate under the right conditions. In the border state of Maryland it was the nomination of a segregationist Democratic candidate for governor in 1966 that led to the election of Republican Governor Agnew. Our final example of a Republican victory resulting from Democratic defections comes from the 1969 Virginia gubernatorial race. There were three major Democratic candidates, and a moderate defeated both a liberal candidate and a conservative, Byrd-organization candidate. Then *both* liberal and conservative Democrats defected to help elect a Republican governor.

## Primaries, registration requirements, and third parties

One of the consequences of one-party domination of state politics in the early 1900s was the widespread adoption of the direct primary, designed to give the voters a choice of candidates within the dominant party at a time when there was little real choice between the parties. Ironically, in many states the operation of the primary has had the effect of delaying the development of strong two-party systems. We will examine the primary more carefully in chapter 4, but some of its effects on two-party competition must be mentioned here. The traditional members of the minority party who live in counties controlled by the party are likely to be overrepresented in the state primary because of their interest in voting in local as well as state nomination contests. This means that they are likely to choose statewide candidates who may have little appeal to the newer members of the party and consequently have little chance of being elected.

In a state that has been dominated by one party for a considerable period there is likely to be strong competition for statewide offices in the majority party primary and little if any competition in the minority party primary. Members of the minority party have little incentive to register and vote in the minority party unless they live in counties where their party controls local offices. The result is that many of those who commonly vote for the minority party in national and even state elections decide to register in the majority party and vote in its primaries. This has been a particularly common pattern in southern and border states where the Democratic primary has usually been decisive.

An example of one-party domination of registration and primary voting patterns is found in Maryland, a traditionally Democratic state. From 1958 to 1974 between 70 percent and 75 percent of the registered voters who designated a party were Democrats and about 80 percent of all primary voters were in the Democratic gubernatorial primary, despite the fact that the Republicans controlled the governorship from 1951 to 1958 and averaged 40 percent of the gubernatorial vote from 1958 to 1974. Nevada, a state with Democratic majorities in state and national elections during the New Deal years, maintained a Democratic majority among those registered with a party that ranged from 61 percent to 67 percent from 1950 to 1976, although the Republicans won three of the seven gubernatorial elections during that period. Florida is an example of a state that has had a steady growth in the Republican percentage of the two-party registration, from 6 percent in 1950 to 17 percent in 1960, and 29 percent in 1976, but it has lagged considerably behind the Republican percentage of the gubernatorial vote, which ranged from 39 percent to 55 percent in five elections from 1960 to 1974.

Data on changes in party registration figures over time should provide a useful measure of changing two-party competition in a state, but such analysis is not possible in a number of states for several reasons: primaries are open and no party affiliation is required at registration,

registration is not required in all parts of the state (particularly in rural areas), or statewide registration data are not readily available. Table 2–3 provides such data over a number of years for a variety of states.

**Table 2–3**
**Variation in Democratic and Republican registration over time in eight states**

| | | Democratic registration as percentage of Democratic and Republican registration | | | | |
|---|---|---|---|---|---|---|
| State | Years | First year | Last year | Highest | Lowest | Average |
| N.Mex. ..... | 1960–76 | 71.3 | 65.5 | 71.7 | 69.5 | 70.8 |
| Nev. ....... | -1950–76 | 66.6 | 64.2 | 67.4 | 61.0 | 64.6 |
| Calif. ....... | 1946–76 | 60.8 | 61.4 | 61.4 | 57.3 | 59.2 |
| Md. ........ | 1958–76 | 71.1 | 74.3 | 74.3 | 71.1 | 72.7 |
| W.Va. ...... | 1950–76 | 59.9 | 67.7 | 67.7 | 59.9 | 64.5 |
| Pa. ......... | 1958–76 | 47.4 | 55.4 | 55.4 | 47.4 | 51.2 |
| Oreg. ....... | 1946–76 | 49.1 | 61.1 | 61.1 | 49.1 | 53.7 |
| Mass. ...... | 1950–76 | 50.7 | 74.8 | 74.5 | 50.7 | 61.9 |

There are some states like Massachusetts in which there has been a clear trend toward one party over a period of 25 years. In Massachusetts the Democratic percentage of the two-party registration has risen steadily from one half to three fourths from 1950 to 1976. (Massachusetts also has an unusually high proportion of voters registered independent—over 40 percent.) Oregon is another state with a steady Democratic gain in registration. The most important conclusion to be drawn from the table, however, is that in most of the states, both highly competitive and one-party dominant, the Democratic and Republican proportions of party registration have remained remarkably consistent over a long period of time. The most stable of these states is California. Between 1946 and 1976 there was large-scale migration into the state, and voter registration rose from about five million to almost ten million. But the Democratic proportion of two-party registration was never less than 57 percent or more than 61.4 percent; it started at 60.8 percent in 1946 and was 61.4 percent in 1976. In fact, the Democratic share of party registration had changed very little since 1936 when it reached 60 percent. (There has been an increase in those registered who were neither Democratic nor Republican, however.)

What difference does it make if there is stability over time in the partisan balance of registration, or if one party has a consistent lead or is gaining? The ratio of Democratic to Republican registrants in a two-party state may not be a very good predictor of the two parties' prospects in state elections. In California, for example, the Republicans held the governorship for almost two thirds of the time between 1947 and 1978, despite having only about 40 percent of the registered vote. One study of California politics (Owens, Constantini, and Weschler, 1970: 134–37), in a section on the "Case of the Disappearing Democrats," suggests several reasons for this. Registered Democrats in California (and in other states) have lower turnout than Republicans. The permanent registration law means that voters may not bother to change party registration as their partisan preferences change. Many California Democrats come from southern states and have relatively conservative viewpoints, more compatible with Republican than with Democratic candidates in California. There are a few states where the proportion of voters who register as independents (or for minor parties) is large enough so that the two-party ratio of registration is less useful. States where one fourth or more were registered as independents in 1976 include: Alaska (56 percent), Massachusetts (42 percent), Colorado (38 percent), Connecticut (37 percent), Iowa (34 percent), Hawaii (29 percent), Maine (28 percent), New Hampshire (27 percent), and New York (27 percent).

Although the balance of party registration may be deceptive, a trend toward one party over a number of years may be a rather reliable measure of a changing balance of party power. This would be the case in Massachusetts (despite the large number of independents). Because changes in the party registration figures often lag behind changes in voting patterns, registration is not so much a predictor of coming change as an indicator that trends in voting behavior may be durable.

Although the precise ratio of party registration in two-party states may not have much effect on state politics, a lopsided margin in party registration and in primary turnout in a state where the minority party is struggling to become competitive does have important implications for the minority party—all negative. Campaign workers for that party have difficulty identifying sympathetic voters because they are registered with the other party. If there is competition in the minority party on occasion, the nomination is made by a small proportion of the party's potential voters. There is a more fundamental consequence of a dominant state primary. One factor that is supposed to maintain the vitality of a two-party system is that voters who become disillusioned with the party in power, for whatever reason, will vote for the opposition party, at least temporarily. Over a period of years any administration in power is likely to antagonize enough voters so that the opposition party has a chance. In a state with a dominant-party primary, however, those who oppose the administration in office are likely to support a challenger in the primary, because they recognize that this is the best vehicle for bringing about change in the administration. The primary, and not the general election, becomes the arena in which conflicts between the major social and economic interests in the state are resolved. Under these conditions, the minority party faces a major obstacle in persuading voters not only to change their party registration (where that is required), but also to change long-established habits of voting in the primary that they perceive to be decisive.

There have also been examples of states in which the minority party's monopoly of the opposition is challenged by a third party. Often that third party is part of a national third-party movement. Most third parties at the state level are short-lived, but if they have any durability they may seriously undermine the second party. They are likely to develop at a time when there is serious discontent with the party in power, and they are able to capitalize on that discontent better than the second party. The best example of a long-term third-party movement can be found in Minnesota. A Nonpartisan League was organized there in 1917, gained support from isolationists and Bull Moose (Theodore Roosevelt) Republicans, and ran statewide candidates in several elections. In 1922 the party was reorganized, with more labor union support, as the Farmer-Labor party, and it ran candidates for governor and for the Senate in every election through 1942. It won several of the Senate races, and it elected governors in 1930, 1932, 1934, and 1936. The impact of the third-party movement on the Minnesota Democratic party was devastating. In every gubernatorial election from 1918 through 1942 the Democratic party placed third and in 9 of the 13 races gained less than 15 percent of the vote. The narrow base of support for the Democratic party was urban, Catholic, Irish, and ideologically conservative. Years of efforts to unite the Democratic and Farmer-Labor parties into one finally culminated in success in 1944, under the leadership of Hubert Humphrey. (See Mitau, 1960; chap. 1; Fenton, 1966; chap. 4.)

Wisconsin provides a good illustration of how a minority party can be handicapped by both the majority-party primary and the competition from a third party. During the first half of the 20th century the traditional Democratic support came from Irish and German immigrants and from major urban centers, particularly Milwaukee. The leadership was both traditional and conservative. As Epstein (1958: 37) says, in Politics in Wisconsin, "In the whole period from 1900 to 1932 Wisconsin politics were fought largely within the Republican party." The Democratic party failed to win the governorship and only once got as much as 40 percent of the vote. The direct primary was initiated in Wisconsin in 1906, and it quickly became the decisive election in the state. Epstein (1958: 37–38) notes:

In view of the openness of the primary, the relevant voters were practically the electorate-at-large, and not a closely defined Republican electorate. Any voter wishing to participate in the only serious election contest simply chose the Republican primary ballot.

Epstein's data show that from 1906 to 1930 the Republican primary vote often was larger than the Republican vote in the general election and usually was between 75 percent and 95 percent of the total primary vote in gubernatorial races (Epstein, 1958: 40).

The emergence of a strong third party in Wisconsin came in 1934 when the LaFollette brothers (sons of Robert LaFollette, the legendary Progressive leader) led their followers out of the Republican party and formed a Progressive party. The Democratic party was too weak and conservative to take advantage of the New Deal realignment, and the Progressive party moved quickly to capture the support of persons who were voting Democratic in national elections. The Progressive party won three of the five gubernatorial races from 1934 through 1942, and in all five the Democratic party placed third. The Progressive party collapsed during World War II, in part because of the issue of isolationism, and many of the more liberal and internationalist members joined the Democratic party. In the postwar period new, more liberal leadership emerged in the Democratic party that was able to lead it to victory, after a decade of gradual growth, in the 1957 and 1958 races.

## PROSPECTS FOR CONTINUED
## TWO-PARTY COMPETITION

Except in a few states in the South, most states have reached a substantial level of two-party competition. During the 1961–78 period there was no state outside of the South in which the governor's office was consistently held by one party—except North Dakota, where the Republicans were shut out after 16 years in office. In the Deep South, only Alabama, Georgia, Louisiana, and Mississippi failed to elect a Republican governor or senator. Except in a few of the southern states the minority legislative party is generally strong enough to have some significant impact on legislative decisions.

There is no certainty that the present pattern of competitive state

politics will last indefinitely. In recent years there has been a Democratic trend affecting a large proportion of states, at both the gubernatorial and legislative level. This has enabled the Democratic party
to win frequent gubernatorial victories and even to win some legislative majorities in states which have long had Republican majorities,
such as New Hampshire, Vermont, and the plains states. Several of the
few states that we have classified as "Republican Majority" appear
to be on the verge of becoming fully competitive. On the other hand,
Democratic legislative control is growing stronger in the southern New
England states, several border states, and California, while the gubernatorial contests remain highly competitive. This Democratic trend
has eroded, or at least delayed, the prospects for stronger two-party
competition in most southern states. The 1976 election and the Carter
Administration may make it even more difficult for southern Republican parties to recover the momentum that they had at various periods
during the 1960s.

There are several forces operating in all or nearly all states that
should be conducive to closer two-party competition. The pattern of
migration from rural to urban and metropolitan areas, while it may be
slowing down, has had the effect in most states of reducing the political
strength of those counties where a single party has had traditional
control. Urban and metropolitan politics is likely to be more competitive and fluid. Similarly, continued migration from state to state has
the effect of weakening traditional party loyalties. At the national
level there is evidence that the party coalitions created during the
New Deal have been crumbling, or at least evolving, for a number
of years, and there are also strong indications that party loyalties are
weakening as fewer voters assert identification with any party and
more of them split their ticket at the polls. We will look more carefully
at the possible effects of these and other trends in the final chapter.

There is one development that has gone largely unnoticed but that
significantly affects the impact of national political trends on state
elections. Table 2–4 shows that since 1932 the number of states having
two-year terms for the governor has dropped from 24 to 4, and almost
all of these states adopting four-year terms have designated a nonpresidential election year as the time for choosing the governor. As a
result, while over two thirds of the states elect a governor in congressional election years, the number electing in presidential years has
dropped from two thirds to less than one third. (Another five hold
gubernatorial elections separate from either presidential or congressional ones.) The effect is to isolate state politics from national, or at

**Table 2–4**
**States holding gubernatorial elections in presidential and nonpresidential years**

| Years | 4-year-terms | | | 2-year terms | Schedule of elections | | |
|---|---|---|---|---|---|---|---|
| | Presidential year | Congressional year | Off-year | | Presidential year | Congressional year | Off-year |
| 1932–34 ............ | 10 | 9 | 5 | 24 | 34 | 33 | 5 |
| 1952–54 ............ | 10 | 14 | 5 | 19 | 29 | 33 | 5 |
| 1974–76 ............ | 10 | 31 | 5 | 4 | 14 | 35 | 5 |

least presidential, political trends to some extent. Key (1956: 28–33) pointed out many years ago that the coincidence of presidential and gubernatorial elections could help a minority party because it made possible the election of a governor on a presidential candidate's coat-tails. As split-ticket voting increases, the timing of elections may make less difference. Nevertheless, it is important that in over two thirds of the states the choice of a governor—the election having the greatest impact on the state political system—takes place only in nonpresidential years.

# 3 ★ ★ ★

# State political party organization ★ ★ ★

The single term, "political party," disguises an enormous range of behaviors and organizational types, from the minimal structure of Southern Democrats through the massive and all-encompassing ruling parties of foreign dictatorships. Classifications of this diversity are not well developed conceptually, much less established empirically, either across national boundaries or within the United States. The judgment, made some years ago, still stands, that "Unfortunately, we have no measures of party organization in the states" (Schlesinger, 1966: 104). This statement applies with equal force to city and county parties as well as to state parties.

The purpose of this chapter is to suggest a typology—a way of looking at and thinking about state political parties. To arrive at that point, we will examine a variety of ways of looking at and measuring parties and their activities. We will first discuss parties as a distinctive kind of organization, and then will examine the topics of formal structure, party personnel, candidate recruitment, and party activity in nominations. We will conclude with a presentation of the types of state political parties.

## PARTIES COMPARED TO OTHER ORGANIZATIONS

Political parties—at least in the United States—are unique forms of organizations. Indeed, whether they are organizations at all is subject to dispute. Perhaps we should simply say that parties are unique forms of human behavior. Parties may be compared to other forms of organization on at least four criteria:

### Membership

Who is a "member" of an American political party, and how does one "join"? Persons can join churches or be employed by (or buy stock in) corporations and thus become members. But what is the equivalent act in a U.S. political party? To whom would one pay dues or submit a membership application? With the exception of some voluntary and unofficial party clubs, the status of "member" does not exist in a U.S. party. In some states, the voter "enrolls" with, or lists a preference for, a party in the voter registration process. But many states lack even that minimal provision. The closest we come to a status of membership is through the public opinion polls which measure "party identification," which essentially is a psychological concept—how the person views himself in relationship to whatever he thinks the parties are. The voter, not the party, assigns himself a party identification. If U.S. parties are organizations, they are organizations without members.

But parties do have participants—self-willed and self-designated participants, who take part in politics and elections on their own terms and for their own reasons. We can indicate several different categories of participants in parties and elections. One set of participants occupy positions in the formal structure of the party—from precinct chairman to national chairman. Another set are elected public officials who were nominated by and carry the label of their party. Another set are the candidates who, though nominated and having run with the party label, were not elected. Still another set of participants are those who work in an election campaign, whether as volunteers or as contributors, and whether for an individual candidate or for the party as a whole.

Volunteers for and contributors to United Way campaigns are a parallel to the volunteers and contributors to individual candidates in an election. If the United Way participants were mainly interested in specific agencies, rather than in the United Way itself, the parallel would be more complete to those volunteers and contributors who are mainly candidate-oriented rather than party-loyal.

A related problem for political parties is that candidates and their followings may enter and leave political parties at will. George Wallace is the best recent example in national politics. After running in the 1964 and 1968 Democratic primaries, he then ran as an independent in the 1968 general election, and again ran in Democratic primaries in 1972 and 1976. For most of that time, he was the Democratic governor of his own state. Whether persons loyal to Wallace would remain Democrats, or become Republicans, or return to the Democratic fold after his independent campaign has been an open question.

There are some parallels in other organizations. Parishioners and clergymen do leave their original church. Some form new churches; others join other existing ones. Their leaving is often preceded by long periods of dissent (sometimes viewed as heresy) within their original church. Employees can quit, or be fired from, corporations and take employment with other and even rival companies, or they can form their own new companies. Soldiers desert, and citizens emigrate and are sometimes expelled from their home countries.

Most other organizations, however, impose a test for membership or for reentry. A corporation can decide to employ a potential employee or not. A church can readmit—often with some form of a ceremony—the supplicant. But who readmits someone to a political party? It is basically the person's own decision. George Wallace decided to, and did, run again in Democratic primaries. When former Mayor Lindsay became a Democrat and Senator Strom Thurmond before him a Republican; those decisions were essentially theirs to make and to implement. In neither case did the new party make an explicit decision that they should be admitted. In neither case was the party capable of making a decision to either admit or not.

The political party is less an organization able to define even minimal conditions for those who seek to enter it than an open forum within which persons participate when and if such participation makes sense to them.

## Timing of activity

The major activity of political parties—elections—is episodic. A party is active and has many participants usually at election time, if at all, while in between it is usually dormant. The periods of episodic— if not frenetic—activity are not synchronized among various governmental levels and offices. While the presidential election occurs every four years, and congressional elections are at two-year intervals, the states have a more varied schedule, and localities even more so. Thus, the various units of the party which concentrate on different offices lurch into activity at different times. Perhaps the closest parallel in private organizations is the summer sales force—new persons are recruited to sell products each summer. Most corporations, however, and most governmental activity, continue at a constant pace throughout the year. The one activity of government which is episodic is the administration of the election system itself, in which workers must be employed and trained for deployment into every precinct at election day. Another parallel might be war time, in which vast resources and manpower are marshalled, only to be dismantled at the end of the war. The annual fund-raising drives of private charities are another example.

## Government-based organization

Parties duplicate the structure of government within their own structure. Government is layered by state, county, and municipality; so are parties. Governmental jurisdictions overlap among town, township, county, city, and special-purpose districts; so do parties. Parties also duplicate the parallelism of the executive branch and the legislature. Both the governor (and a variety of other state executive branch officials) and the legislature are usually elected under party labels and have been nominated by political parties. The differences in electorates and in governmental functions among the offices are built into political parties as well. The structure of parties becomes even more confused in that legislators are selected from legislative districts, the boundaries of which often crosscut all other governmental jurisdictions. The parties create a party unit to accommodate those unique boundaries, thereby crosscutting all of their other organizations and their boundaries. Examples of private organizations which also have a complex internal structure would include General Motors and the Roman Catholic Church. These organizations, however, are free to create and modify their own structures, while political parties are constrained to duplicate the structure of government.

Political parties are, at least potentially, organized in both the electorate and in public office. Parties bridge the public-government gap, or the constituent-official gap. But separate party units are organized for each section; a party committee and chairman for a county, for example, are paralleled by a set of party-labeled public officials in the courthouse. Public officials, more than party officials, are likely to have full-time positions, which provide salary, office space, and employees. These resources give the public officials considerable advantage over other party participants in the event of disagreement among them.

## Variability

The 50 states, the more than 3,000 counties, and the thousands of municipalities vary greatly in the extent to which their parties are organized and how they function. In some localities, we speak of "bosses" and "machines," and think that their parties are "strong," while in other areas we speak of "weak" and ineffective parties. In some instances the parties are not staffed, seldom run candidates, and are not active. This range of behavior is rarely exhibited within any other organization. Government agencies must function at some minimal level of activity and performance; corporations are likely to disband activity in unproductive units. Volunteer organizations, however, such as churches, may more completely approximate the range of activity shown by political parties.

These four characteristics of political parties as organizations make them a unique institution in American life. While any one of the four characteristics is shared with a variety of other organizations, their combination makes political parties among the most open, the most fragmented and decentralized, and the most variable of organizations. We cannot speak of "the" party, but rather, of many different parties and of many different kinds of parties.

## FORMAL ORGANIZATION

The formal structure of state political parties resembles a layer cake more than a pyramid. The latter evokes the imagery of hierarchy and command, while the former, more the notion of strata and autonomy. To be sure, the number of geographic units does diminish from lower (3,000 counties) to higher (50 states) and more inclusive levels, just as, presumably, there are fewer generals than privates in an army. But there is no command structure within political parties. Rather, each geographic unit of the party tends to be autonomous from both those above it and those below it. Each unit is likewise autonomous from the other units at its same geographic level.

Not only is the party structured in horizontal layers (Key, 1964: 316), it is structured (and thus, divided) vertically as well. That is, at each geographic level, the party is likely to have a convention, a committee, and a set of officers and chairman. Since party units tend to parallel governmental units, the party is likely also to have at least some members in government (governor, state legislature) who create their own party units and exist in an uncertain relationship with the other party units at the same geographic level.

## Two main patterns

Table 3–1 diagrams typical elements of the party's formal structure. One consistent feature of the formal party structure is the importance of the county (township takes its place in New England). Below the county level, precincts, wards, or cities may be important also. There are two main patterns within county parties. Most commonly the precinct is the smallest unit of party organization. The precinct chairman (sometimes called "executive") is elected either by the precinct convention (sometimes called a "mass meeting") or by voters in the party primary. The precinct chairman (perhaps with other precinct officers) then becomes a member of the county committee, which, in turn, elects a county chairman. In some states, county chairmen are elected by a county convention, delegates to which are, in turn, elected by precincts.

The other main pattern is to bypass the precinct, making the city or ward the lowest elective level of party organization. In that case, if precincts are organized (as in Chicago), they are staffed downward and appointed from the ward level. If, however, precincts are not organized (as in California), they are only sporadically staffed by volunteers at election time. The arrows in table 3.1 reflect the former and more common pattern. In the latter pattern, the arrow from the primary election would run directly to the ward chairman, with the arrow running downward from that office to the precinct chairman, as in the Chicago instance.

There are, in addition, numerous other practices among state parties. In California, for example, members of the parties' county committees are elected from county "supervisorial" districts, paralleling the structure of the county board of supervisors. In a quarter of the state parties, at least some members of their state-level committees are elected by either precinct or county through the party primary (McNitt, 1976: table 9A). In some instances, public officials, or at least the nominees to public office, fill the formal structure of the state party.

**Table 3-1**
**Formal structure of state political parties**

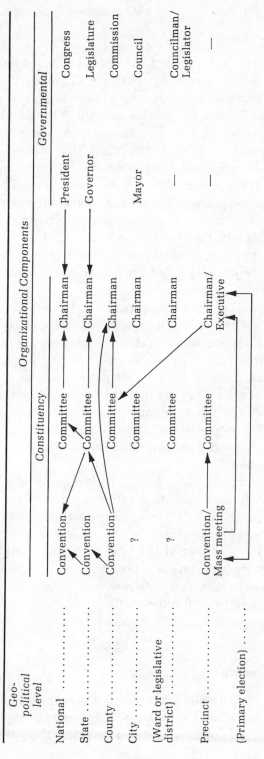

| Geo-political level | Organizational Components | | | Governmental | |
|---|---|---|---|---|---|
| | *Constituency* | | | | |
| National ............... | Convention | Committee | Chairman | President | Congress |
| State ................. | Convention | Committee | Chairman | Governor | Legislature |
| County ................ | Convention | Committee | Chairman | | Commission |
| City .................. | ? | Committee | Chairman | Mayor | Council |
| (Ward or legislative district) ........... | ? | Committee | Chairman | — | Councilman/Legislator |
| Precinct .............. | Convention/Mass meeting | Committee | Chairman/Executive | — | — |
| (Primary election) ...... | | | | — | |

## Potential for control

Whether by precinct, ward, assembly district, county supervisorial district, or county, some geographic unit of the party is staffed through an elective process. Votes are the avenue to power, not only in government, but within the parties as well. The circumstances of the election, however, vary widely among state parties. Most commonly, the elective party position is filled through a primary election. To the party officials concerned, their position is the most important office on the ballot. While the media and the public may be interested in a gubernatorial or presidential contest, those offices are secondary to the party official's own interest in his own party position. It is frequently to his advantage to have a low voter turnout in that primary election. Since the party position, however, is not filled in the general election, party workers may have less concern about the size of voter turnout then.

In almost half of the state parties, the election for party office is indirect. In both parties in Virginia, for example, party officials are selected at "mass meetings," called "caucuses" in most other states (such as Minnesota). As we will note later in this chapter, turnout in such precinct or even countywide mass meetings is very low. Such meetings, except as they are invaded by presidential candidates seeking delegates for the nomination convention, are usually insulated from public awareness and from media attention. The position of party officials is more secure in this system than even in a low-turnout primary election.

Our comments on the degree of control party officials can exercise over their own election indicates only a potential for control. When a number of precincts or other units are linked together in a factional or centralized party organization, that potential for control will ordinarily be exercised. But at the other extreme, many positions in the American party structure are unfilled, and the major task facing a would-be leader is to persuade someone to take the position. Rather than attempting to limit interest, the problem in such situations is to create interest and stimulate involvement.

## National standards

Party officials usually serve terms of two or four years, keyed to the cycle of gubernatorial and national elections. Since most states elect governors in nonpresidential years (and thus their other state officials and the legislature as well), their party officials have tended to remain unchanged through the quadrennial struggles over presidential nominations. Precisely this holdover feature of many state parties was the target of criticism and reform by the national Democratic party since 1968. To increase the representativeness of the presidential selection process, state parties must now select those officials and convention delegates (at all geographic levels) who participate in the presidential selection process, within the year of that election. Hence, for the first time beginning with the 1976 election, all state parties have selected their party personnel in the formal structure in the same year. Although this requirement was developed by the national Democratic party for state Democratic parties, the need for a uniform law within any given state has tended to induce Republican parties to make similar personnel decisions at the same time.

Additional uniformities are being introduced by the national parties into practices at state and local levels. The national Democratic party has now required that the state party delegations in the national convention reflect in their composition the demographic diversity of their electorates (by sex, race, and age) and also reflect proportionately the strength of various presidential candidates. Furthermore, these requirements of balance and proportional composition must be followed at all levels of the state party involved in the presidential selection process, beginning at the precinct. While these changes are more explicitly, and earliest, expressed by the Democratic Party, Republicans are beginning to introduce similar practices if not requirements. For the first time in our long history of a decentralized party system, a small element of national uniformity has been introduced among the states and precincts. To that small degree, our parties are now more centralized than previously.

The national standards apply only to the practices of state parties in the presidential nomination process and only in presidential years. We might expect, however, a spillover effect in how state parties function in other years and for other purposes, for the parties will not change their structure from year to year, but rather, employ a constant structure and set of internal procedures.

## The county level

The county is ordinarily considered the most important geopolitical unit of party organization. A nationwide study of the 1952 presidential nomination process, for example, observed that if effective party organization and leadership were found anywhere in the American party system, it would be at the county rather than at the state level, and most certainly, not at the national level (David et al., 1954: 165). While this observation is usually agreed to, it is not clear why the county level would be the more important unit of party organization. Several reasons have been suggested, but none tested.

1. Several offices are elected countywide. This reason relates to a more general hypothesis: The larger the number of offices filled in a common constituency, the greater the likelihood that candidates cooperate through a party structure (Schlesinger, 1965: 774–86). While this more general statement has a presumptive plausibility, it has not been tested. Neither do we have studies asking what variations occur among county party organizations as the number of county offices changes. Nor do we have studies comparing county party organization with other governmental units which also elect multiple offices, such as the city and state.

2. Patronage is more commonly found at the county level than at other levels of government. As we will later observe, the relationship between patronage and party organization is often commented upon, but seldom studied. But we do not know that, in fact, more patronage is available at the county level than at either city or state levels.

3. Many other office constituencies are built from counties. Indeed, defense of the county was one important argument against redrawing legislative and congressional district boundaries in accord with population size. Either the county chairman or delegates selected by the county party would collectively compose the party committee for the district in question. Although reapportionment has subdivided counties in drawing legislative and congressional districts, the practice of county party representation on the party committees for such offices probably still continues (though this, too, is not known).

4. Finally, the county was and remains an important unit in economic life (trading at the county seat) and in the provision of governmental services (welfare, highways, libraries). Again, this statement is more agreed to than proven.

These four statements are advanced in texts on political parties as reasons why the county is more important and powerful than other geopolitical levels in the structure of American parties. None has been proven. Each is an implicit hypothesis that party organizations vary by that particular factor.

## State regulations

The formal structure of the state parties is shaped mainly by state law. On those matters on which the state statute is silent, each party develops its own bylaws and informal practices, leading to differences, not only among the states, but between the parties within the same state. We have very few compilations of state statutory provisions on political parties (Childs, 1967). We are only told that the states "have enacted a kaleidoscopic variety of legislation . . . that literally defies summary or classification" (Sorauf, 1976: 65). One recent review of state statutes and of party bylaws, however, found that they collectively listed almost 250 different "powers" for the state parties and chairmen. Most of these came from the parties' own bylaws, for the relevant state statutes were more concerned with election administration than with party organization directly (David Davis, cited in Huckshorn, 1976: 14–15).

## Party organization authority

One study has developed a measure of "party organization authority" which combines the size of the employed party staff in nonelection years, the legal authority of the party organization (either the state committee or convention) over nominations, and the lack of competition in the nomination process (Weber, 1969). This particular measure is the most direct and useful one of the several which have so far been reported.

Table 3–2 lists the states by their ranking on the party organization authority factor. The states ranking in the highest category are presumably those with the "strongest" and most capable party organizations. They tend to be located in the industrial Northeast and Midwest, as are most of the states in the "fairly high" category. In the lowest two categories at the other end of the scale, the states having the "weakest" party organizations, tend to be Southern and Western in location (Weber, 1969).

A number of other items in the formal structure of state parties have also been measured. They include the size of the state party committee, the inclusion of office holders in the committee and the convention, the number of steps or layers in the state party structure, and a generalized measure of party centralization. The major finding is that these several available measures of the formal party organization are not re-

**Table 3–2**
**State ranks on factor of party organization authority (1954–1967)**

| Low (7) | Fairly low (12) | Intermediate (16) | Fairly high (7) | High (8) |
|---------|-----------------|-------------------|-----------------|----------|
| Ala. | Alaska | Ariz. | Colo. | Conn. |
| Calif. | Ark. | Hawaii | Ill. | Del. |
| Kans. | Fla. | Idaho | Mass. | Ind. |
| Md. | Ga. | Iowa | Pa. | Mich. |
| Nev. | Ky. | Maine | R.I. | Minn. |
| Okla. | La. | Mo. | Vt. | N.J. |
| Tenn. | Miss. | Mont. | Wis. | N.Y. |
|  | N.H. | Nebr. |  | S. Dak. |
|  | N.C. | N. Mex. |  |  |
|  | S.C. | N. Dak. |  |  |
|  | Utah | Ohio |  |  |
|  | Wyo. | Oreg. |  |  |
|  |  | Tex. |  |  |
|  |  | Va. |  |  |
|  |  | Wash. |  |  |
|  |  | W.Va. |  |  |

Criteria: The categories are based upon the following factor scores: Low, −1.0 or lower; Fairly low, −0.5 to −0.9; Intermediate, −0.4 to +0.4; Fairly high, 0.5 to 0.9; High, 1.0 or more.

Source: Weber, Ronald E. "Competitive and Organizational Dimensions of American State Party Systems." Paper prepared for annual meeting of the Northeastern Political Science Associations, 1969, pp. 19–20, table 5.

lated to one another (McNitt, 1976; Weber, 1969). They do not form patterns among the states. Furthermore, these measures, including the party organization authority measure, are not related to patronage (discussed more fully in a later section). Each state party seems to be individually constructed, and different elements in them are combined in unique formations.

## Party meetings and conventions

Precinct meetings are attended by a very small proportion of those who are eligible—we would estimate less than 1 percent. This estimate is based on personal experiences and observations, for no study has ever been reported of this form of political participation.

Recent reforms—especially by Democrats—of the presidential se- lection procedure, however, have radically altered participation in precinct meetings. Participation in the precinct meetings to begin the selection of the Democratic nominee for president in 1976 in some states was as high as 10 percent to 16 percent of the general election vote for president. And for the first time, national media and the na- tional candidates turned their attention to precinct meetings, espe- cially in the early-selecting states. Iowa, for example, held the earliest precinct meetings, prior to the New Hampshire presidential primary. Carter's narrow plurality in the Iowa precincts gave him his first media-designated "victory."

All party meetings above the precinct are attended by persons selected as delegates. And in some states even the initial-level precinct meetings are attended by persons selected through a primary. In party meetings attended only by delegates, the question of the participation rate is very different from the membership meetings. In these instances, participation measures the extent to which the party is organized in all precincts or counties sufficient to the task of at least selecting and sending delegates to the party meeting.

Participation in state and national conventions of the party is in part a function of one's party office. A Wisconsin study found that while very high proportions (69 percent was the lowest) of several categories of party officials attended state conventions, the proportion was highest for county chairmen. Although the proportions attending national conventions were much lower (33 percent was the highest), county chairmen had the highest proportion in one party and were second highest in the other (Epstein, 1958: table 5A).

The main task of party meetings and conventions is to organize power. At whatever level of activity (or inactivity) of the party and to whatever degree the party is organized (or unorganized), the party is controlled by someone or by some set of political actors. Control and power in conventions are established through the vote. Frequently, some issue or vote is the "test" vote, by which the relative strengths of opposing sides are measured, tested, and usually established for the remainder of the meeting. In national conventions we have seen credentials fights and contests over the rules as the early test votes of rival candidate strength. While the same type of early votes can occur in state and county conventions, more typically their test vote is over selection of the chairman or perhaps "temporary chairman" of the convention.

In some instances, two or more factions organize throughout the state to capture control of the state convention. Their organizational fight begins with the precinct conventions. Each side attempts to gain control of enough precinct conventions to enable them to control enough county conventions to give them a majority at the state convention. At each level, each losing side challenges the credentials of the victors at the next highest level. The losers sometimes hold "rump" conventions, protesting the legality of the winning side. At the state convention, the majority side on the credentials committee seats its adherents from the contested counties, thus solidifying its control in the convention itself. In one such state, public officials commented that they invariably avoided party conventions. One termed them a "meatgrinder" and averred that a candidate could only create enemies for himself by attending or taking any role whatsoever in these intra-party fights. One participant has described how rival slates organized conventions from the precinct through the state level in the McCarthy versus Johnson-Humphrey factional fight in Minnesota in 1968 (Lebedoff, 1972). Another statewide fight occurred among Indiana Republicans in 1954 (Munger, 1960).

The critical function of the convention is to select persons to occupy formal party positions. The chairmanship of the convention is the typical position to be controlled. In presidential years, the delegates to the national conventions are usually the major positions to be filled and hence the object of factional organization. Party conventions usually adopt resolutions or a platform as well. While a good many delegates obviously enjoy the platform debates, are committed to issue positions, and are skilled advocates of their views, such debates occur after the main matters (chairman/delegates) have already been settled. Furthermore, party and factional leaders are less involved in such debates and usually do not interpret the results as affecting their control within the party. The willingness of the Ford leaders in the 1976 Republican National Convention to hold a test vote on the rules but avoid platform fights illustrates the usual practice.

In some instances—perhaps most—party meetings are tranquil, noncontroversial, and poorly attended. Especially at the first, or precinct, level, attendance is usually a problem. The few precinct officials usually have to ask their friends to attend to obtain enough people to hold a meeting.

At the other extreme, such meetings can turn into protracted battles. Local enthusiasts for causes and candidates—most often candidates seeking the presidential nomination of a party—invade precinct meetings and attempt to gain control of the state party delegation to the national convention. (Those states which select delegates through a presidential primary deflect candidate supporter energies from the precinct meetings to the primary election itself.) On these occasions, the formal structure of the party is in danger of capture by persons who perhaps have rarely been active in the party and who are likely to have more loyalty to their candidate than to the party as a whole. The supporters of Senator Eugene McCarthy stimulated turnout in the 1968 Minnesota conventions of the Democratic-Farmer-Labor Party

(Lebedoff, 1972), as did Eisenhower supporters in the previously tranquil Southern Republican parties in 1952 (David et al., 1954). We will return to this issue as we discuss the national impact on state parties in chapter 7.

## PARTY PERSONNEL

We have examined the legal and formal structure of state parties including their conventions. What of the people within them, who participate in them, and who make them work? While we lack studies of most state committees and conventions, we do have some evidence about the chairmen of state parties from nationwide studies.

### State party chairmen

The state chairmen's relationship with their governors is the single most important element of their office. Three types of state chairmen can be identified by that factor. The "political agent" of the governor is usually selected by the governor (though officially "elected" by the state committee or convention), and performs those tasks delegated to him by the governor. These tasks usually include liaison with the state legislature, handling of patronage, and administering the party organization at county and local levels. The state chairman in this role sometimes also serves as a public spokesman for the governor. The "agent" chairman works closely with the governor, has often been his campaign manager, and sometimes is also a close personal friend. (The bulk of the information on state chairmen, and all of the quotations, come from Huckshorn, 1976. The quotations from chairmen and the data on roles are found in Huckshorn's chap. 4.) One chairman, to illustrate the agent type, commented

I am the governor's agent. I am a top appointed official in the party, and I see that as meaning that I am a representative of the governor as the elected top official in the party (80).

While most persons as agents are actively involved in the party with and on behalf of the governor, some are relegated to a less active position, as indicated by a governor:

. . . The state chairman has always been my hand-picked man. I have had three of them. The first . . . was my campaign manager and was the most effective because I trusted him and used him. The next two . . . were chosen because they would be ineffective, and I wanted to be my own state chairman and have total control of the party organization in my office (69).

The second type of state party chairman also serves with a governor of his party, but is "independent" of that governor. This type of chairman occupies that position independently of the governor's wishes, and has perhaps defeated the governor's own choice or has occupied the position for some time before the current governor was elected. In some cases—for example, Democratic chairman John Bailey of Connecticut—the chairman cooperated closely with governors of his party but was a power in his own right, and indeed, was instrumental in their nominations (by convention) and in winning their general election. In other cases—Alabama Democrats and Indiana Republicans—the party chairman has been selected by a faction of the party opposed by the governor. These chairman, as a group, are more concerned with the party than with any single candidate, as indicated by one:

The chairman . . . can concentrate his attention on party-building. He does not tie his fortunes to any single candidate (89).

Indeed, such chairmen are apt to evaluate candidates for the governorship on their potential for contributing to party unity and growth. The Republican chairman in Ohio commented:

The trouble with most chairmen is that they do not have the power base nor the know-how to stand up to party leaders and tell them that they cannot be governor or senator. A strong state chairman must be able to make that statement and to make it stick (88).

These two types of state chairmen share one trait—the governor is of their party. The third type of state chairman comes from the out-party, the party which lost the governorship in the preceding election. For some parties, this loss is chronic—they are long-term minority parties. For others, the loss is temporary, for they are more competitive in their states. Without control of the governorship, the relationship of the chairman to the state committee of the party becomes more important. The state committee may be the forum within which the chairman's election is decided, unless the party's gubernatorial nominee has been able to designate his own choice.

For parties which do hold some other elective offices, however, these officials potentially are able to control the state party and the chairman. For newly developing parties, such as Southern Republicans, which elect U.S. Senators (but not governor), these senators, almost by default, can assume active leadership of their party, as in Texas. But perhaps the more common pattern is that such officials avoid participation in the state party, as indicated by this chairman of a competitive midwestern state:

We have both U.S. Senators but they have neither one ever shown any real interest in the party. They leave us alone and we leave them alone (91).

The competitive out-party may be reasonably well organized and active. In that case, the chairman is an important leader and is active in working with the party toward the next election. Or, as in California, the chairmen mainly mediate factional disputes and avoid any appearance of involvement with candidacies or primary nominations.

Still another variation of the out-party is the chronic minority, best typified by Southern Republicans. Some chairmen accept that chronic condition and do little else than act as a spokesman for their party, and perhaps act as a patronage agent for national Republican administrations. Other Southern Republican chairmen—about half in the 1970s —more actively build a party organization and seek to contest elections. The former category might be termed "electorally quiescent" and the latter "electorally combative."

As of the mid-1970s, state chairmen of both parties were fairly evenly distributed by thirds among the three types. Aside from the in- and out-competitive status differentiating the "out-party independent" from the first two types, competitive status itself is not directly related to variations among state chairmen. Neither is region. We do not know—though we have made some rough guesses—how these three types of state chairman are related to variations in the organization and behavior of the state parties.

State party chairmen indicate that they perform a variety of tasks. The task rated as "very important" was building their party organization. Most also view themselves as fund raisers, campaign strategists, campaigners, and candidate recruiters. Given the stress in the political parties' literature on patronage, we should note that many fewer of the state chairmen rated patronage as "very important" in their responsibilities than rated the previously listed ones. Ranking near the bottom of such responsibilities was serving as a link between local and national units of the party. The rankings of these various responsibilities was quite similar between the two parties (Huckshorn, 1976: 100).

Although we will turn to primary elections in the following chapter, we should note here that state chairmen are quite active in both candidate recruitment and in primary elections. Republicans are a bit more active (80 percent) than Democrats (67 percent) in candidate recruitment, mainly because of the new growth of Republican activity in the South. The state chairmen are mainly interested in county offices and especially in the state legislature (Huckshorn, 1976: 103–5). They tend to be precluded from candidate recruitment to state level offices for two reasons: One, those chairmen who are agents are typically selected by the governor (or nominee), and are thus chosen after recruitment has become a closed question. As a result, state chairmen tend to recruit candidates on behalf of the governor, who seeks support from the local parties and in the legislature. Two, most of the other statewide offices are held by long-term incumbents who predate both the state chairman and governor.

While candidate recruitment is usually quiet and unpublicized, participation in primary elections is more open and visible. Yet 63 percent of the state chairmen indicated they would, or actually have, participated in the primaries of their own parties. They clearly preferred to avoid visible participation, but 15 percent indicated they have intervened openly in their own primaries (Huckshorn, 1976: 107). Our later discussion in this chapter will illustrate the various forms of endorsement procedures used by state parties to indicate choices and preferences among candidates for the party's nomination.

In a separate study, state chairmen ranked as their two most important tasks, first, administration of the state party and, second, promotion of the party's image. Ranking last in order of importance among five tasks was helping to manage campaigns of state candidates. Ranking in intermediate importance were raising of party funds and promotion of the party's policies. We cannot compare the findings between these two separately done studies, for they use different definitions of the chairmen's tasks and measure them differently. We can only indicate that the two studies, at least in this respect, report different findings (Wiggins and Turk, 1970: 329–30, table 5).

State chairmen are not the state party by themselves. They have a governor or nominee, on the one hand, and/or a state central committee on the other. Their relationships with both entities tend to be reciprocal. Chairmen who are agents of the governor pay only perfunctory attention to the state committee, the members of which ratify the governor's selection of the chairmen, and apparently accept either the inevitability or desirability of having the party and its chairman serve the purposes of the governor.

At the other extreme of types of state party chairmen, the out-party independents have the closest working relationship with their state committees. The state committees have selected them, and they remain the only source of authority within the party to remove them. It is the in-party independents who have to balance both a governor and the state committee, each of which is a potential source of threat to continuance in office, and each of which has important resources needed by the chairman to accomplish his tasks (Huckshorn, 1976: 231–32). Kansas Republicans presented a particularly virulent example of conflict in the 1950s between a governor and the chairman of the state party, whom he had originally selected (Smith and Hein, 1958).

Most state parties now have permanent headquarters—offices and staff. In nonelection years, the median staff size is about five persons, which increases to ten during elections. In nonelection years, the median annual costs are about $100,000 for the headquarters, varying from under $25,000 to almost $1,500,000 per state party. These costs can greatly increase during elections. Chairmen now place considerable emphasis upon maintaining a full-time headquarters, most of which have been opened only since the early 1960s.

Four reasons have been suggested for this development. The first is the spread of two-party competition, especially in the South. Southern Republicans created state party offices to aid their growth, thereby threatening and stimulating Southern Democrats to do likewise. The second is the growth of technology. State parties have attempted to take advantage of public opinion polling, computerized information retrieval systems and media services, and have created their own professional staffs to take advantage of such technologies. The third is national party demands. As both national parties have "reformed" their national convention delegation selection process (see chap. 7), they have required the state parties to closely define and monitor their own procedures. As a related development, the reform of campaign finance has also required state parties to keep careful control over and records of their own fund raising and spending. The fourth reason is communication among the state chairmen. In the past decade, state chairmen have begun meeting with one another and have formed their own organizations within the national parties. They have been able to exchange experiences, with the unstaffed chairmen learning from those with headquarters what can be done with such support (Huckshorn, 1976: 254–57).

Another aspect of the state chairman's activity is to maintain liaison with the county and city level parties within the state. These relationships are highly variable. Close to 60 percent of the state chairmen indicate they are active with the county parties, while over 40 percent indicate they do not deal with the county parties at all. This wide variation among state chairman largely reflects the variety of conditions among county parties. Almost 14 percent of the state chairmen report that their county parties are inactive—mostly Southern, we would guess. Another 23 percent, however, indicate the opposite extreme of organization and activity, in that the county parties are autonomous from the state party. Another 6 percent of the state chairmen report that the governor bypasses them to deal directly with county level parties themselves (Huckshorn, 1976: 234).

We have named the governor, the state committee, and the local parties as important constraints on the performance by state party chairmen of their jobs. There is, in addition, another set of constraints upon state chairmen—their own characteristics, perhaps the most important of which is their tenure in office. The average chairman is in office a little over two years. Assuming that a person needs time to become acquainted with his office, and with the people throughout the state (and nation) with whom he must interact, a two-year term leaves little time to either develop or implement plans. Some state parties have a two-year limit on the tenure of chairmen—California, for example. But in most state parties, chairmen leave office through resignation, not through a legal limitation on time.

The reasons for resignation tell us something about the opportunities and constraints upon the chairmen. A little over a third resign for personal and family reasons. Most state chairmen serve part-time, and must continue their occupation to earn an income. They find the drain upon their time (and personal income) more than they had anticipated and more than they and their families wish to continue. Thus, the chronic underfinancing of state parties and the constant turnover in personnel are reinforcing. A survey of state party chairmen in the 1960s found that the only salaried chairmen were some of the full-time ones: Only 39 percent were full-time, and of them, only half were on salary (Wiggins and Turk, 1970: 328, table 3).

In almost two thirds of the cases, however, resignations are political in origin. A sizable proportion resign after suffering defeat. Especially in highly competitive states, the party which loses the gubernatorial election often has its chairman resign, while in other instances, the chairman falls victim to intraparty factional fights (Huckshorn, 1976: 118). The more numerous of the political resignations, by contrast, result from upward political mobility. The chairman resigns to accept appointment to a public office, to become a candidate himself, or to manage an election campaign. That is, the chairmanship becomes a step in an upward career ladder, a way station on the road to other (and presumably better) offices and/or activities (Huckshorn, 1976: 49).

To become a candidate for public office places the chairman in an ambiguous position relative to the rest of the party. He may become a candidate to help the party, to provide the party with a qualified candidate whom other candidates wish to have on the ticket. But, on the other hand, the chairman may become a rival to some other aspirant to the party's nomination, thus jeopardizing the utility of both the chairman and the state party to at least a portion of their own party.

The findings reported here come from recent studies of state party chairmen. While the findings themselves do not measure types of party organization, they do indicate some of the characteristics of state parties and their variations. In some state parties, the chairmen and the state committee merely occupy formal offices because someone has to fill them, but the source of activity lies with the governor and his personal supporters. In some states, the county and city parties are better organized and probably more active than is the state level of the party—at least sufficiently better organized to function autonomously from each other and from the state party itself. While in some states party chairmen have long tenure and independent authority, in most the chairmen have short tenures and serve at the pleasure of either the governor, the state committee, or both.

We have little information on the correlates of various characteristics of state chairmen. Competitive status is one of the criteria defining the three major role-types of state party chairmen, but the same study does not report either competition or demographic characteristics of states as correlates of the other chairmen attributes. The other state chairmen study, although it reports the chairmen's tasks in a noncomparable form, does examine region, with the finding that, by and large, chairmen throughout the nation tended to have a similar view of their responsibilities. There were some party differences within regions, however. Republicans more than Democrats stressed administration of the state party as an important task in the South, Border, and Midwestern states. Democrats, more than Republicans, stressed fund raising in the Border, Midwest, and Northeast states (Wiggins, 1973: 490, table 1).

## County and precinct personnel

Although we have many studies of county and especially precinct-level party leaders, the studies are not evenly distributed around the country. They concentrate within the Northeast and Midwest; the

South, West, and Rocky Mountain areas have been studied infrequently. In addition, most of the studies are confined to a single urban
county. The fairly large number of studies of party personnel do not
constitute a good national sample of events and party elites and, thus,
it is difficult to generalize from them. We will concentrate upon studies of county-level chairmen and parties. The precinct-level studies
are useful for our purposes only if they include two or more states
within the same study or if, at least, they include two or more organizational levels within the same state. We will discuss county party
activity under the headings of precinct organization, campaign activities, and constituent service.

The prerequisite to party activity is party organization, yet many of
the formal positions in the political party are vacant, especially at
precinct and other local levels. Whether in city or countryside, whether
North or South, the lower levels of the party are only partially staffed.
In North Carolina in the early 1960s, for example, in only one third of
the counties were all of the precincts staffed with minority Republican precinct chairmen. By contrast, all of the precinct positions in the
dominant Democratic party were filled in over three quarters (but not
all) of the counties (Crotty, 1968: 298). Throughout the South in the
same time period, about 70 percent of the precincts were organized
by Democrats, while Republicans had organized about 60 percent
(Beck, 1974: 1240). As another example, in over half of the Pennsylvania legislative districts in the late 1950s, something less than 50 percent of their precincts were staffed (Sorauf, 1963: 46, 165–66).

Staffing is a particularly acute problem for minority parties. When
such a party seeks to grow and develop, one of its first tasks is to find
county (much less precinct) chairmen. Such chairmen are usually
volunteers and are appointed by the state level of the party or by a
candidate. In the early 1960s, for example, as the Republican Party was
organizing and growing in Texas, one congressional candidate observed that a tangible accomplishment of his losing campaign was to
find chairmen for his party in most of the counties in his district and
thereby help build the Republican Party. "In every county," he said,
"our workers are more numerous and better organized." In the same
period and state, an urban county Republican chairman pointed to
his success: over half of the city's precincts had been organized by
his party with a chairman and a precinct committee (personal interview).

While staffing is critical, there are some gains to party leaders from
having their party positions in precincts and counties only partially

occupied. The gains relate to intraparty power, and may best be illustrated by conventions. Precincts send delegates to county conventions (and counties to state) whose number of votes is proportional to some combination of population and voting turnout. Not infrequently, at least some precincts (and some counties) will not send a delegation of full strength to the convention. In the mid-1960s, for example, only 45 percent of the precincts sent full delegations to their county Democratic conventions in North Carolina, while for the developing minority Republicans the equivalent figure was only 22 percent (Crotty, 1968: 299, table 3A). The leaders of the precinct (or county) with unfilled delegation seats still cast the full vote allocated to their unit, thus magnifying the voting power of those leaders. That is, for some purposes, party leaders may benefit from not completely filling the positions of convention delegate.

Likewise, county chairmen who desire to obtain and hold their position may evaluate precinct staffing from the same perspective. If not all precincts are already staffed, perhaps filling those positions would have the effect of bringing into the party persons who would disagree with the existing chairman and who might swing the balance of power against him.

In general, the higher the geopolitical level of party organization, the more completely the positions are filled. State chairmanships rarely are vacant for long, though there is rapid turnover; most county chairmanships are filled. Likewise, we think (but do not know) that most positions on party state committees are filled. It is mainly the precinct positions which are vacant. Turnover, however, is probably high at all party levels.

We might expect that the extent of party organization would vary with competitiveness, and that the closer the contest between the two parties, the better each would be organized to fight that contest. A different hypothesis is that party organization is more an urban than a rural phenomenon. The evidence is very contradictory and confused on both points. We suspect that such contradictions reflect both differing realities in different states and also different research designs. There is only one national study, unfortunately, and that uses only one measure of "party organization"—the percentage of precincts which have chairmen. This study found that, at least in 1964, the extent of Republican organization increased with the Republican share of the vote. This finding points to party dominance, not competition. Democratic organization, however, was related neither to the election returns nor to the urbanism of the county (Beck, 1974: 1238).

Sometimes, whole party units may be characterized by inactivity and disorganization. This type of party, though, is "virtually unrepresented in the scholarly literature because it offers so little to study" (Sorauf, 1976: 76). A classic study of Southern politics placed many of the state level Democratic parties in this same category in the late 1940s: "an impotent mechanism," a "framework for intraparty factional and personal competition," and "merely a holding company for a congeries of transient squabbling factions . . ." (Key, 1949: 16, 387–88).

How do party personnel define their responsibilities? Party personnel sometimes emphasize either their organizational tasks or their campaign tasks. An Oklahoma study—in the period of Republican growth in the early 1960s—found that more county chairmen of both parties emphasized their internal organizational role than the external campaign role. In the competitive counties, however, Democratic chairmen placed more stress on their campaign role than did their colleagues in safe counties, while the relationship was reversed for Republican chairman (Patterson, 1963: 351). We might speculate that an internal organizational emphasis is characteristic of a party as it begins to grow and develop. Some support for this interpretation was found in North Carolina in the 1960s. The growing Republican party (at least in the urban sample) at that time was more organization-oriented than were the Democrats, while the majority Democrats were much more campaign-oriented (Bowman and Boynton, 1966, table 2).

Ordinarily, the higher the organizational level of the party, the more the occupants of those positions are concerned with organizational maintenance. We have already noted that state chairmen ranked administration of the state party among the most important of their tasks. Likewise, so did the chairmen of congressional district parties within Detroit. None of the Detroit precinct workers ranked this task as important (Eldersveld, 1964: 247–54), although about one third of precinct workers in Massachusetts did (Bowman and Boynton, 1966).

The most common form of campaign activity by county parties in North Carolina was to use TV; the least common election activity (25 percent of the county parties) was to make personal contact with the voter (Crotty, 1968: 304). The ranking of the county parties in the extent to which they were active in election campaigns did not vary, contrary to the above findings, with the party's competitive status and, furthermore, Republican parties (at an early stage of their Southern development) were as active as were the Democrats. Campaign activity, however, did vary with the extent to which the party was organized and staffed for the minority Republicans, but not for Democrats (Crotty, 1968: 273).

Midwestern state county parties tend to be quite active in election campaigns. At least 70 percent of the parties in 250 counties in seven states purchased newspaper ads, conducted voter registration drives, sponsored public meetings for its candidates, and provided voter transportation to the polls. Over 60 percent of the parties helped raise campaign funds, while over 80 percent of the chairmen themselves helped raise funds (Harder and Ungs, 1966).

A study of a national sample of county parties divided campaign activities into two types—"persuasion" of unconvinced voters and "mobilization" of those voters who already supported the party. An example of persuasion is the use of TV to reach the general public; an example of mobilization is to contact one's known supporters on election day encouraging them to come (or even transporting them) to the polls. There is a consistent nationwide difference between the parties; Republican county parties, in both the North and South, stress mobilization of their own supporters in competitive counties. In counties in which they are a minority, they likewise emphasize mobilization activity in Northern states, but not in Southern states. Supporter mobilization by Democratic parties, however, does not vary with competitiveness in either region. In the North (but not in the South) mobilization activities for both parties also increase with population characteristics of the counties—high proportions of urban, black, and foreign-stock. The external persuasion activities of both parties, however, increase in rural and even predominantly Republican areas in the North, but in the South are not related to either competition or population characteristics (Beck, 1974: 1238–41).

A year-long party activity is that of "service"—maintaining contacts with voters and organizations between elections to handle their requests (or complaints) for various governmental services and patronage. Less activity in receiving and acting upon these requests has been reported for precinct leaders in Seattle, Washington, than in Gary, Indiana (Cutright, 1964: 99). Although the literature widely and firmly speculates that this activity is more commonly found in cities than in rural areas, no data have been reported to test the speculation. Within the two urban areas, however, the constituent service activities for both parties increased with the Democratic share of the vote. Thus the more minority the Republicans, the more service activity they performed. We might speculate that the socioeconomic characteristics of the city precincts made such services useful in some areas of the cities but inappropriate in others.

We have reviewed studies of county party chairmen and those few precinct workers studies which include two or more states or at least two or more organizational levels of the party within one state. The bulk of the party personnel studies examine precinct-level workers within single states or even cities. The precinct studies, however, taken as a group, reinforce the main conclusion from those studies which we have examined in this section: ambiguity and confusion of findings (this literature is reviewed in Wright, 1971: 335–51).

The most commonly tested variables—urbanism and party competition—are not consistently related to either party organization or activity. In some instances, these patterns apply to one party but not to the other within the same state or city. In some cases the logic of the two major variables is contradictory: if party organization and activity increases in urban areas, so does the dominance of the Democratic vote, at least in Northern states.

One complication in attempting to generalize across states is that the available studies are not directly comparable. They use different measures and apply different methods of analysis. But we also suspect that each study is a good reflection of the realities of its particular state or city: each researcher studies what is available to be researched in his particular location. Yet the studies do not constitute a good sample of the nation's states or counties. The one national study—as a sample of counties—found some variables were related to organization and activity for some parties in one region or another. But few variables were consistent for both parties in both regions (Beck, 1974).

## AMATEURS AND PROFESSIONALS

To this point, we have reviewed the formal structures of political parties at the state, county, and precinct levels. We have also examined the characteristics of those persons who fill the formal positions in the official party structure. Now we turn our attention to volunteers and factional participants in party affairs. We also take a different look at the official party personnel, for both types of party participants can be viewed in terms of their goals and incentives. Since the concept of incentives raises the question of patronage, we will take a look at the extent and uses of patronage, as well.

## Incentives and goals

In the 1950s unofficial party organizations (loosely termed "clubs"), were formed in New York City, in the Chicago area, and in California. Particularly in the first two cities, club participants were "reformers," creating a new intraDemocratic faction to wrest power away from "bosses" and "machine politicians" who then controlled the party and held the elective offices. The reformers were "issue-oriented," while, they claimed, the others were "patronage-oriented." They were the "amateurs," while the others were the "professionals."

The California faction, by contrast, did not have much of an organized party to rebel against. Its purpose was to create a party organization and to rejuvenate a moribund structure. Those few Democrats who did hold elective office, however, were not pleased at the growth of a rival center of party power, and, in that sense, the new organization had something to fight against and reform.

All three Democratic reform and amateur movements shared in common a high income, professional occupational, highly educated, and assimilated population base. They were found in suburbia and in high-income city areas. As a group of reformers they did not then hold elective office, hence the term "amateur."

Furthermore, all three amateur club movements stressed issues. To adopt policies on public question was, they claimed, the main purpose of political parties. They reacted against the blandness of the Eisenhower Administration and responded enthusiastically to the Stevenson presidential campaigns. These movements, and their affluent metropolitan areas, have since provided much of the impetus to liberalism in the national Democratic party and to conservatism in the national Republican party, both in Congress and in the national conventions.

They criticized the incumbent Democrats of their areas as either conservative, or what was worse, not interested in or competent to consider public issues. The incumbents were, in their view, more interested in patronage and material incentives than in issues. It is hard to judge the validity of these claims. One leader of the "organization" acidly observed about the reform leaders: "Boy, when it comes to the spoils, they are right there up front!" And a reform leader admitted that while his faction did not want to obtain patronage, "We must appoint our like-minded political friends to existing positions" whenever they won control of the appointment power (personal interviews).

The terminology of these intraparty fights has now entered the political science literature. The terms "amateur" and "professional" are used to distinguish different types of participants in political party activity. By extension, the same terms are used to differentiate between types of political party organizations as well; this usage was the origin of the terms in the first place.

As types of party participants, amateurs have been differentiated from professionals in several ways. First, they were distinguished by their motivations to enter and remain in their party: patronage and an interest in issues were the original categories which were expanded into broader categories of personal or material motives on the one hand, and impersonal or purposive motives on the other (Conway and Feigert, 1968).

A more recent way to measure the difference between amateurs and professionals is to examine their goals or values for their party. Professionals are more concerned with winning elections, more ready to compromise on candidates and issues, and less concerned with intra-party democracy, while amateurs are more concerned with adoption of certain policies, are less willing to compromise to win an election, and are more insistent upon democratic intraparty procedures (Soule and Clarke, 1970; Soule and McGrath, 1975; Roback, 1975).

Most of our studies of the amateur-professional distinction have been conducted in a few local areas. We simply do not know if the concepts, much less their specific measurements, are specific to their locales or not. Nevertheless, two efforts have been made in different localities to test the existence and characteristics of the amateur-professional distinction, rather than to merely assert its presence. One found, in Missouri, that the two concepts could be measured in a population of party participants, and that the measures largely coincided with the membership of divergent factions of the local Democratic party (Nimmo and Savage: 1972). The second found, in Ohio, that the complex of attitudes bound up in the amateur-professional distinction factored into two separate clusters: attitudes toward internal party procedure, and attitudes toward the relative importance of issue consistency compared to an emphasis upon electoral victory. While the several factional groups in the (Democratic, again) party ranked as expected on these two indicators, the first factor—internal procedure—was more important than was the factor of issue orientation (Hofstetter: 1971).

## Patronage

The patronage-oriented party worker is presumably found in that type of party organization termed the "machine." In spite of its original pejorative connotations, that term is now used to designate a certain type of party organization. But what type of organization, and on what basis? The term is frequently used, especially in popular and journalistic discourse, to mark a hierarchical and cohesive party structure, the main (or at least a main) incentive of which was patronage. But the same term "machine" has also been used to designate any party which uses patronage as its incentive, whether or not it is hierarchical or well-organized. Indeed, a good many patronage-based parties have been dispersed and fragmented—for example, Boston and Manhattan Democrats (Wolfinger, 1972: 375–76).

It is commonly claimed that either machines or patronage, or both, are declining. A related claim is that party organizations are less important and less active than in the past (Wilson, 1973: 96–99). Perhaps all of these assertions are true, but we lack the evidence with which to test the claims. We do not have adequate measures of the amount of patronage available in various states, counties, and cities throughout the country, nor do we have reliable or comprehensive measures of cohesiveness or centralization of party organization (a point to be discussed in a later section). We lack these measures both now and for any time in the past (Gump, 1971: 87–88). Those who have not held power, but who sought to gain power by appealing to the electorate, have, at least since the election of Andrew Jackson, claimed to represent a "new" politics, and popular "reform" against the "machines," against the "bosses," and usually against "patronage," too. The lack of evidence on one hand, and the durability of the same appeal by successive generations of reformers on the other, should caution us against accepting any claims on these points.

We are not even certain of the correlates of either patronage or party centralization. If the old and classic "boss" or "machine" was located within central cities with their immigrant poor, not all such cities boasted of that type of political organization. If machines are now in decline, our cities have not lost a corresponding share of the poor or unacculturated. If cities are or have been the locale of party centralization, so have suburbs: Nassau County Republicans (New York), suburban Philadelphia (both Democrats and Republicans), and DeKalb County (Georgia) are examples. If patronage—quite apart from party centralization—has been, or is, a central city phenomenon, it is no less found in rural areas (Conway and Feigert, 1968: 1166; McKean, 1967; Althoff and Patterson, 1966: 47–48; Munger, 1960: 28). If patronage is an East Coast or immigrant poor phenomenon, it is no less found on the West Coast among contractors (Wall Street Journal, Sept. 15, 1976: 1). If it is central city, in location, it is also suburban (Gilbert, 1967).

In California, which we will use as an example of a progressive and reformed state supposedly free of patronage, the governor has about 170 appointments to make of heads and administrators of agencies, including several important regulatory boards. Another 2,200 appointments are made as part-time members of over 300 commissions and councils within state government. The governor also appoints, in the average four-year term, about 160 persons to judicial positions (about 16 percent of all judicial positions). Finally, the governor fills vacancies to otherwise elective positions (e.g., Lt. Governor, U.S. Senator) not only at the state level, but also on boards of county supervisors. Some 40 percent of Los Angeles County's Board of Supervisors were originally appointed by Governor Reagan, as one example.[1]

One study has ranked the states by their "patronage potential." The number of state employees not covered by merit or civil service systems in each state has been calculated as percentages both of the adult population and of the number of all state employees. These measures were not related to any other measures in the same study of party organizational characteristics, and neither were they related to party competition. The states are ranked in Table 3–3 by their patronage potential. Some of the lowest states, such as Connecticut

**Table 3–3**
**States ranked by patronage potential**

| Lowest (7) | Low (15) | Intermediate (8) | High (6) | Highest (14) |
|------------|----------|------------------|----------|--------------|
| Conn. | Alaska | Ala. | Ind. | Ariz. |
| La. | Calif. | Colo. | Miss. | Ark. |
| Md. | Ga. | Fla. | Tenn. | Del. |
| Mass. | Ill. | Minn. | Tex. | Hawaii |
| N.J. | Kans. | Mo. | Wash. | Idaho |
| N.Y. | Ky. | N. Mex. | W.Va. | La. |
| Ohio | Maine | Pa. | | Mont. |
| | Mich. | Vt. | | Nebr. |
| | Nev. | | | N.C. |
| | N.H. | | | N. Dak. |
| | Oreg. | | | Okla. |
| | R.I. | | | S.C. |
| | Va. | | | S. Dak. |
| | Wis. | | | Utah |
| | Wyo. | | | |

Criteria: The categories are based upon the following factor scores: Lowest, −1 0 or lower; Low, −0.5 to −0.9; Intermediate, −0.4 to +0.4; High, 0.5 to 0.9; Highest, 1.0 or more.

Source: Weber, Ronald E. "Competitive and Organizational Dimensions of American State Party Systems." Paper prepared for annual meeting of the Northeastern Political Science Associations, 1969, pp. 11, 15–16.

---

[1] We are indebted to Professor Charles Bell of California State University at Fullerton for these data.

and Ohio, appeared in some of our earlier measures as having well-organized parties. Another feature of the distribution of states is the absence of regional clusters: southern, western and northeastern states, for example, scatter through all of the patronage categories. Those aspects of patronage which have been measured, at least, show no association with the other things we think we know about political party organization (Weber, 1969).

We have little hard evidence about the uses of patronage for political party and election purposes. As already indicated, we do not know its extent or amount (Fair, 1964; Wilson, 1973: 98–99). Direct studies of patronage indicate, furthermore, that patronage has low and uncertain results for the political party. In one Pennsylvania rural county, less than half of the patronage employees worked in election campaigns (Sorauf, 1956). In Ohio, the only election activity which over half of the party county chairmen expected of their patronage holders was to encourage friends and relatives to support the ticket. Just a bare majority of party chairmen used any patronage workers for envelope stuffing and mailing. Some election activities were almost ancillary to the state job: highway crews were asked to tack election posters to utility poles (Gump, 1971).

The patronage system could provide a political party considerable autonomy from other political actors. In the first place, while the level of campaign performance may be spotty, the political party has some campaign workers independently of candidates, interest groups, or volunteers. The party's workers, through patronage, may be expected to be more loyal to "the organization" and its leadership than to any single candidate or to any single issue position. Their participation also might be more continuous through various stages of the electoral cycle, and at all levels of office, than would volunteers or campaign workers recruited by candidates.

Second, and perhaps much more importantly, the holders of patronage are an independent source of the party's finances. Patronage, for this purpose, includes both job holders and the winners of discretionary governmental contracts for goods (office supplies, highways) or services (insurance brokerage, bank deposits). The practice of "macing," whereby government job holders appointed by the party are expected to contribute a fixed percentage of their salary (2 percent), raises a sizeable treasury for the political party, and thus reduces the party's and candidates' dependence upon alternative sources of campaign finance (Tolchin, 1971: 117–18; Munger, 1960).

One difficulty in considering the extent or the party utility of patronage is that patronage is frequently not coordinated through the party. Rather, each officeholder has his own patronage. Our impression is that, in a good many states with fragmented and/or inactive parties, patronage is widely available but is administered separately by each individual officeholder.

Our interviews in several southern fragmented Democratic parties indicate that patronage is a powerful weapon at the disposal of the governor. Government employment is one source of patronage, but another type, of greater importance to the governor, is his power of appointment to boards and commissions, most of which are advisory in function, which meet occasionally but not full time, and which compensate only travel and meeting expenses. These "honorary" positions are eagerly sought, and their allocation by the governor becomes an important means by which he solidifies loyalties in the state party to himself and also by which he wields power over the legislature.

One durable source of patronage is the election system itself. The election and voter registration system is complex, requiring many people throughout the state to operate it. Both the full-time employees and the election-day polling place employees can be, and often are, recruited through the political party. Party control of this resource frequently shifts when party control of the governor's office shifts. One continuing source of Republican patronage in New York City, for example, has been the elections board during Republican governorships.

Another durable source of patronage is the judiciary and district attorney-public defender system (Tolchin, 1971: chap. 4). These positions are particularly attractive to, and are usually monopolized by, attorneys. Not only do the positions represent well-paid, high-status, and long- (or even life-) time offices, attractive personally to the holders and aspirers, but the entire system dispenses many other jobs and services which are valuable to party workers and to faithful voters. Every court, though it has but one judge, has many staff positions. Every court, regardless of how lowly it is, makes decisions with wide discretion about speed of trial, conditions of imprisonment and bail, severity of fines, and the like. Those portions of the judiciary handling probate of wills and guardianships are especially lucrative and discretionary sources of income to attorneys, accountants, and insurance agents. A minority party chairman in a wealthy county was asked about the political value of the county's probate judgeship: "Very. But I did not realize how valuable until we held it for a few months" (for an appointment to an unexpired term). It was precisely for this type of judgeship that Senator Robert Kennedy supported a reform candidate in 1966 against a candidate of the regulars in Manhattan. While many offices were contested between the two factions in that election, this office attracted the greatest attention and intraparty venom.[2]

But there is another form of patronage: discretionary contracts for goods and services. Road construction, architects' plans, building construction, food purchases, purchase of supplies, voting machine purchases, letting of contracts for services and consultants, placement of bank deposits and insurance contracts, release of prisoners on parole —all of these and more are financial and occupational preferments awarded by all levels of government and for which there are few neutral or objective standards (Tolchin, 1971: 119–20; Smith and Hein, 1958: 8–13). Irrespective of types of party organization and extent of two-party competition, irrespective of urban or rural location, irrespective of region, and irrespective of the amateur-professional distinction, the financial and contract patronage (often directed to well-educated and professional and business people) is necessary in every governmental unit throughout the county. While "blue-collar" patronage may vary by region and through time, there is no reason to think that "white-collar" patronage does anything but increase through time. Many of these matters are handled separately by autonomous governmental officials, not subject to coordination either by a governor (or mayor) or political party.

## Voluntary associations

In addition to the formal and legal structure of the political party, numerous informal and voluntary clubs have also existed, and continue to exist, within American political parties. Urban "machines" have often featured "clubs" within the structure of the "regular" and dominant faction of the party. They are usually organized by ward or assembly district, and provide the core of precinct workers for the leadership of the corresponding party unit. The major office and patronage holders of the party are usually the dominant figures in the club (Peel, 1935). Given the ethnic identities of many city neighborhoods, these clubs have also had a strong ethnic flavor. Indeed, the

---

[2] One election night, one of the authors was in the office of a "boss" viewing TV election returns with approximately 30 other persons. I asked a young man seated next to me who these people were. He replied that those sitting next to the boss were judges and that those lined up against the side wall were lawyers who, he said, wanted to be judges. "And what do you do?" the young man was asked. "Oh," he said, "I go to law school."

sense of personal friendship and social solidarity within these clubs has suggested the "solidarity" incentive, in addition to the "material" and "issue" incentives, as a major motive to which party workers respond (Salisbury, 1965–66).

The newer clubs and voluntary organizations have a strong "reform" and "amateur" cast (Sorauf, 1976: 78–80). Beginning with Wisconsin and California Republicans prior to World War II, the voluntary organizations have strongly advocated various positions on issues (whether conservative or liberal), have endorsed candidates in their respective party primaries, and have provided much of the campaign support for candidates in both primary and general elections. Democrats after World War II in these two states also created voluntary associations to fulfill the same functions for their party (Epstein, 1958; Carney, 1958; Bone, 1951).

Volunteer clubs have also been found in Illinois, Pennsylvania, Ohio, Missouri, and New York. The clubs tend to be formed in urban areas, and more particularly in the high-income, highly educated, and affluent areas. That is, even among Democrats, the reform and volunteer clubs tend to be suburban in location.

These newer volunteer club movements share a number of characteristics: (1) They say their main reason for participation in politics is their issue orientation, and, in fact, the clubs hold conventions and adopt platforms after much wrangling which frequently and strongly dissent from the prevailing sentiment of their party. For example, Democratic clubs were the first to overtly dissent from the Johnson Administration's Vietnam policy. (2) As a consequence, they are riven by ideological factionalism. (3) If a club movement is dominated by adherents of one ideology, adherents of another view will withdraw from the first to create a new and rival group. Many of the California Republican groups have been created in this fashion.

All of these groups have an open membership policy. Members are volunteers who pay a fee and thereby become members. They seek a wide if not "mass" membership participation. As a result, they are uniquely susceptible to infiltration by outside elements. The dominant Republican groups in California in the 1950s, as survivals of Earl Warren's governorship, were systematically captured by more conservative factions. Likewise, the New Left captured many district endorsing conventions within the California Democratic Council (CDC) by the simple expedient of swamping existing clubs and by the even simpler device of creating new ones. Among the New York City Reform Democrats, all members of the several clubs are eligible to participate as delegates in the district endorsing conventions. This policy permits rival aspirants for endorsement to "pack" and otherwise manipulate membership rolls and convention attendance to secure results favorable to themselves.

One major consequence of all of the above characteristics of the organized "amateurs" is that elected public officials do not trust them. Indeed, the conflict between the "governmental party" and the "constituency party" is endemic in any governmental system. Most political parties, however, are either sufficiently powerless or acquiescent enough not to pose a major threat to the elected officeholders of their party. The overt ideological and activist orientation of the American amateur groups, by contrast, makes them potentially powerful and active, so that public officials will be wary of them. The most important single questionnaire item differentiating amateurs from professionals in an Ohio study was: "Keep elected public officials strictly accountable to the party organization" (Hofstetter, 1971: 42, table 1). Such groups are most useful to a nonincumbent candidate in his first successful election. But once elected, the same official usually attempts to monitor and perhaps also control events inside the club. The conflicts between former Governor Pat Brown and the California Democratic Council, for example, severely limited the effectiveness and unity of that group, and, in turn, contributed to Brown's defeat by Ronald Reagan.

Two states have had analogous developments. The Michigan Democratic Party is widely cited as an "issue-oriented" party, following its rejuvenation by a combination of labor unions (especially UAW) and liberals in professional occupations. While voluntary clubs were not created, the new activists in the party were liberal and reformist in their attitudes on public policy, and their election activity did further their policy objectives.

Liberal Democrats in Texas formed the "Coalition" against the Johnson-Connally wing of the party. The Coalition consisted of four components or "legs": organized labor, the several black political groups, the Mexican-Americans represented through PASO (Political Association of Spanish-speaking Organizations) and unaffiliated white liberals (in professional occupations, mainly). The Coalition itself did not create a club movement, but, rather, rested mainly upon existing interest groups. Neither did the Coalition adopt platforms, though all of its members were both liberal in policy and loyalist toward the national Democratic party. The Coalition endorsed candidates in the Democratic party, provided campaign workers and funds for those candidates, ran voter registration drives, and attempted to gain control of the state party by contesting precinct and county conventions. The liberal Coalition reached its peak of internal unity and near-success in the early 1960s. The Johnson presidency and the Connally governorship muted the factional disputes among Texas Democrats. The Connally conservatives appealed for black support, the emerging Republicans appealed for Mexican-American support, and organized labor was beset with internal disputes.

Southern Republicans and those southern Democrats who remained loyal to the national Democratic party from Truman to Carter have usually been strongly issue-oriented. With the exception of blacks and Mexican-Americans, southern participants in both parties have fit the profile of "amateurs" elsewhere—well-educated, affluent, and urban. Organized labor has also been a constant participant in such political developments, at least among Democrats, both North and South. The enthusiasm of southern Republicans for Goldwater and Reagan, and the votes cast for McGovern's nomination by southern Democratic delegations in their 1972 national convention, illustrate the issue-oriented base in current Southern politics. The internal struggle among southern Democrats over race relations for 20 years, and its episodic national eruption in the Wallace candidacy, was paralleled by the emergence of Republicans who aspired to contest and even win elections as conservatives, no longer content to depend upon occasional patronage from national Republican administrations.

## CANDIDATE RECRUITMENT

The procedures by which a person becomes a candidate for public office are an important litmus test of the existence and activity of party organizations. We are particularly interested in knowing who the actual or potential candidates talked to in deciding whether or not to become candidates. Did they talk with party leaders? Were party leaders mainly responsible for their candidacy? Or, did they talk with other persons—perhaps interest-group leaders—or did they largely decide on their own initiative? Answers to these questions tell us about the existence and activity of a political party in one of its critical functions—offering candidates for public office.

Competitive and, especially, dominant parties will attract candidates under their labels irrespective of whether or not party leaders have been active in recruiting those candidates. Conversely, a minority party may not have any candidates at all unless party leaders or a party organization actively find them and persuade them to run. But

even in competitive and dominant parties some leaders and organizations are active in candidate recruitment and effectively decide who
shall be the party candidate for a particular office. Thus, while the
party's strategic situation varies with its competitive status, the ability
of a party to recruit candidates is more a function of its organization
and leadership.

## Extent of party recruitment

From a variety of studies of candidate recruitment, we know something of the variability of party activity in finding candidates. Most
studies have concentrated on the state legislature, while we do not
have even a single study of recruitment to candidacy for state-wide
offices (e.g., governor, attorney general). The state legislature is, however, a key position in state politics.

We can roughly rank the states (in which we have recruitment
studies) by the proportion of legislative candidates (or elected legislators) who were recruited to candidacy through the political party
(Table 3–4). Although we noted earlier that state chairmen more often
recruited candidates for the legislature than for statewide offices,

**Table 3–4**
**Party recruitment of state legislative candidates**

| State | Percentage of candidates recruited by party | Source |
|---|---|---|
| Conn. .................... | 83 | Tobin and Keynes (1975):674, table 2 |
| Pa. ....................... | 75 | Tobin and Keynes (1975):674, table 2 |
| N.J. Democrats ............. | 74 | Eulau (1961): 226, table 5 |
| Wash. (mainly Republicans) ............. | 69 | Tobin and Keynes (1975):674, table 2 |
| N.J. Republicans ............ | 66 | Eulau (1961):226, table 5 |
| Pa. (losers) ................ | 65 | Sorauf (1963):102 |
| Minn. ..................... | 63 | Tobin and Keynes (1975):674, table 2 |
| Iowa ...................... | 56 | Patterson and Boynton (1969):257 |
| Oreg. ..................... | 50 | Seligman (1974):73–80 |
| Pa. (winners) .............. | 45 | Sorauf (1963):102 |
| Calif. Democrats ............ | 42 | Eulau (1961):226, table 5 |
| Ga. Republicans ............ | 37 | Parker (1970):145, table 5 |
| Tenn. Republicans .......... | 28 | Eulau (1961):226, table 5 |
| Ohio Republicans ........... | 24 | Eulau (1961):226, table 5 |
| Calif. Republicans .......... | 22 | Eulau (1961):226, table 5 |
| Tenn. Democrats ............ | 15 | Eulau (1961):226, table 5 |
| Wis. ...................... | 13 | Epstein (1958):205, table VII–0 |
| Ohio Democrats ............ | 12 | Eulau (1961):226, table 5 |
| Ga. Democrats ............. | 6 | Parker (1970):145, table 5 |

most recruitment activity for the legislature seems to occur at the county level of the party, not the state level. Thus, strictly speaking, we are measuring within-state variations. Pennsylvania and New Jersey, for example, rank high in the proportion of legislative candidates recruited by their county party leaders, while Tennessee Democrats and Wisconsin rank low on that measure.

The high-ranking states are in the Northeast, but also include some of the border and western states. The low-ranking states are southern and one midwestern state strongly influenced by the Progressive movement at the turn of the century.

The bare numbers, however, may imply more than they should. To place Iowa, Oregon, and California Democrats in the same category as Pennsylvania strains what we think we know about the diffuseness of party organization in the former set of states contrasted with the hierarchical discipline of parties in Pennsylvania. Strictly interpreted, the numbers indicate the proportions of legislators (and, in some studies, of losing candidates as well) who reported that party leaders had talked to them about becoming candidates for legislative office. They do not necessarily imply decisive influence, and in many cases, a variety of other persons and actors were active in their candidate recruitment.

In a four-state study, high proportions of legislative candidates reported candidacy discussions with their party leaders. But in two of the states—Pennsylvania and Connecticut—these discussions were crucial in instigating their candidacy, while in the other two states—Minnesota and Washington—the discussions occurred after the decision to run, and party leaders were informed of that decision after the fact. Nevertheless, the relatively high frequency of Washington candidates holding discussions with party leaders was itself a reflection of the concerted attempt by the state Republican party and its governor to gain control of the legislature by finding, recruiting, and financing legislative candidates (Tobin and Keynes, 1975: 673–77).

Party personnel report themselves to be more active in candidate recruitment than legislators do. Over 86 percent of Wisconsin party leaders reported they were active (but not controlling) in candidate recruitment, while midwestern county chairmen in seven states reported (over 70 percent) that they recruited candidates, if for no other reason than to fill the party's ticket. Over half indicated that they have at least "sometimes" urged persons to run for the party's nomination even though at least one other candidate had already filed (Harder and Ungs, 1966: table 8).

Precinct workers stated they were more frequently consulted by prospective candidates in competitive Massachusetts than they were by either the dominant Democrats or minority Republicans in North Carolina. Within that southern state, however, Democrats were more frequently involved in candidate recruitment than were the Republican precinct workers. Indicative of the newly growing status of that southern Republican party, their precinct workers were more frequently consulted by state than by local candidates. Usually the relationship is reversed, in that precinct-level party workers are more frequently consulted by candidates to local and legislative offices (Bowman and Boynton, 1966: tables 7, 8).

**Correlates of party recruitment**

Common hypotheses are that parties which recruit candidates tend to be competitive in status, rather than either dominant or minority, and that they tend to be urban rather than rural. These hypotheses have been tested only for within-state variations, and do not purport to distinguish among states themselves.

The hypothesis that recruitment activity by party leaders varies by urbanism of the district has produced contradictory evidence. A higher frequency of candidate recruitment has been found in urban than in rural areas in both Iowa (Patterson and Boynton, 1969: 261) and Pennsylvania (Sorauf, 1963: 55), but only small differences in the same direction were found among midwestern county chairmen (Harder and Ungs, 1966).

Evidence for the competitive status hypothesis is not very strong either (Wright, 1971: 109–11; Tobin and Keynes, 1975: 672). Indeed, parties recruit candidates in all competitive statuses. How and why parties recruit varies by these categories, but not the fact of candidate recruitment itself. Some dominant parties (Pennsylvania) recruit candidates as a means of screening among many potential aspirants to insure control of the nomination process (Sorauf, 1963: 119). Other dominant parties, though less well-organized and cohesive, have extensive recruitment activity by many different leaders and factional groups. "Diffuse" recruitment is the term applied to this phenomenon in Oregon (Seligman, 1974), and might also apply to the relatively high rates of recruitment activity found in Iowa.

Minority parties recruit candidates under two circumstances. Some parties are minority in certain sections of a state, but are competitive in statewide politics. Local minority candidates, even if they have little chance to win, can nevertheless aid the statewide ticket by local-level campaigning. Furthermore, such candidates could anticipate future rewards from the statewide party should their party win state-level offices (Althoff and Patterson, 1966).

The other type of minority party is minority in both state and local politics, of which southern Republicans have been an example. But some of these hopeless minority parties actively contest state and some local offices (Olson, 1963). Their candidates may not have much chance of winning any specific election, but run as a means of developing a party organization and increasing their long-run chances. Such "electorally combative" parties actively recruit candidates; they are not likely to attract candidates, given their current minority status, without such an effort.

## Minority party difficulties in recruiting candidates

One of the most difficult problems faced by any minority party is to recruit able, experienced candidates who can run strong campaigns. Ambitious, talented young men and women usually launch their political careers in the party that regularly wins elections. Different types of candidates are willing to run hopeless campaigns in the minority party.

Sometimes what the minority needs to become a majority is an unusually strong candidate who can win election and often re-election for a major office such as governor or senator. In Maine, for example, the Democratic party had rarely won more than 40 percent of the vote for governor or senator for many years until 1954 when Edmund Muskie was elected governor. After being re-elected in 1956, he was elected to the Senate by over 60 percent in 1958 and has since been re-elected by large margins. Subsequent Democratic gubernatorial candidates have consistently won or come very close to winning. In Michigan, G. Mennen Williams won the first of six two-year terms in 1948. When Hubert Humphrey was elected to the Senate in 1948, he was the first elected Democratic senator from Minnesota. His election paved the way for the election of a Democratic governor in 1954, the first since 1914. In Wisconsin, the Democratic breakthrough came in 1957, when William Proxmire won a special Senate election by a wide margin, after several unsuccessful statewide races. In 1958 he won a full term and the party elected a governor for the first time since 1932. Since that time Democratic candidates have consistently won or run rather close races. One symptom of the slowness with which Republican parties have developed in the South is that none of the few Republican governors have been able to win re-election, except for one second two-year term (Rockefeller—Ark.); four southern Republican senators had won re-election, however, up until 1976 (Tower—Tex.; Thurmond—S.C.; Baker—Tenn.; Bellmon—Okla.).

One measure of the strength of two-party competition is the proportion of legislative seats contested by both parties. A strong candidate for statewide office may be necessary for a minority party to win that one office, but its ability to recruit candidates for a large portion of the legislative seats is a better test of the party's durability and geographic spread. The party not only needs names to fill out its ballot, but candidates with enough political strength and ability so that they have a chance of winning if the gubernatorial candidate runs a strong race and can play an effective role in the legislature if they are elected. Legislative candidates are particularly important to a gubernatorial candidate because his chances of making a good record if elected depend in great part on having at least a substantial number (if not a majority) of legislators of his party in office. During Governor Winthrop Rockefeller's two terms as Republican governor of Arkansas, for example, he was severely handicapped by never having more than a handful of Republicans in the legislature to help pass his programs, as was true also for North Carolina's James Holshouser (1973–76). Recruiting and supporting a large number of legislative candidates is difficult for a minority party because it requires a degree of organizational strength and a pool of manpower throughout the state, not just in those sections where its state and national candidates get the most votes.

During the 1950s and 1960s, when southern Republican parties were winning presidential races and in some states races for governor and senator, they were also making serious efforts, with varying degrees of success, to recruit legislative candidates. Table 3–5 summarizes the data from several southern and border states for the 1952–66 period and includes one or more elections from the 1970s to show whether the earlier growth of candidates has been sustained. The most dramatic increase in the number of Republican candidates occurred in South Carolina, which went from none in 1960 to over half in 1966, and has sustained that level. Alabama went from very few in 1958 to over three fourths in 1966, but dropped thereafter. There was a gradual increase in Florida, reaching over half in the 1970s. The number of Republican candidates grew more slowly in Louisiana, while in Texas the number actually declined somewhat after the peak in 1962 and 1964. The

**Table 3-5**
**Proportion of legislative races contested by southern Republican parties (in percentages)***

| State | | 1952 | 1954 | 1956 | 1958 | 1960 | 1962 | 1964 | 1966 | 1972 | 1974 | 1976 |
|---|---|---|---|---|---|---|---|---|---|---|---|---|
| Ky.† | S | 74 | 42 | 68 | 42 | 68 | 47 | 63 | 47 | 84 | 42 | 68 |
|  | H | 48 | 60 | 52 | 52 | 44 | 52 | 57 | 61 | 67 | 59 | 59 |
| Tenn. | S | 33 | 39 | 33 | 33 | 36 | 36 | 42 | 42 | 63 | 53 |  |
|  | H | 40 | 41 | 35 | 36 | 31 | 40 | 57 | 60 | 73 | 65 |  |
| N.C. | S | 46 | 50 | 32 | 42 | 44 | 58 | 58 | 52 |  | 64 | 54 |
|  | H | 53 | 53 | 33 | 49 | 49 | 61 | 67 | 50 |  | 73 | 43 |
| Fla. | S |  | 21 | 21 | 11 | 16 | 26 | 32 | 48 | 70 | 64 |  |
|  | H |  | 20 | 19 | 14 | 18 | 31 | 36 | 52 | 73 | 53 |  |
| Texas | S |  |  |  | 27 | 19 | 48 | 40 | 26 | 39 | 53 | 50 |
|  | H |  |  |  | 19 | 13 | 54 | 49 | 23 | 49 | 37 | 37 |
| La. | S | 0 |  | 8 |  | 20 |  | 15 |  | 39 |  |  |
|  | H | 0 |  | 5 |  | 15 |  | 17 |  | 37 |  |  |
| Ala. | S |  | 0 |  | 3 |  | 17 |  | 74 |  | 6 |  |
|  | H |  | 6 |  | 10 |  | 19 |  | 80 |  | 30 |  |
| S.C. | S |  |  | 0 | 0 | 0 | 4 | 17 | 48 | 41 | — |  |
|  | H |  |  | 0 | 0 | 0 | 17 | 24 | 55 | 63 | 50 |  |

* Data are missing for some states in the earlier years, and also the most recent years. Louisiana and Alabama hold legislative elections only every four years.

† Elections in Kentucky are one year earlier than those in other states, that is from 1951 to 1965, and 1971 to 1975.

Source: Data for the 1952–66 period are from a table in Malcom E. Jewell, *Legislative Representation in the Contemporary South* (Durham, N.C.: Duke University Press, 1967), p. 107.

Republican parties in these states ran legislative candidates first and most consistently in metropolitan counties and in other counties where the presidential or statewide candidates had been most successful.

Kentucky, Tennessee, and North Carolina each have a bloc of mountain counties in which the Republican party has regularly run legislative candidates and in some of which it has consistently elected legislators. In fact, in Tennessee and Kentucky the Democratic party has failed to run candidates consistently in some of these districts. Table 3–5 shows that, despite this head start and some years with unusually large numbers of candidates (like Kentucky and Tennessee in 1971 and 1972), the Republican party in these states failed to raise the proportion of legislative candidates consistently over 60 percent. The parties limited their competitive efforts to safe counties and other areas where their chances were best. Another example is Oklahoma, where the Republicans during the 1960s and early 1970s contested only about half of the legislative seats despite two gubernatorial victories. If the minority party contests half or fewer of the seats it cannot win a legislative majority no matter how powerful the coattails of either its gubernatorial or presidential candidate.

States with relatively strong two-party competition at the state level do not necessarily have contested legislative races in every district. One variable affecting such competition is the distribution of party strength throughout the state. If there are counties where one party has overwhelming voting strength, the other party is less likely to run candidates in such "hopeless" areas. The use of single-member districts in large metropolitan counties reduces the number of contested seats. V. O. Key (1956: 169–96), in *American State Politics* argued that the use of the direct primary, by reducing the party organization's responsibility for nominations, had reduced the number of legislative contests. He noted that Connecticut and Indiana, states where the party still had some responsibility for nominations, had a higher proportion of legislative contests than several other states where there was no such responsibility. If there are no organizational efforts to recruit them, candidates are least likely to appear in the districts where the chances of victory are least.

Where the state party leadership is making a serious effort to overcome a party's minority status, it may offer assistance and financing to candidates who are willing to compete in districts where the chances of success are small. During the 1950s in Wisconsin and the 1950s and 1960s in Iowa, for example, when the Democratic parties were achieving competitive status, they usually succeeded in running candidates in at least 95 percent of the legislative districts.

## CANDIDATE NOMINATIONS AND ENDORSEMENTS

One of the most persistent observations about the introduction of primary elections in American politics is that they have taken from the political party its most important function: the making of nominations. As a consequence, it is argued, the organizational vitality of the parties has been eroded, and they have lost the ability to screen potential candidates in order to present a slate of candidates who represent the major views and interests in the party and who have a good chance of winning.

There are, however, a number of states which have retained for the parties a formal and legalized role in the nomination process. In a very few states one or both parties can use a convention rather than a primary for nominations, although the number of these states is shrinking. In a larger number of states, the party organization is authorized to make some type of formal endorsement of candidates, usually in a convention, before the primary election. An analysis of how these endorsement procedures work in practice will provide us with some additional insights into the operation of party organizations and the relationships between legal requirements and political practice. We will also look at several other state party organizations which have used informal endorsement procedures in the absence of any legislation concerning preprimary endorsements.

In some states preprimary endorsements were included in the law adopting the primary as a compromise required to win legislative approval for the primary. Preprimary endorsements have been a part of the Colorado system since the primary law was passed in 1910. Connecticut and New York, two of the most recent states to adopt primaries for statewide office, have both continued to use the state convention as an important part of the nomination machinery. North Dakota adopted a primary in 1907, but held informal endorsing conventions for many years before giving them legal status in 1967.

## Convention states

As the use of primary elections has expanded, the use of party conventions as the final authority for statewide nominations has become very rare. New York permitted conventions instead of a primary until 1970, and Indiana followed this practice until 1976. Delaware remains the only state in which both political parties use conventions rather than a primary for nominations. Virginia permits each party, at each election and for each office, to decide on its nomination method. Virginia Republicans continue to nominate by convention even though they have won several statewide and congressional offices. The party has used the convention device to prevent any Republican from running against Senator Harry F. Byrd, Jr., a former Democrat who has twice been elected as an independent and who appeals to many Republicans. Virginia Democrats sometimes use conventions instead of primaries to nominate congressional and local candidates in areas of Republican strength. A number of other southern Republican parties continue to nominate candidates by convention rather than by primary under state laws permitting such a choice when a party's vote in the previous election is relatively low. There has, however, been an increase in the number of southern Republican primaries, partly because the party's vote totals have reached the level requiring the party to hold a primary under state law.

Although the convention nomination system is usually criticized as a method of insuring control by a small group of party bosses, a detailed study (Leege, 1970) of the Democratic conventions in Indiana (1956 to 1962) indicates a different pattern there. Delegates were chosen in primaries, sometimes with competition, but seldom were committed to statewide candidates. In some counties the chairman had an important influence on the choices made by delegates, but this was not consistently true. Although many of the delegates held party office or elected or appointed office, few of them felt under pressure from the party leadership, in part because the voting on the convention floor took place secretly in voting machines. Leege (1970: 219) concluded:

Both at the primary stage and at the convention stage, control over outcomes is widely dispersed. Regardless of their level in the party hierarchy, in the Indiana convention leaders act like participants in any responsive democratic system: They attempt to get what they can and learn to tolerate what they must.

The pattern in the New York Democratic convention, which nominated statewide candidates prior to 1970, was very different. Delegates were selected by local party leaders, and were expected to follow absolutely the wishes of these leaders in order to keep the political benefits that they enjoyed and to enhance their chances for more benefits in the future. The local leaders, in turn, followed the suggestions of a handful of top leaders in the state. The result was that the votes of most county delegations were cast as a bloc, and most delegates spent their time at conventions waiting for their leaders to finish their bargaining and issue instructions on how to vote. During the Rockefeller years, Republican conventions were usually orderly and harmonious, but Democratic conventions were characterized by factional fighting, chaotic atmosphere, and often unwise decisions. One observer (Costikyan, 1966: 152) has argued that the failures of the Democratic convention resulted from the fact that the party was

a nonexistent entity comprised of independent local organizations which assembles every two or four years in the hope that it can get through its business without doing too much damage. It rarely does. Normally, the mistakes of the convention take about three years to clear up, by which time the party is ready for another crack at it.

If this appraisal is accurate, it may help to explain not only why the primary law was adopted in New York for statewide nominations but why the new primary endorsements have not had much impact on Democratic primaries since then, either.

## Procedures for endorsement

The principal reason for authorizing preprimary endorsement has been to give the party organizations some influence, but not complete control, over the choice of candidates in the primary election. Another pertinent factor in some states has been the desire to reduce the number of candidates able or likely to run in the primary and thereby increase the chances that the winner will get a majority. The specific devices designed to help the endorsed candidate differ from state to state, and need to be identified to understand the exact effect of laws on the operation of primary elections and consequences for party organization.

In Connecticut and Utah, it is necessary to win votes in the convention to get on the primary ballot. In Connecticut the winner of the convention endorsement becomes the nominee unless challenged, and the only persons eligible to challenge are those who have won at least 20 percent of the votes in the convention; such challengers must also get petitions signed. In Utah, convention endorsement is the only way to get on the primary ballot, but Utah law provides that the convention shall endorse two candidates, both of whom automatically get on the primary ballot, unless one candidate gets at least 70 percent of the convention vote, in which case he is nominated without a primary. In several other states the candidate or candidates who win convention votes automatically go on the primary ballot, but other candidates can get on the ballot by petition. In Colorado any candidate with 20 percent of the convention vote gets on the primary ballot; it is possible but very rare to get on the ballot by petition. The new statewide primary law in New York specifies a 25 percent convention vote to get on the ballot; candidates may also enter the primary by petition and some have done so. North Dakota has a similar provision, though very few signatures are needed on a petition.

In several states the endorsed candidate is either specifically designated on the primary ballot or is listed first on the ballot. Colorado provides that the various endorsed candidates appear on the ballot in order of the number of convention votes received, with any unendorsed candidates appearing below them. In Connecticut and Rhode Island the endorsed candidate is listed first, with an asterisk beside the name. From 1953 until 1973 Massachusetts had a law specifying that an endorsed candidate would be listed first with the endorsement specified on the ballot, in addition to a provision making it easier for endorsed candidates to get on the ballot.

Laws providing for endorsement in primaries can be expected to affect the party organization's influence on the outcome of primaries, and thereby affect its power. On the other hand, the existence of such laws is itself a consequence of organizational strength; it shows that the party has been strong enough to get and keep endorsements as part of the primary system. There may be disagreements between parties or between political factions about the desirability of endorsements. In Massachusetts, where endorsements had been part of the primary law from 1932 to 1937, they were reinstituted in 1953 on the initiative of Republicans and some dissident Democrats, and were again abolished in 1973 by the Democratic legislature.

There are several state parties that regularly make endorsements in primaries even though they have no legal effect. In North Dakota, endorsements were made informally for many years before they were legalized in 1967. Both parties in Minnesota and Pennsylvania, and the Republican party in Wisconsin, make informal endorsements; the Democrats and usually the Republicans in Illinois also follow this practice. In California, preprimary endorsements were adopted by informal organizations in both parties because of the confusion resulting from cross-filing of candidates in both party primaries. Although cross-filing has since been abandoned, the numerous voluntary organizations continue to make preprimary endorsements.

## Effects of endorsements

If a party convention endorses candidates, do they usually win in the primaries? Is the endorsement more likely to be effective in a state where it is sanctioned by law rather than informal, or where convention votes facilitate getting on the ballot? Under what conditions do candidates seek convention endorsement, if they do not have to; and what determines whether unendorsed candidates will challenge the endorsee in a primary? Under what conditions can an endorsed candidate be beaten in a primary?

To answer these questions, it is necessary to examine in more detail what actually happens in endorsing conventions and in the primary campaigns that follow them.[3] A study of the preprimary conventions

---

[3] Information on state laws concerning party endorsements in most cases comes directly from the statutes. Information on the recent history of endorsing conventions is based on accounts in the newspapers of these states, as well as a few books and articles that are cited. We are also indebted to the Republican party organizations in Wisconsin and Minnesota for information.

**Table 3–6**
**Effectiveness of procedures for preprimary endorsement by state party organizations**

| *Effect of endorsement upon primary* | *Convention votes required to run in primary* | | *Other legally specified endorsements* | | *Informal endorsements* | |
|---|---|---|---|---|---|---|
| Endorsement decisive, rarely challenged in primary | Colo. | D–R | Mass. | R | Mass. | R |
| | Conn. | D–R | (1954–72) | | (1974–  ) | |
| | N.Y. | R | R.I. | R | Wis. | R |
| | N. Dak. | D | | | | |
| | Utah | D–R | | | | |
| Endorsement sometimes challenged, rarely upset | | | R.I. | D | Ill. | D |
| | | | | | Minn. | R |
| | | | | | Pa. | R |
| Endorsement usually challenged and occasionally upset | N.Y. | D | Idaho | D–R | Calif. | D–R |
| | N. Dak. | R | Mass. | D | Ill. | R |
| | | | (1954–72) | | Minn. | D |
| | | | | | Pa. | D |

shows that the state parties can be classified into three groups: those in which the convention endorsement is rarely contested; those where the endorsee is sometimes challenged but rarely beaten; and those where conventions are often sharply divided, the endorsee is usually challenged, and he is occasionally beaten in the primary. In Table 3–6 we have cross-tabulated the major types of endorsement procedures with the consequences of endorsement. The table shows that endorsements are most likely to be effective where state law gives the endorsee a distinct advantage in getting on the ballot. Among the other states with legal endorsement procedures, and also among state parties with informal endorsements, we can find examples of endorsements ranging from the most effective to the least effective. Obviously there are factors in addition to the legal provisions that help to determine how effective the endorsement will be. Moreover, there is no obvious geographic pattern distinguishing the effectiveness of endorsements.

The best way to shed some light on the variety of patterns of preprimary endorsements and their effect is to look at a few examples from individual states. We will not take time to examine every state, but these examples may be useful to persons who want to examine convention endorsements in their states. We begin with state parties in which the endorsements have been most effective.

## Endorsement tantamount to nomination

The dominant role of the state convention in the Connecticut nominating system results from party norms and practices as well as legal provisions (Lyford, 1959). The law provides that any statewide candidate who wins convention endorsement will be the party's nominee unless he or she is challenged in the primary, and that, to make such a challenge, a candidate must win 20 percent of the vote on at least one convention roll call and must get 5,000 signatures on a petition. The primary law took effect in 1958, and only one gubernatorial primary was contested between then and 1974—the 1970 Republican nomination. The state party organizations have been strong for many years in Connecticut, and the organizational leaders continue to play a powerful role in the choice of nominees. At the conventions, the goal of the leadership is not only to win endorsement for its candidates but to prevent other candidates from getting the 20 percent vote needed to enter a primary. There is pressure on candidates to accept the verdict of the convention and even to commit themselves to such acceptance before the convention begins. The Democratic convention has rarely had any competition for the gubernatorial nomination, although other offices have been contested. In 1974 one gubernatorial candidate withdrew when it became clear that he could not get as much as 20 percent of the convention votes. The Republican convention has had more close contests. In 1962 there were six gubernatorial candidates, and it was not until the eighth ballot that a candidate won the majority of votes necessary for endorsement; after some delay his major opponent decided not to enter the primary. The only gubernatorial primary occurred in 1970, when a candidate who won only 22 percent of the convention votes challenged the endorsee, criticized the endorsement process in his campaign, but won only 20 percent of the vote in the primary.

Endorsement conventions have been provided by law in Colorado since the primary was established in 1912. The present law provides that any candidate winning at least 20 percent of the vote at the state convention will appear on the primary ballot, and that the candidates will be listed in the order of the votes won in convention. Although candidates can get on the primary ballot by collecting signatures on a petition, this is very rarely done. Even though the Colorado party organizations are not as strong and disciplined as those in Connecticut, and the Colorado primary law is more flexible, there are relatively few contested primaries in Colorado—only 5 out of 18 contested gubernatorial primaries from 1950 to 1974. Contests for other statewide offices are also infrequent. Since 1928 only one gubernatorial candidate has defeated the top endorsee in a primary of either party (Eyre and Martin, 1967: 51). The fact that voters consistently support the top choice of the convention may be a reason why so few primaries are contested.

Generally, when a state has a law authorizing endorsements it indicates that the political parties favor such endorsements and are powerful enough to get such legislation passed. Where the parties disagree about endorsements, however, there are likely to be frequent changes in the law or differences in how the endorsement procedure operates. In Massachusetts, for example, the Republicans enacted a law mandating the use of preprimary conventions in 1954. It was repealed in 1973 by a Democratic legislature, which had to override the veto of a Republican governor. In Republican hands, the endorsing convention was consistently a device for deciding the nomination. The Democratic convention, on the other hand, was only the first step in an often bitter primary battle. The Republican party continued to hold informal endorsing conventions after the repeal of the law in 1973.

Seven of the eight Republican gubernatorial nominations from 1954 through 1970 in Massachusetts were settled in the convention without a primary. (The only exception occurred in 1958 when the endorsed nominee died and another candidate had to be substituted in the primary.) There were very few gubernatorial contests in the convention, and the losers made no move to challenge the outcome. There was a hard-fought primary for attorney general in 1962 between Edward Brooke and Elliott Richardson (subsequently a senator and a member of the Nixon-Ford cabinets, respectively) after an extraordinarily close vote in the convention. In 1974, after the repeal of the endorsement law, the Republican party held an informal convention; its endorsement of the incumbent governor was challenged unsuccessfully in the primary by a more conservative Republican who had won about a third of the convention vote.

The Wisconsin Republican party is an example of a state party that has made very effective use of informal endorsement procedures. The state law does not authorize endorsements; in fact, the effective Wisconsin party organizations are informal, extralegal ones, because of legal restrictions on formal party activities. The Democratic party in that state makes no endorsements. The Wisconsin Republican party has been making endorsements in its conventions consistently since 1950, as provided by its constitution. These endorsements have been very effective in determining nominations, partly because the party organization's funds, as well as its manpower, are available to assist the endorsed candidate if a primary is contested. In 1946 the convention endorsed an opponent to the incumbent Republican governor, and the endorsee lost. Since that time (through 1974) the endorsed gubernatorial candidate has won every primary, and been challenged only four times. The last very close convention contest was in 1962. Many of the Republican primary contests have followed a liberal-conservative alignment, but the ideological division within the party has declined as many of the old Progressives have left to join the Democratic party.

## Endorsements often challenged

We have identified several state parties in which the endorsed candidate is often challenged in the primary but is rarely defeated. Rhode Island, like Connecticut, is a state with strong party organizations that was very slow to adopt the primary. The Rhode Island law, in effect since 1950, permits the state party committees to make endorsements in the primary and provides that endorsed candidates appear first on the ballot and are marked with an asterisk. We have classified the Republican party as one in which endorsements are tantamount to nomination because in only two of 13 elections from 1950 to 1974 was the endorsee challenged, both times without success. Democratic primary competition in the governor's race has been a little more frequent: 5 of 13 endorsees were challenged. Although none of these challenges was successful, there were four very close gubernatorial primaries between 1958 and 1964, with factional conflicts—some of which had an ethnic base—eroding party discipline. Incidentally on two occasions, in 1960 and 1976, an endorsed Democratic candidate for the Senate has been defeated.

There is no legal provision for party endorsements in Illinois, but the Democratic party for many years has endorsed candidates for state and local office. The endorsement was made by a screening committee of the state party committee, and on occasions other partisan groups have made endorsements, one example being the Independent Voters of Illinois, a Democratic reform group. The screening committee is dominated by members from Cook County (Chicago) which meant that it was dominated by the late Mayor Daley. The organizational endorsements are important because the party organization is powerful and well-disciplined. If there is primary competition, the endorsed candidate can count on assistance from an army of party workers who will, among other things, distribute sample ballots on which the endorsed candidates are listed. The party screening committee interviews prospective candidates and then makes its endorsements just a few days before the filing deadline for the primary. Nonendorsed candidates often find it impossible to collect enough signatures on petitions without organizational help in the brief time before the deadline

(Sittig, 1962). In 1936 a Democratic endorsee was beaten in a gubernatorial primary, when the organization made the mistake of refusing to
endorse the incumbent governor. Since that time, endorsed candidates
had won consistently until 1972, when Paul Simon was beaten in the
primary by Daniel Walker, who did not seek endorsement and who
campaigned against the state party and particularly the Cook County
organization. In 1976, the endorsed challenger defeated incumbent
Governor Walker, but was in turn defeated in the general election. In
both 1956 and 1960 nonendorsed candidates announced that they
would run with or without endorsement, and did so unsuccessfully.

### Endorsements usually challenged, sometimes beaten

There are several examples of states in which decisions of endorsing conventions are usually challenged and sometimes reversed. The
most notable of these is the Massachusetts Democratic party. Between
1954 and 1974, all but one of the eight gubernatorial endorsements
were contested in the primary, and on two occasions the endorsee was
beaten. While Republican conventions were usually harmonious,
Democratic decisions on endorsements were usually close and
achieved only after long and bitter struggles. The party for many years
has been torn by personal rivalries and factionalism. Instead of settling
these differences, the convention system seemed to exacerbate them.
Party workers who had supported losing candidates in the convention
were often angered by the tactics used and pressures exerted by the
winning candidate, and worked even harder for their candidate in the
primary. Democratic politicians increasingly became convinced that
either a convention system or a primary would serve party interests
better than a preprimary convention, and eventually they succeeded in
abolishing the state requirement for a preprimary convention (see Barbrook, 1973). The party endorsement was thought to be useful in small
towns where party workers usually knew most of the voters personally
(Levin, 1962: 244–45).

After many years of making statewide nominations in convention,
New York adopted a primary law, with an endorsing convention, that
took effect in 1970. The law provided that one candidate would be endorsed, but that any candidate getting 25 percent of the vote on any
convention ballot could get on the primary ballot without having to use
petitions. We might expect that, as in Connecticut and Rhode Island,
the convention decisions would not be seriously challenged in the
primary—at least during the first years of its use. This did not prove
to be the case in the New York Democratic party. In 1970 the conven-

tion endorsed Arthur Goldberg for governor, but he announced that he would also collect signatures on a nominating petition to avoid the charge that he was simply an organization candidate. He was challenged in the primary by Howard Samuelson, who got less than the 25 percent minimum at the convention, and Goldberg won a relatively narrow victory. Four years later the convention endorsed Samuelson over Hugh Carey. Carey got a little more than the 25 percent minimum (aided by some votes from Samuelson supporters who did not want it to appear that their candidate was handpicked by the organization). Carey proceded to overwhelm Samuelson in the primary, with 61 percent of the vote. (The three other endorsed candidates who had opposition were also beaten). After two elections, it appeared that the Democratic convention had become, like that in Massachusetts, simply a preliminary skirmish for the primary election.[4]

In Minnesota the preprimary conventions are strictly informal, without any legal basis, but have been used to make endorsements consistently by the Democratic-Farmer-Labor party (DFL) since 1944 and by the Republican party with some regularity since the party amended its constitution in 1959 to permit them. Although most gubernatorial primaries in both parties have been contested, the endorsed candidate has usually won, often by large margins. In some elections the primary opposition has come from candidates who did not seek convention endorsement. There has often been pressure on a candidate who failed to get endorsement to not enter the primary, and in a few cases they have been persuaded to accept endorsement for other offices. Leaders of both parties favor the endorsement system as a way of enhancing party unity and also minimizing the effect of cross-over voters in an open primary state. The DFL has made extensive use of sample ballots to make voters aware of its primary endorsements.

The most notable failure of the DFL convention system occurred in 1966, when the convention refused to endorse the incumbent DFL governor, Karl Rolvaag. Many members of the party were convinced that he could not be re-elected. A bitterly-divided state convention re-

---

[4] The 1976 New York Democratic convention deserves brief mention if only because of its success in defying the laws of mathematics. For reasons that are too complicated to explain but involve a high order of tactical sophistication, the convention decided to endorse Paul O'Dwyer for the U.S. Senate nomination (requiring more than 50 percent of the vote), but also voted to qualify three other candidates for the primary ballot, without their having to get petitions signed (requiring that each get 25 percent of the vote). This miracle was accomplished by shifting votes from the first to second to third ballots. It is worth noting that some of those who eventually voted to endorse O'Dwyer (who ultimately got 85 percent of the convention vote) did so in the belief that he would become vulnerable to charges of being the candidate of the bosses. He lost in the primary.

quired 20 ballots before finally endorsing Lieutenant Governor Keith for the gubernatorial nomination by the two thirds margin then required. Governor Rolvaag launched a campaign that was effective enough to win a 68 percent majority in the primary, and obviously picked up a large sympathy vote from those who believed that he deserved the party's endorsement. The badly-divided party was defeated in the general election.

The preprimary endorsements in California are not part of the legal nominating structure, but are made by several unofficial party organizations. The practice was started by the California Republican Assembly in 1942 and adopted by the California Democratic Council (CDC) in 1954. Prior to 1958, state law permitted cross-filing, a practice under which candidates could run in the primaries of both parties, and endorsements helped to reduce the chances that a primary would be won by a candidate from another party. In the early years both endorsing organizations were highly successful. Not only did their candidates usually win the statewide primaries but those who were not endorsed often dropped out of the primaries. In the 1940s and 1950s, almost all of the Republican Assembly's candidates were nominated, and from 1954 through 1960 all of the CDC's statewide candidates won. In both 1964 and 1968, however, the CDC's senatorial candidates lost in the primaries. In recent years the CDC has been divided by sharp ideological splits and has earned the opposition of several top Democratic officeholders. On the Republican side there has been a proliferation of endorsing organizations. In 1974 endorsements in the Republican race were made by the conservative United Republicans and the liberal Republican League as well as the Republican Assembly. That same year the CDC failed to endorse any candidate because none of the seven contenders was able to win the required 60 percent of the vote. The favorite among the CDC delegates, Jerome Waldie, eventually placed fifth in an 18-person primary, while the primary winner, Edmund Brown, Jr., had only one sixth of the convention vote. In a state where party discipline is weak and parties are fragmented along ideological, regional, and other lines, it is not surprising that the endorsements of informal party groups have failed to have a decisive impact on the primary.

## Legislative endorsements

While our previous discussion has concentrated on statewide offices and state-level party decisions, similar practices can, and do, occur in district elections to the state legislature. Our evidence, how-ever, is much more fragmentary than for the statewide offices, though we speculate that the practice is much more widespread.

Among four states which have been compared directly, Connecticut and Pennsylvania had relatively high proportions of legislative candi-dates who were endorsed by their parties, while that practice was less often encountered in Minnesota and Washington. In the latter state, the endorsements were mainly by Republicans, while in the intermedi-ate-ranked state, Minnesota, the endorsements were mostly by Demo-crats. We cannot tell whether party endorsements cause a reduction of competition in the primary election, although that effect is probably intended by party leaders. The best we can conclude is that endorse-ments and lower rates of contested nominations occur together, while higher rates of competition and the absence of party endorsement also occur together (Tobin and Keynes, 1975: 676–79).

This statement, however, was not true in the 1958 Pennsylvania legislative primary elections. In that year, at least, competition oc-curred more often in those districts in which the party organization had endorsed a preferred candidate than in districts in which the party had not. This finding was more pronounced for Democrats than Re-publicans. As a consequence, we cannot infer, from the absence of primary competition, the presence of party organization and party ac-tivity (Sorauf, 1963: 112–14). It is precisely this confusion which be-devils much of the analysis of political party organizations.

Our discussion of legislative endorsements begs an important ques-tion—Which party units make the endorsements? While we have pre-sented evidence and illustrations of the active involvement of state chairmen and governors in recruitment of legislative candidates, most recruitment and endorsement activity occurs—if at all—at local levels of the party. Usually the county unit of the party is the best organized and most capable of making endorsements. Furthermore, the county was customarily the unit from which legislative districts were formed. In rural areas, several counties would be joined to form a single dis-trict, or in urban areas, several legislators would be elected at-large from a single county. These districting arrangements gave the county party maximum opportunity to act as a unit in recruiting and endors-ing candidates to the state legislature. Court decisions on the "one man, one vote" principle have greatly reduced the number of at-large districts. In their place, several smaller single-member districts have been drawn within and across county lines. The result has been either to deliver the endorsement power to smaller units of the party or to simply reduce the ability of any party unit to effectively select and endorse legislative candidates in the primary. Once elected, an official can develop his own ties to his own electorate, and thereby increase his independence of the party. Indeed, perhaps possession of a strong but localized base of support displaces the political party in the initial recruitment and nomination process (Jewell, 1969: 11).

In some cities, such as New York and Baltimore, the legislative district (or assembly district) is the basic unit of party organization, while in other cities, such as Chicago, the ward is that basic building block of party organization. The necessity of frequently moving legislative district boundaries to accommodate population shifts also disrupts the party organization and its ties to its electorate.

## FACTIONALISM IN STATE PARTIES

Few parties are homogeneous and monolithic. Rather, they contain many different elements, each being a potential source of controversy, disagreement, and opposition to the others. The mere division of a state into counties, legislative districts, judicial districts, and cities provides an ample supply of designations by which party activists can define themselves in opposition to others. The division of state government between executive and legislature, and, within the executive branch, among various elective offices, also provides an ample supply of differing sources of power and ambition. Theoretical literature and evidence are almost totally lacking on factionalism, though it is one of the more frequently used words in politics.

### Factional bases

We can indicate the more common bases for the formation of factional groups within state parties. Regionalism is one basis of factionalism within states. California is divided north versus south, Tennessee into three regions, Mississippi into the delta and the rest of the state. An urban versus rural distinction is important in many states, and is often superimposed upon the regional division, as, for example, the place of Boston in Massachusetts and Chicago in Illinois politics. The otherwise common urbanism of San Francisco and Los Angeles disappears into their regional differences, and the "upstate" cities of New York usually have more in common with the rural "upstate" areas than with New York City. Georgia politics is frequently a case of the Atlanta metropolitan area against the rest of the state. Pennsylvania politics, particularly among Democrats, is dominated by the differences between Pittsburgh and Philadelphia.

Ethnic and demographic differences among a state's population are frequently the bases of factionalism within parties. Religion in Louisiana, Idaho, New York, and Connecticut is particularly important. When added to ethnic differences, the number of separately defined groups grows rapidly. The European nationality differences among Catholics between Irish and Italian, and between Polish and Ukranian, are examples. Race has been one of the major factional bases in Southern states, and is growing in northern urban states as well.

Other factional bases are also important in selected states. We have earlier discussed, for example, the reform versus "regular" split among Democrats in New York City, Illinois, and Ohio. The ideological splits among California Republicans and among several of the southern democratic state parties are another example.

Political generations can form the bases of factional leadership and opposition. Senator Harry F. Byrd, Sr., and Mayor Richard Daley were examples of dominant factional leaders in Virginia and Chicago, respectively, whose control over their parties continued until their deaths. Other dominant officeholders, such as Governor Earl Warren in California, Governor George Wallace in Alabama, Senator Styles Bridges in New Hampshire, and Lyndon Johnson in Texas, were not seriously challenged in their control, or at least leadership, of the party while they remained in public office. Of these dominant party leaders, only Byrd and Daley inherited an already-made state political organization. All the others, in effect, created an organization which did not, however, outlast their own tenure in office. But during their political lifetime (whether that coincided with their physical life or not), they dominated politics of their state, they dominated their own party, and factionalism within the party was formed in support of and/or opposition to them. Dominant leaders can dampen the open expression of intraparty rivalry. Only upon their death or retirement from office, will the latent factionalism erupt into open view and overt expression. The battles of succession, especially if won by a subsequent dominant leader, become the best barometer of a party's factionalism, even though they erupt only once every political generation rather than in every election.

Economic-based organizations are also a source of factionalism within state parties. Organized labor in many state Democratic parties (and some unions in some state Republican parties, too), specific companies, and associations of either businessmen or farmers are major

participants in the parties of their states, are a major source of resources and leadership, and are an object against whom others organize
within the party. Among Democrats, white-collar liberals (and especially the New Left) are different from, and are opposed by, organized
labor. Republicans in some states are not entirely happy with the dominant role within their party played by companies, either (Huckshorn,
1976: 133).

A generalized labor-management conflict pervades the politics of
many states. Whether or not a state should have a "right-to-work" law
is a particularly visible and dramatic issue. Workman's compensation
is a more continuous though less publicized issue over which labor
and management dispute. These issues are perhaps most commonly
expressed through interparty competition, as in Michigan (Fenton,
1966: chap. 2), but in at least some states, the labor-management conflict is found within parties as well (Smith and Hein, 1958). The more
a single party is dominant within a state, the more likely this type of
economic-based conflict will be fought within it. Southern state Democratic parties particularly have been riven by such a conflict. But competitive Republican parties of such states as New York, Pennsylvania,
and California, have also had important sources of labor union support
along with management.

Aspiring candidates are another source of factionalism. They can
attract supporters, and can finance a paid staff, especially if they already hold a public office. These supporters and staff may have more
loyalty to the one candidate than to any other type of participants
within the party. They will work for that candidate in whatever elections he enters and will perhaps serve with him in staff positions upon
his attaining a new office.

Still another source of factionalism consists of new participants in a
political party. Parties grow by attracting both voters and elites who
have previously participated in the other party. The new participants
bring not only needed votes and support, but also distinctive views.
The surge of Eisenhower supporters into southern Republican parties
in 1952 swamped the prior combination of "post-office" and Appalachian Republicans, and the Goldwater surge of 1964 again brought in
new participants who tended to displace the leadership of the Eisenhower era. The same type of personnel displacement seems also to
have occurred in the transformation of the northern Democratic parties into a New Deal party (Sorauf, 1954: 695–96; Fenton, 1966:
142–45).

Party switchers reduce the factional strife in their former party by the act of leaving it. That not enough leave-taking has already occurred in southern Democratic parties is indicated by this comment from one state party chairman in speaking of his own party's county chairmen:

I would be glad to drive them all out of the party and into the Republican party so we could start fresh. They are all Wallaceites (Huckshorn, 1976: 239).

## Interparty tactics of factionalism

Why should, or do, the various factions remain within their party, particularly if they do not control the party or at least have not achieved their self-defined goals? In some instances they do not remain in their original party. To change parties is an extreme step, but is probably one occurring frequently today. The growth of southern Republicans is accomplished by former Democrats who become Republicans, in the same way that former Republicans in New England and the Midwest became Democrats in the 1930 to 1960 period (Fenton, 1966: 221). The Progressives of Wisconsin, for example, were first a Republican faction, and then at various times in national politics a third party. Now many of their former members are Democrats (Epstein, 1958: chap. 3). Similarly, Senator Strom Thurmond, originally elected a Democrat, was the Dixiecrat candidate for President in 1948, but not until the 1964 presidential election did he become a Republican. John Lindsay of New York, Congressman and Mayor, and Congressmen Reid (New York) and Riegle (Michigan) became Democrats after they won office as Republicans, while John Connally has become a Republican after serving as Democratic governor of Texas. In each case, the change of party has been ideologically consistent; each was unhappy in and disagreed with his original party. In each instance, the new party has been more agreeable with those persons' views on public policy.

Another tactic available to factions is to form a separate party, as have Liberals and Conservatives in New York, and the Freedom Democratic Party in Mississippi. Whether such third parties should be regarded as factions of a major party or as separate political parties in their own right is open to question, and is a matter of disagreement among their own leaders and supporters. Each, however, often attempts to influence the decisions of a major party, particularly on nominations. The Liberal Party in New York will withhold its endorsement of Democratic candidates of whom it disapproves, hoping that Democrats will fear they would lose the office if they lost the added votes brought by the Liberal Party's customary voters (Bone, 1946: 277–78). The New York Conservative Party acts similarly upon Republicans. The potential impact of this strategy was shown in the 1970 New York Senatorial election, in which the Conservative Party nominated its own candidate (James Buckley) who won against both the Democratic and incumbent Republican candidates. Buckley promptly joined the Republicans in the Senate, and later obtained the support of the state Republican leaders for their nomination in his re-election campaign in 1976. In return, the Conservative Party would adopt the Ford-Dole ticket and place the Republican candidates under its name on its own line on the ballot. Having the Republican national nominees on the Conservative Party's ballot line would add to their totals the latter's normal share of the vote. The Conservative Party did fulfill the bargain, but only by a reluctant three-vote margin in its state committee, for Reagan had been its strong preference for the Republican nomination (*New York Times,* September 19, 1976, p. A34).

The Mississippi Freedom Democratic Party is mostly black in leadership and voter support, and was organized as a separate party during the voter registration campaigns of the 1960s to provide a means of political expression for voters who had been excluded from the state's Democratic party. It acted as a faction of the state party, especially in contesting against the "regular" party for possession of the state's seats in the national conventions. In the 1976 presidential primaries, however, members of both party groups met in the same party caucuses (though they largely voted for different candidates), formed a joint delegation to the national convention, and jointly supported the Carter-Mondale ticket in the fall.

Third parties are sometimes transition vehicles for factions to move from their original party into the other major party, as has occurred with the Progressives of the 1920s and the Dixiecrats of the 1940s. The supporters of George Wallace appear to have gone different ways: some have become Republicans, attracted by Goldwater in 1964 and the Nixon southern strategy in 1972. Others, however, have remained Democrats. Governor Wallace himself remained within the Democratic primaries in 1976, and supported Carter in the November election.

Other third parties, however, retain a separate existence, for they are not so much "in between" the major parties as "off to one side." The Liberal and Conservative parties in New York, for example, are positioned to the ideological left and right, respectively, of the Democratic and Republican parties. Although the Liberal party on occasion supports Republican candidates, and the Conservative Party, Democratic ones, that tactic is a protest against decisions made by the other major party.

## Intraparty tactics of factionalism

One strategy for a faction which remains within a party but which is not in agreement with that party is to work for the election of a candidate of the other party. This strategy is usually confined to a single election and single office, and is a protest to the nomination of a single candidate. Perhaps the most notable example occurred in the Maryland gubernatorial election of 1966, in which liberal Democrats supported the Republican candidate, Spiro Agnew, after their own candidate had been defeated in the Democratic primary by a racial segregationist. Liberal Democrats in Texas have on several occasions supported Republican candidates in general elections when a conservative had won the Democratic nomination, especially for the U.S. Senate.

A less drastic strategy is to withhold support from the nominee of one's party, though not to work overtly for the other party's candidate. In presidential politics, Republican moderates withheld support from Goldwater in 1964, Democratic dissenters from the Vietnam war withheld support from Humphrey in 1968, and some conservative Republicans withheld support from Ford in 1976. In state politics, the "regular" Pennsylvania Democratic organization was less than enthusiastic for their nominee for Governor, Milton Shapp in both 1966 and 1970, and organized liberal Democrats in California shared a similar disenchantment with their gubernatorial nominee, Jesse Unruh, in 1970. Organization Democrats in Illinois did not work overly hard for the Democratc gubernatorial nominee, Daniel Walker, in 1972, and in 1976 were able to defeat him in the Democratic primary.

One means candidates have to defend themselves against party desertion is to become independents. Maine elected an independent as governor in 1974, and Senator Harry Byrd, Jr., has run as an independent in Virginia, as did the two major candidates for governor in Virginia in 1973. To become an independent increases one's appeal to the other party. It also has the great merit of evading the nomination process of one's original party. Senator Byrd, in particular, was in danger of losing the Democratic primary because of the rapid growth of that state's electorate by the addition of urban and black voters.

There are a variety of means by which parties can attempt to contain, if not ameliorate, the enmities of factionalism. One classic method is the balanced ticket, in which each claimant group, especially ethnic and religious groups, obtains at least one nomination on the party's "ticket." The ascent of ethnic names up the ticket from lower to higher offices has been used as an index of the rise of various ethnic groups in social acceptability and political power (Lubell, 1951: 67–78). Representation of the state's regions can be achieved through the same device. Ideological and economic-group factionalism, however, is less easily accommodated by this or any other procedure.

The same result can be achieved in a de facto manner if various candidates and factions are attracted to different offices. In a state with several elective executive offices, various economic groups may concentrate on that office of greatest concern to themselves. Given the long incumbencies common in these offices, an interfactional struggle will usually occur only at those infrequent intervals when the office becomes vacant. Otherwise, incumbents will not be seriously challenged for renomination, not even in a primary.

Patronage is a classic device both for rewarding one's friends and placating factional opponents. Yet, as our previous discussion indicated, we have little systematic knowledge of the use of patronage—of either the personnel or white-collar varieties.

## TYPES OF STATE PARTIES

To this point, we have highlighted the differences among state parties, and have discussed their component parts. Now we can attempt to draw the parts together to develop general categories into which state parties may be placed and among which they can be compared.

### Criteria

We will categorize state parties by the alignments among the participants within them. We will use V. O. Key's concept of the competitive patterns among factions within each party. If the party appears united, if the various participants and factions can agree on a wide variety of matters, we will place that party in the "cohesive" category. If, by contrast, the party appears dominated by two major sets of contenders which typically oppose one another, we will term that party "bifactional." If, however, there are many uncoordinated factions and sets of participants within the party, we will term that party "multifactional," or a party of low cohesion and coordination (Key, 1949: chap. 14; Lockard, 1963: 188; Olson, 1971: 127–29).

We are judging the end product of what could be a long and complicated process of intraparty negotiation and discussion. In some—perhaps many—instances, intraparty battles are openly fought in primaries, for which the election results are one major indicator of internal party coherence and power. But we also want to know what lies behind the election statistics. What happened at the earlier stages of candidate recruitment, of fund raising, and of endorsement negotiation to produce the number of candidates, the patterns of support and the eventual election outcome? Where we have such pieces of evidence —as discussed in earlier sections of this chapter—we will use them to place state parties in our categories. Where we have little other than the convention or primary election results, we will use them. In all circumstances, however, our placement of the 100 state parties is meant to be suggestive, for the evidence is uneven among the states and very weak for most. (If our guesses are wrong, but stimulate others to generate more extensive data, our purposes will be well served.)

While internal cohesion is our major criterion for categorizing state parties, we will also employ the parties' competitive status relative to one another. The parties' competitive status defines the strategic context within which candidates and party leaders function. Factionalism does not occur in a vacuum, but within parties in relationship to one another within their respective states. We will use the five competitive categories defined in Chapter 2 for the 1960–76 period. The 3 categories of internal cohesion matched against the 5 different competitive categories yields 15 possible types of state political parties (see Table 3–7).

## Electorally quiescent parties

But there is a 16th type—the electorally passive and hopeless minority party, fast becoming a relic of the past—which we will discuss first.

Southern Republicans and some New England Democrats were electorally quiescent. Their purpose was to support national factions in the presidential nominating conventions. They received, in return, a few federal patronage appointments. The "post-office" southern Republicans first began to change from this status in the 1952 Eisenhower election. By the time of the Goldwater 1964 election, most southern Republican parties became electorally active, rather than

**Table 3–7**
**Types of state political parties**

| Two-party status and party | Factional pattern | | |
|---|---|---|---|
| | Cohesive | Bifactional | Multifactional |
| **Dominant** | | | |
| D ........ | Va. 1930–65 | Ala. / Texas, 1950s, '60s / S.C. / La. 1940s / Ga. 1930–60 | La. 1960s, '70s / Tex. 1970s / Ga. 1970s / Ark. / Miss. |
| **Majority** | | | |
| D ........ | R.I. | Va. 1970s / Tenn. 1950s / Hawaii / Ky. | N.C.  N. Mex. / Md.  Mo. / Fla.  W.Va. / Okla. / Tenn. 1960s, '70s |
| R ........ | Colo. | Vt. | Wyo.  Kans. / S. Dak.  Idaho |
| **Competitive** | | | |
| D ........ | Conn. / Del. / Ind. / Minn. | Pa. / Ill. / Mich. | N.Y.  Oreg.  Utah / N. Dak.  Ohio  Calif. / Wis.  Maine  N.H. / Alaska  Nev.  Mass. / Iowa  Mont.  N.J. / Ariz.  Wash.  Nebr. |
| R ........ | Nev.  Ohio  Minn. / Conn.  Ill.  Mass. / Wis.  Del.  Iowa / Pa.  N.Y. | Mich. / Ariz. / Ind. | Calif.  Maine  Alaska / Oreg.  Neb.  Wash. / N.D.  Mont.  N.H. / Utah  N.J. |
| **Minority** | | | |
| R ........ | Va.  Hawaii / Ky.  Okla. / R.I.  Md. / W.Va. 1950s | Tenn. / N.C. / Fla. | Mo. / N. Mex. / W.Va. 1970s |
| D ........ | S. Dak. / Colo. | | Kans.  Vt. / Wyo.  Idaho |
| **Electorally combative** | | | |
| R ........ | La.  S.C. / Miss.  Ga. | Tex. | |
| **Quiescent** | | | |
| R ........ | | | Ala.  Ark. |

quiescent. In the mid 1970s, only the Republican parties in Alabama and Arkansas seem to have returned to the electorally quiescent mold. Their organization is minimal and their activity is sporadic; for them, questions of internal control and patterns of factionalism are irrelevant. Thus, they constitute a distinctive, if now rare, type of state political party.

The remaining 98 state parties are distributed among the three categories of internal cohesion and among the five categories of competitive status.

## Cohesive parties

The cohesive party has a single source of leadership. That single source might be a powerful individual, recognized as the "leader" or the "boss," examples of which were the late Senator Harry Byrd, Sr., of Virginia and, at the city level, the late Mayor Daley of Chicago. The single source of leadership might also be a state chairman (John Bailey of Connecticut) or a governor (Nelson Rockefeller of New York). The leadership might be more collegial—a state committee or an informal council of regional or county party leaders, as among Republicans in Pennsylvania. The ability of the state party to cohere into a unified entity might best be expressed through the state convention, as has usually (but not always) been the case in the DFL of Minnesota. The states we have earlier identified as having party endorsement conventions are in this category, if their endorsements are usually ratified in the primary by a sizable share of the vote (table 3–6). State parties which nominate by convention—Delaware and several of the southern Republican parties—are also placed in this cohesive category. We place primary states in this category if their gubernatorial nominations are seldom contested or are usually won by a large margin (Table 4–1). We use those data in the absence of any other information about the internal dynamics of the party.

The highly cohesive party does not lack factions. Its distinction stems from its ability to compromise factional differences internally, and, in the end, to present a unified front in both the primary and general elections. We would guess that the major factions within this type of party are ethnic and geographic, rather than economic or ideological. Ideological differences, especially, are difficult to negotiate, while the other factional bases present more of an opportunity to share nominations and to distribute power.

With the exception of the former dominant-status Virginia "Byrd machine" and Colorado Republicans, all of the cohesive parties are either competitive or minority in status. By contrast, many of the highly cohesive county and city organizations are usually majority if not dominant within their respective jurisdictions. Republican state parties outnumber Democratic ones in the competive category, while only Republican parties, among the minority parties, are highly cohesive. Judging from scattered case studies, the cohesion of some state parties has changed in the past 20 years: Rhode Island Democrats and West Virginia Republicans were, in earlier studies, highly cohesive parties, while in the 1970s they both appear fragmented instead (Lockard, 1959; Fenton, 1957).

Each of the four electorally combative Republican parties in the southern states still dominated by Democrats would appear to belong in the cohesive category. All four developed active Republican parties during the Goldwater surge of 1964; perhaps they lack the urban economic conservatives who became active during the Eisenhower period but for whom race was a relatively minor consideration. They also lack a sizable Appalachian area with its traditional Republicans dating from the Civil War.

## Bifactional parties

Bifactional parties are dominated by two main opposing groups. One basis of internal division within a party may be disagreement over issues; among southern Democrats, a general liberal-conservative split has been joined with disagreement over loyalty to the national party. A second basis of internal division may be geographic, either between different regions of the state, or between a large city and the remainder of the state. A third may be a split between the "regulars" and the "reformers" as among New York Democrats. Any or all of these splits may be joined to a split between a governor and the chairman of his state party, as has been illustrated by Democrats in both Alabama and Pennsylvania. The minority Southern Republican parties show a different form of bifactionalism—a split centered upon their control of two, but not many, state offices, especially governor and U.S. Senator.

The bifactional parties are distributed among all five categories of competitive status. Among dominant parties, the bifactionalism of Louisiana and Texas Democrats seems to be disappearing in the 1970s in both states, while growing among South Carolina Democrats (see Chapter 4).

In the majority party category, Virginia's Byrd machine is both dissolving and facing more extensive opposition. Kentucky Democrats have long had a bifactional pattern, as have Vermont Republicans.

In some competitive parties, bifactionalism is expressed by conflicts between the governor and his internal opposition, as for example among Illinois Democrats.

Michigan Democrats illustrate the perils of factionalism accompanying new growth: The party was revitalized in the 1940s by a coalition between organized labor, on the one hand, and middle class liberals, on the other. The two wings of the coalition have later disagreed over nominations and retain separate identities (Fenton, 1966: chap. 2).

The successful southern Republican parties, having achieved a "minority" status and no longer electorally quiescent, are experiencing the same factional stresses as have Michigan Democrats. They tend to have several overlapping splits: (1) between the occupants of two major offices such as governor and senator; (2) between major cities such as Dallas and Houston; and (3) between the Eisenhower and Appalachian Republicans, on the one hand, and those brought in with or since the Goldwater campaign of 1964, on the other.

## Multifactional parties

The multifactional parties are more numerous than the other categories, perhaps because this category is both least well-defined and the most diverse. Parties in this category have at least several different competing groups within them. They could be based upon any or all of the potential bases of factionalism noted earlier. In addition, parties which have gained at least competitive status may have won some of the minor statewide offices, the long-term occupants of which become fairly independent of the remainder of the party. The safer parties create an ample supply of potential state-wide candidates because they already occupy legislative and county offices throughout the state. Minority parties are also found in this category. Their gubernatorial primaries have been frequently contested and often won by modest margins (Table 4–1).

The low-cohesion parties are found in all competitive statuses except the electorally combative minority. Judging from the southern Republican parties in the 1960s and 1970s, the effort to become electorally active is associated with high rather than low cohesion.

Although we lack comprehensive evidence on the low-cohesion state parties, we might speculate that they, in turn, fall roughly into three subcategories. In one, the participants in a state party will tend to be episodic, changing from one election to the next and from one office to the next. They will tend to be attracted by a current issue or candidate, but will soon drop out of political activity. In the next two subtypes of state parties, the participants will tend to be fairly constant over time, but differ in characteristics of their alignments. In one type, the same participants will have roughly the same set of allies and opponents, and will face one another through a number of elections, and perhaps also over a range of offices. In the other type, the participants will change alliances. That is, even though the participants will be fairly continuous, the alliances among them will shift by time and office. While at least some of the participating groups may themselves be well organized internally, their very numbers and diversity precludes their ability to either cohere or dominate. California and Florida Democrats perhaps illustrate the first subtype, Texas Democrats the second, while Maryland and New York Democrats the third.

## ATTRIBUTES OF PARTY TYPES

The three major types of state political parties probably vary on a number of attributes (Table 3–8):

**Table 3–8**
**Attributes of types of state political parties**

|  | Party types | | |
| --- | --- | --- | --- |
| *Attributes* | *Cohesive* | *Bifactional* | *Multifactional* |
| Electoral cycle stage .......... | All | All | Segmented; varied |
| Scope of office .............. | Wide | Wide | Office or candidate specific |
| Geographic coordination ...... | High | High | Low |
| Staffing and activity .......... | High | High | Low |
| Formal structure ............. | Independent chairman | Conflict between governor, chairman | Agent chairman |
| Electoral reliance ........... | Party | Faction | Candidate |

## Stage of electoral cycle

Recruitment, nomination and general elections are three main stages, sequenced through time, of an election. The types of state parties differ in the extent to which they are active in all stages of the electoral cycle.

The cohesive parties are highly active in all stages of the electoral cycle. Their leaders either screen among potential aspirants (if competitive, majority, or dominant) or recruit aspirants for the party's nomination (if minority). The leaders seek to have suitable candidates but also wish to avoid contested primaries. Those parties which nominate through conventions (Connecticut, both parties; Virginia, Republicans) more easily achieve this objective than the more numerous primary states (Pennsylvania, Republicans). The minority party, however, has a decision to make which is foreclosed for the other status parties—for which offices shall it offer candidates? Southern Republican parties, in particular, developing with the Goldwater surge and the Nixon southern strategy, have had their decisions in this respect greatly complicated by considerations of their national nominees and administration.

The point of avoiding contested nominations is to avoid splitting the party. When contests do emerge, parties respond differently. The strategy of Pennsylvania Republicans is to endorse a candidate and then to campaign for that candidate in their own primary. The strategy of officials in the formal structure of the low-cohesion California Republicans is to avoid participation, leaving nomination campaigning to the voluntary clubs within the party.

The likelihood that the party will actively participate in the general election campaign is increased if the potential bitterness of primary contests can be avoided. The cohesive parties generally avoid primary contests and actively campaign in general elections for its nominees (Olson, 1971: 140–45). In bifactional parties, each faction, having recruited and supported its candidates for the party's nomination, tends to campaign in the general election for those party nominees who come from its own faction. The consequences for the bifactional minority party can be disastrous. In multifactional parties, candidates tend to create their own support organizations and bypass the formal party structure altogether. The electorally quiescent minority party avoids these problems by not attempting to run candidates in the first place.

## Scope of offices

Both cohesive and bifactional parties tend to wage campaigns for the entire ticket—for all offices on the ballot. In multifactional parties, by contrast, participants tend to concentrate on a single office or on those offices confined to a specific geographic area or governmental level. While some parties are more concerned about their own county, such as Chicago and Cleveland Democrats, or about their own state, such as the Virginia Byrd machine, others are mainly interested in national politics, such as both Wisconsin parties and Oregon Democrats (Fenton, 1966: 137; Sorauf, 1954: 703; Seligman, 1974: 77). Electorally combative minority parties experience this dilemma less than majority ones simply because they contest fewer offices. But they experience this tension more acutely, because they must consciously choose the offices for which they do run candidates. Furthermore, since much of their growth stems from national politics, they tend to view in-state offices for the support those campaigns could give to preferred presidential candidates, and vice versa.

### Geographic coordination

The many county and city parties within a state may be linked to state-level politics in a variety of ways. In the cohesive party, overt and long-term negotiations occur among the county and city leaders together with state-level leaders, especially over candidacies and nominations. In cohesive parties, the local leaders usually believe in the need for and efficacy of statewide coordination. They may even express this view in terms of loyalty to "the organization" or to "the leader." Some participants justify their own coordinated activity by claiming that every organization, whether business, religious, or military, needs and has a leader. In their view, political parties are no different. That viewpoint is one of the major ways in which their respective parties are markedly different from most other state parties in the country.

In bifactional parties, each faction may largely control a separate set of counties and cities. Such control gives factional leaders their base of operation within the state party. But in other states, the counties and cities themselves may be split by factionalism, so that the same factional struggle in state-level politics is duplicated around the state in a variety of local settings. In these instances, state conventions are preceded by acrimonious county conventions, with numerous credentials fights one result at the state convention.

In multifactional parties, regions of the state, if not also county and city parties, may be important sources of competing candidacies and also of policy views. Their uncoordination is signaled by numerous candidates in primaries and by "friends and neighbors" patterns in the vote (Key, 1949: 37–52). Local offices might be more frequent sources of state wide candidacies, while the state legislature would become the main arena within which localities meet and bargain with one another (Schlesinger, 1966: 87, 96–98).

### Staffing and activity

Although most state parties have chairmen and national committeemen, not all of them are very active or necessarily important decision-makers in their party. One of the problems facing newly growing parties is to find chairmen for all of the counties, while even long-term majority parties usually do not staff all of their thousands of precincts throughout the state. In the cohesive parties we would expect a higher portion of party positions to be filled and reasonably active, than in the other types of parties. Bifactional parties might have as high a proportion of filled positions, but those persons would be split—and perhaps immobilized—by the two major factions in the state. Given the growth of new Republican parties in the southern states in which most Democratic parties are weakly organized, the electorally combative minority is often better staffed and more active, at least in its target areas, than are the dominant or majority Democrats. The electorally quiescent minority does not staff even those positions mandated by state law. When such positions are filled, they are either inactive or could even be members of the majority party (Rakove, 1975: chap. 6).

### Place of the formal structure

In the cohesive party, the state chairman is likely to be "independent," as discussed in a previous section. This chairman is autonomous from the governor if their party holds that office, is likely to both predate and outlast the governor's tenure in office, and is able to weld the state committee into an effective instrument of his own choosing.

The state chairman is more likely to be dependent upon the governor in the multifactional states. There, the official party is little more than an instrument for the governor's use. In the absence of any group able to control the gubernatorial nomination over time, gubernatorial candidates are likely to come from different segments of the party and to bring with them personal supporters and allies into state government and into the state party as well. At least some governors deliberately intend to emasculate the formal party and to keep it inactive and unimportant.

The relationship of the governor and the state chairman is much more complicated in bifactional parties. The two factions may divide control of the governorship and state party's chairmanship, in which case the two persons are intraparty enemies. For most of George Wallace's tenure as governor, for example, the state chairman has been loyal to the national Democratic party and has been an opponent in intraparty activities both in the state and nationally. In the mid 1970s, similar disputes occurred between the governor and the state chairman among Democrats in New York, New Jersey, and Connecticut. In such instances, the legislature becomes a battleground resolving, if not mediating, the intraparty disputes. Republicans witnessed similar struggles in the 1950s in both Indiana and Kansas (Smith and Hein, 1958; Munger, 1960).

In other bifactional states, of which Texas Democrats in the 1950s and 1960s are an example, the out-faction makes a valiant effort to capture control of the state convention and state committee. But the chairman is always selected personally by the governor. Once selected, the chairman's main task is to both reduce the activity and importance of the formal party and to keep the out-faction out. Because the formal structure of the party has a potential importance, control over it is important even when it is inactive.

## Electoral reliance

To what extent do candidates campaign together and with the party? This question is perhaps the critical one to which the previous attributes of state parties contribute and in which they culminate. One of the few theories of party formation argues that the candidate seeking an office is the "nuclear" unit of the party (Schlesinger, 1965: 774–86). The more offices are shared within a given geographic area (having the same electorate), the greater the likelihood that the candidates will combine in a joint effort and hence, the greater the likelihood that a party organization will develop. This theory accounts for the relative importance of county courthouses in party organization. States, however, also have many elective statewide offices, the results of which, it is argued, decentralize the executive power and diminish the ability of the governor to effectively manage the executive branch. One of the "good government" reforms in Virginia in the early 1930s—to streamline state government and reduce the number of separately elected state offices—materially contributed to the ability of the "Byrd machine" to dominate the state party until the late 1960s. Indeed, the rates of competition vary greatly among state offices. In general, the top offices, such as governor, are much more competitive than are other state offices, such as secretary of state or auditor. The occupants of the latter set of offices have a personal longevity, irrespective of the party fortunes in the governorship or state legislature. They would perhaps wage independent campaigns, and separate themselves from their party, particularly if they expected their party to not do well in a coming election.

In cohesive parties, candidates for all offices customarily wage a joint campaign among all geopolitical levels within the state. A candidate for county sheriff and governor in the same party will campaign together: they will share speaking engagements, campaign literature, and both will urge a straight party vote. The cohesive minority party, however, may react differently. In the first place, it may have candidates for some offices and in some areas, but not all. Secondly, it will urge a straight ticket vote among its own voters, but may wage separate campaigns in the wider electorate. At this point its candidates may implicitly campaign against one another by urging the wider (and presumably majority) electorate to selectively split their tickets. Under this threat, majority party candidates may react defensively by attempting to avoid their party colleagues against whom a split ticket is being urged. That is, the threat of competition reduces the likelihood of joint partywide campaigning.

In bifactional parties, the factions customarily "cut" one another's candidates from their own campaigning in the general election. Candidates, at all stages of the electoral cycle, rely on the factions. Although the average voter may not care or even know, party activists are often more concerned about possession of the nomination than of the public office. If a factional opponent wins the party's nomination, the loser's adherents may either avoid the general election or actively support the candidate of the other party. Texas liberal Democrats have supported Republican candidates in preference to conservative Democratic nominees, for example.

Candidates typically form their own support organizations and wage independent campaigns in multifactional parties. The candidates tend to be self-recruited, but even if party-recruited, the party has little to offer the candidates in either primaries or general elections. Candidates raise their own funds, find their own volunteers, and make independent appeals to the electorate. They may not even list their party affiliation in their campaign materials, but rather, emphasize their own name and qualifications. In most states and counties, irrespective of competitive status, the occupants of the formal positions in the multifactional party, and the volunteer and unofficial clubs as well, genuinely seek to help the candidates of their party (or faction). But they are limited in their resources: minimal or inactive staffing, strong factionalism, perhaps unpopular top-of-ticket candidates, and an inability to raise campaign funds, all limit their well-intentioned efforts. Whether candidates personally wish it or not, they are forced in this long-run and chronic debilitation of their party—given their own short-run needs to win an election—to develop their own campaign and to hope for the best.

## CONCLUSION

We have suggested three basic types of political parties, differentiated by the degree of internal cohesion. We have also suggested a fourth type, distinguished not by its internal cohesion, but its electoral passivity. Our first three basic categories distinguish among parties which at least make an effort to contest elections. They, in turn, may be allocated among five different categories of competitive status, resulting in a total of 15 types of state political parties.

While it might be desirable to work with a smaller number of types of parties, considering that we have 100 state parties (plus numerous third parties in various states), these categories should be able to accommodate the diversity of state parties over a long period of time. Various state parties change categories; for example, some of the southern Republican parties are now "minority" rather than electorally quiescent, with a corresponding change in the competitive status of the Democratic parties of their states. Likewise, parties change in their internal characteristics; the Virginia Democrats are no longer highly cohesive, and Texas Democrats no longer bifactional.

The diversity among state political parties, their autonomy from the national parties, and the frequent autonomy of county and city units from them, continue into the present the characteristics present from their beginnings. Some of the American state parties are among the oldest parties in the world, simply because we were the first nation to widely extend the suffrage. Their origins trace back to the colonies. They began at different times and in different ways in response to local conditions in their separate colonies. Just as the colonies, and later the separate states, united to form a common national government, so their parties formed alliances across state boundaries to create national parties. American parties today retain the decentralization and the diversity of their origins while most of our other institutions are increasingly centralized—such as government, business, labor, and even religion and entertainment.

# 4 ★ ★ ★

# The nominating process ★ ★ ★

The nomination of candidates for public office is one of the most important steps in the political process, and consequently the study of how the nominating process varies in practice from state to state is basic to an understanding of variations in American state politics. An examination of nominations can shed light on many significant characteristics of state politics, including:

The character and level of two-party competition.

The nature and strength of party organizations.

The elements or factions that make up the two parties.

Nominating systems differ in various ways, but the basic dimension for comparing nominations among the states is the breadth of participation in the selection of nominees. At one extreme is the case in which a few party leaders select the nominee, and their choice is not challenged in any primary election. At the other extreme is a primary election in which there are several candidates, there are no efforts by the party organization to influence the choice, a large proportion of the eligible voters turn out, and the outcome is close. In order to measure participation in the nominating process, we need to collect information on the following:

Laws defining who may vote in the primaries.

The extent of competition, specifically the number of candidates who run and the closeness of outcomes.

The proportion of voters who turn out for primaries.

The factors that explain the outcomes of the nominating contests.

The characteristic that distinguishes nominating systems in American states from those in most foreign countries is, of course, the use of primary elections for most nominations. In Key's words (1964: 371): "Throughout the history of American nominating practices runs a persistent attempt to make feasible popular participation in nominations and thereby to limit or to destroy the power•of party oligarchies." During the Jacksonian period the legislative caucus was replaced as a nominating device by the convention attended by popularly elected delegates. The convention system in turn came under attack at the end of the 19th century because too often the selection of delegates and the decisions of the convention were tightly controlled by the party organization, which often meant a small group of bosses. The Civil War had created a pattern of Democratic control in the South and Republican control in many of the northern states, a pattern that was reinforced by the 1896 election. Even in those northern states that were more competitive, most counties and cities were dominated by one party. The effect of tight organizational control over nominations in a dominant party was to deny voters any effective choice in the elections.

The primary election came into use first in the area most completely dominated by one party, the southern states, late in the 19th century, initially as a result of party rules and later as a result of state law. In some southern states it was one manifestation of the Populist movement. Outside the South the campaign for direct primary elections was an important ingredient in the Progressive movement, and it represented a direct challenge to the conservative political leaders who dominated one or both parties in most states. The speed with which this reform spread among the states is impressive. Wisconsin adopted the first relatively comprehensive statewide compulsory primary law in 1903. Within five years similar laws had been adopted in most of the plains and western states where the Progressive move-

ment was strong, and by 1917 the direct primary had been adopted
in all but a handful of states (Key, 1964: 371–76; 1956: 87–97). Most
of the states that were slow to adopt the primary or did not use it consistently were eastern or midwestern states with relatively high levels
of two-party competition and strong party organizations, such as New
York, Connecticut, Rhode Island, Delaware, and Indiana. When Connecticut adopted a limited form of the direct primary in 1955, no state
remained that relied entirely on the convention system. In the last
three decades a number of states have enacted laws changing the
number of offices covered by the primary or the authority of party
conventions to endorse candidates in the primary, but there has been
no clear trend toward either greater organizational control or greater
popular influence in the legislation enacted.

## LAWS REGULATING PRIMARIES

In order to understand differences among the states in the nomination process, we must first look at differences imposed by law. We are
particularly concerned with statewide nominations because of our
interest in state political systems. Statewide candidates must be nominated by primaries in all states except Delaware. (In some southern
states the law permits Republican candidates to be chosen by convention.) The most recent states to apply the primary to statewide offices
were New York, where it took effect in 1970, and Indiana, where it
took effect in 1976.

One aspect of the law on nominations that significantly affects
the primary system is the definition of voter qualifications for participation in the primary. The basic distinction is between closed primaries, which are limited to members registered with a party, and open
primaries, which are open to anyone qualified to vote in the general
election. A closer examination of primary laws discloses wide variations in the qualifications for voting in a party's primary. Not all primaries are equally "closed" or "open." We can define a closed primary
as one in which a person must be registered in a party, usually in
advance of voting, and a record is kept of this registration. Most closed
primary states set a deadline by which a person who wants to shift his
registration from one party to the other must do so, but there are great
differences in the lead time required. At one extreme there are two
states, New Jersey and Rhode Island, that until recently have required
voters to miss one or two primary elections if they wished to shift

party registration.[1] The courts have ruled that the requirements in these states were unconstiutional because they disenfranchised voters for one or more primaries.[2] Six other states require a shift of registration six months or more before a primary. Most of the other closed primary states have deadlines of one to three months before a primary. In a few states the deadline is even shorter, and in Iowa and Wyoming a voter may shift his registration at the polls.

There are also significant differences in the "openness" of open primaries. In a few states a person must declare his party preference at the polls, but no record is kept of his choice. More common is the open primary in which the voter need not declare any preference. He can vote in either primary, and the mechanics of the election permit him to keep secret which party primary he participated in. Finally, the "blanket" primary used in Washington and Alaska permits a voter to participate in both primaries in a single election, voting in the Democratic primary for governor, the Republican primary for senator, and so forth.

The rationale for a closed primary is that the selection of candidates should be limited to persons who are willing to be identified with that party, through the process of registration, and that this identification should remain reasonably stable over time. It is argued that, in an open primary, the party is vulnerable to being "raided." Voters who normally vote in one primary might enter the other primary to vote either for the weakest candidate or for a candidate whose personality or views are particularly attractive. Very little is known about what actually happens in open primary states, and what proportion of voters shift how frequently from one party to another. It does appear that few voters shift primaries in a deliberate effort to choose the weaker candidate. They are much more likely to shift because they are particularly attracted to a candidate in the other party or because the other party has closer, more interesting primary contests.

The basic argument for an open primary is that voters should be able to participate freely in primaries without revealing their party preferences. The open primary preserves the secrecy of political

---

[1] Although Illinois did not require that registration records list party affiliation, it did require anyone seeking to vote in the primary to declare a party preference, maintained a record of that, and prohibited a person from voting in the other party primary for a period of 23 months. This prolonged lead time was ruled unconstitutional by the U.S. Supreme Court in 1972, resulting in an open primary in Illinois.

[2] Both the New Jersey and Rhode Island laws were ruled unconstitutional in 1972, and in both states the immediate result was that the primaries became open.

choice, and thus the secrecy of the ballot. In those closed primary states where a voter may shift party registration within a month or two of the primary, it would seem to be almost as easy for a determined voter to cross over as in an open primary state. But in fact we know very little about how much shifting of party registration occurs during a primary campaign in such states.

Most of the states with open primaries are midwestern or western states. Many of them are states in which the Progressive movement was strong. On the other hand, most of the states in which the closed primary has required a long lead time for switching parties are ones in which party organizations are strong and have been able to maintain considerable influence over nominations despite the primary. It seems clear that the leaders of party organizations prefer closed primaries and want to discourage voters from frequent shifts of party registration. The laws on qualifications for primary voting reflect the strength or weakness of party organizations at the time the laws were adopted, the status of organizations since that time, and the force of habit or tradition in state politics. In recent years there has been some trend toward greater openness in primaries. Several open primary states have eliminated the requirement that a voter specify a party or have abolished the possibility of challenging his right to vote in a particular party. We have also noted court decisions that have invalidated long waiting periods for shifting party registration. How much effect the closed or open character of primaries actually has on the strength of party organizations and their ability to influence nominations is difficult to determine because so little is known about the behavior of voters in primary elections.

In the past the open or closed character of primaries has not been important in southern states because only the Democratic party has held primaries. Moreover, it has been common for state laws to leave the question of qualifications for primary voting in the hands of the Democratic party. (At a time in the past when black voters were excluded from the primary, this was a device for accomplishing this goal.) At present, all southern states restrict the primary to party members, but in many of these states there is no registration by party, and voters simply declare at the polls which party primary they wish to vote in.

Most southern primaries are distinct from those in other states in another respect. In ten southern states (all but Tennessee) and also in Oklahoma, a runoff primary between the top two candidates is held if no candidate gets a majority of the first primary vote. The purpose is to insure that the winner will have majority support. Because the

Democratic primary has usually been the decisive election in southern states, it has often attracted a substantial number of candidates, more than in most nothern states, and consequently the risk of a nominee getting much less than half of the vote would be considerable if there were no runoff. At the same time, the existence of the runoff has probably contributed to the large number of candidates, some of whom run in the hope of bargaining with the leading candidates before the runoff.

In the previous chapter on state party organizations we described another aspect of the laws affecting nominations: laws in a number of states that authorize state party conventions or committees to endorse candidates running in a primary and in many cases give the endorsed candidate some advantage in the primary. We will discuss later in this chapter the evidence concerning the effect that these laws have on the levels of competition and of popular participation in the primaries. It is clear that laws making it impossible or difficult to enter the primary without getting a minimum number of convention votes have the effect of reducing the number of candidates and giving the party organization some kind of veto over candidates. The effect of laws simply permitting designation of the endorsee on the ballot depends on the extent to which party workers and voters are swayed by such endorsements.

If we were to rank order the states in terms of the influence that party organizations have over nominations as a consequence of legal provisions, we would have the following scale:

1. Party conventions making nominations without a primary.
2. Closed primary system, including endorsement by party conventions.
3. Closed primary system without party endorsements.
4. Open primary system (with several levels of openness).

In fact, several states do not fit this ranking because they have combined legal preprimary endorsements with open primaries; Utah, North Dakota, and Idaho (from 1963 to 1970) are three examples. (Three other open primary states—Minnesota, Wisconsin, and Illinois—have informal endorsements by one or both parties.) We might expect that in states where the party organizations were strong enough to make endorsements and even get legal authority for them, they would be strong enough to get a closed primary law adopted. However, in a state with an open primary the party organization might find it more necessary than in a closed primary state to make endorsements in an effort to reduce the uncertainties of an open primary. In any case, our rank ordering of party organizational influence over nominations works better in theory than it does in practice.

## LEVELS OF PRIMARY COMPETITION

The purpose of nominating by primary elections is to enable voters, rather than a party organization or leaders, to choose the nominee. That purpose is thwarted if the voters find only a single candidate's name on the primary ballot for an office. The choice has already been made by the potential candidates who choose not to run and/or by the party organization that supported and encouraged one candidate and discouraged others. The greater the number of candidates in the primary, the greater the opportunity for the voter to find one who suits his preferences. A relatively close election may be a better measure of competition, because it suggests that the voters can choose among two or more candidates who are strong enough to be serious contenders, rather than having to choose between one powerful candidate and several nonentities. These criteria suggest three ways that we can measure competition in the party primary for any office:

1.   The proportion of primaries that are contested.
2.   The average, or median, number of candidates.
3.   The average percentage of votes for the winning candidate.

Why are some primaries more competitive than others? To answer this question, we need to discover the reasons why potential candidates decide to run or not to run. At the individual level, these decisions may be affected by a person's education, wealth, occupation, career goals, and psychological motivations, among other reasons. But we are concerned with influences on candidates that are characteristic of certain states or types of elections. Do some states consistently have higher levels of primary competition than other states, and if so why? Why do the two parties in some states differ in primary competition? Are certain types of primary elections regularly more competitive than others?

We can start with the basic (and very logical) assumption that a potential candidate's likelihood of running increases as he perceives a better chance of winning the primary and general elections. This assumption leads to several hypotheses about differences in levels of competition that occur from state to state, party to party, or election to election:

1.  There will be less primary competition in those states where there are strong party organizations that endorse candidates, because nonendorsed potential candidates will frequently decide that they cannot win the primary. Competition will be particularly low in states where preprimary endorsements are provided by law.

2.  The greater a party's chances of winning, the more competition there will be in that party's primary. If this general principle is correct, states with strongly competitive two-party systems should have a high proportion of contested primaries in both parties. In states dominated by one party, however, that party should have highly competitive primaries, while the other party should have less competition and probably some uncontested primaries.

3.  The presence of an incumbent in a particular primary election will reduce the level of competition, because incumbents are usually difficult to beat in a primary.

To test these hypotheses, we can measure competition in gubernatorial primaries in 47 states (excluding Delaware, which uses conventions, and New York and Indiana, which used them until 1970 and 1976, respectively). The time period runs from 1950 (or in some states 1946 or 1948) to 1976.[3] We concentrate on gubernatorial elections (as in other parts of this book) because of their central importance in state primaries. We can also look at data on legislative primaries for several of the states over shorter periods of time.

We begin by looking at the impact of incumbency on primary competition. There were incumbents running in 31.7 percent of all the gubernatorial primaries in nonsouthern states, including 23.4 percent of the 474 contested primaries and 50 percent of the 210 uncontested primaries. Only 51.1 percent of the primaries with an incumbent running were contested, in contrast to 77.7 percent of the primaries without any incumbent. In the southern states almost every Democratic primary was contested, and only 29.9 percent of the contests had incumbents running.

Because incumbency is so important, and the proportion of incumbents running varies from state to state, when we make comparisons

---

[3] Throughout this chapter the tabulations on contests and participation in primaries include all elections from 1950 through 1976. In states where four-year gubernatorial terms were used consistently, the 1946 or 1948 election was included to insure that there would be at least eight elections covered.

among the states and parties it is necessary to distinguish between primaries with and without incumbents. This has been done in tables 4–1 and 4–2, which show several measures of competition in the non-southern and southern states. In both tables the states are ranked according to the proportion of contested primaries. The tables show that in most states competition is greater when there are no incumbents running. There were 60 state parties (in all states) in which at least some of the primaries had incumbents. In 33 the median number of candidates was higher without incumbents, in 11 it was higher with incumbents, and in 16 there was no difference. In 50 of these parties the average winning margin was greater when there were incumbents in the race; in only 10 cases the margin was less with incumbents running, and the differences were usually small. We can conclude that in most state parties the presence of an incumbent in the primary discourages other candidates from running and often leads to one-sided contests.

Table 4–1 shows impressive differences in competition among the nonsouthern states. In roughly half of them both parties have contests in all or most of the primaries; in about one-fourth of the states one party's primary is much more competitive than the other; and in the remaining states both parties have moderate to low levels of competition. The state parties with fewer contests tend to have a smaller number of candidates in contested races. The southern states (Table 4–2) vary somewhat in the number of candidates and closeness of races, though nearly all primaries are contested. Given the important effect that incumbency has been shown to have, it is worth noting that several of the nonsouthern states with the highest proportion of contested primaries rarely had incumbents running: Missouri, Kentucky, Oklahoma, Pennsylvania, and West Virginia; and only three southern states had more than two primaries with incumbents. (These states where incumbents rarely ran are ones where there is or has been a constitutional ban on consecutive terms for a governor, and incumbents ran only after succeeding to a vacancy in the office or else after that ban had been repealed.)

We have hypothesized that primary competition would be least in states where parties make preprimary endorsements of candidates, and this is borne out by Table 4–1. If we look at the states at the bottom of Table 4–1, we find Connecticut (with a challenge primary), Rhode Island, Colorado, and Massachusetts (all with legal preprimary endorsements during all or most of the period), Wisconsin (informal Republican endorsements), and North Dakota (informal endorsements

**Table 4–1**
**Levels of gubernatorial primary competition in nonsouthern states, 1946–1950 to 1976 elections***

| | | | Democratic incumbents | | |
|---|---|---|---|---|---|
| State | Years | No. of contests, D & R | Contested | Median no. running | Average winning (percent) |
| Missouri | 8 | 16 | 1/1 | 3 | 85.5 |
| Washington | 8 | 16 | 3/3 | 4 | 75.1 |
| Kentucky | 8 | 16 | 2/2 | 3.5 | 70.4 |
| Nebraska | 11 | 21 | 3/3 | 3 | 84.2 |
| Oklahoma | 8 | 15 | 1/1 | 3 | 37.4 |
| California | 8 | 15 | 3/3 | 4 | 62.9 |
| Pennsylvania | 8 | 15 | 1/1 | 3 | 70.6 |
| West Virginia | 8 | 15 | — | — | — |
| Alaska | 5 | 9 | 3/3 | 3 | 71.6 |
| Hawaii | 5 | 9 | 2/2 | 2.5 | 66.3 |
| New Hampshire | 14 | 25 | 0/2 | — | — |
| Maryland | 8 | 14 | 4/4 | 5 | 61.5 |
| Nevada | 8 | 14 | 5/5 | 5 | 74.3 |
| Oregon | 9 | 15 | 1/1 | 3 | 62.0 |
| Ohio | 9 | 15 | 3/5 | 3 | 67.6 |
| Idaho | 8 | 13 | 1/2 | 3 | 60.2 |
| New Jersey | 8 | 13 | 1/2 | 2 | 90.9 |
| Utah | 8 | 13 | 1/3 | 2 | 56.6 |
| Montana | 8 | 12 | 0/2 | — | — |
| Minnesota | 10 | 15 | 4/5 | 3.5 | 82.4 |
| Wyoming | 8 | 12 | 0/1 | — | — |
| Kansas | 13 | 19 | 0/5 | — | — |
| Illinois | 8 | 11 | 1/2 | 2 | 53.9 |
| New Mexico | 12 | 16 | 2/3 | 3 | 51.1 |
| Iowa | 13 | 15 | 0/3 | — | — |
| Maine | 10 | 12 | 1/2 | 2 | 63.2 |
| Arizona | 12 | 14 | 2/3 | 4.5 | 37.3 |
| North Dakota | 11 | 12 | 0/4 | — | — |
| Massachusetts | 11 | 11 | 1/4 | 4 | 49.6 |
| Vermont | 14 | 13 | 1/3 | 2 | 84.4 |
| Wisconsin | 12 | 11 | 2/3 | 2 | 74.1 |
| Michigan | 11 | 10 | 1/6 | 2 | 85.5 |
| South Dakota | 13 | 10 | 1/3 | 2 | 65.9 |
| Rhode Island | 14 | 8 | 3/7 | 2 | 66.7 |
| Colorado | 9 | 5 | 0/3 | — | — |
| Connecticut | 5 | 1 | 0/2 | — | — |

* In some states the first election included was 1950; in states where four-year terms were used consistently, the 1946 or 1948 election was included to insure coverage of at least eight elections.

| Democratic nonincumbents | | | Republican incumbents | | | Republican nonincumbents | | |
|---|---|---|---|---|---|---|---|---|
| Contested | Median no. running | Average winning (percent) | Contested | Median no. running | Average winning (percent) | Contested | Median no. running | Average winning (percent) |
| 7/7 | 5 | 62.2 | 1/1 | 2 | 91.7 | 7/7 | 3 | 64.9 |
| 5/5 | 4 | 46.0 | 3/3 | 4 | 82.8 | 5/5 | 5 | 65.0 |
| 6/6 | 4 | 53.0 | — | — | — | 8/8 | 3 | 69.1 |
| 8/8 | 3 | 54.7 | 4/4 | 2.5 | 69.7 | 6/7 | 5 | 56.3 |
| 7/7 | 8 | 35.5 | 0/1 | — | — | 7/7 | 3 | 63.5 |
| 5/5 | 6 | 58.1 | 2/3 | 3.5 | 89.9 | 5/5 | 3 | 72.1 |
| 7/7 | 3 | 64.2 | — | — | — | 7/8 | 3 | 70.2 |
| 8/8 | 4 | 49.7 | 0/1 | — | — | 7/7 | 4 | 58.5 |
| 2/2 | 3 | 64.3 | — | — | — | 4/5 | 4 | 48.7 |
| 3/3 | 2 | 72.1 | 1/1 | 2 | 57.0 | 3/4 | 2 | 76.6 |
| 11/12 | 3 | 58.5 | 8/8 | 3 | 56.9 | 6/6 | 5.5 | 55.1 |
| 4/4 | 5.5 | 51.1 | 1/1 | 4 | 80.0 | 5/7 | 3 | 74.5 |
| 3/3 | 4 | 51.4 | 0/2 | — | — | 6/6 | 2 | 72.3 |
| 6/8 | 4 | 54.1 | 5/6 | 2 | 73.8 | 3/3 | 5 | 66.6 |
| 4/4 | 4 | 53.3 | 2/2 | 2 | 75.7 | 6/7 | 3 | 64.6 |
| 6/6 | 3 | 40.8 | 3/4 | 2 | 58.9 | 3/4 | 3 | 47.0 |
| 4/6 | 3.5 | 55.6 | 2/2 | 2 | 65.0 | 6/6 | 3.5 | 52.8 |
| 5/5 | 2 | 59.4 | 2/2 | 2 | 70.3 | 5/6 | 2 | 58.5 |
| 6/6 | 5 | 45.4 | 2/3 | 3.5 | 63.8 | 4/5 | 2 | 54.9 |
| 5/5 | 2 | 75.3 | 1/3 | 5 | 89.8 | 5/7 | 3 | 87.1 |
| 5/7 | 3 | 53.0 | 2/3 | 4 | 57.7 | 5/5 | 3 | 52.9 |
| 7/8 | 2 | 53.3 | 3/4 | 2 | 70.6 | 9/9 | 4 | 49.6 |
| 3/6 | 2 | 56.7 | 3/4 | 2 | 68.2 | 4/4 | 4.5 | 62.9 |
| 8/9 | 4 | 43.0 | 1/4 | 2 | 55.8 | 5/8 | 2 | 56.4 |
| 8/10 | 2 | 61.6 | 2/7 | 2.5 | 53.2 | 5/6 | 3 | 45.2 |
| 5/8 | 2 | 51.6 | 1/4 | 2 | 59.3 | 5/6 | 3 | 58.0 |
| 8/9 | 3 | 61.2 | 0/6 | — | — | 4/6 | 3 | 47.1 |
| 3/7 | 2 | 66.5 | 2/3 | 2 | 56.9 | 7/8 | 2 | 65.1 |
| 7/7 | 2 | 57.1 | 1/5 | 2 | 63.3 | 2/6 | 4 | 60.2 |
| 2/11 | 2.5 | 49.4 | 2/5 | 2 | 65.7 | 8/9 | 2.5 | 52.6 |
| 5/9 | 2 | 66.1 | 0/5 | — | — | 4/7 | 2 | 70.4 |
| 3/5 | 3 | 55.3 | 2/4 | 2 | 82.9 | 4/7 | 3.5 | 47.6 |
| 2/10 | 2 | 59.6 | 1/5 | 2 | 58.2 | 6/8 | 3 | 55.2 |
| 3/7 | 2 | 65.1 | 0/4 | — | — | 2/10 | 2.5 | 79.3 |
| 2/6 | 2.5 | 54.1 | 1/4 | 2 | 60.5 | 2/5 | 2 | 63.9 |
| 0/3 | — | — | — | — | — | 1/5 | 2 | 71.4 |

**Table 4–2**
**Levels of Democratic gubernatorial primary competition in southern states, 1946–1950 to 1976 elections**

| State | Years | No. of contests | Incumbents | | | | Nonincumbents | | | | No. of contested Repub. primaries |
|---|---|---|---|---|---|---|---|---|---|---|---|
| | | | Contested | Median no. running | Average winning (percent) | No. of run-offs | Contested | Median no. running | Average winning (percent) | No. of run-offs | |
| Ark. ......... | 14 | 14 | 10/10 | 4 | 54.4 | 2 | 4/4 | 6.5 | 34.7 | 3 | 6 |
| Tenn. ........ | 10 | 10 | 5/5 | 4 | 57.2 | — | 5/5 | 6 | 37.6 | — | 3 |
| Ga. .......... | 9 | 9 | 2/2 | 4.5 | 47.3 | 0 | 7/7 | 6 | 48.6 | 3 | 2 |
| Fla. ......... | 9 | 9 | 2/2 | 5 | 60.1 | 0 | 7/7 | 5 | 34.6 | 6 | 4 |
| Ala. ......... | 8 | 8 | 1/1 | 5 | 64.4 | 0 | 7/7 | 8 | 38.9 | 4 | 0 |
| Miss. ........ | 8 | 8 | — | — | — | — | 8/8 | 5.5 | 36.0 | 7 | 0 |
| N.C. ......... | 8 | 8 | — | — | — | — | 8/8 | 4.5 | 50.3 | 4 | 4 |
| La.* ......... | 7 | 7 | 1/1 | 5 | 80.6 | 0 | 6/6 | 9.5 | 34.3 | 5 | 1 |
| Tex. ......... | 13 | 12 | 8/9 | 4 | 60.8 | 2 | 4/4 | 6.5 | 41.8 | 3 | 5 |
| S.C. ......... | 8 | 6 | — | — | — | — | 6/8 | 4.5 | 50.4 | 3 | 1 |
| Va. .......... | 8 | 6 | — | — | — | — | 6/8 | 2 | 58.5 | 1 | 0 |

* The figures for Louisiana do not include the 1975 nonpartisan primary.

legalized in 1967). South Dakota, Michigan, and Vermont are the only states not using endorsements that have half or fewer of the primaries contested. The informal preprimary endorsements in Minnesota and California did not lead to fewer contests, although most Minnesota races were lopsided. The Utah preprimary endorsement system always produced two candidates until the 1968 and 1972 elections when one or both parties endorsed a single candidate as a result of changes in the law, permitting endorsement of a single candidate by a large margin in the convention. We conclude that both legal and informal endorsing procedures help to explain why several states have very low proportions of contested primaries.

We have also hypothesized that primary competition is greatest in parties that have dominated the politics of a state and that where two-party competition is strong, both primaries should be competitive. In the southern states the fact that victory in the Democratic primary has been tantamount to victory in the general election (until very recent elections in some states) is an obvious reason for the high level of primary competition. Only very recently have contested Republican primaries become common in the South. Table 4–2 shows that these have been concentrated in a few southern states. Most have occurred since the mid–1960s. (See Black and Black, 1973.) Outside the South, there are few if any states where a single party has dominated politics consistently in recent years. There are, however, several states that might be described as traditionally dominated by one party, where that domination has extended back to the turn of the century or at least to the start of the New Deal and where that party has remained the stronger party, if not a dominant one, up to the present time. Vermont, Kansas, North Dakota, and South Dakota are examples of Republican-dominated states in which the Republican primary has been much more competitive than the Democratic one. Traditional Democratic dominance can similarly explain greater competition in the Democratic primaries of Arizona and New Mexico. In the traditionally Republican states of Maine and New Hampshire, however, there are no major differences in the levels of competition. Missouri, Kentucky, Oklahoma, West Virginia, and Maryland are all border states in which the Democratic party has held the upper hand since the start of the New Deal (and earlier in Oklahoma), and yet both parties have had contested primaries in almost every election. It is true that the Democratic party has generally had closer primaries than the Republicans in Kentucky, Oklahoma, and Maryland.

It is also true that most of the states with high levels of two-party competition in recent years have had a high proportion of contested primaries in both parties, but there are exceptions in states like Connecticut, Colorado, Michigan, Wisconsin, Massachusetts, and Illinois, and there are competitive states like Pennsylvania and Minnesota where contested primaries are seldom close.

No single factor explains the levels of competition in the states. There is evidence that organizational endorsements, the relative strength of the two parties, and the presence of incumbents in primaries all affect the level of competition, and in particular states they may have contradictory effects. For example, the dominant party is more likely (by definition) to have incumbents running in the primary unless there is a constitutional ban on successive terms. Several of the states with close two-party competition (which might lead to contests in both primaries) have preprimary endorsements that discourage competition. The states with the highest proportion of contested primaries include several that are closely competitive and several others in which incumbents rarely run (most of which have traditional one-party dominance), in addition to the southern states. The states with the lowest proportion of contests include several with preprimary endorsement, and several others where a traditional minority party has had few contests.

These findings are similar to those of V. O. Key (1956: 104–18), who studied competition in gubernatorial primaries for about half of the states from the introduction of the primary until 1952. He found that primary competition was closer in races without incumbents, and that for both races with and without incumbents there was closer competition in a party's primary in those states where that party had greater electoral strength.

Essentially the same factors that influence primary competition at the gubernatorial level affect it in legislative races. V. O. Key (1956: 172) suggested that: "The extent to which a party's nominations are contested in the primary by two or more aspirants depends in large measure on the prospects for victory for the nominee in the general election." Key's examples, and data collected from several northern states in the 1940s and 1950s, demonstrate that this is true in legislative races.[4] Another important factor is incumbency. Data from a number of southern states in the 1950s and early 1960s (when Republican opposition was rare) show that when there was no legislative

---

[4] Key (1965: 175) also found that in cases where the party's strength was very high there was a drop in the proportion of contests, a fact generally explained by the higher proportion of incumbents in such cases.

incumbent running there was a larger proportion of primary contests, the races were closer, and more runoffs were necessary. Data from both northern and southern states show that more legislative primaries were contested in metropolitan than in nonmetropolitan districts, if other variables such as incumbency and levels of party competition are controlled (Key, 1956: 175–78; Epstein, 1958: 133; Jewell, 1967: 28–34).

It is also important to note that, in southern legislative primaries at least, there is substantial variation from state to state in the frequency of contests and the closeness of competition, and this remains true if such variables as incumbency and the metropolitan-rural character of districts are controlled. The two southern states (out of seven studied) with the most legislative primary competition, Louisiana and Alabama, also rank high in gubernatorial primary competition; North Carolina ranks low in both levels of competition; South Carolina ranks much higher in legislative than in gubernatorial competition. These comparisons suggest that, at least in southern states, there are some pervasive characteristics of the political system producing stronger primary competition in some states than in others.

## VOTER PARTICIPATION IN PRIMARIES

### Problems of measuring turnout

In order to assess levels of participation in the nominating process, we need to measure not only the frequency and closeness of contested primaries but the number of persons who vote in contested primaries. In states where the primary turnout of voters is low, party organizations are likely to have more influence over the outcome, and those who vote in the primary may be unrepresentative of those who are likely to vote for the party in the general election. Large differences in primary turnout between the two parties may tell us something about the character of two-party competition in a state. There are, of course, many factors that affect whether an individual will vote in any particular election, including socioeconomic, attitudinal, and perceptual variables, some of which are not pertinent to our study. We are interested in characteristics of particular states, parties, or elections that may encourage or discourage persons from voting. Because we do not have survey data on motivations for voting in primary elections, we must look for political variables that are associated with differences in the aggregate level of primary voting.

We would expect a voter to be more likely to vote in a primary election if:

The election laws and procedures make it relatively easy.

He has become accustomed to voting as a matter of habit.

The voter has some sense of loyalty to or identification with the party that is holding the primary.

He is urged to vote by workers for party or candidate organizations.

The voter thinks his vote will affect the outcome, because the primary election is close and/or because the party is likely to win the general election.

He perceives that there are some real alternatives in terms of the number or characteristics of candidates or the issues that they stand for.

Primary elections are usually held for several offices at one time, and there is no certainty about what contests for which offices are most likely to generate voter turnout. We will concentrate on turnout for gubernatorial primaries because it is one of the major offices on the ballot and because the governor plays a central role in state politics. There are several problems with measuring turnout in primaries that need to be mentioned so that the techniques we use can be understood. We will measure the turnout only in *contested* primaries, for several reasons: in some states data are not readily available on the vote in uncontested primaries; turnout is likely to be lower in uncontested races so that comparisons with contested races are misleading; and there is no theoretical utility in measuring how many persons vote when there is only one candidate. The standard technique for measuring voting turnout is to compare it with the total population of voting age (as measured by the Census Bureau). We will use turnout as a proportion of voting age population when we are measuring the total turnout in both parties' primaries for governor in one year—which is only useful in years when both primaries are contested. It is also possible in those years to calculate what proportion of the total primary vote was cast in each party's primary.

The problem arises in trying to calculate turnout in a single party primary because there is no obvious way of calculating what the maximum possible turnout is, or what proportion of the voting age population can be considered Democrats or Republicans. Consequently, there is no sure way of estimating whether a larger proportion of Democrats or of Republicans turn out in the primary. In states that require and keep records of party registration, if the data are available, we can calculate and compare the percentages of registered Democrats and Republicans who voted in the primary. However, some states do not require registration in all counties and cities or do not keep statewide registration data. In addition, the open primary states do not require registration by party. The inconsistency of registration requirements makes it impossible to use registration data for comparative purposes in all states.

The inconsistencies in state requirements are important not merely because they prevent the use of party registration data for 50-state comparisons. Because of these inconsistencies, the concept of turnout for a party's primary has a different meaning in some states than in others. In states with a closed primary, there is a specific group of voters registered as Democrats who constitute the maximum number of participants in one primary, and a similar group of potential Republican participants. It is not likely that during the primary campaign large numbers of voters will shift their registration from one party to the other for the specific purpose of voting in the other primary— particularly where there is an early deadline for shifting. In the open primary states, on the other hand, there is no way of calculating the maximum possible turnout for each of the two parties and so no standards for measuring the level of turnout. It would be theoretically possible in open-primary states for all registered voters to vote in one of the parties' primaries. We do not have any accurate records of how much cross-over voting actually occurs, and whether a significant proportion of voters in open primary states frequently shifts from one primary to the other depending on candidates or issues that attract their interest.

Another way of measuring turnout that we have used is to compare the vote in a party's gubernatorial primary with the vote cast by that party's candidate in the general election. This makes it possible to measure each party's primary separately, even in years when only one primary was contested. It is necessary to recognize, however, that the vote cast for the Democratic candidate in the general election may include the votes of independents or Republicans who were not eligible (in a closed-primary state) to vote in the Democratic primary. Although the ratio of primary to general election vote is an imperfect measure of turnout, and may be affected by sharp variations in the general election vote, it provides a way of comparing primary turnout among states and between state parties over a period of years.

## Primaries outside the south

The first step in analyzing turnout is to compare the levels of turnout among the states in the two primaries combined for years in which both are contested (Table 4–3). (Connecticut is omitted from the table because there were no years with contested primaries in both parties.) The first conclusion we can draw from the comparison is that primary turnout is substantially heavier in some states than in others. The average proportion of voting age population voting in the primary ranges from about one fifth to almost one half, with ten states under one fourth and six over 40 percent. If primary turnout is compared to general election turnout, the range is from about one third to 95 percent, and there is a rough similarity in the rank order of the states, using these two measures (a correlation of .786). A comparison of columns *A* and *C* shows that the variation in primary turnout are not simply a reflection of differences in general election turnout; the rank order correlation is only .378. In other words, the primary turnout is affected by some factors that are of lesser or no importance in explaining general election turnout. Moreover, an analysis of registration and voting laws shows that the states with the strictest laws do not have the lowest primary turnout.[5]

No single factor can account for the differences in primary turnout from state to state, but there are several factors that, taken together, help to explain the differences. These are summarized in Table 4–4, which is based on the data in Table 4–3. There are not dramatic differences between states with open and closed primaries, but closed primaries with long waiting periods for shifting registration have low turnout rates; open primaries with no required party identification have high turnout; and Washington and Alaska—states with a blanket primary—have particularly high turnout.[6] States with a high proportion of contested primaries have higher levels of turnout in contested primaries than do states with less frequent contests. There is some

---

[5] The rank order of primary turnout in the states was compared with two rankings of the restrictiveness of registration and voting laws, compiled by Blank (1973) and Kim, Petrocik, and Enokson (1975). In both cases the relationship was very weak.

[6] Note that in Tables 4–3 and 4–4 the states are classified by type of primary (open or closed) according to their status for the bulk of the time covered, and not their status at the end of the time period. Hawaii is excluded from the tabulation of the type of primary in Table 4–4 because it shifted from open to closed about halfway through the period, and Illinois is excluded because the peculiar system it used during most of the period defies classification.

**Table 4–3**

**Total gubernatorial primary turnout in both parties, general election turnout and contested primaries in nonsouthern states, 1946–1950 to 1976 elections**

| State | No. of years | Total vote in two-party primaries averaged for years when both are contested: As percentage of voting age population (A) | As percentage of two-party general election vote (B) | Average of two-party general election vote as percentage of voting age population (same years) (C) | Open or closed primaries* (D) | Percentage of primaries contested in both parties, entire period (E) |
|---|---|---|---|---|---|---|
| W.Va. ........ | 7 | 46.7 | 65.9 | 71.0 | C | 93.8 |
| Mont. ........ | 4 | 46.1 | 68.3 | 67.4 | O | 78.6 |
| Wyo. ........ | 5 | 43.9 | 73.2 | 60.0 | C | 75.0 |
| Hawaii ....... | 4 | 42.6 | 80.4 | 53.6 | O/C | 90.0 |
| Okla. ........ | 4 | 40.8 | 94.7 | 43.5 | C | 93.8 |
| Wash. ........ | 8 | 40.2 | 62.9 | 64. | O–B | 100.0 |
| Calif. ........ | 7 | 38.7 | 77.0 | 50.7 | C | 93.8 |
| Utah ......... | 6 | 38.1 | 54.4 | 72.0 | O | 81.3 |
| N. Dak. ....... | (2) | (38.0) | (67.6) | (58.4) | O | 55.0 |
| Oreg. ........ | 6 | 37.9 | 70.0 | 54.5 | C | 83.3 |
| Alaska ....... | 4 | 37.8 | 78.9 | 48.7 | O–B | 90.0 |
| Idaho ........ | 6 | 36.0 | 59.7 | 61.0 | O | 81.3 |
| Nevada ...... | 6 | 35.8 | 75.2 | 47.7 | C | 87.5 |
| S. Dak. ....... | 3 | 33.8 | 52.8 | 66.9 | C | 38.5 |
| N. Mex. ...... | 5 | 32.7 | 61.0 | 54.0 | C | 66.7 |
| Minn. ........ | 5 | 32.2 | 50.9 | 64.0 | O | 75.0 |
| Mo. .......... | 8 | 29.9 | 47.1 | 64.0 | O–I | 100.0 |
| Neb. ......... | 10 | 29.1 | 49.4 | 59.7 | C | 95.5 |
| N.H. ......... | 11 | 29.0 | 50.3 | 58.8 | C | 89.3 |
| Ky. .......... | 8 | 28.8 | 68.5 | 41.7 | C–6 | 100.0 |
| Ill. ........... | 4 | 28.0 | 42.4 | 66.4 | O–I–6 | 68.8 |
| Kans. ........ | 6 | 27.4 | 50.4 | 54.2 | C | 73.1 |
| Ariz. ......... | 3 | 26.7 | 58.4 | 45.6 | C | 58.3 |
| Pa. .......... | 7 | 25.3 | 48.3 | 52.3 | C–6 | 93.8 |
| Wis. ......... | 3 | 25.2 | 43.8 | 57.9 | O | 45.8 |
| Maine ........ | 4 | 24.8 | 55.9 | 47.9 | C–6 | 60.0 |
| Md. .......... | 6 | 24.6 | 63.0 | 38.9 | C–6 | 87.5 |
| Mass. ........ | (1) | (23.7) | (55.7) | (42.5) | C | 50.0 |
| Vt. ........... | (2) | (23.0) | (45.8) | (49.8) | O–I | 46.2 |
| R.I. .......... | (1) | (22.9) | (36.9) | (62.1) | C–6 | 26.9 |
| Ohio ......... | 7 | 21.5 | 42.4 | 51.8 | O–I | 83.3 |
| Mich. ........ | (1) | (21.1) | (41.7) | (50.6) | O | 45.5 |
| Iowa ......... | 3 | 21.0 | 32.2 | 65.8 | C | 57.7 |
| Colo. ......... | (1) | (20.9) | (44.2) | (47.3) | C | 27.8 |
| N.J. .......... | 5 | 16.9 | 34.0 | 50.0 | C–6 | 81.3 |

\* C = Closed; C–6 = Closed, no shifting of party registration 6 months or more before primary; O = Open; O–I = Open, but voter must declare party preference at polls; O–B = Open-blanket—voter may vote in both primaries. These are the categories used during all or most of the period included.

**Table 4–4**
**Total turnout in gubernatorial primaries for both parties in years when both primaries are contested, by categories of nonsouthern states, 1946–1950 to 1976 elections**

| Categories of states | No. of states | Turnout as percentage of voting-age population |
|---|---|---|
| **Type of primary** | | |
| Closed—6-month limit on changing registration | 6 | 23.8 |
| Other closed primaries | 15 | 32.5 |
| Open—party identification needed | 3 | 24.8 |
| Regular open primaries | 7 | 33.8 |
| Open blanket primaries | 2 | 39.0 |
| **Percentage of primaries contested** | | |
| 90–100 | 10 | 35.0 |
| 70– 89 | 12 | 32.5 |
| 50– 69 | 7 | 27.8 |
| 27– 49 | 6 | 24.5 |
| **Average two-party turnout in general elections as percentage of voting-age population** | | |
| 60–73 | 12 | 35.1 |
| 50–59 | 13 | 29.7 |
| Under 50 | 10 | 28.7 |
| **Party competition** | | |
| Democratic majority | 8 | 33.7 |
| Republican majority | 6 | 30.8 |
| Competitive two-party | 21 | 30.3 |
| **Region** | | |
| West | 13 | 36.9 |
| Border | 4 | 36.5 |
| Midwest | 10 | 27.7 |
| Northeast | 8 | 23.8 |
| **Pattern of party endorsements** | | |
| No endorsements | 26 | 31.7 |
| Party endorsements | 9 | 30.0 |
| Average of all states | 35 | 31.3 |

tendency for states with higher turnout in general elections to have higher turnout in primaries, though the differences are modest. The states with strong two-party competition (as measured by gubernatorial races) do not have higher primary turnout than states dominated by one party. Turnout is substantially higher in the western and border states than in the Midwest and Northeast. Some of the states where organizations make endorsements in primaries have lower turnout, as well as less frequent contests, but there are some exceptions: Utah, North Dakota, and California have high turnout despite the use of endorsements.

We can get a better understanding of the reasons for differences in turnout and also learn more about two-party competition by comparing turnout in the Democratic and Republican primaries in each state. Table 4–5 uses two methods to compare turnout rates: the percentage of the total primary vote cast in each of the party primaries when both are contested (col. A) and the vote cast in each contested primary of a party in proportion to its vote in the general election (cols. B, C, D). Although these measures are quite different, the rank order correlation (columns A and D) is .958. There are 20 states having more voters in the Democratic than in the Republican primary, and 15 states with a larger turnout in the Republican primary, with more of the lopsided advantages occurring in Democratic states.

The states in which one party or the other has a much higher turnout (using either of the measures in Table 4–5) are generally ones that have been traditionally dominated by one party. This includes traditionally Democratic states in the Border and the Southwest states and traditionally Republican states in the Great Plains and northern New England. In a number of the Democratic states the Democratic primary vote averaged almost as much or even more than the Democratic vote in general elections. There is also a tendency for the party that has won more general elections during the contemporary period (column E) to have higher primary turnout, but the current level of two-party competition seems to be less important than traditional patterns of competition in determining levels of primary turnout. There are a number of states, such as Maryland, Rhode Island, New Mexico, North Dakota, Iowa, Kansas, and Maine, in which the party traditionally in the minority has won a substantial proportion of gubernatorial elections in recent years, but still has a primary turnout much lower than that of the traditional majority party.

In other words, there appears to be a time lag, often of many years, between the growth of two-party competition and the development of balance between the parties in primary turnout. Voters have been more willing to cast votes in one or more elections for the candidates of the traditional minority party than to shift their vote to that party's primary. The ratio of the primary vote to the party's vote in the general election is higher for the traditional majority party (column D); it is also generally true that the traditional majority party's share of the total primary vote is larger than its share of the general election vote. This means that decisions in the traditional minority party primary are being made by its long-established voters, not by its newer supporters;

**Table 4–5**
**Comparison of gubernatorial primary turnout in two parties and measures related to primary turnout in nonsouthern states, 1946–1950 to 1976 elections**

| State | No. of years | Average percentage (A) | Dem. (B) | Rep. (C) | Difference | (D) |
|---|---|---|---|---|---|---|
| | Vote in Dem. primary as percentage of vote in both, averaged for years when both contested | | Average primary vote as percentage of party's vote in general election, entire period | | | |
| Okla. .......... | 4 | 85.9 | 144.2 | 29.2 | D | 114.6 |
| Md. ........... | 6 | 80.1 | 96.2 | 28.9 | D | 67.3 |
| Mass. .......... | 1 | 79.7 | 64.2 | 30.6 | D | 33.6 |
| Ky. ............ | 8 | 79.3 | 98.8 | 31.1 | D | 67.7 |
| R.I. ............ | 1 | 76.5 | 52.2 | 12.3 | D | 39.9 |
| N. Mex. ........ | 5 | 74.6 | 93.2 | 31.4 | D | 61.8 |
| Hawaii ........ | 4 | 72.8 | 104.1 | 49.5 | D | 54.6 |
| Mo. ........... | 8 | 68.7 | 59.8 | 32.9 | D | 26.9 |
| Nev. .......... | 6 | 66.0 | 90.4 | 70.2 | D | 20.2 |
| W.Va. ......... | 7 | 65.4 | 82.3 | 50.0 | D | 32.3 |
| Ill. ............ | 4 | 61.2 | 58.2 | 37.0 | D | 21.2 |
| Ariz. .......... | 3 | 60.5 | 91.9 | 44.0 | D | 47.9 |
| Mont. ......... | 4 | 58.1 | 82.2 | 63.1 | D | 19.1 |
| Colo. .......... | 1 | 56.9 | 42.8 | 35.6 | D | 7.2 |
| Calif. .......... | 7 | 56.7 | 91.3 | 59.5 | D | 31.8 |
| Wash. ......... | 8 | 53.6 | 68.9 | 57.1 | D | 11.8 |
| Oreg. .......... | 6 | 51.7 | 78.9 | 67.2 | D | 11.7 |
| Mich. ......... | 1 | 51.2 | 43.1 | 47.3 | R | 4.2 |
| Minn. ......... | 5 | 50.9 | 50.8 | 45.6 | D | 5.6 |
| Ohio .......... | 7 | 50.7 | 45.5 | 42.2 | D | 3.3 |
| Idaho ......... | 6 | 49.3 | 59.4 | 58.1 | D | 1.3 |
| Alaska ........ | 4 | 48.7 | 83.0 | 90.3 | R | 7.3 |
| Wyo. .......... | 5 | 45.3 | 66.3 | 77.5 | R | 11.2 |
| Wis. .......... | 3 | 45.1 | 40.3 | 55.3 | R | 15.0 |
| Utah .......... | 6 | 43.8 | 49.0 | 66.5 | R | 17.5 |
| N.J. ........... | 5 | 43.7 | 28.3 | 42.9 | R | 14.6 |
| Pa. ............ | 7 | 43.2 | 43.9 | 53.5 | R | 9.6 |
| Vt. ............ | 2 | 40.1 | 44.0 | 77.5 | R | 33.5 |
| Maine ......... | 4 | 38.0 | 34.3 | 79.6 | R | 45.3 |
| Nebr. ......... | 10 | 37.6 | 41.8 | 58.8 | R | 17.0 |
| Kans. ......... | 6 | 33.7 | 33.6 | 65.6 | R | 32.0 |
| S. Dak. ........ | 3 | 32.6 | 35.0 | 69.5 | R | 34.5 |
| N.H. .......... | 11 | 29.7 | 32.2 | 66.6 | R | 34.4 |
| Iowa .......... | 3 | 28.4 | 23.0 | 47.4 | R | 24.4 |
| N. Dak. ........ | 2 | 21.1 | 39.2 | 82.3 | R | 43.1 |
| Conn. ......... | 0 | — | — | 22.5 | R | 22.5 |

| No. of yrs. | Party that won general election | | No. of contested primaries | | Average percentage of candidate winning primary | |
| --- | --- | --- | --- | --- | --- | --- |
| | Dem. | Rep. | Dem. | Rep. | Dem. | Rep. |
| | (E) | | (F) | | (G) | |
| 8 | 6 | 2 | 8 | 7 | 35.8 | 63.5 |
| 8 | 5 | 3 | 8 | 6 | 56.3 | 75.4 |
| 11 | 5 | 6 | 8 | 3 | 56.2 | 61.2 |
| 8 | 7 | 1 | 8 | 8 | 57.3 | 69.1 |
| 14 | 10 | 4 | 6 | 2 | 65.9 | 79.3 |
| 12 | 6 | 6 | 10 | 6 | 44.6 | 56.3 |
| 5 | 4 | 1 | 5 | 4 | 69.8 | 71.7 |
| 8 | 7 | 1 | 8 | 8 | 65.1 | 68.3 |
| 8 | 5 | 3 | 8 | 6 | 65.7 | 72.3 |
| 8 | 5 | 3 | 8 | 7 | 49.7 | 58.5 |
| 8 | 4 | 4 | 4 | 7 | 56.0 | 64.9 |
| 12 | 4 | 8 | 10 | 4 | 56.4 | 47.1 |
| 8 | 4 | 4 | 6 | 6 | 45.4 | 57.9 |
| 9 | 4 | 5 | 2 | 3 | 54.1 | 62.8 |
| 8 | 3 | 5 | 8 | 7 | 60.0 | 77.1 |
| 8 | 3 | 5 | 8 | 8 | 56.9 | 71.6 |
| 9 | 2 | 7 | 7 | 8 | 55.2 | 71.1 |
| 11 | 6 | 5 | 4 | 6 | 62.9 | 59.4 |
| 10 | 6 | 4 | 9 | 6 | 78.5 | 87.5 |
| 9 | 5 | 4 | 7 | 8 | 59.4 | 67.3 |
| 8 | 2 | 6 | 7 | 6 | 43.5 | 53.0 |
| 5 | 4 | 1 | 5 | 4 | 68.7 | 48.7 |
| 8 | 3 | 5 | 5 | 7 | 53.0 | 54.3 |
| 12 | 5 | 7 | 7 | 4 | 68.4 | 70.4 |
| 8 | 4 | 4 | 6 | 7 | 58.9 | 62.1 |
| 8 | 5 | 3 | 5 | 8 | 62.7 | 55.8 |
| 8 | 4 | 4 | 8 | 7 | 65.1 | 70.2 |
| 14 | 5 | 9 | 3 | 10 | 61.1 | 55.2 |
| 10 | 5 | 4 | 6 | 6 | 53.5 | 58.2 |
| 11 | 6 | 5 | 11 | 10 | 62.7 | 61.7 |
| 13 | 6 | 7 | 7 | 12 | 53.3 | 54.9 |
| 13 | 4 | 9 | 3 | 10 | 61.7 | 55.6 |
| 14 | 3 | 11 | 11 | 14 | 58.5 | 56.1 |
| 13 | 5 | 8 | 8 | 7 | 61.6 | 47.4 |
| 11 | 6 | 5 | 3 | 9 | 66.5 | 63.2 |
| 5 | 4 | 1 | 0 | 1 | — | 71.4 |

moreover, decisions in the traditional majority party primary are being made by voters some of whom frequently do not support that party in the general election.

We might expect that if one party had more frequent and closer contests in its primaries than the other party, it would get higher turnout in its primaries. Voters would prefer to register (if necessary) and vote in the primary that was more interesting because it was more competitive. We have already noted some tendency in states that have been dominated by one party for that party to have more competitive primaries. With very few exceptions, Table 4–5 shows that in states where one party clearly has a higher level of primary turnout, that party has a higher proportion of contested primaries or else both parties have the same proportion (sometimes 100 percent). On the other hand, in some states large differences in turnout occur despite a high proportion of contests in both parties' primaries. If we look at the closeness of competition in contested primaries (column G), we find that 18 of the 20 states with higher Democratic turnout (based on column A) had closer Democratic primaries, but only 8 of 15 states with higher Republican turnout had closer Republican primaries.

Obviously a table that shows averages may conceal significant variations or trends. We cannot tell from Table 4–5 whether primary turnout was consistently higher for one party in a particular state. By calculating the standard deviation of the percentages in column A, it is possible for us to identify those states with the greatest variation (the highest standard deviation) in the percentage of the total primary vote that was Democratic. One possible cause of greater variation would be a long-term trend, as in Minnesota, where the percentage of primary voters choosing the Democratic primary rose from the 38 percent to 40 percent range in 1950 and 1952 to the 61 percent to 64 percent range in 1958 and 1966. A second factor could be the existence of an open primary, which makes it easier for voters to shift primaries from one election to another. There is evidence that both factors contribute to variation in the Democratic and Republican proportion of the primary vote. There are 13 states with a standard deviation of 5.0 or less, and 11 of these had closed primaries. Of the 18 with standard deviations of 5.8 to 16.6, there were 9 states with open primaries, and in some of these there was also evidence of a long-term trend; in 8 of the remaining 9 there was a discernible pattern of growth in the primary vote for one party or the other during the period of time covered by the data.

Obviously the turnout in any particular primary contest may be affected by specific situations or events—the popularity of a candidate, factional divisions in a party organization, or an issue that is salient to many of the voters. But it is difficult to find variables that are measurable and that have consistent effects on individual elections. Although primary turnout tends to be higher in state parties that generally have close primaries, in less than one fifth of the parties does it appear that turnout consistently varies from election to election with the closeness of the primaries, and half of these are in open-primary states. Although the absence of incumbents may lead to closer primaries, there is no consistent pattern of higher turnout with or without incumbents in the race. In the open primary states there are scattered examples, but no consistent pattern, of higher turnout in one party's primary, either when that party alone had a contest or when that party had a closer contest than the other one did. There is some evidence that relative turnout levels in the two primaries vary more in open primary states, but the shifts of voters that appear to contribute to this seem to be caused less by voters' beliefs about the closeness of primaries than their interest in other aspects of the primaries, such as the attractiveness of candidates. In states electing a governor during presidential years, we might expect higher turnout if the gubernatorial primary is held on the same day as a presidential primary. In fact, very few states have had the two types of primaries coinciding over a period of several years. Only in West Virginia does this practice appear to have raised turnout, and there the levels of turnout and competition have been higher and more consistent in gubernatorial than in presidential primaries.

## Southern primaries

Southern primaries differ from those in other states in several respects. In most southern states the Republican party has not used the primary until very recent years and has used the party organization to nominate when it ran any candidate. Because of the absence or weakness of Republican candidates, at least until the last few elections, the Democratic party primary has usually been the decisive election and has attracted more attention and more voters than the general election. In every southern state except North Carolina the average number of voters in the Democratic gubernatorial primary has been higher than the average Democratic vote in the general election. The use of the

runoff election if no candidate has a majority is another distinguishing characteristic of southern primaries (execpt in Tennessee and, until recently, Virginia).

In southern states there is little point in measuring primary turnout
as a percentage of the Democratic vote in general elections because the
weakness or absence of Republican candidates causes wide variations
in the general election vote. It is more useful to measure the vote in the
Democratic primary as a percentage of voting age population, as we
have done in Table 4–6. There are obviously large variations among
the states (col. A), with the lowest percentages occurring in states with
greater Republican strength.

**Table 4–6**
**Turnout in Democratic primaries and in both party primaries in southern states,
1946–1950 to 1976 elections**

| State | Basic turnout (A) | Average Democratic primary vote as percentage of voting-age population | | | Average adjusted turnout in both party primaries as percentage of voting-age population (E) |
| | | Adjusted turnout | | | |
| | | All elections (B) | With incumbent (C) | No incumbent (D) | |
|---|---|---|---|---|---|
| La.* | 47.3 | 51.9 | 52.6 | 51.8 | 52.0 |
| Miss. | 42.1 | 51.1 | — | 51.1 | — |
| Ala. | 32.9 | 36.9 | 32.8 | 37.5 | — |
| Ark. | 34.8 | 36.1 | 35.8 | 36.9 | 37.0 |
| Ga. | 29.5 | 32.5 | 36.4 | 31.4 | 33.0 |
| S.C. | 26.5 | 31.2 | — | 31.2 | 31.5 |
| Fla. | 28.7 | 30.1 | 25.2 | 31.5 | 32.2 |
| Tenn. | 28.6 | 29.6 | 27.9 | 31.3 | 31.6 |
| Tex. | 25.8 | 26.4 | 25.9 | 27.5 | 26.9 |
| N.C. | 22.8 | 24.5 | — | 24.5 | 26.5 |
| Va. | 12.3 | 13.5 | — | 13.5 | — |

* The figures for Louisiana do not include the 1975 nonpartisan primary.

Until the mid-1960s blacks were discouraged or prohibited from
voting in many parts of the South. Discrimination tended to be greater
in states where primary turnout was highest. Because we are interested
in measuring differences in turnout that were not affected by discrimination against blacks, we have calculated an adjusted turnout figure
(col. B). The calculation requires some explanation. Data are available
on the percentage of voting-age blacks who were registered at various
times in the past. We assume that, in the absence of discriminatory
measures, roughly one third of the blacks would not be registered (a

figure that is accurate for southern whites and blacks where there were no obstacles to voting). For each election year we have estimated the percentage of voting-age blacks not registered, subtracted 35 percentage points from that figure, and then multiplied the resulting percentage by the percentage of the state population that was black to get an estimate of the percentage of the state's voting- age population that was eliminated by discrimination. That percentage was subtracted to get an effective voting-age population, which was the base for calculating the percentages in column B of Table 4–6. The effect of these calculations is to increase the range of variation in turnout among the states.

Since the early 1960s contested Republican primaries have become rather common in several of the southern states, particularly Arkansas, Florida, Tennessee, Texas, and North Carolina. There have been fewer contested Republican primaries for governor in Louisiana, Georgia, and South Carolina, and none in Mississippi, Alabama, and Virginia.[7] Column E of Table 4–6 shows the total vote in both party primaries as a percentage of the adjusted voting age population. It would be helpful to know whether a contested Republican primary increases total turnout by attracting voters who have not participated in Democratic primaries, or whether it lures voters away from the Democratic primary, at least in states where it is relatively easy to shift party affiliation (See Black and Black, 1973). In three of the southern states, Florida, Tennessee, and North Carolina, the result of including Republican primary votes is to increase the turnout rate by several percentage points, but in all three the turnout in the Democratic primary has been dropping as the number voting in Republican primaries has increased—and only in North Carolina has the result been a net increase in total primary turnout. In 1970 in Florida almost one third of the total vote was cast in the Republican primary, while the actual number of voters in the Democratic primary dropped to the lowest level since 1954. In Texas and Arkansas the percentage of the total vote cast in Republican primaries has never been high enough to make an estimate possible about whether these primaries have been attracting new voters or former Democratic primary voters. (In 1970 there was a contest in the Re-

---

[7] Prior to the 1976 primary, the Louisiana legislature abolished the partisan primary for governor and some other offices. Instead there was established a single primary for both Democratic and Republican candidates—with a runoff between the top two—replacing the general election. Consequently, the Republican party cannot hold its own primary and cannot have a candidate in the runoff unless its candidate runs first or second in the first primary.

publican but not the Democratic primary in Texas; the Republican primary vote was almost identical to that in 1968 and 1972, years when both party primaries were contested.)

One way of putting southern primaries into perspective is to compare the turnout in them with the turnout of voting age population in nonsouthern states. A comparison of Tables 4–3 and 4–6 shows that (using adjusted turnout) Louisiana and Mississippi had higher turnout than in any nonsouthern state, and that 8 of the 11 southern states had turnout of at least 30 percent (or 7 of 11 if only southern Democratic primaries are counted) compared to two-party primary turnout of at least 30 percent in almost half (16 of 35) of the nonsouthern states. Obviously the generally high southern turnout results partly from the fact that primaries are usually more important than general elections in the South. Moreover, most of them are contested. In 8 of the 11 southern states all of the Democratic primaries were contested; in South Carolina there were 6 contests out of 8, in Texas 12 out of 13, and in Virginia 6 of 8.

It is not easy to explain the differences in turnout that we find among the southern states, except for the lower levels in Virginia, North Carolina, and Tennessee, where the Republican party has had some strength for many years. Party organizational endorsements do not occur in any southern primaries, nor has there been much chance until very recently for voters to move back and forth between Democratic and Republican primaries. In some southern states, because of constitutional restrictions or traditional constraints, few if any incumbents seek renomination, and so it is important to control for incumbency in comparing turnout. Columns *C* and *D* of Table 4–6 show that incumbency has little effect on turnout.

There are substantial differences in the closeness of competition (with incumbency controlled because races without incumbents are generally closer). Louisiana and Mississippi, which have the highest turnout, are two of the four states with the closest primaries. Virginia and North Carolina, with the lowest turnout, are two of four states with the most one-sided primaries. Virginia, which for many years was controlled by the Byrd machine, had much lower turnout than any other state, and the turnout was lower in individual elections in which the primaries were won by the largest margins.

In general we can conclude that in a number of southern states the Democratic primary turnout is relatively high compared to two-party primary turnout in other states. The differences in turnout among the southern states is substantial (and would still be so even if a correction were not made for the effect of racial discrimination). The states with the highest turnout tend to be those that are most solidly Democratic and/or those with the closest competition. Those with the lowest turnout tend to be ones with a longer and stronger record of Republican competition in general elections and/or those with a lower level of primary competition. Although incumbency is associated with levels of competition, it seems to have no independent and consistent effect on turnout.

## FACTORS AFFECTING THE OUTCOME
## OF PRIMARIES

In Chapter 3 we described in some detail the efforts by party organizations in some states to influence the outcome of primary elections by endorsing candidates, and we summarized the limited information available concerning the success of these efforts. When primaries are contested, the influence of the party organization on the outcome should be less when voter turnout is high, because the organization can be expected to exercise the most influence over a relatively small group of supporters. We have shown in this chapter that levels of voter participation vary widely from state to state and also between the two parties in a state.

We now want to determine, if possible, what factors determine who will win contested gubernatorial primaries in those cases when the organization's influence is not decisive. The first step is to find out what categories of voters are most likely to vote in primary elections. We know that outside the South turnout is usually lower in primaries than in general elections. What kinds of voters who often vote in general elections also vote in primaries, and what kinds stay at home? Second, we want to look at whatever clues we can find (and they are very few) about how voters make their choices in primaries. Finally, we want to examine a factor that has been peculiar to primaries in some southern states: durable factions that have some impact on voters' choices.

### Who votes in primaries?

Obviously voters who stay at home cannot influence the outcome of primaries, and so it becomes important to determine whether certain types of voters are more likely than others to vote in primaries. Compared to voters in general, are those who vote in primaries likely to be better educated, more loyal to their party, more liberal or conservative, more likely to live in certain parts of the state?

There are not enough surveys to provide definitive answers, but we do have a few clues. We know that the characteristics influencing turnout in general elections have an even greater impact on voting in primaries. For example, surveys have shown that persons with higher socioeconomic characteristics (education, income, occupation) and higher age (over 30) are more likely to vote in general elections. National surveys (for the years 1958, 1964, 1966, and 1968) have produced similar findings about primary voters. Those who vote in primaries include a higher proportion of college graduates and of business and professional persons, and also more persons 30 and over, than are found among those who vote only in general elections, although there are no consistent differences by income (Scheele, 1972: chap. 3). There are also more Protestants among the primary electorate, but this may result from higher primary turnout in the South; studies of primary turnout in individual northern states have not found any consistent differences by religion. Similar findings about primary voting being higher among socioeconomic and age groups have resulted from surveys in Wisconsin (Ranney and Epstein, 1966; Ranney, 1968). We can conclude somewhat tentatively that the primary electorate is a higher status and slightly older group than those who vote only in general elections.

Voting behavior studies have frequently shown that the stronger a person's identification with a party the more likely he or she is to vote in a general election. We would expect party identification to have an even greater effect on voting in a primary. Persons who are strongly identified with a party should be particularly interested in the choice of its nominees. Persons who consider themselves independents not only are less interested in the nominations of either party but may be reluctant to register with either party in closed primary states. Scheele (1972: 48) has summarized data from four national surveys (1958, 1964, 1966, 1968) on the relationship between voting in primary and general elections, as follows:

|  |  |  |  |  | Independents | |
| --- | --- | --- | --- | --- | --- | --- |
| Percent voting | Strong Dem. | Strong Rep. | Weak Dem. | Weak Rep. | Leaning Dem. | Leaning Rep. |
| In primary ........... | 46 | 53 | 37 | 38 | 28 | 33 |
| In general election .... | 72 | 82 | 61 | 70 | 62 | 70 |

It is clear that in these elections the strength of party identification had a greater effect on primary voting than it did on general election voting. Although there are larger proportions of Republicans than of Democrats voting in each category, the differences are smaller in the case of primary elections, and it is also true that the proportion of Republicans voting in primaries varies more from year to year than is true for Democrats. A national survey such as this probably conceals important differences that occur between the parties from state to state. Our findings on participation, for example, suggest that persons identified with the dominant party in a state are more likely to vote in primaries. There may even be differences in the effects that strength of party identification has on voting. The Wisconsin survey showed that Republicans more strongly identified with their party were more likely to vote in primaries, but that among Democrats the stronger identifiers were less likely to vote in primaries (Ranney, 1968: 237). It may be worth noting that Wisconsin has open primaries, and so independents are free to vote in either party.

It is commonly assumed that the highest rate of voting in primaries is found among a particular subgroup of strong party identifiers, those who play some active role in the party organization. Moreover, it is assumed that this group of voters is highly responsive to the advice given by organizational leaders about the choice of candidates in primaries. If these assumptions are true, the organization can have the greatest effect on the outcome of primaries in those states where it commands a large number of party workers and where the total primary turnout is relatively low. In fact we have found that turnout tends to be low in a number of states, particularly in the East, which have traditionally had strong party organizations. If many voters assume that the party can determine the outcome of primaries, they have less incentive to vote and their assumption is more likely to become reality. Despite all of these assumptions about the influence of loyal party workers on primary outcomes, we do not have survey data from any state to show what proportion of the voters play some role in the party organization. It seems obvious, however, that the number of party workers voting in primaries is relatively stable, at least in the short run, and that their effect on the outcome will be less in primaries with high turnouts. Moreover, in states where the size or cohesiveness of party organizations is declining, the impact of party workers on the outcome of primaries should also be declining.

Is there any reason to believe that voters representing particular

points of view—liberals or conservatives, perhaps—are more likely
to take part in primary elections? If, in either party, a particular ideological component is overrepresented in the primary electorate, we
might expect the candidates nominated by that party to reflect that
preference. For example, if the more conservative Republicans are
more likely to vote in primaries, they might choose the more conservative of two Republicans in the primary. If that candidate, because of
his conservatism, did not have enough appeal to independents and
Democrats, he might lose the general election. This question remains
largely unanswered, and a scattering of evidence from several surveys
produces inconsistent results. One national survey indicated that primary voters in both parties were more conservative on some issues
than those who voted only in general elections (Scheele, 1972: chap.
4); this finding is consistent with some studies of presidential primaries. The Wisconsin study shows that primary voters differ significantly on a very few issues from general election voters (Ranney,
1968). There is no reason to expect that—as more studies are completed—we will find any consistent pattern. Factors that are peculiar
to a state are likely to affect the issue orientation of primary voters.
Moreover, turnout will vary from one election to another, depending
on the candidates who are running. For example, if the only two candidates in a Democratic primary are generally perceived as liberals, conservative Democrats may not vote in that primary. The question of
whether certain viewpoints are consistently overrepresented in primary elections of either party in a state depends on more fundamental
questions about the causes of turnout.

We have been discussing several types of voters that are likely to be
disproportionately represented in the primary electorate of both parties compared to those voting in general elections. Earlier in this chapter we noted that if one party dominates state politics, the primaries of
that party attract a larger share of the voters than that party usually
gets in general elections, in part because the dominant party is more
likely to have competitive statewide primaries. At the local level the
majority party is also more likely to have competitive primaries, and
this fact has an important influence on county-by-county primary turnout rates within each party. V. O. Key first explored this phenomenon
in the early 1950s. Key (1956: 145–46) advanced the hypothesis that in
statewide primaries of a party

a disproportionate part of the vote would be cast by residents of areas
strongly attached to a party. Virtual one-party Republican counties, for
example, would be agitated over Republican nominations for local office

and the Republican primary turnout would be exceptionally heavy in such counties. Their contributions to the total vote in statewide nominations would incidentally also be large. In the same counties Democrats, faced by hopeless prospects in local races, would vote in small numbers in the primaries and incidentally contribute a relatively small proportion of the state vote in gubernatorial primaries. In counties controlled locally by Democrats the reverse of this pattern of participation would be expected to prevail.

If voters in the counties of traditional Republican strength are over-represented in the Republican primary, it means that the statewide Republican nominees are likely to be persons who come from, or particularly appeal to, the traditionally Republican areas in the state. The same principle would apply, of course, in Democratic primaries. If this is the pattern found in the dominant or stronger party in a state, it will determine which candidates get elected as well as nominated. If the pattern is found in the minority party in the state, it may mean that that party will fail to choose nominees who can win votes outside the areas of traditional party strength, among independents and members of the majority party. In other words, such a pattern of primary participation may doom a minority party to continued status as a minority.

Because our principal focus is on state politics, we have said very little about primaries at the local level, but it is important to realize that the decisions of some voters about which party to register in and whether or not to turn out for primary elections may be affected as much or more by local candidates and contests than by those at the state level. Moreover; in a large proportion of counties, particularly in rural areas, local politics is dominated by one party and most primary contests are in that party. Local primaries, of course, may include contests for legislative as well as county offices.

The link between local and state primaries has two aspects which need to be distinguished. In a closed-primary state the voters' choice to register for one party or the other may be based in part on a desire to participate in local primaries. Once that choice has been made, these voters must vote only in the same party's primary at the state level, whether or not there are contested local primaries in that party in a given year. This has a long-term effect on patterns of primary voting. The second point is that voters may make a decision about going to the polls or staying home on primary election day in part because of the presence or absence of competition in local primaries, and not just because of statewide primary competition. This would be true in open as well as closed primary states, and may help to explain why in open primary states there is not usually a large shift of voters to the party primary which has the closest competition for major statewide offices. (It should be remembered that, while almost all states elect some legislators in gubernatorial years, some states have county elections only in off years, and in these the short-run effect of local primaries on state primary turnout would be reduced.)

V. O. Key's hypothesis is a logical and significant one, but we need data to determine to what extent it fits voting patterns in the states. The collection and analysis of primary and general election data in every county of all the states for a number of years is far too large a job for us to undertake. We must be satisfied with a few examples covering single-state elections. Anyone interested in primary voting patterns in his state can use the same method to test the hypothesis in one or more elections. In order to examine voting patterns in each county, we will use several measures (most of them employed earlier in our examination of state turnout):

The percentage Democratic and Republican of the total primary vote for governor (when both primaries are contested).

The percentage Democratic and Republican of the general election vote.

For each party, the ratio of the vote in its gubernatorial primary to the vote cast for its candidate in the general election.

The index of primary participation distortion (a term used by Key), which is the difference between these two ratios (Democratic and Republican).

The average number of Democratic and Republican elected officials in each county. (If the data were readily available, we should measure the levels of Democratic and Republican primary competition for local offices. In the absence of such data, we can calculate the party distribution of local officials on the assumption that where one party regularly wins most local offices, it is likely to have more local primaries.)

Key provided tables for Ohio (1944) showing that in counties where one party had a larger share of the primary vote, that party also had a larger ratio of primary to general election turnout and a larger share of local officeholders, and that this pattern was clearer when the larger and smaller counties were examined separately. He examined several other states and found similar relationships, although in some states the relationship was weaker and there were many counties that did not conform to the pattern (Key, 1956: 148–52).

We can begin our examination of recent state and county voting patterns by replicating Key's analysis of Ohio. The data for the 1970 primaries in Ohio are arranged in Table 4–7 in approximately the

**Table 4–7**
**Pattern of voting in Ohio counties in 1970 gubernatorial primary**

| Number of counties | Range: Dem. percentage of primary vote (A) | Average Dem. primary vote as percentage of Dem. vote in general election (B) | Average Rep. primary vote as percentage of Rep. vote in general election (C) | Average Dem. percentage of general election vote (D) | Column B Minus column C (E) | Average no. of Dem. county officials (out of 11) (E) |
|---|---|---|---|---|---|---|
| 3 ...... | 70–73 | 75.1 | 45.8 | 60.9 | 29.3 | 10.5 |
| 6 ...... | 60–69 | 63.6 | 50.5 | 63.2 | 13.1 | 8.5 |
| 10 ...... | 50–59 | 53.8 | 58.5 | 55.8 | − 4.7 | 7.2 |
| 10 ...... | 45–49 | 58.4 | 65.5 | 50.9 | − 7.1 | 6.2 |
| 17 ...... | 40–44 | 50.6 | 70.1 | 50.1 | −19.5 | 3.3 |
| 19 ...... | 35–39 | 47.8 | 66.4 | 45.6 | −18.6 | 2.5 |
| 8 ...... | 30–34 | 40.3 | 67.2 | 46.2 | −26.9 | 1.6 |
| 11 ...... | 25–29 | 39.9 | 74.4 | 41.3 | −34.5 | 1.0 |
| 4 ...... | 23–24 | 38.9 | 78.9 | 39.3 | −40.0 | 0.5 |

same form that Key used for his analysis. The table suggests several conclusions:

In both parties there is a wide range in the ratio of primary to general election turnout.

In most counties the Republican ratio of primary to general election turnout is higher than the Democratic ratio, and so the index of primary participation distortion heavily favors the Republicans.

There is a consistent pattern of higher ratios of primary to general election turnout for the party which has the most local officials (averaged over two time periods).

There are 8 counties where the average number of Democratic officials was 9 to 11 (out of 11); they had an average Democratic ratio of primary to general election turnout of 66.1 and a Republican ratio of 51.9. The 33 counties averaging 9 to 11 Republican officials had a Democratic ratio of 44.2 and a Republican ratio of 72.4. If we examine separately the larger counties (over 100,000 population), we find (as Key did) that in these counties the Republican ratio remains higher—even in Democratic counties—than the Democratic ratio or than the Republican ratio in smaller counties. Finally, we can conclude that in Ohio the partisan division of county officials is better than the partisan division of the general election vote (for governor) as a predictor of the index of primary participation distortion.

We have examined county-by-county patterns of primary voting in a number of other states. Although there is not enough space to provide tables for each of the states, we can summarize some of the similarities and differences that stand out. A table for the 1958 election in Pennsylvania similar to that for Ohio would show that the index of primary participation distortion ranged from +35 for the 9 most Democratic counties to −28 for the 7 most Republican. There is a general pattern of higher party ratios of primary to general election turnout in counties with elected officials of that party; the great majority of the counties have a higher ratio for Republicans and a majority of Republican office holders. The electoral system in Pennsylvania counties usually gives the minority party some county offices, a fact that may encourage the minority to participate in local and state primaries. Among the large number of Republican counties, there are many variations in the ratio of primary to general election turnout that are not explainable by the number of Republican officeholders.

In Michigan, where there are fewer contested primaries for governor, we compared turnout in the 1960 Democratic primary with that in the 1964 Republican primary. For both years and both parties it is clear that the ratio of primary to general election turnout was much higher in the counties where the party controlled local government, but among those counties there were variations in that ratio not explainable by the number of local officials in that party. For example, among 47 counties having only Republican officials during two time periods, there were 9 where the Republican ratio of primary to general election turnout was 70 or over, and 19 in which it was less than 50; of the 10 counties with no Republican officials, none had a Republican ratio of 50 or over.

We would expect that the county-by-county variations in the party ratios of primary to general election turnout would be greatest in those states where a large proportion of the counties are consistently dominated by one or the other party. Kentucky is such a state, having many rural counties that have been traditionally Democratic and a smaller number of traditionally Republican counties in the southeast mountain area. In the 1959 Democratic primary the ratio of primary to general election turnout averaged 135 in 20 counties with the strongest long-term pattern of Democratic voting in state elections and the Democratic ratio averaged 78 in 18 counties with long-term Republican voting patterns. In Arizona, a state where most counties have been traditionally Democratic, the Democratic ratio of primary to general election turnout was highest, and the Republican ratio lowest, in such Democratic counties.

California differs from the other states that we have been discussing because very few of its counties have been traditionally dominated by a single party. It is a state with a tradition of nonpartisanship and with a high level of population mobility, factors not conducive to rigid geographic patterns of party control. At the time of the 1966 primary, when Democratic registration (as a percentage of two-party registration) was between 50 percent and 70 percent in 54 of the 58 counties, the Democratic percentage of the total primary turnout for governor ranged from 40 percent to 63 percent in 53 of the 58 counties, and in most counties lagged from 3 percent to 7 percent behind the Democratic percentage of two-party registration. There was no clear, consistent relationship between the ratio of primary turnout and party strength as measured by voting in general elections.

Two writers, Merle Black and Earl Black (1973), have studied Republican primary voting patterns in three southern states—Tennessee, North Carolina, and Florida—where the Republican party has begun to have a substantial turnout and frequent competition in its primaries. There are areas of traditional Republican strength in eastern Tennessee and in the western and Piedmont areas of North Carolina; and in the 1950s and 1960s the Republicans developed strength in the metropolitan areas of central Florida. In comparing Republican primaries in the early 1970s with those in the early 1960s, the authors show that the base of Republican turnout is spreading, particularly in Tennessee and Florida, into those areas where the party is also winning general election votes. The Tennessee primary is attracting more voters from the middle and western areas, and particularly the Memphis area, and the Florida Republican primary is attracting more voters from both the northern and southern regions. Despite these trends in primary turnout, in all three states the ratio of Republican primary to general election turnout is much higher in the areas of traditional or long-standing strength than in new areas. In the 1970 gubernatorial election in Tennessee, for example, this Republican ratio averaged 171 in the eastern part of the state, where most counties are controlled by Republican officials, compared to 74 in the west and only 43 in the middle part of the state. In western Tennessee the ratio was highest in the metropolitan counties, including Memphis, where the party has won some local races. In all of these states it remains true that the counties of traditional Republican control are overrepresented in the Republican primary electorate, and consequently have disproportionate influence on the selection of the party's candidate.

The Blacks (1973) have also studied the effects of variations in turnout rate in these states on the fortunes of particular Republican candidates. The best example is in the 1970 Tennessee gubernatorial election. One of the candidates, Winfield Dunn, was strong in the west (particularly his home city of Memphis), where the Republican primary turnout ratio was low, and was relatively weak in the east, where the Republican primary ratio was high. As a consequence, he won only 33 percent of the votes, but won the primary because several eastern candidates divided the eastern Tennessee vote. His subsequent victory in the general election can be explained in part by the fact that his areas of political strength coincided with Republican strength in the general election. On the other hand, if there had been a single eastern Tennessee candidate in the primary, he might have beaten Dunn and then lost in the general election because of lack of voting strength outside the traditional eastern counties.

We have been seeking answers to the general question: Who votes in primaries? Two more specific questions, both very difficult to answer, are: Who votes in which primary? and To what extent, and why, do voters switch from one party primary to the other? We can start out with the assumption that persons who consider themselves Democrats vote in Democratic primaries and those who identify as Republicans vote in Republican primaries. National surveys (between 1958 and 1968) have shown that this is usually true but that on the average about 4 percent of the Democrats and 12 percent of the Republicans reported voting in the primary of the other party in the year of the survey (Scheele, 1972: chap. 2). The most obvious reason for this difference is that, in states where one party is dominant and more frequently has contests in its primary, persons who identify with the minority party are likely to register (if necessary) and vote in the majority party primary in order to have greater influence on the choice of candidates. The much higher proportion of Republicans voting in the opposite party can be explained by the larger number of states (mostly southern) where most competition is in the Democratic primary. This principle is illustrated by a 1968 survey in Missouri, a state where the Democratic primary has greater competition and where Democrats are usually elected: 21 percent of the Republicans voted in the Democratic primary, while only 3 percent of the Democrats voted in the Republican primary (Scheele, 1972: chap. 2).

We have noted that some of the states with open primaries have relatively high variations in the primary turnout for each party. (See Smith, 1973: chap. 2.) Using aggregate data alone, however, we cannot tell to what extent this is caused by persons shifting back and forth from one primary to another, and to what extent it results from persons shifting from nonvoters to voters within one primary. One bit of survey data from Minnesota, an open primary state, provides some clues, however. In 1966 the Democratic-Farmer-Labor party (DFL) there had an unusually close and bitter campaign after the state convention endorsed a candidate who was running against the incumbent DFL governor. The Republican primary was of little interest because the convention-endorsed candidate had only token opposition. There was a maximum incentive for Republicans to enter the DFL primary, which had stirred up great statewide interest, and there were rumors about which DFL candidate the Republican leaders considered easier to defeat. The Minnesota Poll, conducted just before the primary, found that almost twice as many independents planned to vote in the DFL primary as in the Republican one (though only just over half of them intended to vote). But it showed that only 4 percent of those who identified themselves as Republican intended to vote in the DFL primary, and that these would constitute only 2.5 percent of the DFL primary electorate. The unusually heavy turnout in the DFL primary apparently came from Democrats who usually stayed home and independents who usually either stayed home or else voted in the Republican primary.

## Voter preferences in primaries

In the absence of well-established factions or of strong party organizations that endorse and work for candidates, what factors determine how voters make choices in state primaries? The honest, direct answer to the question is: We don't know. There is an almost complete absence of survey data on the choices made by voters and the reasons for these choices in state primaries. It is very difficult to draw implications or extrapolate from general election surveys because these consistently emphasize the importance of party identification, a variable that by definition cannot tell us which candidate will be chosen, or why, in a primary election.

Our analysis of how voting decisions are made in a primary has to be based largely on guesswork and general knowledge about voting behavior. We know that in general elections knowledge about the candidates is second in importance to party identification, and so we assume that in primaries it is the most important factor. The voter will usually prefer a candidate whom he or she has heard of to one whose name is unknown, and the more a voter knows about a candidate, the more likely he or she is to vote for that candidate. If there is roughly the same amount of knowledge about two or more candidates, the question is which one has the most favorable image in the voter's mind? Obviously voters may differ in the qualities they prefer in a candidate, but a candidate might be expected to gain if he has the image of being experienced, intelligent, forceful, honest, articulate, a good family man, and so forth.

If these assumptions are correct, it is obvious why an incumbent governor (or any other quite visible office holder) has a substantial advantage in the primary. He is very likely to be better known than other candidates, he is usually perceived as experienced, and he has the opportunity to create a favorable image of himself through the use of the media. If he is skillful and knows how to utilize speeches, press conferences, and television appearances, he ought to be able to create in the voters' minds a clear and favorable impression. The challenger starts out at a disadvantage because he is almost always less known and less experienced. Only rarely is the public so disillusioned with politicians in general that a challenger can capitalize on being inexperienced, and then only if he can create a favorable image as a new type of political leader. A national voter survey conducted in 1968 (Wright, 1974: 93) sheds some light on the reasons for the gubernatorial vote in the 21 states having contested gubernatorial general elections, though it does not directly apply to primaries. The data show that voters were likely to have a greater awareness of the incumbent governor than of the challenger and that there was a tendency to vote for the more familiar candidate. Presumably both of the relationships would be stronger in a primary election because party identification would not be a factor diluting the importance of candidate awareness.

In addition to having an image, the incumbent has a record of performance, but this is not necessarily an asset. If the governor is perceived by the voters as having improved education, built some new highways, and established a new state park or junior college in their community, they may vote for him. But if he is held responsible for raising taxes or tolerating scandals in his administration, they may vote against him. The 1968 survey (Wright, 1974: 103) also showed that when all gubernatorial elections are considered together, and when positive and negative references to candidates by voters are calculated, the incumbent's image is helped by his personal characteristics and experience but is hurt by policy issues and impressions of group benefits—in other words, by the perceptions of his record.

If the incumbent gains recognition and builds an image throughout the course of his term in office, the nonincumbents must try to accomplish these goals during a campaign, and this requires skillful and often very expensive use of the mass media. The development of modern campaign techniques for utilizing the media and the erosion of traditional state and local party organizations in many states have changed the strategy for winning statewide primary elections. Candidates used to rely more heavily on the support of the organization in the primary and often worked their way slowly up the ladder of elective offices with organizational assistance. Now it is possible for a candidate who does not have strong ties to a party organization and whose name is hardly a household word to become well known to the voters through sophisticated, large-scale campaigns, primarily on television. There have been a number of examples in recent years of relatively unknown but well-financed candidates winning gubernatorial or senatorial nominations. This is not to suggest that skillful advertising techniques can turn an inarticulate incompetent into a winning candidate, but that a candidate with attractive personal qualities but limited experience and visibility to voters can make a strong impression on voters during a campaign of a few months if he can afford to buy a lot of television time and to hire individuals who know how to make effective use of the media.

We know from surveys of general elections that relatively few voters make a choice between candidates because of specific issues raised by the candidates. This does not mean, as we have pointed out, that the record of an incumbent makes no impression on the voters. Nor does it mean that issues never have a major influence on many voters in either a general or primary election. It is not difficult to recall issues that clearly have had an impact on gubernatorial campaigns in one or more states in recent years: desegregation of schools and of residential areas, school busing, capital punishment, corruption in government, conflicts between environmental protection and economic development, promises to lower—or not to raise—taxes, and charges that such promises have been broken. Any survey of voters in a single state in a single election year can tell us very little about the impact of issues, because that impact—and the nature of the salient issues—will vary, depending on timing, circumstances, and the ability of particular candidates to exploit the issue. Not every candidate who promises to cut taxes gets elected and, perhaps surprisingly, not every governor who violates a promise concerning tax reduction or stability gets defeated for renomination. Not every southern gubernatorial candidate who has promised to prevent desegregation or busing has been nominated, but, since the mid 1950s, it has been a salient issue in many primaries.

Political scientists tend to be skeptical about the effect of ideology on voting behavior, in part because few voters seem to have a clearly defined and consistent ideology. A study of gubernatorial (and also senatorial) primaries in California by William Bicker (1972: 22) has shown, however, a rather strong correlation between ideology and the votes cast. Voters were asked to identify themselves as liberals, moderates, or conservatives. In the 1966 and 1970 Democratic gubernatorial primaries liberals were more likely to vote for the more liberal candidates, Governor Pat Brown (1966) and Jesse Unruh (1970). Conservatives were more likely to vote for Mayor Yorty of Los Angeles, a conservative who ran in both races, or (in 1970) for some other candidate. Moderates took a middle position in their votes. A similar pattern was found in the 1966 Republican primary, when Ronald Reagan did better among conservatives and moderates than among liberals. In all of these races, the correlation was stronger among the better-educated, and for all educational levels it was stronger at the end of the campaign than earlier, when less was known about the candidates.

## Factionalism in southern Democratic primaries

Southern Democratic primaries deserve separate attention for several reasons. Until very recently in most southern states the Democratic primary has been decisive because of the weakness or absence of Republican candidates—and that remains true in some of the states. Primary turnout has generally been higher than the Democratic vote—and sometimes the two-party vote—in general elections. Most southern Democratic primaries have included a runoff if no candidates got a majority. In no southern state has the Democratic party played either a legal or informal role in the nominating process through preprimary endorsements.

A variety of factions have appeared from time to time within southern Democratic parties, but most of them have borne little resemblance to northern state party organizations. Writing in *Southern Politics*, V. O. Key (1949: 16) said that:

the South must depend for political leadership, not on political parties, but on lone-wolf operators, on fortuitous groupings of individuals usually of a transient nature, on spectacular demagogues odd enough to attract the attention of a considerable number of voters, on men who have become persons of political consequence in their own little bailiwicks, and on other types of leaders whose methods to attract electoral attention serve as substitutes for leadership of a political organization.

He concluded that the Democratic party in most southern states is:

merely a holding-company for a congeries of transient squabbling factions, most of which fail by far to meet the standards of permanence, cohesiveness, and responsibility that characterize the political party.

This pattern of transitory and highly personalized multifactionalism remains the dominant pattern in southern states today, as it did in the period of the 1930s and 1940s that Key was describing. Now, as then, there are occasional examples of a more structured factional pattern appearing in some southern states. Where there are two identifiable factions contending for power over a period of years, we call it a bifactional system; where a single faction maintains a dominant position, it can be called unifactionalism. As defined by Key (in the quotation above) both of these factional structures should be characterized by cohesiveness, durability, and responsibility. More specifically, this would mean that over a period of years a number of candidates would command the support of the same group of political workers and would consistently win the votes of certain groups of voters. The system would be responsible in the sense that voters would recognize the factional linkages among politicians and hold them collectively responsible for decisions made in office. In these respects a bifactional system would resemble a two-party system, and a unifactional system would be like a one-party dominant one.

There is no southern state in which the factions have had the cohesiveness, durability and responsibility of most northern two-party systems, but there are some in which we can find some evidence of these characteristics, just as Key found such evidence in some states a quarter-century ago. In some of the states where sectional, urban-rural, or major group conflicts occur, political factions may develop that draw their support from particular groups or areas. A strong political leader who runs in a series of elections may win the loyalty and votes of the same groups of voters time after time, an alliance that may parallel or cut across regional and group alignments. Even

where these factions are neither very cohesive nor durable, they are
interesting because they give southern Democratic primaries at least
some temporary pattern, and they may be forerunners of two-party
systems.

If there are traces of factions in southern politics, how do we find
them? There is sometimes evidence from journalistic sources to show
that politicians and other observers believe that factions are present.
We do not have survey data available to tell us whether voters recognize the existence of factions or even follow a consistent voting pattern
over a period of years. For hard evidence, we are almost entirely
dependent on interpreting aggregate voting data. In *Southern Politics,*
V. O. Key (1949: 17–18) suggested that one sign of factionalism was the
extent to which the primary vote for governor was won by one or two
candidates, in the first primary. If a single candidate won a large majority, it was a sign of unifactionalism; if two candidates shared nearly
all of the vote, it indicated bifactionalism. Table 4–8 provides Key's
data on this for the 1920–48 period and our data for the years 1954–76.
Note that, as Key did, we have excluded primaries with incumbents
running. Key found that primaries in Virginia, Tennessee, and Georgia
were usually dominated by two candidates. Virginia has remained in
that category, and has been joined by South Carolina. These are the
only states that at times approach unifactionalism. North Carolina and
Alabama continue to rank above average in the percentage of votes
won by two candidates. Florida continues to rank near the bottom,

**Table 4–8**
**Factionalism in southern gubernatorial primaries without incumbents running**

|  | 1954–1976 | | 1920–1948* | |
| --- | --- | --- | --- | --- |
| State | Median percentage, top two candidates | Median percentage, highest candidate | Median percentage, top two candidates | Median percentage, highest candidate |
| Va. ................. | 100.0 | 62.7 | 98.3 | 72.6 |
| S.C. ................. | 100.0 | 61.1 | 63.2 | 35.1 |
| N.C. ................. | 78.5 | 46.8 | 77.4 | 40.2 |
| Ala. ................. | 77.4 | 42.0 | 75.2 | 43.4 |
| Ga. ................. | 72.7 | 42.5 | 91.6 | 51.7 |
| Miss. ................. | 69.0 | 35.8 | 62.9 | 33.5 |
| Tenn. ................. | 61.0 | 33.4 | 98.7 | 58.8 |
| Fla. ................. | 57.1 | 29.9 | 57.0 | 29.5 |
| La. ................. | 54.5 | 33.1 | 69.1 | 41.5 |
| Ark. ................. | 53.8 | 31.2 | 64.2 | 36.3 |
| Tex. ................. | 51.8 | 29.8 | 63.2 | 33.9 |

* The data for 1920–48 are found in V. O. Key, Jr., *Southern Politics* (New York: Alfred A. Knopf, 1949), pp. 17–18.

joined by Louisiana, Arkansas, and Texas. (It should be noted that a large majority of primaries in Arkansas and Texas have incumbents running, and in these races the proportion of votes won by the top two candidates is very high.)

A second measure of factionalism, one more difficult to compile, is the extent to which several candidates over a series of elections win most of their support from the same groups of voters. A rough estimate of this can be gained by studying county-by-county voting patterns over time, but little of this research has been done in recent years in southern states.

For many years Virginia was the prime example of a unifactional system. The dominant faction, led by Senator Harry Byrd until his retirement in 1965, maintained its control through tight discipline and close coordination with local officials throughout the state and by keeping the size of the electorate unusually small. Key (1949: chap. 2) estimated that from 1925 through 1945 an average of less than 12 percent of the voting-age population voted in primaries. Organization candidates almost invariably won statewide nominations, usually by large margins, with their strongest support coming from rural areas. The organization pursued policies that were both highly conservative and segregationist. The decline of the Byrd faction and the growth of an opposition faction or factions had many causes; among the most important were the growth of metropolitan areas and the enfranchisement and increased political effectiveness of blacks (Eisenberg, 1972). The breakdown of the Byrd organization was most drastically illustrated in the 1969 primary, when its candidates were defeated in the three major statewide races and its gubernatorial candidate won less than one fourth of the vote and finished third behind a moderate and a liberal candidate. The badly splintered party then lost the gubernatorial election to a Republican. In the 1973 elections the Democratic party was in such a shambles that it had no gubernatorial candidate, and the governor's race was between two former Democrats, the winner running as a Republican and the loser running as an independent. It remains uncertain what new factional structure, if any, will develop in the Democratic party of Virginia.

V. O. Key (1949: chap. 6) presents evidence of a persistent bifactionalism in Georgia from 1926 to 1948. The stronger faction was led by Eugene Talmadge and later by his son Herman, now a U.S. senator. The Talmadges not only won support from a consistent bloc of voters but were able to transfer much of that support to candidates they endorsed. Talmadge support was particularly strong in many of the black-belt counties (among whites) in the central part of the state, and more generally was concentrated in the rural counties. The Talmadge faction benefited from a county-unit system of voting in primaries, a system somewhat like the electoral college, that gave about 60 percent of the county unit votes to the rural counties that had only about 40 percent of the population. (The system was invalidated by the Supreme Court in 1962.)

In recent years the character of bifactionalism in Georgia has changed but it has not disappeared. After Herman Talmadge's election to the Senate in 1956, the pro- and anti-Talmadge alignment of Georgia politics came to an end, and, as table 4–8 shows, primary votes were no longer monopolized by two candidates. But there has been a continuity to the voting pattern in most gubernatorial primaries, with the alignment roughly along urban-rural lines. One student of Georgia politics, Numan Bartley (1970), has shown that there are high correlations among the votes received by conservative candidates in most gubernatorial primaries from 1946 through 1966. These candidates are strongest in the rural areas and southern and central Georgia, somewhat less strong in the rural areas and particularly the towns of northern Georgia, and weakest in the urban and metropolitan counties, particularly Atlanta. In the 1966 primary the vote was split among several major candidates, and the voting support for Lester Maddox, who won the runoff, did not fit the conservative pattern very well, Maddox, however, like several recent candidates who have stressed racial issues, did particularly well among lower-income white voters in urban counties. Democratic primaries in Georgia are no longer based on a bifactional structure, but the major candidates still draw much of their voting support from clearly definable groups within the electorate, and urban-rural differences remain important.

Perhaps the most interesting example of southern bifactionalism is found in Louisiana. From Huey Long's election as governor in 1928 until the election of his brother, Earl Long, in 1956, Louisiana politics centered around two factions. According to Allan Sindler (1955: 643), Huey Long deserves "the lion's share of the credit for the pervasiveness, durability, and substantive meaning of recent Louisiana bifactionalism. . . . The distracting appeals of localism and personality were reduced to minimal influence as the bulk of voters affiliated themselves, in a close approximation to the two-party system, with the two major factions, Long and anti-Long." The Long faction was not merely a personal dynasty, although the personalities of the Longs tended to arouse passionate emotions, favorable or unfavorable, in the minds of the voters. The Long faction, and its opposition, each drew its support from distinctive socioeconomic groups and geographic sections of the state. According to Sindler (1956: 249), "The heart of Longism lay in the cut-over uplands of northern and west-central Louisiana, populated by relatively few Negroes and by many poorer white farmers." Huey Long's economic programs appealed to lower-income voters, and antagonized the well-to-do. Moreover, there was a close alliance between the statewide factions and those at the local level. One consequence of that was that candidates for governor were often aligned, or "slated," with candidates for the legislature. Obviously this made it possible for a governor to have unusually strong political ties with a substantial number of legislators, much like the ties that would be found in a bipartisan legislature.

In one respect, Louisiana was untypical of bifactional states: Most gubernatorial primaries had a large number of candidates (see table 4–8), and the top two did not monopolize the vote, but the factional identity of most was known, and the runoff usually pitted a Long candidate against an anti-Long candidate. An analysis of 9 statewide races from 1928 through 1956 shows that, if the parishes (counties) are ranked in terms of their percentage vote for Long candidates, 22 of them ranked among the top half (out of 64) in at least 7 elections, and 22 others ranked in the bottom half in at least 7 (Sindler, 1956: 249–251; Jewell, 1967: 78).

With the departure of Earl Long from the political scene, the old factional alignments have broken down. In the 1960 and 1964 runoff primaries, racial issues and the religious identification of the candidates assumed importance. Since that time both urban and black voters have played a larger role in Louisiana politics. But the passing of the Long era appears to have ended not only a particular factional alignment but the bifactional structure of Louisiana politics for the time being (Howard, 1972).

Tennessee is another state in which the passing of powerful political leaders has brought an end to bifactionalism. The dominant Democratic faction in the 1930s and 1940s, as described by Key (1949: chap. 4), was led by "Boss" Crump of Memphis and was based geographically in the western counties around Shelby county (Memphis) and in the Republican counties in the east. Crump's power ended with the defeat of his senatorial and gubernatorial candidates in the 1948 primary. During the 1950s and early 1960s a liberal-populist faction could be identified among the supporters of Senators Estes Kefauver and Albert Gore, but there was no clearly defined bifactionalism in

gubernatorial politics, and the winning margin for gubernatorial candidates (in the absence of a runoff primary) has been 33 percent or less
on several occasions. The badly divided nature of the Democratic party
may have helped the Republicans elect a governor in 1970, but in 1974
a Democrat (Ray Blanton) was elected governor after winning only 26
percent of the primary vote.

The most durable factions appear to be those that do not merely
have a socioeconomic or geographic base but are built around individual leaders who have a powerful and persistent impact on their state.
It is difficult to find examples in the southern states today to match
the Byrds, Talmadges, Longs, or Crump. (Neither Senator Russell Long
of Louisiana nor Senator Harry Byrd, Jr., of Virginia dominates the
politics of his state in the sense that his father did.) Orvall Faubus won
a series of six gubernatorial primaries in Arkansas from 1954 to 1964,
in all but the first by a majority that made a runoff unnecessary. Despite
his dominance of state politics for 12 years, Faubus was unable to
influence the choice of his successor, and in 1970 when he sought a
seventh term as governor he was defeated in the primary.

The other recent southern politicians with a durable impact on state
politics has been George Wallace in Alabama. After losing a gubernatorial runoff primary in 1958, he won the primary in 1962, managed
his wife's nomination and election to succeed him in 1966, carried the
state by a large margin in the 1968 presidential election, won a runoff
primary in 1970 and (after the constitution had been amended to permit
successive gubernatorial terms) won easy renomination and reelection
in 1974. Although his primary victories in both 1962 and 1970 were
rather narrow ones requiring runoffs, Wallace has obviously maintained a broad base of support in Alabama for a prolonged period. It
is not yet evident whether the Wallace movement is more than a personal faction—that is, whether he can transfer his support successfully
to any other candidate (except his wife).

The state of Texas is too large and diverse and its politics too complicated to be encompassed by any simple label, such as bifactional.
The Democratic party has a liberal wing that is usually in the minority
and a conservative wing that is larger, more diverse, and in constant
danger of losing supporters to the Republicans. Labels such as "liberal"
and "conservative" are inevitably vague and imperfect, but they are
used more frequently in Texas than in most states by both candidates
and observers of the political scene. Democratic factionalism in Texas
is based less on individual personalities and dynasties than on ideology
and socioeconomic interests. The liberal wing of the party is strongest

in a number of counties in eastern and southeastern Texas. In the booming metropolitan areas, the liberal base resembles that in northern cities: ethnic minorities (both black and Chicano), labor unions, and lower-income groups. The conservative wing of the party is strong in rural counties scattered through west central and south central parts of Texas, and its urban base is in the higher-income sections of the urban and metropolitan counties. The Republican base of support over-laps that of the conservative Democratic wing, particularly in the metropolitan areas (Weeks, 1972; McCleskey, Dickens, and Butcher, 1975: chap. 4).

Some prominent Democrats, notably Governor Allan Shivers in the mid-1950s, have supported Republican candidates at the presidential level. Other Texas Democrats, such as Sam Rayburn and Lyndon Johnson, have been strong supporters of national Democratic candidates. In the mid 1960s it appeared that Governor John Connally, a close ally of Johnson, had succeeded in establishing a broad base of Democratic support from a position close to the center of the party, but since that time Connally has defected to the Republican party, the leadership of the state Democratic party has been shaken by scandals, and the party is once again deeply divided, with the liberal wing in a minority position. On the frequent occasions since the early 1950s when an incumbent governor (with a two-year term) has run for reelection, he has usually been renominated by a comfortable margin and without a runoff, but in three primaries without an incum-bent in the race (1956, 1962, and 1968) the primary race has been close and a runoff has been necessary. As long as the Democratic party re-mains the dominant one in state politics—and most conservatives do not defect to the Republicans—the party will continue to encompass a wide range of interests and a broad spectrum of ideology, and will continue to be deeply divided in many of its primary elections.

## THE IMPACT OF PRIMARIES ON
## GENERAL ELECTIONS

The primary election has a number of effects on the general election that follows; some are obvious and some are difficult to discover and measure. The choice of a candidate in the primary obviously affects the party's ability to win the general election. It is by no means certain that the primary voters will choose the strongest candidate. We have already noted that a low and unrepresentative turnout of primary voters may lead to the nomination of a candidate who does not have

enough support among other voters in his party and among independent voters. If a party is badly divided into factions or wings, the nomination of a candidate from one faction may lead voters who are allied
or sympathetic with the other faction to stay home on election day,
or vote for the other party. In recent years there have been a number
of southern state elections in which a liberal candidate has defeated a
conservative in the Democratic primary, only to lose the general election because of defections by conservative Democratic voters.

It is much easier to find such examples than it is to estimate how
often and in what fashion a divisive primary leads to a party's defeat in
the general election. Is it simply the outcome of a divisive primary or
also the manner in which the primary campaign was waged that leads
to defeat in the November election? What determines the attitudes
and behavior of voters who supported a candidate who lost the primary? The role played by that candidate, the concessions (or lack of
them) made by the primary winner, or perhaps the actions of campaign workers who supported the loser?

There have been several attempts to measure, through aggregate
election statistics, the effects of divisive primaries on the outcome of
general elections. Andrew Hacker (1965: 110) studied 220 senatorial
and gubernatorial elections between 1956 and 1964 and concluded that
"a divisive primary, in and of itself, bears little relation to a candidate's
prospects at the general election." Piereson and Smith (1975) examined
every gubernatorial primary outside the South from 1903 to 1968. They
sought to measure the effects of divisive primaries on general election
margins as well as outcomes. They concluded that "primary divisiveness has no systematic impact upon general election outcomes,"
whether measured by the won-lost record or by electoral margins,
although there was a slight tendency in competitive states for winners
of nondivisive primaries to have greater success (561–62). There are
several reasons for these negative findings. We have noted earlier in
this chapter that the party with a better chance of winning is likely to
have more competition in its primaries when there is no incumbent,
and consequently it is likely to have more divisive primaries. Moreover, statistical analysis measures divisiveness in terms of the primary
winner's margin, not in terms of the bitterness of the campaign or the
depths of ideological or interest divisions within the party.

One clue to the ways in which divisive primaries affect elections
lies in the behavior of the political workers who have been active in
primary campaigns, and particularly those who supported the loser.
Donald Johnson and James Gibson (1974), studying a 1970 congres-

sional election in Iowa that followed well-organized and hard-fought primaries in both parties, surveyed workers who were active in the primary twice (before the primary and before the general election). They found that supporters of the primary losers in both parties were less likely than supporters of winners to work in the fall election campaign. Only about one fourth of those who had supported primary losers planned to work for the winning candidate; almost half did not plan to work in the fall congressional campaign (although some would work for the party in other races), and one fifth indicated that they would work for the other party in the congressional race. We need similar studies in other states in order to understand more fully the impact of worker defection.

There is survey data available from a few states (summarized by Scheele, 1972: chap. 5) that permits us to trace the behavior of voters from the primary to the general election and measure how many of these supporting primary losers shifted their vote to the other party in the general election. We must be cautious about generalizing from a few election surveys, however, because there are so many factors that vary from one election to another. Earlier in this chapter we described the bitter gubernatorial primary in the Minnesota Democratic-Farmer-Labor party following a convention in which the party had endorsed Lieutenant Governor Keith over incumbent Governor Rolvaag. Rolvaag won the primary, but lost the general election. A Minnesota Poll showed that 92 percent of those voting for Rolvaag in the primary would support him in the general election, but that only 57 percent of those voting for Keith would vote for Rolvaag in November. This is a prime example of how both an endorsing convention and a hard-fought primary can divide a party so deeply as to assure large-scale defections and electoral defeat.

A very different picture emerges from a poll of voters in the 1968 Democratic senatorial primary in Missouri, in which Thomas Eagleton defeated incumbent Senator Long and several other candidates. The poll showed that 13 percent of those supporting Eagleton and 24 percent of those supporting the losers planned to vote Republican in November. In order to understand this pattern of defection, it is necessary to look at the party identification of voters, and to recognize that in that state a substantial number of voters in the Democratic primary are persons who identify as Republicans (according to the poll, 9 percent of those in the 1968 primary). The survey shows that over 90 percent of those primary voters who intended to vote Democratic in the fall identified as Democrats, only 3 percent were Republicans, and the rest were independents. But 40 percent of those in the Democratic primary who planned to vote Republican were Republican identifiers; moreover, defectors who supported the loser were mostly Democrats, but defectors who had supported the winner were mostly Republicans. In a state where the majority party attracts voters from the other party to its primary, a voter who appears to be a defector may have intended to vote for the other party whatever the outcome of the primary.

A third situation prevails in California. We have noted the evidence that ideological divisions (liberal-conservative) in both parties affect the outcome of primaries. There is also survey evidence, analyzed by Bicker (1972: 35–40), on intended defections between the primary and the general election. The data from the 1966 and 1970 primaries show that primary voters usually stick with their choice in November if he wins the primary. If their choice is defeated, their decision to defect is related to the perceived ideological position of the winning candidates in both parties. The conservative voter whose conservative candidate loses the primary will be more likely to defect if he thinks the candidate of the other party is more conservative than his own party's candidate.

These illustrations suggest why it is impossible to make valid generalizations about the causes and frequency of voter defections between the primary and the general election. No two elections are exactly the same, and state parties differ in the depth and nature of their divisions. A party's chance of losing the election because of a divisive election is greater if there is close two-party competition; the party has a history of factionalism or divisiveness; the major primary candidates represent distinct factions or wings and the primary becomes particularly heated; and if the other party succeeds in avoiding similar divisiveness in its primary.

# 5 ⋆ ⋆ ⋆

# General elections:
# Participants and resources ⋆

In a democratic society, an election intervenes between the desire of a person to hold public office and the fulfillment of that desire. An election is a way of attaining a governmental position, a means of personnel selection which is an alternative to coup by force, inheritance by birth, or appointment by authority.

Not all public offices in a democracy need be elective—just those considered either "representative" or "policy-making," and of those, only the most important. In all states, the legislature as the representative body is elective, and so is the governor as the major policy-making officer. Presumably, the legislature is also a policy-setting body, while the governor is also representative in character.

The states vary, however, in their definition of other elective offices. Some 27 different offices are elective across the states, exclusive of both legislative and judicial positions. Of these various executive or administrative offices, some include multimember boards and commissions. Of these offices, only the governor is found in all states. Even the lieutenant governor is elected in only 38 states, while the attorney general is elected in 42. Half the states elect offices such as superintendent of education and state auditor, while such offices as fish and game commissioner and custodian of voting machines are elective in only one state each (Schlesinger, 1971: 219).

Although statewide offices are elective, they are not equally competitive. That is, elections are more closely contested for some offices than for others within the same state, even when the elections for those offices are held at the same time and on the same ballot. The offices at the "top of the ticket"—governor and U.S. senator—are most competitive among the states, while other statewide offices such as treasurer, secretary of state, and even attorney general, are much less so (Schlesinger, 1971: 212).

Table 5–1 measures two forms of turnover in state offices—party

**Table 5–1**
**Party and personnel changes in state offices (1914–1958)**

| Office | Number of states* | Percentage of change in elections of: | | Index of difference |
| | | *Personnel* | *Party* | |
|---|---|---|---|---|
| Governor | 32 | 59 | 31 | 28 |
| U.S. senator | 48 | 48 | 24 | 24 |
| Attorney general | 40 | 52 | 15 | 37 |
| Treasurer | 29 | 43 | 16 | 27 |
| Auditor | 24 | 36 | 15 | 21 |

* States which do not permit reelection to an office are excluded.

Source: Adapted from Joseph A. Schlesinger, *Ambition and Politics: Political Careers in the United States* (Chicago: Rand McNally, 1966), table IV–1.

and personnel. In almost 60 percent of the elections for governor ("Personnel" col.), the office changes hands, but in only 31 percent of gubernatorial elections does the office also change party ("Party" col.). The difference in rates of change applies equally between the two types of turnover to all the offices (last col.). But the rates of change— whether for party or person—decrease as offices descend the ballot (Schlesinger, 1966: 60–62).

## RULES AND PROCEDURES

### Plurality and districts

The statewide offices are quite uniform among the states in their election procedures. With few exceptions, they use the plurality method of deciding the winner. That is, the candidate with the most votes, wins. In a two-party race, that winner automatically has the majority. In a three-candidate race, however, the winner need only have a plurality of the votes. The sole exceptions are Georgia and Vermont, which require statewide office winners to have an absolute majority of all votes cast for that office. If not, the choice among candidates is made by the legislature. The Georgia legislature, for example, selected Lester Maddox, the Democratic candidate, as governor in 1966 even though he did not have the plurality over "Bo" Callaway, the Republican candidate. In 1977 the Vermont legislature chose a Republican for lieutenant governor over the Democrat who had finished first in a three-way race.

Election rules for state legislators are much more diverse. They represent districts smaller in size than the whole state. Districts must now have equal numbers of population throughout the state—but that requirement (one man, one vote) did not become effective until extensive court action in the mid-1960s.

Whether equal in population size or not, there are many different ways to draw district boundaries. The very term "gerrymander" grew out of the artful drawing of districts in the early 1800s for the Massachusetts state legislature. Two types of districts are used in U.S. state legislatures: the single-member and multimember districts. Almost 42 percent of the members of the lower house of state legislatures are elected from multimember districts, while only 18 percent of the state senators are (Patterson, 1976: 152, table 2). Multimember districts are used in 22 states in the 1970s (Book of the States, 1974–75: 67, table 2). The use of multimember districts follows no obvious pattern. While in some states, such as Texas, multimember districts are used mainly in populous urban areas, in other states, such as Arizona and New Hampshire, multimember districts are used throughout these largely rural states.

We have invented two election systems for the multiple-member legislative district. First, in the general at-large system, illustrated by North Carolina cities, the voters cast as many votes as there are seats to be filled (e.g., seven), and the highest-vote candidates (e.g., the seven highest candidates) win. Second, in the seat or "place" system, illustrated by Texas cities, each seat is a separate contest, in which each candidate specifies which seat he is seeking. Dallas County, Texas, for example until recently elected as many as 18 legislators countywide by the numbered place system. The voter cast a single vote for each seat, with the top vote candidate (i.e., plurality) winning that specific legislative seat (Young, 1965; Klain, 1955; Olson, 1963; Seligman, 1974: 46–50).

## Partisan-nonpartisan

One procedural rule helps define both the candidates and the eligible electorate; that rule is whether an office is partisan or nonpartisan. Most statewide offices and state legislators are partisan—that is, candidates appear on the general election ballot under party labels, and are placed on that ballot through their party's nomination process. Exceptions are a few lower-level state offices (such as state superintendent of instruction in California). Only one state legislature is nonpartisan—Nebraska—as was Minnesota's until the early 1970s. Judicial offices are a more numerous exception. Judges are elective in 32 states, of which 17 use partisan elections and 15 nonpartisan (Schlesinger, 1971: 280, table 2).

Most county offices are partisan, though both California and Wisconsin are nonpartisan in courthouse elections. There is much more variation among the states in municipal offices: virtually all municipalities use partisan elections in Pennsylvania, for example, while all municipalities are nonpartisan in California and Oregon. The northeastern and midwestern states tend to have partisan city elections, while southern and western states tend to use nonpartisan elections.

## Ballot form

Citizens vote by written communication—they place a mark upon, or pull a lever adjacent to the printed name of a candidate and/or a political party. At one early time, we had oral voting; later, we used paper ballots printed by the parties. The publicly provided paper ballots and the accompanying secrecy of the vote were brought to the United States at about the turn of the century from Australia. Like the primary, referendum, and nonpartisan elections, the Australian machines.

Ballots now used in the United States are mainly of two types, the office-block ballot and the party-column ballot. In the latter, used in a majority of the states, candidates' names appear in a column (or row) by political party, while in the former, candidates' names are organized by the office they seek. In most states with party-column ballots, and in a few with office-block ballots, a voter can cast a vote for the entire party ticket by marking a single circle or square on the ballot or pulling one lever on the voting machine.

Candidates and parties act as though their placement on the ballot affected their chances for election victory. They seek to have their name placed first on the ballot. Usually the party having won a designated previous election obtains the first column (or top row) on a party-column ballot. In office-block ballots candidates most commonly are listed in alphabetical order or the candidates draw lots or have the names rotated in different precincts; similar steps are taken in primary elections. There is evidence that first-listed candidates are more likely to win election (Hecock and Bain, 1957).

Two consequences have been traced to the differences in ballot forms. In states where the ballot form makes it easy for voters to cast a straight party vote, they are more likely to vote for candidates for minor offices than in states where the vote for each candidate has to be marked separately (Walker, 1966). Moreover, voters are more likely to cast a straight party vote in those states where the ballot form facilitates such a vote. The ballot form makes a greater difference for voters who identify only weakly with the parties (Campbell and Miller, 1957: 299–308). One other effect of ballot form should be mentioned. In states where the ballot form or the operation of a voting machine makes it difficult to write in the names of candidates, write-in candidates are handicapped.

## RESOURCES AND PARTICIPANTS

Campaigns for elective office may be thought of as the acquisition and application of resources to appeal for the votes of the electorate. Funds, campaign workers, issue information, mass media, and party support, are among the important resources in the conduct of an election campaign. The analytic question then becomes: Which type(s) of participant(s) are important in providing these resources? More particularly, the question is: What is the importance and role of the political party, compared with other participants, in providing campaign resources?

The political party is important, at least potentially, in three respects. First, for those offices which are partisan, nomination occurs through a party-labeled process. Second, the political party serves as a reference group to the electorate through the dynamic of "party identification"—a rather stable property of the electorate which forms part of the "strategic environment" within which specific campaigns are conducted. As the Goldwater and McGovern presidential campaigns illustrate, however, the candidate can alienate major segments of a party's normal supporters. The preceding two factors are background elements, in which the party's label is the essential ingredient. The party can be important to a campaign in a third respect: It possesses sufficient personnel, leadership and cohesion to be an active participant in the electoral process. The question of the relative contribution of each actor to a campaign concerns the political party in this third and more active role.

Candidates, parties, and interest groups may be expected to take a pragmatic, even manipulative, view toward each other. Each type of actor may be expected to calculate what the other can do for it. Each participant may be expected to calculate what it is lacking to achieve a particular purpose, and to consider what resources others possess which would be helpful to the first.

In elections, these mutual calculations proceed in uncertainty, at least if the particular office and election are not overwhelmingly safe for a particular party. In that instance, uncertainty may transfer from the general to the primary election.

Surrounded by uncertainty both about the final electoral result and also about precisely what campaign efforts do succeed, candidates and parties are likely to seek diffusely any and all sources of support, and any and all avenues of access to the electorate. We will discuss candidates, political parties, interest groups, the mass media, and campaign management firms as types of participants in election campaigns.

## Candidates

In a previous chapter, we discussed the role of political parties in the recruitment of legislators. We do not have similar studies of the recruitment of gubernatorial or other statewide candidates. We can speculate that potential support groups and candidates consider candidacy for years in advance of running for state office, especially the higher state offices. Gubernatorial candidates typically have had years of prior political experience in other (and lower) offices, especially in the legislature and in law-related offices (Schlesinger, 1966: chap. 6).

This extensive prior experience gives candidates time to develop statewide contacts (a seat in the legislature in particularly well-suited for this). If the political party is well-organized and an effective campaign instrument, prospective candidates need time to become known to and acceptable to party workers and leaders around the state. If candidates develop their own personal campaign organization, time is required for that purpose as well.

While mass media advertising and the skills of professional public relations firms are used in most states, "lateral entry" candidates are more dependent upon media advertising than are those with office experience and a network of personal and party contacts. Governor Romney of Michigan illustrates the lateral entry candidate—known by virtue of being the executive of an automobile company and for his leadership in state constitutional revision—who had not served in lower political offices. Governor Shapp of Pennsylvania illustrates the lateral entry of a candidate opposed by his own cohesive majority party. He employed mass media advertising and a professional public relations firm to campaign not only for the office but, more important, for the party's nomination. Mass media advertising became his weapon against the party (Agranoff, 1972: 33–37).

State-wide candidates typically develop their own campaign staff in a state headquarters. A manager, a press secretary, a fund raiser, speech writers, a scheduler, and a host of staff to handle separate segments of the electorate (youth, minorities, etc.) and different geographic areas of the state are typical. The staff for the 1968 Republican Danforth campaign for attorney general in Missouri, for example, consisted of a manager, two public relations agency consultants, a media director, a research and issues director, a committee chairman, a scheduler, a chief of volunteers, a press secretary, a driver, and a secretary. A clerical staff was also needed in the state campaign office (Agranoff, 1972: 72). Managers are also frequently recruited from, or placed in, most counties and sometimes in geographic areas such as congressional districts.

The relationship of the candidate's staff to the party is a key question. Members of the staff themselves may have long experience in the party and be party loyalists. Or they may, by contrast, be newcomers or else have obtained their experience mainly outside the party, perhaps in advertising firms or as personal staff to the candidate. Whatever the prior experience of the campaign staff for an individual candidate, the relationship of that staff to the party can be structured in different ways. At one extreme, the campaign is conducted through, and essentially by, a preexisting party organization. The state chairman and headquarters staff, and the county chairmen and precinct workers, bear the main brunt of campaigning. At the other extreme, the candidate develops a personal following at local as well as at state level, and barely associates himself with the party or with other candidates of the party. An intermediate stance is for candidates to cooperate, perhaps working from different rooms of a common headquarters. Perhaps more commonly, the party structure does work for the whole ticket, but individual candidates also develop personal organizations. They may depend upon the party to mobilize the normal party share of the vote, but develop their own followings to reach nonparty voters.

The time, energy, and skills of the candidate are perhaps the single most scarce resource in a campaign. He is the portion of the campaign that is most visible to the electorate and most reported by the media. Where he goes, who he sees, what he says, the appeals he makes, the letters he signs and the ads he appears in are usually prepared for him by his staff. Indeed, the candidate may have little sense of the general course of the campaign, since he spends virtually every waking hour on the campaign trail. Family members, too, are sometimes used in the same way for the campaign.

Most candidates tend to enjoy campaigning in public. They especially enjoy handshaking in crowds. While their skills in public speaking and their impromptu syntax may boggle the mind, candidates find that being the center of attention in large crowds and shaking hands with and smiling at many people in a short period of time are usually pleasing, even exhilarating, experiences. The reactions of Lyndon Johnson to his crowd reception in 1964 illustrates that of candidates in general (White 1965: 364–67). Banquet dinners may serve terrible food, cuff links may be seized as souvenirs, and candidates may suffer exhaustion, but through it all most candidates seem to enjoy the experience and thrive on the positive and reinforcing responses they receive from the people whom they meet on the campaign trail.

## Political parties

Successful parties outlive their founders and outlast any specific candidate. Further, parties are concerned with, or at least their labels are used for, a wide variety of offices at all levels of government. Thus, parties have a more inclusive and longer-range concern than any one candidate seeking any one office at any one time.

These differing perspectives begin to indicate the potential for disagreement between any one candidate and the party in the course of a campaign. A candidate may want the party to expend more effort on his particular campaign than the party does. In a situation of scarce resources, many candidates may have the same wish, but the party is incapable of meeting those inherently contradictory demands. Party leaders may estimate that one candidate has a better chance than the others; they may then concentrate party resources on their one best chance to the exclusion of the other candidates and their campaigns. The choices, and perils of those choices, are indicated by one state party chairman:

"The decision to tie ourselves to the governor was not universally popular. Quite a few of our legislative candidates felt that we neglected them and of course, everybody always wants more money, more speakers, and more help than you can actually give" (quoted in Huckshorn, 1976: 117).

The conflict between an individual candidate and his political party can be illustrated by congressional campaigns in California. Nonincumbent candidates were in "sharp dispute" with their county party committees. Either the candidates felt that the county parties "were siphoning off resources that should have been committed to the campaigns," or they found that the county party was disorganized and inactive. The nonincumbent candidates—most of whom lost—ended the campaign "embittered" at their county parties. Some candidates, especially Democrats in contrast to the better-organized Republicans, felt that their county parties "discouraged" active campaigns "because the power structure on the committee would have been disturbed if a party candidate had been elected . . ." in the 1962 campaign (Leuthold, 1968: 42–43).

In general terms, party leaders are concerned with organizational maintenance, while candidates are (usually) concerned with winning. The former is collective, while the latter is usually individualistic. Party leaders are concerned with maintaining internal party unity and worker morale; candidates are concerned with obtaining votes. Party leaders look inward; candidates look outward.

These differing perspectives—stated as general tendencies—are greatly complicated by the varying goals and factional positions of candidates and parties alike. A gubernatorial candidate and state party leaders may come from different factions of the party; both the nomination and the general election then become contests for intraparty power. Possession of the office greatly strengthens the factional position of the candidate; hence, party leaders may be less than enthusiastic in supporting him in the general election. This same struggle may be repeated for any office, and at county as well as at state levels. The geographic factionalism of Ohio Democrats, and the ideological as well as geographic factionalism among New York Democrats, have greatly handicapped their chances of winning statewide elections.

State parties' chairmen and headquarters staff appear to take one of three different stances toward their candidates in general elections. One set of state party chairmen are not active at all. They neither have many resources to use, nor do they view campaign support as an important activity for them and the state party. This type of state chairman is mainly found among the dominant and majority Democratic parties of the South. They are unaccustomed to serious two-party competition, and continue to practice personalistic factional politics, in which the party is either inert or an instrument of the governor (Huckshorn, 1976: 118–19).

The Carter 1976 presidential campaign induced a much greater degree of partywide activity in southern Democratic parties than previously in the general election. Particularly in those few states simultaneously electing governors, the Democratic candidates ran a statewide campaign and issued publicity emphasizing the presidential candidate as well as themselves.

A second set of state party chairmen are active in general elections to build their party organization. They have little expectation of winning, but recruit candidates and use the campaign as a means of attracting party workers and developing previously nonexisting party organizations. This form of party activity is found mainly among the minority southern Republicans.

The third and largest group of state party chairmen are active in election campaigns for the whole party ticket. One chairman gave this view of the state party's activity:

"Our headquarters concentrated on legislative races. The top candidates (for attorney general and U.S. Senate) wanted to run their own campaigns. . . . We put out party policy papers, speech kits, organized a speaker's bureau . . . to serve all the party's candidates. We were also able to give each of the candidates some support through a series of statewide ads pushing the whole ticket" (quoted in Huckshorn, 1976: 118).

Chairmen in this group actively recruit candidates, raise funds, and help develop policy positions, all to aid the whole party ticket. But if the chairmen just quoted is typical, most of the state party's activity is directed to the legislative candidates, as was their recruitment, which we noted in an earlier chapter. The top candidates have run their own campaign organizations and funds, and the lesser statewide candidates have the advantage of long-term incumbency. At more local levels, the candidates and issues are too diverse for a state party to provide much help. The state legislature, thus, provides the only state-level offices for which the state party can provide the most tangible assistance. Since governors must depend upon the state legislature, to work with party candidates for that office is also an important means of assisting the party's gubernatorial candidate.

The single term "party" disguises wide variations in the organizational capacities of parties among the states. These variations were summarized into three major types of parties in chapter 3. The electoral relationship between candidate and party in the general election varies with those organizational types.

The cohesive party is marked by joint campaigning, up and down the ticket. The candidates campaign together and urge votes for the whole party list (from the White House to the court house). Candidates raise money collectively, not individually, and rarely issue their own campaign literature. The cohesive party is usually well-staffed in the counties and precincts, and their party workers campaign for the whole ticket. This type of party has usually been able to resolve its intraparty differences well before the nomination, and its agreed-upon slate is usually nominated in the primary. The result is that in the general election the party faces the electorate as a single and capable election participant.

The bifactional party has two hostile entities, each of which is organized and acts as does the single cohesive party. But the two factions more despise the other than fear the opposite party. Bifactional parties which are either majority or dominant in competitive status usually have little to do in general elections; their main battleground is confined to the primaries. But the competitive and minority bifactional parties have two battlegrounds—the primary and general elections. If their candidate is defeated in their own primary, they will continue to work against the intraparty victor of the other faction by opposing him in the general election. If they can defeat that candidate then, they have deprived that faction of an additional base of power within the party. For them, the general election is but a continuation of their intraparty wars by other means.

Multifactional parties of low cohesion continue into the general election the individualistic and local politics of their primares. Each candidate campaigns individually in the general election just as he did in the primary. The parties are not well-staffed or well-funded at the state level. If they are well-staffed in the counties, it is probably in a minority of counties, and the county parties usually do not cooperate with one another. The parties have little to offer, and candidates must develop their own campaign organizations, resources, and voter support.

We may suggest several other factors which affect the liklihood of political parties becoming active participants in general election campaigns:

**Congruence of office jurisdiction and electorate with party unit.** County parties will be more active in elections to county offices; state parties more active in elections to state level offices. Yet we have noted previously that the state party chairmen seem to be more active in state legislative elections than in statewide ones. Nevertheless, the state party rarely participates in county or city elections; even if it is not active in many state wide races, it may be active in district elections to a state office, the legislature.

**Executive offices will be of more concern to parties than legislative offices.** In part, this distinction overlaps the above, for executive offices are elected from the whole jurisdiction and its electorate. While legislative districts may match the boundaries of a governmental unit, they are typically either smaller than such a unit, or include several such units. Either way, effective party activity in legislative elections is dependent upon their ability to coordinate efforts across their respective organizational boundaries. Another consideration is that executive offices (state auditor, sheriff, not to mention the main ones) make important decisions and act upon them in their own right, while legislative decisions are collegial and thus less certain, direct, or simple. Even among legislative offices there is a distinction: parties are apparently more active in elections to the state legislature than to the U.S. Congress (Kingdon, 1966: 71; Sorauf, 1976: 350–52).

**Incumbency.** Incumbent candidates are generally in a stronger position in elections than are nonincumbent candidates. Incumbents have gained familiarity (and competence) in office, have established relationships with interested clientele groups, and have had an opportunity to placate opposed groups and voters. The office itself is usually a source of issue information, campaign workers, and funding subsidies, which are at least as useful in a campaign as in the conduct of office in between campaigns. Given the frequent turnover rates for governor, this asset is more commonly found in lower-level state offices. Whether incumbents cooperate more closely with parties than nonincumbents, however, varies with the competitive status of both the incumbents and the party.

Incumbents usually win. Even incumbent governors tend to win. For this reason, if for no other, party leaders tend to value the incumbency of their candidates, resolve any factional differences they may have had in the initial nomination, and attempt to protect their chances for renomination. Incumbents, in turn, expect their party to protect their renomination (Sorauf, 1963: 105). This expectation and practice is widespread throughout the United States, and is found in most types of political party organizations.

To the extent that incumbents gain personal advantages, however, they need party support less. But they can simultaneously and for the same reasons better afford to lend their support to the party. The secure candidates have "surplus" assets they can use for the party. While we have no direct evidence on how state office candidates view this calculus of relative advantage, congressional candidates have indicated they at least wish to aid their party in campaigns as their personal election becomes more secure (Olson, 1977).

**Competitive status.** Candidates whose party label is competitive or minority in status need the help of party organizations more than those whose are either majority or dominant. Yet, of the competitive parties, less than one third are cohesively organized (Table 3–7); the other two thirds, either bifactional or multifactional in organization, are unable to provide much campaign assistance to their candidates. These statements are inferences, for we do not have comparative evidence among the states with which to test the inferences. The several studies which examine competitiveness at the county level within states, however, produce findings in disagreement with one another (Beck, 1974; Crotty, 1968; Bowman and Boynton, 1966; Cutright, 1963; Epstein, 1958).

**Urban-rural characteristics.** While the above factors apply to both counties and states, the urbanism of a jurisdiction is perhaps more relevant (it certainly has been better studied) at county and district than at state levels. That is, this factor measures within-state variations better than variations among states themselves. By and large, urban parties do seem to be more active in campaigns than are rural parties, in at least some states (Epstein, 1958: 143–44; Sorauf, 1963: 48). Suburban parties show considerable variation. While suburban areas outside Chicago seem less active than city parties (at least the city Democratic party), suburban parties outside both Philadelphia and New York are very active and also cohesive (Snowiss, 1966; Gilbert, 1967; Ippolito and Bowman, 1969). Although the urban hypothesis does seem to distinguish party campaign activity within at least some states, a national study found mixed results in which competition and the Democratic-Republican distinction complicated and obscured any impact of ecology upon party activity (Beck, 1974).

What can a political party offer a candidate? Perhaps the most important resource available to a candidate for a party is its nomination of other candidates. To the extent, however, that parties cannot control their own nomination process, neither the party leaders nor any candidate can select those nominees who might provide maximum assistance in the general election. The identity of the nominees, especially for the higher offices of the ballot, is a factor beyond the control of, but which affects, lower-level nominees. It is a circumstance to which they react after the fact. If the top nominees are thought popular in any given state or district, lower nominees happily attach themselves to "the ticket." But if the top-office nominees are feared unpopular, the lower nominees dissociate themselves from that ticket. A county party leader noted that, in the 1964 Johnson-Goldwater presidential contest, his party did not

press our people in the presidential election. If they vote Democratic for president, we want them to vote Republican in other offices (personal interview).

Candidates of the same party evaluate each other in the same way. State or district candidates will be concerned about the vote-getting quality of lower-level candidates, and county or multiple-member district candidates will evaluate one another on the same basis. If their support comes from different factions, or from different segments of the electorate, their choice is either to form an alliance in which each candidate would campaign for the ticket among his own constituencies, or to avoid one another. Our guess is that candidates more often campaign individually from fear than collectively from hope.

Candidates expect parties to provide several types of election support: voter registration drives, provision of polling place workers, placement of poll watchers, and get-out-the-vote drives. All four activities are better performed through some collective means than by individual candidates. Voter registration, for example, presumably helps all candidates, not just any single one.

Parties can also undertake a wide variety of other election tasks, but these additional tasks are performed much less consistently than are the four just mentioned. Publicity for the candidates can be communicated to voters by mass media advertisements, by letters, and by personal distribution by precinct workers. All three forms of voter communication can be done by the party, and also by individual candidates. In a recent North Carolina gubernatorial campaign, for example, well over 250,000 personal letters had been sent by the leading candidate just for the primary election alone. Since telephoners can be employed, and computer and mailing firms contracted, any single candidate with sufficient funds can pay for such services. We would guess that since individual candidates use these methods of voter contact in primary elections, they find it easy to continue their individualistic campaign organizations and activities into the general election.

Fund raising can be competitive among candidates of the same party. The primary election system almost insures competition for scarce resources among candidates seeking the same nomination. But in general elections the same competition can occur, particularly between the top-office nominees and the candidates for lesser offices. The top-office candidates tend, in the view of lower-office candidates, to drain off locally available campaign funds. Presidential nominees, in particular, are viewed as sweeping into a state or city on a campaign swing, and leaving with a sizable portion of the area's potential campaign funds. With federal financing of presidential general elections in 1976, the presidential nominees adroitly began to make themselves available to state candidates (congressional in particular) to raise money for them. They also began to raise funds for party-sponsored voter registration drives. Thus, one consequence of public financing of presidential elections may be to strengthen partywide collaboration among candidates and to increase the importance and extent of party activity.

Some state parties—no city or county parties that we know of—have mass media and polling staff. They attempt to provide at least technical assistance to candidates in the general election about how to engage the services of professional firms and how to use and evaluate their product. Some state parties hold workshops for their candidates, and for candidate staff, to help them prepare for their election campaigns.

A particularly ambitious party project was undertaken by the Minnesota Democratic-Farmer-Labor Party to aid their legislative candidates in the 1968 general election campaign. The party assembled a professional staff, identified and established priority rankings for all legislative districts, and helped recruit candidates. A general campaign strategy was developed for voter contact and for emphasis upon selected issues. The candidates were brought to state party workshops, and the state party had field men travel among and monitor the districts. Funds, too, were raised and disbursed centrally (Agranoff, 1972: 96–116). This two-year statewide program is the most ambitious of any state party activity of which we are aware. It is particularly notable because it involved local legislative districts, rather than statewide offices. The services which a political party could provide candidates are indicated by a candidate who lamented their absence in his own election:

I cannot count on the party to do what it should—like registration, hand out literature, arrange coffees and meetings, and turn out the vote. The party should also at least provide poll watchers, but often in the last election, the only poll watchers were ours (personal interview).

The few carefully constructed studies of party effectiveness there are measure the effect of personal contact work among precincts within a city or county. Only one study attempts to measure the effectiveness in a state among counties of party campaign activity. Their general conclusion is that party contact work with voters does appear to increase the party's vote by about 5 percent. In a close election, that margin would be crucial. The impact of precinct canvassing seems to be greater in low-visibility elections (primaries, referenda, local offices) than in high visibility elections (general elections, presidential) (Sorauf, 1976: 258–59). In the statewide study, however, the impact of party activity was slightly greater in presidential and gubernatorial elections than for more local offices, especially in competitive counties (Crotty, 1971: 446).

Legislative candidates in the 1972 Illinois general election rated the importance to them of several different sources of support, including both the local and state parties. Both the winning and losing candidates rated the value of the state parties in their campaigns as "slight." Local parties were rated as more important, though the winning candidates rated them as of "great" importance while the losing candidates rated them as "uncertain" in degree of importance (Dunn and Glista, 1973). By contrast, Wisconsin candidates who won averred the parties were of little importance to them, while the losing candidates more often affirmed the importance to them of their parties, but then blamed the parties' failures for their own defeats (Kingdon, 1966).

Like most other studies of parties, candidates and campaigns, these studies were done at different times, in different locations, and with different research designs. The best we can conclude from these few and disparate studies is that party activity does seem to make a small difference.

## Interest groups

Interest groups, or private associations, are at least potential participants in election campaigns. Having an organization in place in advance of any specific election gives the group a ready-made means of participating in elections. While we have many examples of participation by interest groups in elections, we have little systematic evidence.

Usually, interest groups avoid identification with any single party. Most groups are "nonpartisan" in their organizational positions, even though their members (and officers) may deeply and consistently prefer one party to another. They do, however, engage in "concealed promotion." That is, while their officers may favor one candidate (or party) over another, they do not lend organizational support in any overt or publicly visible way.

These statements are usually made about interest groups which interact with legislatures, governors, and administrative agencies on a wide range of matters of interest to the group. The reason for their avoidance of overt election participation is that they fear the loss of access to those public officials (Truman, 1951: chaps. 9, 10).

Interest groups have undertaken three different roles in elections: (1) They serve as vehicles for a personal acquaintance campaign; (2) they publicize elections and candidates to their members; (3) and their organization staffs may provide a variety of services to a candidate and provide access for the candidate to the membership.

The first, most elemental, and pervasive electoral function of organizations is to provide a means of acquiring friendships, building reputations, and providing the locale for informal communication about elections among the members. Most candidates for public office have a wide variety of group memberships in professional, church, civic, and luncheon clubs and in fraternal orders. When asked what help these clubs can be in a campaign, legislative candidates replied that their memberships are a source of friends and reputation. They become known to a wide circle of persons and hope to acquire a good reputation among the members. Friendships and reputation are translatable into votes. The candidate need not ask the members for their vote, although some candidates do send mailings to the members of such organizations. More commonly, candidates hope the fact of friendship and shared group membership converts by itself—in the absence of other factors—into votes for the candidate (Olson, 1963: 42). This mechanism has been termed in a study of California nonpartisan cities as the "politics of acquaintance" (Lee, 1960: 120–22). Group membership is a potent source of such personal acquaintance. Luncheon meetings of civic and service clubs provide an opportunity for all candidates to appear informally as the guest of a member of and also provide a speech forum for major candidates.

Commonly, endorsement letters for candidates will be mailed to an organization's membership and signed by a member of the organization. The organization provides a means of acquaintance and a common bond which can be utilized by a member in support of a candidate. Sometimes the mailing list of the organization can be easily obtained; in other instances the organization staff or officers will permit the mailing list to be used on behalf of only approved candidates.

A second frequent type of electoral activity by interest groups is to publicize the election and candidates to the groups' memberships. Publicizing elections and candidates is a respectable nonpartisan activity not requiring organizations to publicly select candidates, to be identified with any, or to campaign on their behalf. If the interest group wishes future public officials who are informed about or sympathetic toward the goals of the group, that purpose is accomplished by inviting candidates to attend a group meeting or to respond to a written questionnaire. In the 1962 legislative primary elections in a Texas city, for example, approximately 20 local units of state interest groups asked the candidates to address forums of the membership or reply to questionnaires for distribution to the membership. The candidates clearly viewed these invitations with mixed feelings. On the one hand, the candidates needed to meet personally as many potential voters as possible. On the other hand, they disliked having to express something akin to promises and solicitude for any particular group, and viewed with distaste those candidates who obviously slanted their remarks to each group (Olson, 1963: 42).

The manner in which a statewide interest group uses a questionnaire may be illustrated by the Texas State Teachers' Association. It submits a uniform questionnaire to all statewide and legislative candidates on items concerning state support and regulation of public schools. The replies are published in *The Texas Outlook,* the membership journal. Members are enjoined to:

Study carefully the legislative poll results . . . [in] this issue. Coupling this with other knowledge of the candidates, gained by close observation and perhaps personal contact, Texans can and must elect to the Legislature those persons who sincerely support a favorable climate for education in Texas (April, 1960, p. 10).

The teacher membership was likewise told by an editorial in the same journal:

We respectfully suggest that teachers carefully check the record of the incumbent to determine what his position has been on education. . . .

Groups of voters of all kinds—racial, business, labor, and other professions—determine who their legislative friends are and try to support them. Teachers have the same right—and obligation, if they expect to continue their successful efforts for better educational opportunities in Texas (April, 1962, p. 14).

The organization's relationship to the legislative candidates is indicated by its letter soliciting their replies to the group questionnaire:

The Texas State Teachers Association frequently receives requests for an evaluation of the general attitudes of State officials and candidates for State offices, including the Legislature, toward the improvement of public school education. In order that we might have information available to answer such requests, we submit the following questionnaire. . . .

It has been our policy to list in *The Texas Outlook,* the TSTA official publication which is mailed to approximately 90,000 teachers and other readers, a list of the candidates who reply to the questionnaire and a summary of the answers which they make to the various questions (Texas State Teachers Association letter "To all Candidates for the Legislature and Other State Offices," Austin, Texas, 1962).

The third electoral role performed by interest groups is the provision by group staff of a variety of campaign services to either a candidate or a party. Organizations can provide staff assistance in designing campaign publicity and in managing the campaign. They can give mailing lists of their membership and use their office equipment machines to stuff, address, and stamp envelopes. On occasion, the group's headquarters has become the candidate's headquarters, especially for functionally specialized offices such as school superintendent. Campaign letters mailed to some group's memberships have been written originally by an officer or staff member of the association, even though the letters were signed by the candidate.

These group staff services are generally secured by statewide and legislative candidates by seeking out and talking with interest group personnel. Interest group spokesmen, in turn, want to meet and talk with prospective and announced candidates for state and legislative posts. Staff and group officers view these consultations as an integral part of their job. If the professional staff of associations approve a candidate, they will provide introductions for the candidate to potential contributors and supporters within their membership.

An example of the role of an interest group in campaign finance was found in a trucker-railroad dispute in the Pennsylvania legislature. The Pennsylvania Motor Truck Association gathered some $76,000 from over 600 truckers, and distributed those funds between the two parties. The same association also urged its members to contribute individually to local candidates for the state legislature (Hacker, 1962: 333).

The staffs of different organizations do not merely talk to candidates and members. They also consult with one another on their reactions to candidates, finding that they can cooperate in some races, while they must oppose each other in other races.

The selection of the speaker by the lower house in the Texas legislature provides a major focus of interest group effort in that state. Publicly, the speaker's race becomes a dramatic contest when the legislature casts a series of ballots to break a deadlock between competing candidates. The speaker's race, however, begins two years prior to formal balloting. Many interest groups align themselves with various candidates for speaker and try to secure a majority vote in the legislature for their favorite. This effort requires that interest groups be concerned with all legislative candidates—beginning with party primaries. Allegedly, interest groups in cooperation with "their" candidate for speaker have recruited legislative candidates to run against other would-be speakers in their own legislative districts. Legislative candidates have found that local members of interest groups have been alerted by their state staffs to require "pledges" of support to the correct aspiring speaker as the price of support in their own contests. The process of securing "pledges" for the speaker's race begins considerably in advance of the party primaries, and continues until a speaker has been selected by a formal vote of the new legislature (Olson, 1963: 24–25).

A variant of the interest group is the "electoral" group, which is a private association organized expressly to participate in elections. It is created to run the risks of the loss of access referred to above. A near-relative is the "electoral auxiliary," a specialized subunit of an existing interest group; the auxiliary participates in elections while the parent group maintains its stance of noninvolvement.

The electoral group's campaign efforts are directed toward its own constituency rather than toward the entire electorate. It seeks to develop a high rate of voting by its population target, and to produce a high percentage vote for its endorsed candidates from within that population group. It does not attempt to develop by itself enough votes within the entire electorate to win public office. While the electoral group wishes its endorsed candidates to win public office, it contributes to that goal by cultivating votes only from its own population. Its role is supplemental to the efforts of a candidate or party to appeal to a larger portion of the electorate. It can also supply funds and campaign workers which in turn are useful in the wider campaign. This tactic was used by the Los Angeles County AFL-CIO in the 1958 general election, for example, in which "one hundred or more union-paid, precinct workers were supplied [by the union] to each assembly district office on election day" (Anderson, 1959: 292).

One of the most common membership bases of electoral groups is ethnic minorities, of which Latin-American and black groups are the most common. An ideological commitment can also generate electoral groups. The John Birch Society, the older Freedom in Action group, and the National Committee for an Effective Congress are prime examples.

The Committee on Political Education (COPE) of the AFL-CIO is the best-known example of an electoral auxiliary group. For legal, tax, and public relations purposes an interest group may establish a formally separate unit to participate in elections. The interest group is active with the government in various ways, but also creates a separate unit in which the group concentrates its electoral activity. Although the electoral auxiliary is separately financed, its officers invariably are active members—if not officers—of the sponsoring interest group, and the two units have a common staff. Once created, the electoral auxiliary functions precisely in the same manner as does the electoral group. Other early examples of the new proliferating electoral auxiliaries are the Teamster's Democratic-Republican-Independent Voter Education (DRIVE) and the American Medical Association's American Medical Political Action Committee (AMPAC).

The impact of legal restraints upon an organization's political activities is illustrated by this excerpt from a membership solicitation pamphlet of the Texas (medical) Political Action Committee (TEXPAC):

Regularly established medical organizations, county, state and national, are prohibited by law from providing direct support to candidates.

TEXPAC can—and does—perform this vital function, vigorously upholding office-seekers and incumbents who are pledged to and have a record of strongly backing in Congress those measures dedicated to our cherished freedoms and to battling those who would socialize and destroy these freedoms ("TEXPAC" 1962).

Candidates—generally a full slate—are often endorsed in both primary and general elections. The group then attempts to create for its endorsees a sizeable preponderance of votes among its own membership or population category. The groups may display public posters and window signs, advertise in selected newspapers, and may mail pamphlets and endorsement cards to the groups' electorates. COPE more often relies upon union membership lists, while ethnic electoral groups can use lists of registered voters within ethnic precincts. Electoral groups may also provide free transportation to the polls, distribute handbills outside polling places, and telephone potential voters before and on election day.

## Media

The media of mass communications are involved in the electoral process both as neutral communicators of news and advertisements and as active participants for and against particular candidates and parties (Banfield and Wilson, 1963: chap. 21). Management of the media, especially electronic, has in turn given rise to the involvement of professional media consultants in electoral politics.

The mass media are a means by which candidates may bypass political party organizations to communicate directly with voters. The mass media are rivals to political parties in a double sense. First, the candidate may use the media and the party as alternative means of voter communication, and may choose to emphasize one more than the other. Second, a candidate may be opposed by his own party's organization, and use media not only to bypass the party but to campaign against the party and its candidate. In this second sense the mass media have a particular potency in party primaries. Governor Shapp, for example, was opposed by the party organization in the Pennsylvania Democratic primary. The organization marshalled its campaign workers, while Shapp, using personal funds, employed a professional management consultant (Joseph Napolitan) to manage his media-centered campaign. Likewise, in New York City many of the "reform" candidates (who are sometimes also wealthy) challenging the "regular" candidates in the Democratic primary heavily use media and professional campaign consultants. One spokesman for the regulars commented, perhaps in equal amounts of sorrow and anger, that a poor man cannot afford to run for office anymore.

Mass media and party organization make different appeals to different segments of the electorate. A party with a precinct organization at campaign time makes personal contact with voters living within neighborhoods. Mass media, however, are more diffusely aimed at the generality of the public through impersonal means. The result is that party precinct workers mobilize preexisting segments of voters and appeal to their preexisting attitudes, especially of party identification, while the mass media tend more to create ad hoc voter segments by flexible appeals to candidate images and issue attitudes. This distinction is critical for minority-party candidates (Agranoff, 1972: 19–20).

If candidates have any reason to doubt either the motives or the effectiveness of party organization as a campaign instrument, candidates and their managers would rather work through mass media than through the party organization. Reason: The media are much more flexible than are party leaders and precinct workers. Party personnel must be motivated, and if party positions are unstaffed, workers must be found and recruited. Media, by contrast, need only money. Newspaper space or radio-TV time are purchased at standard rates, known in advance. The skills of media professionals are available for paid employment. Even if media personnel volunteer, a handful of volunteer professionals are much easier to mobilize and instruct than are hundreds for precinct-level party workers. Media personnel are also a means of bypassing existing factional fights within the party.

Mass media have been more used by single candidates than by political parties; media more often project messages about candidates and issues than about parties (Graber, 1972). One possible reason is that an individual candidate's personality and issue positions are more easily presented through mass media than are political party identities. An alternative explanation is that candidates, more than parties, purchase media time and skills, and thus media will tend to reflect the purposes and interests of their paying clients. Another possible explanation for media emphasis upon individual candidates is that the media's news reporting concentrates more on individual actors than upon either collective institutions (e.g., the U.S. Congress) or upon issues. The "authoritative source" of a newspaper column, or the interview on the evening newscast are with individuals, not institutions or collective social forces.

The candidate and strategists spend more time and effort upon the media than any other single activity or purpose in the campaign. Media —especially television—are the largest single monetary expenditure in a campaign; hence, most of the fund raising is directed to media purposes. The media are also one of the most efficient ways of raising money, so that the media-fund nexus becomes circular in effect. Furthermore, many events of the campaign are "media events" staged for the mass media to report. The airport arrival, the parade, the speech, and handshaking tours can directly reach only a small portion of the electorate; through the media, however, those activities are projected to the nation (or state or city). Crowds are useful, not so much because the voters in them will be swayed, but because their presence might influence the media-viewing audience (or the impressions of the reporters). Thus, campaign events are scheduled at times (prior to 2:00 in the afternoon) convenient for the news organizations and particularly the evening network newscasts. A symptom of our preoccupation with the technique of media campaigning was McGovern's 1972 acceptance speech: the reaction and commentary emphasized its bad timing (prime time in Guam) rather than its content.

The utility of various media to a campaign varies with the congruence between the location of the office's constituency, on the one hand, and the viewing-circulation audiences of the media, on the other. Candidates for offices whose voters are a small share of a television station's viewing audience, for example, are less likely to use that station than are candidates whose electorates are more completely included within the viewing area. The small-district candidates are also less likely to advertise in wide-area newspapers or attempt to receive their editorial endorsements. Neighborhood newspapers or personal canvassing are more likely to be used than metropolitan-wide media by small-district candidates (Riggs, 1963; Jacobson, 1975: 782–83; Olson, 1963: chap. 4).

States and cities differ widely in the extent to which they are congruent with "media markets." About 90 percent of the Utah electorate, for example, is reached by the Salt Lake City media. By contrast, New Jersey does not have a single commercial TV station. In that state, the home TVs point either north to New York City or south to Philadelphia. The western portion of Connecticut is reachable by New York TV, but not by Connecticut TV. Commercial advertising rates on the Philadelphia stations include the sizeable viewing audiences in New Jersey and Delaware. Texas, with its wide-open spaces, has 18 "markets" for TV viewing, thus greatly increasing the cost of that medium in statewide politics. (The use of media in several state campaigns is discussed in "Politicking on Television," and "Reagan vs. Brown: A TV Image Playback," reprinted in Agranoff, 1972).

Media give more coverage to presidential elections than to any other office. State- and local-office elections obtain a lesser amount of coverage. Elections to the U.S. House obtain the least amount of coverage, while U.S. senatorial elections receive an intermediate amount of coverage. Of these statements, the lack of congressional election coverage is best documented; a national study of newspaper coverage of congressional campaigns was abandoned because of the lack of that coverage (Converse, 1966: 143). On the other hand, candidates to the state legislature felt they obtained even less newspaper coverage than did candidates to either congressional or statewide offices, at least in Wisconsin (Kingdon, 1966: 52). At any given government level, executive-office elections probably receive more media attention than do either judicial or legislative office elections. In-office activity, however, is better covered by the press for elected, especially legislative, than appointed officials (Dunn, 1969: 159–63).

So far, we have discussed the media as communicators. The media, however, are staffed by human beings with their own political preferences. They are also sizable economic enterprises, with salaries, property, and investments. They are subject to governmental regulation both as employers and in their special status as beneficiaries of First Amendment freedoms and, in the case of electronic media, are subject to regulation by the Federal Communications Commission and Congress.

Newspapers play a more active role in local and state politics than do radio and television stations. Newspapers have been reported as candidate recruiters and fund contributors more in local and state politics than they have in national elections (Wilson, 1959). One possible reason for this is that the bulk of advertising revenues for newspapers come from local retail stores, and the bulk of the paper's investments are in the same local area. While the latter is also true for any given radio-television station, the bulk of their revenues are not as locally based and, further, they are directly regulated by the national government. Thus they may be more active in congressional elections, particularly as a source of financial contributions, than in local or state elections.

Newspapers and magazines, more than radio and television, express political preferences in elections. The "print" media more often express local biases (newspapers) or target a selected audience nationally (magazines), while stations and especially the national networks of the "electronic" media more explicitly attempt to reach the largest and most diverse audience possible. Perhaps the print media also more reflect the prevailing practices of their muckracking origins (yellow

journalism) in the late 1800s, while the much newer electronic media
are more oriented to a bland public relations ethos. The expression of
political preferences is most pronounced through editorials, but selec-
tive news coverage and biased reporting are also found—or at least
alleged—in the media.

Candidates and party workers often complain about biased coverage
of their campaigns by the media (Levin, 1962: 252–66). Somehow, they
find bias toward the other candidate or party, not toward themselves.
One study of press coverage of statewide campaigns probed the degree
of bias, finding—in general terms—that while newspapers were partisan, they did not overtly show bias in their news coverage or use of
headlines or pictures. The biases of newspaper coverage toward the
parties were not evenly distributed around the state (Pennsylvania).
Metropolitan papers preferred Democratic candidates (at least in the
1958 elections), while papers in smaller towns preferred Republicans
(Markham, 1961).

Examples of newspapers which are active and well-known protago-
nists in state politics include the Manchester (N.H.) *Union Leader,* the
*Atlanta Constitution,* the Portland *Oregonian,* Virginia's Richmond
*Times-Dispatch,* the Nashville *Tennessean,* and the *Chicago Tribune.*

Candidates are perhaps more interested in "coverage" by the newspapers than in editorial endorsements. A Wisconsin candidate observed, even though he did have most of the endorsements of newspapers in his district,

> . . . editorial backing does not help unless they give you a story every day
> and push it. Five percent of the readers read the editorial page.

Wisconsin Democrats, more than Republicans, complained of the lack
of press coverage. A losing Democrat found that the "editors are Republicans and just would not print" the candidate's news releases
(both quotes in Kingdon, 1966: 51). On the other hand, newspaper personnel repeatedly complain that candidates must make news before
the papers have anything to report, and that a mere press release
hardly qualifies. Here is another respect in which incumbents have
office-based advantages over challengers.

Media personnel enter public and political employment as a consequence of their having occupied positions in the media. Candidates,
elected officials, governmental agencies, interest groups, and actors
and musicians all have press agents, many of whom are former reporters. Whether or not the possibility of future employment with a

successful candidate has an impact upon reporting of that candidate has not been researched.

Whether the media have much of an impact on the electorate—and if so, how—does not have a simple answer. One study suggests that the relationship between candidate spending for broadcast advertising and the resulting vote varies by office, by the distinction between primary and general elections, by incumbency, and by the normal voting patterns of the electorate. The relationship was least for incumbent U.S. House members and for presidential candidates, but was greatest in nomination contests for governor and U.S. Senate (Jacobson, 1975: 792).

A somewhat different type of effect was measured by examining the salience of issues to the electorate compared with issue emphasis in the media. This question was explored in one state (Kentucky), with the finding that there was a strong correspondence of public awareness of issues with issue attention in newspapers but not in the broadcast media. In the longer view, however, the same study indicated that whether the correspondence between public views and newspaper coverage began with the newspapers themselves, or began with the public to which the newspapers then responded, was an open question (Tipton et al., 1975).

## Campaign management firms

Commercial advertising and public relations firms have turned their skills toward electoral campaigns because candidates and referenda promoters found such skills useful and were willing to pay for them. Tasks such as preparation of advertising copy and the purchase of media time or space have spawned a new industry—professional campaign management firms, whose major activity and source of income is management of election campaigns.

While campaign management firms will undertake to design and manage an entire campaign for elective office, they more commonly manage the entire campaign for referenda issues. Professional campaign management apparently began with referenda campaigns in California in the 1930s. Referenda lack a human being as candidate who is likely to possess his own stubborn notions about campaigning. Rather, referenda issues are likely to be initiated by a corporation or interest group which does not itself wish to campaign and which has few preconceptions about how to win the campaign.

Campaign management firms place more emphasis upon the single candidate than upon parties or groups of candidates. Media design, news reporting, slogan preparation, and public opinion surveying are more easily accomplished when the "product" is a single human being than a collectivity (Agranoff, 1972: 26). In addition, campaign management firms are more employed by single candidates than by collectivities. The long-term effect is both to train an electorate to respond to individual candidacies and to train candidates to act independently rather than collectively. (The activities of media specialists and consultant firms are discussed in "How the 'I Dare you' Candidate Won," and "Media Marketing Strategy in a Major Campaign," in Agranoff, 1972.)

Many professional campaign firms in state and national politics work mainly with candidates defined by party, ideological, and factional preferences. This identification is less marked for occasional participants than for the consistent and full-time firms. This identification might also be less pronounced in local elections than in state and national politics.

Campaign management firms are rivals to political party organization through displacement. Displacement (or perhaps replacement) occurs as a firm provides to candidates and to the electorate all of the campaign services which could be provided by a party organization: fund raising, voter communication, scheduling, campaign events and appearances, voter canvassing and polling, and election-day staffing of polling places. A broader statement of this hypothesis is expressed in temporal and causal terms: Parties first decline in their capacity to provide these services, and then professional firms develop to take the party's place. Campaign management firms are also rivals to political party organizations through hostile competition, as discussed earlier in the media section.

Political party organizations are making some attempt to develop their own skills in campaign management. Beginning with publicists in the 1920s, national committees and local parties have employed specialized personnel to write and distribute publicity materials. More recently, the national committees (the Republican Congressional Campaign Committee and the Democratic Study Group), as well as a few state parties (Minnesota DFL, discussed earlier), have attempted to raise funds, provide media guidance, commission and distribute public opinion polls, and train candidates (Huckshorn and Spencer, 1971: 129–39, 244–47).

## CAMPAIGN FINANCE

Rumors, allegations, and charges about rival candidates' campaign finance and expenditures are almost a commonplace in U.S. campaign rhetoric, whether for president or dogcatcher. We have had, until recently, little reliable information on the subject. Prior to Watergate, the laws regulating campaign finance were vaguely written, narrowly interpreted, and indifferently enforced, more so at state and local levels than for federal offices. But concern with campaign finance practices was leading to new regulations even before Watergate. Indeed, the federal regulations which went into effect in April 1972 were instrumental in providing sufficient information with which to begin press and public investigations into the subsequent Watergate burglary and its financing.

Regulation of campaign finance practices usually takes several forms. One method is to require public disclosure. Another is to limit the amount of funds which can be raised and the sources from which funds can be contributed. A third method is to limit the amounts of campaign expenditures. The fourth method, much more widely used in European democracies than in the United States, is to have public financing of campaign expenditures.

We will confine our attention to what is known about campaign finance, and will have little to say about what the regulations ought to achieve or how they work. Most of what we know—which probably is not very much—comes from the public disclosure requirements and from personal interviews.

We do know that campaigning is expensive, and that costs continually rise. The use of mass media advertising and professional campaign management firms has greatly increased the costs of campaigning (Crotty, 1977: 107–110). In states of any size at all, candidates ordinarily spend a million or more dollars each in gubernatorial campaigns. In the 1974 gubernatorial campaign in New York, for example, the successful candidate, Hugh Carey, spent $5 million in the primary and general election combined, with $1.5 million being spent on the media, primarily TV (Alexander, 1976a: 305). In Georgia, a medium-sized, rural southern state, the successful gubernatorial candidate reported having spent $1,150,000 in two primaries (the first plus a runoff) and the general election (Alexander, 1976a: 215).

State legislative campaigns vary enormously in cost, from a few hundred dollars up to $100,000 per candidate. In part, at least, this difference reflects the vast differences in legislative districts, from the single-member, rural, and sparsely-populated district to the multi-member, urban, highly-populated district. Costs also vary with competition—and we suspect that many seats are not closely contested in either the primary or general election or both. The average amount spent in contested Massachusetts state senate races in 1968 was $4,500 (Mileur and Sulzner, 1974: 89–99). In Florida, the average amount spent by winning legislative candidates in 1974 was close to $11,500 (Alexander, 1976a: 55–57).

## Sources

The sources of campaign finance are wonderfully diverse. They are also often obscure. Contributors sometimes do not want publicity of either their identity or the amount of their contribution. In some instances, the contribution would be illegal, either in size or because of the source (e.g., corporations in half of the states). But in all states, the sources and amounts of campaign contributions are subject to attack by opponents and the press. The recent efforts nationally and in some states to tighten disclosure requirements have provided much more information about the sources of campaign contributions than we had previously (Crotty, 1977: 119–35).

One source of campaign funds is the candidate himself. Governor Briscoe of Texas, for example, in his 1974 reelection campaign provided $645,000 in contributions and loans from his own funds (Alexander, 1976a: 308). In the same year, a losing Georgia gubernatorial candidate spent over $1 million in the Democratic primary, of which he personally contributed $235,000 and personally secured $350,000 in loans. After the campaign, he had $200,000 left in unmet expenses, which he paid personally (Alexander 1976a: 209–10).

Family is another source. The brother of winner Hugh Carey in the 1974 New York gubernatorial campaign gave and lent over $1 million to Carey's campaign. Not only was the dollar amount sizable, but it was timely, in the early stages of the campaign, and the brother's firm was the source of accountants and other skilled professionals who conveyed the funds both discreetly and legally (Alexander, 1976a: 305).

Labor unions provide a sizable portion of campaign funds for many Democratic candidates. In the 1974 Ohio gubernatorial campaign, for example, unions contributed $400,000 to the unsuccessful reelection campaign of then-Governor Gilligan. Unions accounted for almost all of his contributions of over $3,000 each, and for almost 40 percent of his campaign budget (Alexander, 1976a: 305).

State employees are a source of campaign funds in at least some states. In Governor Shapps' 1974 reelection campaign in Pennsylvania, some $300,000 was raised from that source. The fund raiser for the Democratic State Committee levied the following assessments in the state's highway department: $60 per laborer, $120 per foreman, and also $100 per snow removal machine used by the contractors (Alexander, 1976a: 305). State employees and public school teachers collectively were among the sources of the largest amounts of campaign contributions in the 1974 California campaigns for both governor and the state legislature. Collectively they contributed over $1.7 million. A gubernatorial candidate received, from the organized teachers, $25,000, as did his running mate for lieutenant governor. Legislative candidates obtained as much as $10,000 each, though most contributions for that office from the teachers' association were under $5,000 each (Alexander, 1976a: 128–29).

The business sector is an important source of campaign funds in all states. Those businesses and professions which obtain incomes from state contracts are especially frequent campaign contributors. Construction contractors, insurance firms, engineers, architects, and the unions of employees of such firms, are included in this category. These sources were particularly noticeable in contributions to Governor Mandel's 1974 reelection campaign in Maryland. The Kansas election in the same year featured a scandal over the awards of architectural contracts to campaign contributors (Alexander 1976a: 308–9, and 214 for Georgia and 263–64 for Ohio).

Banks are a separate category of campaign contributor simply because they control large reservoirs of assets and cash. The successful 1974 gubernatorial campaign in Georgia illustrates the potentially critical role of banks. Both George Busbee, the winner, and other candidates including Lester Maddox and Burt Lance, obtained personal loans from Georgia banks. These loans were not infrequently signed by other public officials, both elected and appointed. The loans were made by the banks, and were cosigned by supporters, in the knowledge that the funds would pass in the form of personal campaign contributions directly to the campaign. Not only did this system raise large amounts of funds, but it also: (1) disguised their source for reporting purposes; (2) distributed liability for personal debt among a number of people; and (3) deferred until after the financial reporting deadlines the raising of funds to repay the original loans (Alexander, 1976a: 201–8).

Corporations are a type of campaign contributor, either directly or through a "political action committee," though corporation campaign contributions are illegal in about half of the states (Alexander, 1976b: 173). In many instances the preferences of a corporation are inferred from the pattern of giving by its directors and officers, even though there is no record of overt activity by the corporation itself. California does permit legal contributions directly from corporations. In that state's 1974 campaign, a total of $480,000 was contributed by oil companies, and $234,000 by horse racing interests. Associations of realtors gave $224,000, and doctors and dentists contributed over $640,000. Various committees gave funds: The Good Government Committee of the savings and loan companies and the Citizens for Responsible Government of executives of the Pacific Telephone Company are examples. Lobbyists are another source of business contributions. One lobbyist funneled funds through the Consumer Action Committee in his capacity as lobbyist for the Professional Astrologers of California. The same person also contributed through the Environmental Action Committee, which consists of sandblasting and painting contractors. An example of consistent campaign contributions by individual directors and officers of a single corporation is provided in Georgia; officers and directors from different branches of the same bank contributed $27,400 to a single, and winning, gubernatorial candidate (Alexander, 1976a: 126–28, 207, 291–92).

Wealthy individuals are still another source of campaign finance. As an example, successful candidate Jerry Brown, in his 1974 California gubernatorial primary campaign, received $33,250 as contributions and another $40,000 in loans from a single person. These funds were received by separate campaign committees, most of which were created expressly to receive these contributions and to permit the individual to escape paying gift taxes on individual donations over $3,000. The largest single contribution to the Republican candidate in the same general election from an individual was $70,000. In Georgia, one unsuccessful gubernatorial candidate in the 1974 Democratic primary obtained over $100,000 from such persons, usually in amounts ranging from $1,000 to $5,000 each (Alexander, 1976a: 131, 209).

Candidates are themselves a source of campaign funds to one another. In one form, candidates of a party aid one another in the general election. An apparent winner, especially at the top of the ticket, will either raise or channel funds to other party candidates, especially those trailing in the polls, as did Reagan for fellow Republicans in the 1966 California campaign (Alexander, 1976a: 129). Several state legislatures (e.g., Illinois') have party campaign committees in each house which raise, disburse, and channel funds to party candidates in legislative races.

In another form, however, intercandidate fund raising is an expression of intraparty factionalism. This form has occurred in contests for presiding officers of legislatures in both California and Texas. Rival candidates for speaker (or president pro tem) within a party seek pledges of votes from legislators in advance—sometimes four years in advance. Candidates in the intervening legislative elections will be asked to pledge to the rival aspirants for presiding officer, who in turn will help raise funds for those who pledge properly. In addition, campaign contributors, including lobbyists, will fund candidates who pledge to the aspirant for presiding officer whom they support (Alexander, 1976a: 89, 130; Olson, 1963: 24–24).

Intercandidate fund raising can occur after an election. After the 1976 North Carolina election, for example, Democratic members of the state senate were invited to purchase tickets to a fund raising dinner for their presiding officer, the Democratic lieutenant governor. The invitations were issued to senators while that official was deciding upon their committee assignments. One senator commented, "That sort of puts 'em on the spot, doesn't it?" The official's campaign manager replied:

I'm not aware of any impropriety. . . . They live out there in the political world and they're aware of the trials and tribulations involved . . . (Greensboro *Daily News,* Jan. 7, 1977, p. A23).

Even this successful candidate had $85,000 remaining in unpaid campaign expenses after the election.

## Benefits

What do contributors receive in return? This question is perhaps the most vexing one in campaign finance. If citizens presumably vote for candidates whom they favor, and maybe even agree with, would not contributors make the same calculation? But the problem is more acute because of the suspicion that contributors either expect or receive, or both, tangible and monetary favors.

The overt participation by banks in Georgia politics illustrates—

though we simply do not know if this illustration is typical—the problem. An observer of Georgia politics wrote:

. . . the almost total absence of effective consumer credit legislation in Georgia is related to the bank's willingness to lend money to politicians for personal and campaign purposes. . . . [In] 1975, banking lobbyists were busily and successfully at work ramming through the General Assembly a new banking code which in effect allows banks to charge whatever rate of interest they like on consumer loans (Howell Raines in Alexander, 1976a: 196).

Maryland provides another illustration of the potential connection between public responsibilities and private gains by both public officials and campaign contributors. An engineering consulting firm, belonging to two of Governor Mandel's most important fund raisers,

began receiving the largest portion of contracts for work on a new Chesapeake Bay bridge almost immediately after Mandel became Governor. Although the firm was practically unknown in Maryland before then, its assignments on the new bridge increased its public works earning from $2 million to $5 million (Jerome Kelly in Alexander, 1976a: 17).

The same governor and the same fund raisers were indicted in the mid-1970s on allegations of fraud in race track investments. In the same state, the county-level practices of suburban expansion led to the indictment of then-Vice President Agnew for bribery.

A much different view of the exchange relationship between a candidate and a contributor is expressed by the term "access." Whether or not a contributor has any immediate legislative objective in mind, and quite beyond any question of an immediate personal gain by either the official or the contributor, contributors want some assurance that in the future, when they do have some matter requiring governmental attention, they can communicate their views to the appropriate official. One long-term lobbyist and former state senator in Texas expressed this view:

I don't think they [most politicians] would put up with contributions with ties. Naturally, contributors expect a better entrée to present their case. They establish a rapport with the person being helped (Alexander, 1976a: 91).

Most of the information we have presented on campaign finance in state politics comes from a series of studies in ten states and their 1974 elections (Alexander, 1976a). Thanks to new financial disclosure regulations, we now have some notion of how much money is raised and spent, and of how it is raised.

## State financing

Just as the U.S. government now finances (and regulates) presidential campaigns, so nine states (as of early 1977) also publicly finance election campaigns within their states. All nine raise funds through an income tax checkoff system, similar to the national one. Two of these states, plus a third, also use a tax surcharge system, by which taxpayers may add one or two dollars to their taxes to be used for campaign financing.

The states differ in the place and role of the political party in the receipt and disbursement of state campaign funds. In five states—Idaho, Iowa, Rhode Island, Utah, and Kentucky—public funds are distributed to the parties to be used by them without restriction. In Iowa, for example, the state Democratic party allocated $20,000 of their $93,000 state allotment for 1974 to their candidates in two statewide races and in the six congressional campaigns. The remainder was spent on partywide activities—publicity, voter identification, and on the state legislative elections. Iowa Republicans allocated most of their funds directly to candidates for statewide and congressional offices.

In the other states—Montana, Minnesota, North Carolina, and New Jersey—the state parties do not have much discretion in their use of public campaign funds. In Minnesota, for example, 40 percent of the funds must be allocated among five statewide candidates, 30 percent to the state senate candidates, and the remaining 30 percent to the state representative candidates. For each office, the funds must be divided equally among the candidates (Alexander, 1976b: 182–85).

These variations among the states will provide an opportunity to see what the results will be of different ways of allocating public campaign funds. We would guess that the more a state party has discretion, the more the leaders (and the whole legal structure) of the party organization will be strengthened. They will become more important, and political elites will more frequently attempt to enter and to control the party. The party itself will have the resources with which to become an active participant in election campaigns. By the same token, we would guess that to the extent to which parties are bypassed in the campaign finance system, their importance will diminish and their autonomy will be reduced.


## Are spenders winners?

Probably the balance of campaign resources between two candidates in the general election (or among several candidates in a primary) is a more important consideration in affecting the outcome than is the absolute amount of dollars spent and raised. High spenders do not always win. Perhaps one of the more important consequences of public financing of campaigns will be that each candidate will have at least the necessary minimum amount of funds with which to wage a viable campaign.

Prior name recognition is an important consideration. This asset is possessed both by "lateral entry" candidates and, presumably, by incumbents. The former have obtained recognition through nonpolitical activities (e.g., actors, war aces), while the latter have built a record of performance and service in office. Both sets of candidates probably need campaign funds less, but are able to raise funds more easily than relatively unknown challengers (Crotty, 1977: 111–19). In the 1974 U.S. senate races, for example, all but one incumbent outspent their challengers. In one instance, the higher-spending incumbent was even defeated by his challenger—in Colorado (*Congressional Quarterly Weekly Report*, April 19, 1975: 789).

A sizable and early expenditure of funds is probably a major advantage for unknown candidates in primary elections. In John Connally's first campaign (1962) for the Texas governorship, for example, the first public opinion polls showed him with less than 5 percent support in the electorate. That low, if not poor, showing was interpreted as a "name recognition factor," and the first purpose to be achieved in the early stages of the campaign was to make the candidate's name known widely by the public. But we can cite an instance in which the same strategy failed. One of the unknown candidates for lieutenant governor in Kentucky in 1975 spent $644,000 and still came in third in the Democratic primary, while the much-better–known winner spent only about $50,000.

Now that we are beinning to obtain more complete reports of campaign expenditures, we can begin to do more than only cite contradictory examples. One study (Glantz et al., 1976) has compared expenditures (reported) with election results for California Assembly elections and for all U.S. House of Representatives races in 1972 and 1974. The major finding is that the vote results are more closely related to the campaign expenditures of the challengers than of the incumbents. Very few challengers did win election in races for either office, but nevertheless, the margin of defeat was narrowed in proportion to their expenditures. The authors estimated the funds which theoretically would have provided challengers' victories: between $66,000 and $69,000 for the California Assembly and $168,000 for the U.S. House of Representatives.

## ACCESS TO THE ELECTORATE

An election campaign can begin years in advance of election day. The campaign's early stages of candidate recruitment, and of obtaining group support and financial contributions usually take months (if not years) and proceeds with very little public visibility. But as election day approaches (two separate days months apart for the primary and general election), candidates increasingly appeal overtly to the electorate. The purpose of the campaign in its later stages is to reach the voter directly. Advertising appears, the candidates speak at rallies and tour shopping centers and factories, and the parties adopt platforms. All of this frenetic activity is directed at the voter. It is also something tangible which reporters can report. Thus, the voter receives (or is exposed to) a double dose of the overt campaign.

How the electorate should be approached is itself a subject of long-term study and decision within the campaign organization. Which portions of the electorate are likely supporters; which are known opponents; which segments can be persuaded—all of these questions are probed through public opinion polling in advance. Which appeals should be made; which issues and which "images" should be stressed or avoided; to which segments of the electorate these appeals should be directed; how those voters should be reached—these, too, are planned in advance.

We will illustrate the range of state campaigns by citing examples from Jimmy Carter's gubernatorial campaign in Georgia, and from Minnesota campaigns for the state legislature. The Carter campaign illustrates the individual, candidate-centered campaign, while the Minnesota campaign illustrates the roles of an active political party.

### Georgia: The candidate campaign

Jimmy Carter's quest for the Georgia governorship took six years. After losing the 1966 primary election, he began campaigning again, winning the 1970 election. The campaign appeals, and methods of delivering those appeals, were carefully calibrated among the candidate, the pollster, and the advertising firm. The campaign theme could be termed "new-style populist," in which the candidate identified himself with the "common man" on an economic and class basis, differentiating himself from the racial appeals of one candidate and the metropolitan and wealthy identifications of another. Personal visits and speeches and media advertisements were the major means of reaching the electorate (Clotfelter and Hamilton, 1972).

**Minnesota: The party campaign**

The statewide orchestration of campaigns to the state legislature
by the Democratic-Farmer–Labor Party in Minnesota was certainly
unusual in U.S. politics, but illustrates some of the possibilities of
tangible help which a state party could extend to candidates in legislative districts around the state. The services provided by the state party
have been discussed in an earlier section. Within the districts, candidates formed three major committees for finance, publicity, and coordination. Candidates, along with the state party's field men, decided
specific matters such as fund raising events, advertising, issue selection, and candidate image. Each district candidate and his campaign
produced three plans: a daily calendar of campaign events, a budget
for both revenue and expenditures, and a block work plan showing
the exact location for door-to-door campaigning each week. The state
party used a number of indicators to measure progress by the individual candidates and their campaigns: number of volunteers, number and
type of groups before which the candidate had appeared, the dates of
literature distribution, the amount of candidate canvassing in residential areas, and the amount of funds raised (Agranoff, 1972: 103–7).

**Candidate appeals**

Some of the slogans, appeals and means of reaching the electorate
may be illustrated by brochures used in recent campaigns. The Republican candidate for governor in Oklahoma in 1974 issued a newspaper,
*The Campaign Special*. One article was headed, "Meet Jim Inhofe—
The Taxpayer's Governor," and another, "Jim Speaks to Rural Oklahoma." A special box in the paper headed "Flip-Flops" quoted his
Democratic opponent in a series of contradictory statements. Another
article stressed the merits of Republican nominees to the other state
offices as "qualified and enthusiastic candidates . . . to oppose some of
the old guard politicians who have opposed reform." In a similar vein,
a common flyer sheet was distributed for all the Republican state candidates, headed "Vote Republican . . . for a 'Clean Slate.' "

A common characteristic of candidates, especially southern Democrats, is that they campaign individually. In 1974, however, with a
Democratic sweep likely, at least some North Carolina Democrats campaigned together. The candidates for U.S. Senate and attorney general
issued a joint campaign button with both of their names. The Senate
candidate's committee also issued a newspaper, *The Democratic Team*,

which featured the Democratic candidates for state offices (attorney general and supreme court justices) and for each of the congressional districts. In an urban county, electing two members to the state senate and five to the lower house (all at large), the whole Democratic slate campaigned together and issued a common folder "Forsyth Democratic Team" picturing each candidate together with a short biography, and listing "Our Goals," including "The restoration of honesty and integrity in representative government" and "Fair allocation of highway funds and restoration of Forsyth County's role as a leader in the General Assembly." In the same year, in an adjacent urban area the county Democratic party issued a sample ballot with, on the reverse side, pictures and descriptions of every Democratic candidate for state, county, and legislative office. The Republican candidates of both counties tended to campaign separately, each fearing (correctly) their collective defeat.

Much of the overt campaign consists of advertisements of the names of the candidates, with or without a simple slogan. "Bentley" was the only word on the bumper stickers for the Republican candidate for the Georgia governorship in 1970, while the Democratic sticker read "Speak up—Elect Jimmy Carter." A Texas candidate for the United States Senate had a bumper sticker reading "This car for Carr!", to which the opposition retaliated with, "This car not for Carr."

## EXPLAINING THE RESULTS

During any state election campaign, the press carries predictions and speculation about which candidate will win and why; after the election, reporters, politicians, and other observers try to explain the outcome. Though impressionistic and unscientific, these are often the best sources available to us in trying to understand state elections. Most of us who are familiar with politics in our own state rely on the same sources in explaining political developments. Such explanations are often idiosyncratic ("Jones was much too liberal for this state," "Smith's campaign was poorly organized and financed," "The Democrats never recovered from a bruising primary fight"), but it should be possible to draw some conclusions about gubernatorial elections by aggregating the impressions of individual campaigns.

With this goal in mind, we have examined the explanations of election outcomes drawn from the media in all gubernatorial races in which the incumbent was defeated from 1962 through 1974, a total of 37 races. We have concentrated on elections in which incumbents lost because these elections are among those most likely to be decided by characteristics of particular campaigns. Most such outcomes do not result from traditional party loyalties, and by definition they cannot be explained by any advantage of incumbency (though some may illustrate the liabilities of incumbency). The results are summarized in table 5–2, which shows the number of elections in which each factor

**Table 5–2**
**Factors affecting outcome of gubernatorial elections in which incumbents were defeated, 1962–1974 (37 elections)**

| Factors | *Major factor* | *Contributing factor* | *Total* | *Percentage of elections* |
|---|---|---|---|---|
| Partisan factors (51 percent of elections) | | | 19 | |
| Dominant party strength | 3 | 5 | 8 | 22 |
| Losing party: split or divisive primary | 10 | 1 | 11 | 30 |
| Winning party: unusual unity | 4 | 3 | 7 | 19 |
| Personal characteristics (41 percent of elections) | | | 15 | |
| Personality of winner or loser | 4 | 7 | 11 | 30 |
| Office-holding experience or lack of it | 3 | 2 | 5 | 14 |
| Record of incumbent administration (73 percent of elections) | | | 27 | |
| Taxes | 10 | 2 | 12 | 32 |
| Scandals | 1 | 2 | 3 | 8 |
| Anti-third term, or time for change | 0 | 6 | 6 | 16 |
| Other major issues | 2 | 12 | 14 | 38 |

*Importance of factor by number of elections*

Note: More than one factor may be counted as affecting an election. Consequently, the numbers and percentages within any broad category may add to more than the total for the category as a whole. All percentages are based on a denominator of 37 elections.

appears to have been either of major importance or a contributing factor in the election outcome. In half of the elections the traditional party strength of one party and/or extent of unity in one or both parties help to explain the outcome. In over 40 percent of the elections, the personality or experience of one or both candidates assumed particular importance. In almost three quarters of the races, some aspects of the incumbent governor's record were credited by the media with playing a substantial role in his defeat, with taxes being the issue in almost half of these cases.

The strength of the dominant party contributes to an incumbent's defeat in cases when a governor from the minority party is unable to win reelection. Examples may be found in the defeat of several Republican governors in southern and border states in 1970: Rockefeller in Arkansas (after two two-year terms), Kirk in Florida and Bartlett in Oklahoma (both after a single four-year term). Kirk was also handicapped by the fact that the minority Republicans had become seriously divided into factions and by his own controversial personality.

In almost one third of the elections in which incumbents were defeated, their party was seriously divided, usually as a consequence of a divisive primary. An incumbent governor usually wins renomination without serious opposition and consequently a major challenge to him in the primary suggests serious dissatisfaction with his performance or else deep factionalism within the party. Sometimes the party that is out of power manifests an unusual degree of cohesion and nominates a candidate who succeeds in pulling the party together. In Massachusetts, during the 1974 election, both factors were at work. The Massachusetts Democratic party is usually a seething mass of personal factions, but in 1974 Michael Dukakis succeeded in winning a contested primary without alienating supporters of his opponent, and he had united Democratic support in the general election. The Massachusetts Republicans, by contrast, are usually models of decorum and cohesion, but in 1974 the party had its first lively gubernatorial primary in 24 years, as a conservative candidate challenged the relatively liberal Governor Sargent. The unusual combination of Democratic unity and Republican disunity, in a state with a normal Democratic majority, led to the Republican governor's defeat.

The Minnesota election in 1966 provided another example of costly party disunity. Many Democrats believed that their incumbent governor, Karl Rolvaag, would have difficulty being renominated. The Democratic party's preprimary convention endorsed another candidate; the governor won renomination in the primary after a bitter, divisive campaign; and the Republicans won the election. It is impossible to tell, of course, whether the governor could have been reelected if he had had the party's endorsement and no primary opposition. A much different sequence of events occurred in the New York Democratic party in 1974. Although he was not endorsed in the preprimary convention, Hugh Carey won an impressive primary victory—doing well among most of the ethnic and religious groups considered essential to Democratic victory. Party leaders, anticipating victory, rallied to his support, and he defeated the incumbent governor, Malcolm Wilson, who had succeeded to that post when Nelson Rockefeller became vice president.

The costs of a divisive primary can be measured more accurately in California, where survey data are available for the 1966 and 1970 gubernatorial races. In 1966, Democratic incumbent Governor Pat Brown was renominated with only 53 percent of the vote, while Ronald Reagan won the Republican nomination with 65 percent of the vote. Survey data show that not only was the Democratic primary closer, but the divisions in that party were deeper than those within the Republican party. Among Democrats, 93 percent of those who had supported Brown in the primary, but only 26 percent of those who had supported his conservative opponent, Sam Yorty, were willing to vote for Brown in the general election. Among Republicans, Reagan had the support of 99 percent of his primary supporters and 65 percent of those who had voted for his primary opponent. Four years later, while Governor Reagan was unopposed in the primary, Jesse Unruh won the Democratic nomination by 64 percent (once again over Yorty), but could count on the votes of only 37 percent of the Yorty supporters in the general election.

The personal strengths and weaknesses of all candidates could have some effect on the outcome of all elections. The 11 elections which are classified under "personality" in Table 5–2 are ones in which personal characteristics of winners and/or losers attracted particular attention in the press. In the 1974 New York election, for example, Governor Wilson was pictured in the media as a colorless figure and a weak campaigner who for years as lieutenant governor had been overshadowed by Governor Rockefeller. Governor Gilligan, who was defeated in Ohio in that same year, was often described as bad-tempered, arrogant, or erratic. In the 1966 California race, Ronald Reagan was described as a vigorous campaigner and a new figure in politics in contrast to Governor Brown, who was often pictured as a tired, sometimes bumbling, familiar politician. In the 1962 elections, George Romney in Michigan and Harold Hughes in Iowa were attractive, vigorous newcomers, both good campaigners, who swept out of office not only incumbent governors with less personal magnetism but entrenched political parties. If the media accurately reflect the voters' perceptions of these candidates, these personal characteristics presumably played a significant part in the election outcomes.

Five of the governors who lost were men who had not been elected to that office but who had moved up, usually from the post of lieutenant governor, to fill a vacancy. In some of these cases the winner had held important elective offices and was better known than the incumbent governor. We have already mentioned the example of Governor

Wilson of New York, who was beaten by Hugh Carey, a veteran congressman. Another example is Samuel Shapiro of Illinois, a "pleasant, genial, faithful party workhorse" who had assumed the governorship less than six months before the 1968 election (Wright, 1974: 108). His opponent had been a very visible office holder in Cook County (Chicago). Survey data show that voters were less familiar with the governor than with his opponent. A candidate who inherits the governorship not only has had no opportunity to demonstrate his ability to win the office, but may have had little opportunity to acquire visibility and the other assets that are normally associated with incumbency.

One of the most common explanations for the defeat of incumbent governors can be described in the following scenario. The candidate promises faithfully and frequently during the campaign that he will not raise taxes, but that he will improve and expand state programs. As soon as he takes office, he discovers that revenue projections based on the existing tax structure will not even provide enough money for the normal growth of existing state programs, to say nothing about financing his campaign promises. The tentative budget he has inherited from his predecessor includes a very large deficit. The governor announces that he has no choice but to recommend an increase in taxes. The legislature either enacts his tax proposal or engages in a prolonged struggle with him resulting in tax increases that are somewhat different from, but just as politically painful as, what he proposed. Four years later, he loses his bid for reelection to an opponent who constantly reminds the voters of the governor's broken promises and higher taxes, and who promises that he will hold the line on taxes, or even decrease them.

This scene is not only familiar, but factual. Governors in recent years have constantly been confronted with demands for increasing services and pressure from the federal government to provide matching funds for programs devised in Washington. Gubernatorial candidates have been reluctant to admit the inevitability of new taxes, but governors have frequently had to recommend them. Taxes are frequently an issue in campaigns, an issue that generally appears to be salient to the voters. The question is: How often does the tax issue contribute to the defeat of incumbents? Our summary suggests that the tax issue played a role, usually an important one, in about one third of the defeats of incumbents (12 cases). At the same time we should remember that many of the governors who were criticized for raising taxes won reelection anyway.

A few examples may help to explain some of the conditions under which the tax issue can be fatal to a governor seeking reelection. In 1969, Illinois Republican Governor Richard Ogilvie persuaded the legislature to adopt the state's first corporate and personal income tax, which produced more than $1 billion in its first year of operation. His 1972 campaign for reelection featured the claims that the tax "saved the state from bankruptcy" and that he was "a governor with guts." His opponent, Daniel Walker, accused Ogilvie of having opposed such a tax during the 1968 campaign, and in turn promised to cut $.5 billion in waste from the budget and to freeze taxes for four years. Walker defeated Ogilvie. Governor Norbert Tiemann of Nebraska came under attack in the 1970 election because, during his term of office, the state adopted both its first income tax and its first state sales tax. He, too, boasted that his administration was "willing to bite the bullet hard," but he barely survived a primary contest and was defeated in the general election by an opponent who promised no increases in taxes. In 1964 Republican Governor Knowles of Wisconsin was beaten in part because of a sales tax; he had promised to veto any sales tax, but when the legislature refused to adopt his alternative revenue program, he was forced to break his promise and accept the sales tax. In 1962 Republican John Chafee campaigned successfully for the governorship of Rhode Island, labeling the incumbent "Mr. Income Tax" and charging him with having concealed a plan for an income tax during the previous campaign. Though the legislature had refused to adopt the governor's income tax, his proposal contributed to his defeat. Six years later Governor Chafee openly advocated an income tax during the campaign and claimed that the only alternative would be an increase in the regressive sales tax. His opponent proposed instead a tax on investments, and won.

There are, of course, a wide variety of other aspects of a governor's record that come under attack during a campaign and may contribute to his defeat—though probably none of them are as salient to voters as the issue of taxes. Perhaps surprisingly, we found only three cases in which charges of scandals in the governor's administration were seen by the media as contributing to his defeat. There were several states in which governors sought reelection in defiance of well-established traditions against a third term—and lost; and there were several other examples of governors apparently being hurt by a general feeling that they had been in office too long. In several western states the governor's record on environmental questions has become an issue—but its salience is hard to judge. In the 1968 election the governor of

Delaware was charged by his opponent with having made excessive use of the National Guard during a period of riots; this is the kind of issue likely to be perceived differently by different voters. Ronald Reagan, campaigning in 1966, criticized the Brown administration's "soft" policy toward student demonstrations at Berkeley. In several cases the governor's inability to get along with the legislature, and resulting stalemate in government, has been a dominant theme of the challenger's campaign. Perhaps we should conclude this list of examples with another reminder that the judgments of reporters and other observers about what are the major or decisive issues in a campaign are not completely reliable, in the absence of survey data on whether either the voters or candidates perceive these issues as important and how they reacted to them.

# 6 ★ ★ ★

## Voting behavior in state elections ★ ★ ★

What factors lead the voters in state elections to make the choices that they do, particularly in elections for governor and for state legislators? Have these factors recently been changing in relative importance? Under what conditions does a particular factor assume importance? Most studies of voting behavior in this country have dealt with presidential and congressional elections. Is voting behavior fundamentally the same at both the national and state levels, or do different factors assume importance in the election of state officials? As we have done in other chapters, we will concentrate our attention on the major office in state politics, the governorship, and later in the chapter try to explain some of the factors that determine the selection of state legislators. Our analysis of state voting behavior is heavily dependent on aggregate voting data. The voter surveys that provide so much of our knowledge about presidential and congressional elections have only rarely been replicated at the gubernatorial level. We will utilize whatever surveys of gubernatorial voters are available, but their utility is limited because they cover only a few races in a few states.

The advantages of aggregate voting statistics are many. They are available, at the state and county level, for all states for long periods of time. It is possible to generalize from such data about all states and to measure trends over time. It is sometimes possible to estimate the voting pattern of certain groups (such as black or rural voters), but it is not possible to draw conclusions about the perceptions and motivations of individual voters. Survey data can provide much more specific information about the variables associated with voting and can make possible a number of inferences about motivations. If we had enough data from surveys of state elections, we could be much more confident in drawing conclusions about a number of important questions, such as: Which types of voters participate in state elections? How consistently do voters follow their party identification? How frequently do voters split their tickets, and which ones do so? How much do voters know about the candidates for state office?

The shortage of survey research on state elections can be partly explained by the greater interest of scholars in national elections and their desire to achieve findings that are valid for the nation as a whole. In order to generalize about gubernatorial elections in this country, it would be necessary to conduct surveys in all of the states (unless we could assume that some states were "typical" of others), and the rules of sampling make it almost as expensive to conduct a survey in one gubernatorial election as to conduct a national survey in a presidential election. National surveys have occasionally included questions on state elections, and the data provide a few answers of use to us. There is more useful information in a 13-state survey conducted in 1968, but unfortunately gubernatorial elections were held in only 4 of the states. Because most surveys of state elections are recent, and because surveys have not been replicated in a single state over several elections, survey data are almost completely useless for studying trends in state electoral behavior. We must always be cautious about interpreting survey data from a few state elections, not only because states differ so much in their political and electoral systems, but also because voters' perceptions and choices in any single election are affected by the idiosyncracies of particular candidates and campaigns.

## FACTORS INFLUENCING VOTING BEHAVIOR

In Chapter 2 we discussed the variations that are found in the level of two-party competition from state to state. In some states a single party has dominated elections for long periods of time, its comfortable majorities based on the dependable support of loyal party voters. But in many of these states, the dominant party has been upset and party loyalties have apparently changed in recent years. If we understood more about voting behavior in state elections, we would know why this happens. What combination of circumstances leads to change in established voting patterns in a state? To what extent are such changes at the state level influenced by national political trends, and to what extent are they caused by particular characteristics of candidates and issues that are salient to the voters? In this chapter we are going to examine four factors that affect voting in state elections, and try to determine the conditions that contribute to the importance of each. These four are: the party loyalties of voters, national political trends, incumbency, and the characteristics of candidates and issues in particular elections. We will then examine briefly levels of voting turnout in gubernatorial races in the various states.

## Party loyalties of voters

We know from voter surveys conducted during the last 30 years that a large proportion of voters identify with a political party, that many individuals maintain their identification with a party for long periods of years, and that those who identify with a party are likely to vote for the candidates of that party unless some particular issues or perceptions of candidates lead them to vote differently. We also know that in recent years the proportion of voters identifying with a party has declined (roughly from three fourths to two thirds), and that party identification has also declined in utility are a predictor of voting (Asher, 1976: chap. 3; Dennis, 1975: 192–98). Although most of our data on party identification comes from national studies, there are several reasons for expecting that party identification has at least as great an influence on state elections.

The stable patterns of voting in state elections that are evident in an examination of county voting returns strongly suggest that a large proportion of voters are loyal to state parties and usually vote in accord with those loyalties. One-party domination of many counties and cities has helped to reinforce those loyalties. In a town where most voters are Democrats, it is easy for a voter to remain a Democrat. There is very little data to show whether, for many voters, there is any difference between their loyalties to national and to state parties. The erosion of party loyalty evident in recent years has occurred partly because of the disillusionment of some voters with the national party.

An obvious example is the changing attitude of many southern Democrats toward the national Democratic party. In states where many such
voters remain satisfied with the policies and candidates of their party
at the state level, we might expect to find more stability of party loyalties. On the other hand, the increase in patterns of migration within
and between states in recent years has resulted in some erosion of
party loyalties. A lifelong Democrat who moves into a heavily Republican area may begin to lose his party identification because the reinforcing effects of his old neighborhood are gone. Just as the stability
of voting patterns in state politics and one-party domination of many
states in earlier years were both symptoms of strong, stable party
loyalties, so the changing pattern of state politics and the growth of
party competition suggest that party identification is becoming less
important in state politics.

Obviously the best way to measure the strength and stability of
party loyalty and its effects on voting would be to use survey data;
but, as we have noted, it is rarely available for state elections. Data on
party registration, a possible but imperfect surrogate for party identification, are not compiled in all states, and even where compiled, are
not readily available over extended periods of time. To a large extent,
we must rely on aggregate voting data. We can estimate the basic,
persistent voting strength of a party by determining its minimum
vote for statewide offices over a period of years. And we can gain
some impression of the stability of voting patterns by looking at party
voting percentages at the county level over a number of years. It is
reasonable to assume that, if a county consistently produces a vote that
is 60 percent to 70 percent Democratic, a large proportion of those
casting Democratic ballots are persistent voters who identify with that
party.

## National political trends

The outcome of congressional elections is very much affected by
national political trends. A party that wins a presidential election by a
landslide—as the Democrats did in 1964—is likely to make substantial
gains in Congress. In some off-year congressional elections, such as
1958 and 1974, one party gains a large number of seats while losing very
few. It is generally true that the party winning the presidency gains
some congressional seats and is likely to lose some seats two years
later. Despite such recent examples as the 1974 landslide, there is considerable evidence that national political trends are weaker and less

consistent than used to be the case. In 1956 and 1960 the party winning the presidency lost more seats than it gained in the House, and in the 1972 presidential landslide the Republican party had only a small net gain in the House and a slight loss in the Senate. Senatorial elections appear to be much less affected by national trends than in the past, apparently because of the political strength of many incumbent senators (Jewell and Patterson, 1977: chap. 4; Kostroski, 1973). As party loyalty declines in importance as a factor influencing national elections, there is less straight-ticket voting for presidential and congressional races, and national electoral trends lose some of their force (DeVries and Tarrance, 1972; Cummings, 1966: chap. 2).

To what extent are gubernatorial elections influenced by national trends? Are incumbent governors, like incumbent senators, better able than in the past to win reelection despite national trends in favor of the other party? To some extent state elections are insulated from national politics. Five states—Kentucky, New Jersey, Mississippi, Virginia, and Louisiana—hold gubernatorial elections separate from the time of either presidential or congressional elections. As we pointed out in Chapter 2 (Table 2–4), the number of states electing a governor in presidential years dropped from 34 to 14 between 1932 and 1976. There continue to be trends or cycles in partisan control of governorships, and we shall see that these sometimes coincide with and sometimes appear inconsistent with partisan trends in Congress.

Aggregate voting data can be used to compare gains and losses in gubernatorial races with those for presidential and congressional races, and to measure changes in percentages of votes as well as won-lost records. More elaborate statistical techniques are also available to measure the extent to which gubernatorial races are affected by national trends. Survey data can provide information about straight-party voting and ticket-splitting, but it is difficult to determine from surveys to what extent individual voters are influenced by national trends. In order to make judgments about why some candidates are swept out of office by national trends and others are able to resist these trends, we need to look more carefully at individual races.

### Incumbency

Does an incumbent governor have an advantage over a nonincumbent, other factors being equal? Do governors enjoy as much of an advantage from incumbency as senators and representatives apparently do? Is any such advantage greater now, or less, than it was a few years ago? Obviously in a state where one party has been traditionally dominant, incumbents may win reelection because of their party's advantage. But in more competitive states it is important to isolate the advantage of incumbency. An incumbent might be expected to have an advantage for several reasons. He is likely to be better known than his opponent, and congressional voting surveys have shown the importance of that factor. Some voters may believe that experience is a major asset for a candidate. An incumbent governor can usually command political resources, such as funding, and in some states he can command the loyal support of a strong party organization. An incumbent may have liabilities. Voters may hold him responsible for increased taxes, scandals, and programs that they dislike. A governor bears more individual responsibility for the performance of state government than any senator or representative does for the actions of Congress. Recent political history is strewn with the political corpses of governors who were unable or unwilling to keep their political promises (particularly not to raise taxes) and were defeated in reelection bids.

It is relatively simple to measure the won-lost record of incumbent governors, and to note any trends in this record; it is also possible to control for other factors, such as political party, affecting that record. In order to know why incumbency helps some candidates and hurts others, we must rely on the scattered results from survey data. Specifically we want to know whether incumbents are better known than nonincumbents, and whether voters cite such factors as experience and particular policies and accomplishments of the governor in explaining their votes.

## Candidate and issue characteristics

Questions about the effects of incumbency lead us inevitably to examine a broader range of questions: What characteristics of candidates and what kind of issues affect the decisions of voters in gubernatorial races? We want to know several things:

The level of voters' information about candidates.

The characteristics of candidates that they consider important—experience, personality, record, image, background.

The kinds of issues that are salient to voters—taxes, busing, education, corruption in government.

The obvious difficulty that we face is that the answers to these questions presumably differ from one election to another. Newspaper accounts can provide some examples of particular races, but not much solid evidence about what factors influence voters. Survey data are available from only a few races, and can provide us with only a few clues about the candidate and issue characteristics that are salient to voters and affect their voting decisions. When we ask these questions, we are asking what went on in the minds of millions of voters in a large number of election campaigns scattered over 50 states. However great our faith may be in survey research techniques, it is too late to answer that question with any precision for most states in recent elections and for any states in any earlier elections. In short, any conclusions we draw must be very tentative.

## THE EFFECTS OF STATE PARTY STRENGTH

We turn to an examination of each of the factors affecting the gubernatorial vote, starting with the basic strength of each party in a state. Voting data in national elections indicate that party voting is on the decline. If this is occurring in state elections, one or both of two trends must be occurring: party loyalties of voters are becoming less stable than in the past, or voters are less influenced by partisanship in voting for governor and for other state offices. We know that patterns of voting and party competition have been changing more rapidly in some states than in others. This fact leads us to expect that established party loyalties must have more impact on gubernatorial voting in some states than in others. Consequently we must look for evidence of interstate differences in the stability of party voting.

In any state that has long been dominated by a single party, we assume that a substantial majority of the voters have a high level of loyalty to that party. One reason why the majority party loyalists have little incentive to defect is that the minority party seldom runs candidates who are strong enough or whose campaign is visible enough to encourage defection. Often the closest contest and the most visible campaign occurs in the majority party primary. There may be a substantial minority of voters who are loyal to the minority party, many of them perhaps living in counties where that party holds a majority position. Despite the stable pattern of party loyalists in such a state, there may be considerable variation from year to year in the percentage vote for governor won by the majority party because of differences in the degree of campaign effort and the credibility of the candidate representing the minority party.

In a state previously under one-party domination where the minority party is gaining competitive status, we would expect to find unstable voting patterns and a number of voters abandoning their traditional voting habits. For the minority party to win gubernatorial elections, for example, it must win the vote of independents and presumably at least some votes from persons who have been identifying with the majority party. Voters who abandon their party to vote for the minority party in a governor's race may split their ticket and remain loyal in other races. Consequently, in a state where the minority party is becoming more competitive, we would expect to see it winning a larger percentage of votes for governor than for Congress. Differences in the party's vote from office to office indicate that factors other than party loyalty are explaining some of the outcomes.

Among the states where the two parties are highly competitive, we may expect to find two patterns of voting. In some states each of the parties has a large, very stable, traditional bloc of voters, representing different counties, interests, ethnic groups, and so forth. Each party may hold a stable majority in different groups of counties. The swing vote that determines the outcome of elections may be very small. Another pattern of competition is found in states where the traditional blocs of Democrats and Republicans are smaller, and a larger proportion of voters are rather volatile or independent. The trends that are occurring in state politics reflect a decline not only in the number of one-party states but in the number of states having a high proportion of traditional bloc voters, or party loyalists.

The most direct measure of the effect of party loyalty comes from survey data. Table 6–1 was compiled by Andrew Cowart (1973) from national surveys of voting in the election years 1964 through 1970. It shows that national party identification is highly correlated with voting for governor; strong Democrats usually vote Democratic, strong Republicans usually vote Republican, and the weaker the identification with the party, the less predictable the vote. During the short span of time covered in the table, there is no evidence of any decline in the relationship between party identification and voting for governor.

In order to measure the effects of party identification in individual states, we need surveys with an adequate sample of voters in a single state, and very few such surveys are available. Table 6–2 provides data on one or more gubernatorial elections in 7 states, as well as data on 20 states holding gubernatorial elections in 1968. In each state it is

**Table 6–1**

**Percentage voting Democratic for governor by party identification, 1964, 1966, 1968, 1970**

| Year | Strong Democrats | Weak Democrats | Independents | Weak Republicans | Strong Republicans |
|------|-----------------|----------------|--------------|------------------|--------------------|
| 1964 .......... | 88 (155) | 70 (115) | 59 (96) | 22 (55) | 5 (57) |
| 1966 .......... | 86 (107) | 65 (130) | 44 (111) | 13 (88) | 4 (71) |
| 1968 .......... | 83 (88) | 73 (86) | 37 (82) | 25 (40) | — |
| 1970 .......... | 86 (133) | 72 (120) | 42 (149) | 23 (99) | 1 (77) |

Note: The figures given are percentages; entries in parentheses are the total Ns on which percentages are calculated. Empty cells are ones in which the N was too small for specification.

Source: Andrew Cowart, "Electoral Choice in the American States," *American Political Science Review* 67 (September 1973), p. 843.

**Table 6–2**

**Percentage of voters voting Democratic, by party identification, in gubernatorial races in selected states**

| State | Year | Party identification Democratic | Party identification Independent | Party identification Republican |
|-------|------|------------|-------------|------------|
| 20 states .......... | 1968 | 82 | 43 | 10 |
| Tex. .............. | 1968 | 85 | 52 | 14 |
| N.C. .............. | 1968 | 86 | 43 | 11 |
| S. Dak. ........... | 1968 | 73 | 33 | 10 |
| Ill. ................ | 1968 | 80 | 38 | 6 |
| Iowa .............. | 1964 | 96 | 72 | 31 |
|  | 1966 | 94 | 71 | 22 |
| Minn. ............. | 1966 | 87 | 39 | 6 |
|  | 1970 | 90 | 40 | 9 |
| Calif. ............. | 1966 | 70 | — | 12 |
|  | 1970 | 73 | — | 8 |

Sources: The figures for 20 states and for Texas, North Carolina, South Dakota, and Illinois are based on unpublished data from the Comparative State Elections Project conducted by the Institute for Research in Social Science at the University of North Carolina. The figures for Iowa and Minnesota are from the Iowa and Minnesota Polls, on file at the University of Iowa. The figures for California are from William E. Bicker, "Ideology is Alive and Well in California: Party Identification, Issue Positions and Voting Behavior." Paper prepared for annual meeting of American Political Science Association, 1972, pp. 13–14.

obvious that there is a strong relationship between party identification and the vote for governor. In some states (Texas and North Carolina, for example) we find elections in which both candidates drew approximately the same proportion of the vote within their own party and roughly split the independent vote. There are also examples of candidates (the Democrat in both elections in Iowa and the Republican in both elections in California) who won a very high proportion of the vote in their own party while winning roughly one fourth or more of the vote in the other party. Although we do not have data from enough state elections to generalize with any certainty, the evidence that we do have supports the assumption that party identification usually has an important impact on gubernatorial elections.

For the most part we must draw conclusions about the stability of party loyalty and its impact on gubernatorial voting from aggregate data. We can look for evidence about the size of the minimum or stable vote that each party regulary gets in a state. We can look at the size of differences in the votes cast for various offices as a measure of straight-party voting, which in turn indicates the strength of partisanship in voting. We can examine data available from a few states on the relationship between party identification and aggregate voting, over time.

As one measure of the stability of party voting patterns, we can calculate the smallest percentage of the gubernatorial vote won by Democratic candidates over a period of years (1946–74), and the smallest percentage won by Republicans. In Delaware, for example, the lowest Democratic percentage was 48 percent (in 1956), and the lowest Republican percentage was 46 percent (in 1948); the combined minimum vote for the two parties was 94 percent, the highest figure for any state. We cannot say with any certainty what proportion of the Delaware voters are party loyalists who regularly support the candidates of one party. But we can say that voting patterns in that state appear to be remarkably stable. It is interesting to see what other states have had a high level of voting stability in gubernatorial elections during this period. (In the following listing the combined minimum percentage vote for the two parties is listed in parentheses.) Among the most stable states are several that have been highly competitive, at least since the 1930s or 1940s: Illinois (90), Washington (88), Montana (87), Indiana (86), New Mexico (86), Michigan (83), Pennsylvania (83), Ohio (81), Wyoming (81), New York (80), and Wisconsin (80). Several of the other stable states are ones generally dominated by one party, in which the minority party has a particularly stable bloc of voters, including West Virginia (87), Kentucky (85), Missouri (83), Arizona (80), and even Alabama (82). At the bottom of the list, the states with much lower percentages for the combined minimum vote for two parties include most of the southern states plus Oklahoma; several states traditionally dominated by Republicans—Vermont (54), North Dakota (65), Nebraska (70), New Hampshire (70), South Dakota (70); and several more competitive states—Rhode Island (59), Utah (60), and Minnesota (68). Instability may be a sign of major shifts in partisan balance, as in Minnesota, which has shifted from being heavily Republican to being moderately Democratic. Rhode Island, though solidly Democratic in congressional races, has swung sharply back and forth in recent gubernatorial races.

We would expect that in a state with a high proportion of party loyalists and stable patterns of voting there would be a relatively high degree of straight-party voting. Although this can be measured precisely only by survey data, it can be roughly estimated from aggregate data. Paul David (1972: 21–23) has calculated, for the 1932 to 1970 period, the average differences between each party's percentage of the vote for each of four races: president, governor, U.S. senator, and U.S. representative (statewide).[1] The states that had the smallest differences (and thus the most stable voting) are listed below (the two numbers following each being the average percentage interoffice differences for the Democratic and Republican party):

| | |
|---|---|
| Indiana (3.2, 3.0) | South Dakota (5.3, 5.5) |
| Missouri (3.7, 3.5) | New York (6.2, 4.8) |
| Illinois (3.8, 4.0) | New Jersey (5.5, 5.7) |
| West Virginia (4.2, 4.2) | Iowa (5.5, 5.7) |
| Delaware (4.0, 4.5) | Wyoming (5.7, 6.0) |
| Pennsylvania (4.2, 4.5) | Michigan (5.7, 6.2) |
| Connecticut (4.8, 3.9) | Kansas (5.8, 6.1) |
| New Mexico (4.9, 4.7) | Kentucky (6.0, 6.2) |
| New Hampshire (4.9, 5.2) | |

The states with the largest differences among the various offices are almost entirely southern states.

It is worth noting that these two rough measures of stable party voting, which cover different time periods, have some similarities. Several states appear near the top of both lists, and can be regarded as ones

---

[1] David calculated the difference between the percentage vote for the six possible pairs of the four offices, averaged these for each year, and then compiled a state average for each party for the whole time period. In years when there was no race for an office, interpolation was used to produce an average figure so that there would be a figure for each office every two years.

where party voting has been particularly stable for a prolonged period: Illinois, Indiana, Delaware, West Virginia, Pennsylvania, Missouri, New Mexico, New York, Michigan, Wyoming, and Kentucky. Some of these are states with long histories of two-party competition; others are ones dominated by a single party in most elections of recent decades. What these states appear to have in common is a division of their electorates into two relatively stable blocs of party loyalists, concentrated (in most states) in certain well-defined geographic areas.

Because we are primarily interested in current patterns of politics, our next step is to identify those states in which there has been some recent trend away from stable voting patterns, states in which the outcomes of gubernatorial elections have begun to differ from other election results. There is no single set of voting figures that can be considered a norm or an index of party strength, but the statewide total of votes cast for U.S. House seats has been used in some other studies. One reason for using House elections is the assumption that candidates for the House are unlikely to create enough attention during campaigns to lure voters away from their established voting habits, or least less likely than candidates for president, governor, or senator. A second reason is that the statewide total for House candidates, being a summary of individual races, tends to submerge the individual impact of particular candidacies. On the other hand, it is possible that the vote cast for House candidates may be influenced more by national trends than are votes for governor and senator.

Comparing the two-party distribution of the vote for governor and for the U.S. House, we find that the differences have been very small (usually 2 percent or less) in many of the states that we have defined as stable, up through the 1974 election. This is the situation in Delaware, Illinois, Indiana, Pennsylvania, Missouri, and Wyoming, as well as in Wisconsin and Connecticut. Massachusetts, Rhode Island, and West Virginia are examples of states in which large differences have appeared in recent years, with the Democrats usually having solid majorities of votes for the House, while the gubernatorial contests are much closer. Similarly, in North Dakota and South Dakota the Republicans maintain their comfortable lead in House races but not in gubernatorial contests. There are many other states in which the voting patterns have been unstable for a number of years. Generally it is true to say that the differences were larger in the late 1960s and the early 1970s than had previously been the case, but all of these states had examples of instability during the 1950s. Generally what happened in such states was that the party that had enjoyed majority status in the past maintained its advantage in House races, while the party that was emerging from minority status was more successful in gubernatorial than in House races. This was the case in the traditionally Republican states of Iowa, Kansas, Maine, Vermont, and New Hampshire. In two large and competitive states, California and New York, the Republicans quite consistently did better in gubernatorial contests. In several other states the vote in congressional races has been relatively stable, while the gubernatorial vote has been quite volatile, giving first one party and then the other a larger percentage than it had in congressional races. Examples of such states are Maryland, Michigan, Ohio, Colorado, Utah, and Washington.[2] We can conclude that gubernatorial voting is becoming less stable, less closely tied to other elections, but that the degree of this variation and its duration over recent elections both vary considerably from state to state.

If we had adequate information over time in each state about the party identification of voters, we could make some comparisons with aggregate voting patterns. The more closely voting was correlated with party identification, the more voters would appear to be casting votes in accord with—and largely as a result of—their party loyalties. There is some longitudinal data on party identification for Iowa, Minnesota, and California. In all three states the proportion of voters who call themselves independents has grown. Unfortunately, questions used to identify independents are not the same in the three states (and have changed over time in the Iowa survey). Consequently it is impossible to rely on such data to demonstrate that party loyalty has more influence in one state than the other, and in Iowa (because of changes in questions) it is hard to tell how much the proportion of independents has grown. We can conclude that a growth in the number of independents should mean that party loyalty has a declining impact on voting.

We can also examine changes in the proportion of Democrats and Republicans among those who identify with either party, and compare that data with the votes for governor and U.S. House seats. Table 6–3 provides this information for Iowa and Minnesota (including only nonpresidential years). Both of these are states in which the Democratic party made gains after World War Two—somewhat more rapidly in Minnesota. We would expect changes in party identification to lag

---

[2] We have excluded southern states from this analysis because many of them have not consistently had contests for governor and/or contests for all or most U.S. House seats.

**Table 6–3**
**Patterns of partisan identification and voting in Iowa and Minnesota (as percentages)**

| | Iowa | | | | | | Minnesota | | | | | |
| | Dem. and Rep. identifiers | | Vote for governor | | Vote for U.S. House | | Dem. and Rep. identifiers | | Vote for governor | | Vote for U.S. House | |
| Year | Dem. | Rep. | Dem. | Rep. | Dem. | Rep. | Dem. | Rep. | Dem. | Rep. | Dem. | Rep. |
|------|------|------|------|------|------|------|------|------|------|------|------|------|
| 1950 .... | 45 | 55 | 41 | 59 | 39 | 61 | | | | | | |
| 1954 .... | 44 | 56 | 48 | 51 | 42 | 58 | 54 | 46 | 53 | 47 | 53 | 47 |
| 1958 .... | 46 | 54 | 54 | 45 | 50 | 50 | 57 | 43 | 57 | 42 | 53 | 47 |
| 1962 .... | 46 | 54 | 53 | 47 | 46 | 54 | 59 | 41 | 50 | 50 | 50 | 50 |
| 1966 .... | 50 | 50 | 55 | 44 | 48 | 52 | 64 | 36 | 47 | 53 | 48 | 52 |
| 1970 .... | 47 | 53 | 47 | 51 | 50 | 50 | 60 | 40 | 54 | 46 | 53 | 47 |
| 1974 .... | 51 | 49 | 41 | 59 | 54 | 46 | | | 65 | 31 | 59 | 41 |

Sources: Iowa Poll and Minnesota Poll data at the University of Iowa.

behind changes in the competitive balance of the parties, with voters changing their voting patterns more quickly than they changed their identification. In Iowa there has been a shift in the balance of party identification, as the Democrats have gradually been gaining a position of equality. Since the mid-1950s there has been a shift in the vote for U.S. House seats that has roughly paralleled the shift in party identification. Voting for governor has been much more erratic; the Democratic margins in 1956, 1958, and 1964, and the Republican margin in 1972 were much larger than could be explained by party identification. The data for Minnesota show a clear pattern of Democratic growth in party identification from the early 1950s to the late 1960s and early 1970s. But there has been no comparable growth in Democratic voting for the governorship or the U.S. House (except for lopsided Democratic victories in 1974). Since the early 1950s, when the Democrats achieved a position of approximate parity at the polls, there has been a very close balance between the two parties. The polls do show that the proportion of independents is high in Minnesota and has risen from about one fourth to about one third. Taking all voters into account, the proportion of Democrats has remained about the same, Republicans have declined, and independents have increased. The fact that the voting balance has not changed much suggests that many Republicans who have changed to independents have continued to vote Republican.

Data on voting, party identification, and registration for California are perplexing. Data on identification are available for the period from 1962 to 1971, during which there has been a growth of independents, but of those identifying with a party, most of the time from 58 percent to 61 percent have been Democratic. Although we would not expect party registration necessarily to reflect identification, it is noteworthy that from 1944 to 1974 the Democratic proportion of those registered with either party has almost always been between 57 percent and 61 percent. At the polls, however, the Democrats have consistently been much less successful. Only in the 1958 governor's race and U.S. House races has the Democratic party won a percentage of the vote close to its share of the party identifiers or those registering with a party. Its share of the gubernatorial vote has been as low as 35 percent and its share of the U.S. House vote has several times been below 45 percent. The stability of party registration and identification over many years is remarkable, given the large influxes of population during that period. But it is clear that in California party loyalty provides a very poor and limited explanation of voting patterns (Owens, Costantini, and Weschler, 1970: 130–42).

## THE EFFECTS OF NATIONAL TRENDS
## AND INCUMBENCY

In most states gubernatorial elections are not completely isolated from presidential and congressional races. Ten states choose governors only during presidential elections, 31 do so only during off-year congressional elections, and 4 elect governors every 2 years; only 5 states have gubernatorial races that do not coincide with either presidential or congressional elections. In most states, therefore, it is reasonable to assume that strong national political tides will have some effect on gubernatorial races. We want to know how great that effect is and whether it is growing or declining.

Table 6–4 compares the partisan net gains and losses of gubernatorial seats with the net changes in the composition of Congress from 1948 to 1976. It is evident from the table that the balance of governorships usually changes in the same direction as partisan shifts in Congress, but the magnitude of changes is sometimes quite different. It also appears that gubernatorial elections are becoming more independent of national trends. During the 1950s the changes were roughly parallel (although in 1954 Democratic gains were proportionately greater among governorships). In 1964, however, Democratic congressional gains were not matched in governors' races; in 1970 Democratic gubernatorial gains far exceeded the modest shift in the House, and Democratic gubernatorial gains in 1972 and 1974 were inconsistent with the congressional pattern. Gubernatorial races are somewhat like those

**Table 6–4**
**Changes in partisan control of governorships compared to U.S. House and Senate,**
**1946–1974 elections**

| | | Governorships | | | | U.S. House net gains and losses | | U.S. Senate net gains and losses | |
| | | Total held after election | | Net gains and losses | | | | | |
| Year | Number elected | Dem. | Rep. | Dem. | Rep. | Dem. | Rep. | Dem. | Rep |
|---|---|---|---|---|---|---|---|---|---|
| 1946 | 33 | 20 | 23 | | | | | | |
| 1948 | 33 | 26 | 17 | + 6 | − 6 | +75 | −75 | + 9 | − 9 |
| 1950 | 33 | 19 | 24 | − 7 | + 7 | −29 | +28 | − 6 | + 5 |
| 1952 | 30 | 14 | 29 | − 5 | + 5 | −21 | +22 | − 1 | + 1 |
| 1954 | 34 | 22 | 21 | + 8 | − 8 | +19 | −18 | + 1 | − 1 |
| 1956 | 30 | 24 | 19 | + 2 | − 2 | + 2 | − 2 | + 1 | 0 |
| 1958 | 34 | 30 | 14 | + 6 | − 5 | +49 | −47 | +17 | −13 |
| 1960 | 28 | 29 | 16 | − 1 | + 2 | −20 | +20 | − 2 | + 2 |
| 1962 | 35 | 29 | 16 | 0 | 0 | − 4 | + 2 | + 4 | − 4 |
| 1964 | 25 | 28 | 17 | − 1 | + 1 | +38 | −38 | + 2 | − 2 |
| 1966 | 35 | 20 | 25 | − 8 | + 8 | −47 | +47 | − 3 | + 3 |
| 1968 | 21 | 16 | 29 | − 4 | + 4 | − 4 | + 4 | − 5 | + 5 |
| 1970 | 35 | 27 | 18 | +11 | −11 | +12 | −12 | − 4 | + 2 |
| 1972 | 18 | 28 | 17 | + 1 | − 1 | −12 | +12 | + 2 | − 2 |
| 1974 | 35 | 32 | 12 | + 4 | − 5 | +43 | −43 | + 3 | − 3 |
| 1976 | 14 | 33 | 11 | + 1 | − 1 | + 1 | − 1 | 0 | 0 |

Note: Five states having gubernatorial elections that do not coincide with congressional elections are omitted: Kentucky, New Jersey, Mississippi, Louisiana, and Virginia; the congressional totals, however, include these states.

for the Senate; the candidates (particularly incumbents) are well enough known to inspire some ticket-splitting, and elections are not held in every state that has congressional races. Table 6–4 shows, however, that in recent years there have been more net partisan changes in governorships than in Senate seats.

Very little effort has been made to measure the effects of national political forces on gubernatorial voting through survey data, but Piereson (1975) has analyzed the effects of presidential popularity on gubernatorial voting in one midterm election (1970). His data show that, among those identified as independents, voters who gave President Nixon a favorable rating were more likely to vote Republican in gubernatorial races. There was some tendency for Democrats to follow the same pattern, but there was no such relationship among Republican voters, most of whom gave Nixon a high rating.

The first step in explaining the effect of incumbency on gubernatorial elections is to find out how often incumbents run, and what happens to them. This information is summarized from 45 states for the 1958–76 elections in Table 6–5. (The five omitted states are ones

**Table 6–5**
**Fate of incumbents and partisan turnover in gubernatorial elections in 45 states holding elections during congressional elections**

| Year | No. of elec- tions | Elections with incumbents | | | Elections with no incumbents | | Per- centage of in- cum- bents who lost | Percentage of party turnover | | Per- centage of all elections with in- cumbents |
| | | Total | Inc. won | Inc. lost | Total | Party turn- over | | With incum- bents | No incum- bents | |
| 1958 ..... | 34 | 21 | 12 | 9 | 13 | 4 | 43 | 31 | 69 | 62 |
| 1960 ..... | 27 | 14 | 8 | 6 | 13 | 7 | 43 | 54 | 46 | 52 |
| 1962 ..... | 35 | 26 | 16 | 10 | 9 | 3 | 38 | 33 | 77 | 74 |
| 1964 ..... | 25 | 14 | 12 | 2 | 11 | 3 | 14 | 27 | 40 | 56 |
| 1966 ..... | 35 | 21 | 14 | 7 | 14 | 6 | 33 | 43 | 54 | 60 |
| 1968 ..... | 21 | 13 | 9 | 4 | 8 | 5 | 31 | 63 | 44 | 62 |
| 1970 ..... | 35 | 24 | 17 | 7 | 11 | 8 | 29 | 73 | 47 | 69 |
| 1972 ..... | 18 | 9 | 7 | 2 | 9 | 3 | 22 | 33 | 40 | 50 |
| 1974 ..... | 35 | 22 | 17 | 5 | 13 | 8 | 23 | 62 | 38 | 63 |
| 1976 ..... | 14 | 7 | 5 | 2 | 7 | 5 | 29 | 71 | 28 | 50 |
| Total .... | 279 | 171 | 118 | 54 | 108 | 52 | 32 | 48 | 51 | 61 |

in which gubernatorial and congressional elections do not coincide.) We can draw several conclusions from the data:

The proportion of elections with incumbents has been just over 60 percent, with no trends obvious during the period. (There are a few states, of course, where only a single consecutive term is permitted.)

The proportion of incumbents who get defeated, of those seeking reelection, has averaged less than one third, and has been declining since the early 1960s. (By contrast, only one sixth of the U.S. senators who sought reelection from 1952 to 1974 were defeated in general elections.) These data do not include defeats of incumbents in primaries, which are counted as nonincumbents running in general elections.

The party in office is defeated much more often, nearly half the time, when the incumbent is not running for reelection.

During the more recent part of this period, 1964–76, party turnover has occurred 26 percent of the time with incumbents and 50 percent of the time without incumbents, a contrast suggesting that recently incumbency has been a major asset in gubernatorial races.

We can gain further perspective on the successes and failure of incumbent governors over a longer time span from a study done by

Stephen Turrett (1971), which included only 19 of the most competitive states for the years 1900–1969. Turrett finds that the proportion of elections in which incumbents have run has increased from about half in the first half of the time period to roughly two thirds in the period since 1940. During the more recent period (1940–69) the proportion of incumbents winning election (of those seeking it) in general elections has remained at just about the same level—two thirds. It is also true, however, that roughly half of those who have won reelection have had a smaller margin of victory than in their previous election. (See Table 6–6.)

**Table 6–6**
**Vulnerability of governors in 19 states, 1900–1969**

| | | Elections with incumbents | | *Percentage of incumbents who ran and:* | |
|---|---|---|---|---|---|
| *Time period* | *Number of elections* | *Number* | *Percent* | *Were defeated* | *Got a smaller percentage of vote than previously* |
| 1900–1909 .......... 76 | | 35 | 46.1 | 28.6 | 69.0 |
| 1910–1919 .......... 77 | | 44 | 57.1 | 45.5 | 68.2 |
| 1920–1929 .......... 77 | | 37 | 48.1 | 29.7 | 67.6 |
| 1930–1939 .......... 75 | | 44 | 58.7 | 25.0 | 59.1 |
| 1940–1949 .......... 72 | | 49 | 68.1 | 34.7 | 65.3 |
| 1950–1959 .......... 68 | | 44 | 64.7 | 36.4 | 68.2 |
| 1960–1969 .......... 50 | | 42 | 72.9 | 34.9 | 62.8 |

Source: J. Stephen Turrett, "The Vulnerability of American Governors, 1900–1969," *Midwest Journal of Political Science* 15 (February 1971), pp. 117–18.

Turrett also provides data that compare the effects of incumbency with two other factors that concern us: state party strength and national political trends. He finds that during the 1960s, for the first time, incumbent governors were running significantly ahead of their party's statewide percentage of the votes in U.S. House races, averaging 9 percent ahead during that decade. In previous decades they had averaged only slightly ahead of or behind their party's statewide House vote. In other words, not only are incumbent governors becoming more successful at the polls, but their success is less related than in the past to the strength of their party in the state. Turrett's data also show that the vulnerability of incumbent governors is affected by national trends. In presidential years (1900–1968) 20 percent of those governors who belonged to the winning presidential party and 43 percent of those belonging to the losing party were beaten. In nonpresidential years governors belonging to the party out of power were less likely to lose (by a margin of 26 percent to 42 percent of defeats). These differences remained true in the more recent periods of his study.

Survey research studies provide some additional clues as to the importance of incumbency in gubernatorial elections. Andrew Cowart (1973) has studied patterns of straight-party voting and split-ticket voting in the 1964, 1966, 1968, and 1970 elections, based on a national sample of voters. He finds that incumbency explains a large amount of ticket-splitting. For example, when a Democrat splits his ticket by voting for a Republican candidate for governor, that candidate is usually an incumbent. When a Democrat votes for a Democratic candidate for governor, but splits his ticket for other offices, there is usually a Democratic governor running. Further analysis of Cowart's data, combining straight-party and split-ticket voting, shows that voters who identify with a party vote for the gubernatorial candidate of that party five sixths of the time when he is an incumbent, but only two thirds of the time when he is not.

Gerald Wright (1974) has made a more detailed effort to explain how incumbency affects gubernatorial voting, using survey data from a national sample and a 13-state sample in the 1968 election. That year there were gubernatorial elections in 21 states but in only 4 of the states in the 13-state sample. (In other words, in all but four states the sample of gubernatorial voters in each state is very small.) He concludes that in the 1968 races the net advantage of incumbency was very small, and that it was infinitesimal after the effects of party were controlled. That does not mean, of course, that it was not a significant asset —or liability—in some states. (By contrast, he found Senate incumbency to be a major asset.)

Wright also tried to determine what characteristics of incumbency might have some importance, either in helping or hurting incumbents. He found that in races where an incumbent was running, 37 percent of the voters had more awareness of the incumbent, 22 percent were more aware of the challenger, and 41 percent were equally aware of both. It is not surprising that respondents indicated more familiarity with incumbent governors than with their opponents; the surprise is that more than a few apparently knew more about the challenger.

It is generally true that, if other variables are controlled, voters are more likely to vote for candidates with whom they are more familiar. But if we look more closely at the reasons voters give for voting for one candidate and against another, we can see that incumbency, like familiarity, may breed contempt. Wright classifies voter responses into several categories, and finds that gubernatorial incumbents tend to have several advantages over their opponents in terms of personal characteristics and, to a lesser extent, their status as a party representative and their leadership and experience. But incumbents draw less praise and more criticism than their opponents with respect to policy questions. Wright (1974: 97) suggests why governors are so vulnerable to criticism in this area:

The state chief executive is a central figure in virtually every controversial policy issue that arises in state politics. The reason for his prominence is the high visibility of his office coupled with public *perceptions* that he has considerable if not enormous power in *all* state-level policy areas and conflicts, although in fact gubernatorial powers are limied.

In contrast, as Wright notes, incumbent senators are not perceived as being responsible for national policy-making, do not suffer in comparison with their opponents on the policy-making dimension, and gain much more than governors do from an image of having experience and exercising leadership. We will look more closely at this question of perceptions and images when we examine the characteristics of individual elections. The point to stress here is that, although some gubernatorial incumbents do very well at the polls, incumbency carries with it liabilities as well as assets.

Turrett's study (1971) referred to earlier, indicates that all three variables—party strength, national trends, and incumbency—have had some effect on gubernatorial voting. In order to evaluate more precisely the importance of these variables, it is useful to examine a recent study that uses multivariate analysis of aggregate data. This can give us a better impression of trends that have been occurring in the relative importance of each variable. It can also show to what extent gubernatorial voting can be explained by the three factors taken together, and how much remains to be explained by particular characteristics of individual election campaigns, such as the salience of issues and the images of candidates.

James Piereson (1974) has analyzed data on gubernatorial elections from 1910 through 1970, excluding only the 11 southern states and several other states (such as Kentucky and most New Jersey elections) that have held gubernatorial elections in years when no congressional elections were held. His purpose is to measure the separate and combined effects of the three variables we have been considering on the percentage of votes received by gubernatorial candidates. The variables are measured as follows:

The strength of the parties in each state is measured by the state-wide party votes for the U.S. Senate and House (using the lowest figure over a three-year period in an effort to approximate basic party strength).

National political trends are measured by each party's percentage of the national vote for the U.S. House.

Incumbency is simply the presence or absence of an incumbent in the general election.

Piereson uses a multiple regression analysis to measure the relative impact of each variable, and the three combined, on the gubernatorial vote percentages. In Table 6–7 the standard regression coefficients, or Beta weights, measure the relative importance of each variable; the $R^2$ measure tells us what percentage of the variance in gubernatorial vote is explained by these three variables, rather than by other factors.

It is evident from Table 6–7 that party strength has been the most important predictor of the gubernatorial vote over the 1910–70 period, and more important for Democrats than for Republicans. National

**Table 6–7**
**Relationships between vote for governor and party strength, incumbency, and national tides, measured by Beta-weights, over time, 1910–1970**

| | Beta weights | | | |
|---|---|---|---|---|
| Time period | Party strength | Incumbency | National tides | $R^2$ |
| Republicans .............. .43 | | .12 | .29 | .37 |
| All presidential elections ............ .43 | | .12 | .36 | .45 |
| Nonpresidential elections ............ .42 | | .12 | .20 | .29 |
| 1910–20 ............... .34 | | −.03 | .54 | .52 |
| 1922–30 ............... .43 | | .13 | .20 | .26 |
| 1932–40 ............... .51 | | −.01 | .35 | .39 |
| 1942–50 ............... .65 | | .16 | .11 | .53 |
| 1952–60 ............... .44 | | .14 | .31 | .41 |
| 1962–70 ............... .02 | | .33 | .27 | .16 |
| Democrats .............. .55 | | .16 | .16 | .46 |
| All presidential elections ............ .53 | | .20 | .20 | .49 |
| Nonpresidential elections ............ .58 | | .13 | .13 | .45 |
| 1910–20 ............... .49 | | .18 | .17 | .34 |
| 1922–30 ............... .68 | | .08 | .08 | .51 |
| 1932–40 ............... .64 | | .07 | .24 | .44 |
| 1942–50 ............... .58 | | .22 | .10 | .50 |
| 1952–60 ............... .46 | | .17 | .38 | .48 |
| 1962–70 ............... .03 | | .36 | .27 | .22 |

Source: James E. Piereson, "Determinants of Candidate Success in Gubernatorial Elections, 1910–1970." Unpublished paper, 1974, tables 4, 5, 6.

political trends have been of secondary importance, assuming more significance in presidential years, as we would expect, and having more impact on Republican candidates. Incumbency has been less important, but it has generally been an asset to members of both parties. These three variables explain almost half of the gubernatorial vote for Democrats, and almost half for Republicans in presidential years but less than one third for them in nonpresidential years.

If we look at changes over time, we find that established patterns of state party strength were very important for a long time, particularly in the 1920s, 1930s, and 1940s, but they began to lose their impact in the mid-1950s and almost disappeared during the 1960s. Incumbency has varied in importance over time and has sometimes been a net liability rather than an asset. A more detailed examination of recent election years shows that incumbency was a major, positive force in explaining gubernatorial election outcomes in the 1952 to 1956 elections and again from 1964 to 1970. It is also worth noting that the combined effect of these three variables was much less important in explaining gubernatorial elections in the decade of the 1960s than in any previous period, primarily because of the declining importance of state party strength. In summary, it is clear that state politics has begun to change in recent years, with gubernatorial candidates winning in states where their party has traditionally lost. These upsets have resulted not so much from national trends but from the strengths of particular candidates and other aspects of individual campaigns.

## EFFECTS OF CANDIDATES AND ISSUES IN GUBERNATORIAL CAMPAIGNS

If traditional patterns of party loyalty are declining in importance and the effects of national political trends do not always reach gubernatorial contests, we must learn more about the factors that are peculiar to specific campaigns—the relative political strength of candidates and their appeal to particular groups, the issues salient to voters, the record of the state administration, and campaign organizational strengths and weaknesses, for example. We have already noted the difficulties of measuring these factors: survey data are scarce and other sources tend to be impressionistic. Most important is the simple fact that every election is different. Generalizations about factors most likely to be important in campaigns may tell us very little about why Jones beat Smith in a particular state. Survey data can tell us what characteristics of candidates and what types of issues voters most often mentioned in explaining their vote. Other sources can tell us what the candidates were talking about, how well-organized their campaigns were, and what tactics they pursued that may have helped or hurt their chances at the polls.

A 1968 survey of voters in 21 states with gubernatorial elections provides some clues to the images of gubernatorial candidates that influence voting decisions (Wright, 1974). Most voters have some impressions about such candidates, at least as much as they have about senatorial candidates. The dimensions of candidate image which have the most impact on the choices of voters are those related to specific policy stands taken by candidates or perceived benefits for particular groups (areas that we have noted tend to be a liability for incumbents) and those related to political leadership and experience. A third dimension concerns the partisan affiliation and campaign tactics of candidates. The least significant aspect is the personal characteristics of candidates, according to the survey.

The difficulty of applying such findings to individual state elections can be illustrated by data from four states in this survey in which large samples of voters permit more detailed analysis. In only one of these states (Illinois) was leadership and experience the most important aspect of candidate image. The incumbent governor was seriously handicapped because he had only recently moved up from the post of lieutenant governor, while his opponent was a highly visible office holder with an anti-boss image. In three other states the party affiliation of candidates overshadowed other aspects of their image; all three —Texas, North Carolina, and South Dakota—have traditionally been dominated by one party. The aspect of policy and group benefits was of moderate importance in all four states but less important than it was in the national survey.

During our discussion of gubernatorial campaigns in the previous chapter we described factors that appeared (according to press accounts) to contribute significantly to the defeat of incumbents. We noted that partisan factors (domination, unity, and disunity) were pertinent half the time; personality characteristics and experience influenced 40 percent of the elections; and the administration's record— particularly regarding taxes—was costly to incumbents in almost three fourths of the cases. Presumably these same factors are among the most important in other elections that do not involve the defeat of an incumbent. The qualities of a candidate that emerge as most important or the most salient issues in a particular election, however, are difficult to predict.

A study by Bicker (1972) of the 1966 and 1970 gubernatorial elections in California demonstrates, in his words, that "ideology is alive and well in California." We noted earlier (Table 6–2) that voting in those elections was closely related to party identification, but Table 6–8 shows that ideology and partisanship both contribute to an ex-

**Table 6–8**
**Ideological and partisan identification of voters in California gubernatorial elections (in percentages)**

| Election and candidates | Voting intentions of Democrats | | | Voting intentions of Republicans | | |
|---|---|---|---|---|---|---|
| | Lib- eral | Mod- erate | Conser- vative | Lib- eral | Mod- erate | Conser- vative |
| 1966 election | | | | | | |
| N = | (181) | (228) | (161) | (44) | (148) | (202) |
| Brown (Dem.) ............ | 72 | 55 | 47 | 30 | 11 | 7 |
| Reagan (Rep.) ............ | 14 | 25 | 38 | 50 | 75 | 88 |
| Don't know .............. | 14 | 20 | 15 | 20 | 14 | 5 |
| 1970 election | | | | | | |
| N = | (116) | (82) | (85) | (18) | (38) | (166) |
| Unruh (Dem.) ............ | 78 | 65 | 53 | 33 | 8 | 4 |
| Reagan (Rep.) ............ | 14 | 23 | 42 | 56 | 82 | 93 |
| Don't know .............. | 9 | 12 | 5 | 11 | 11 | 4 |

Source: William E. Bicker, "Ideology Is Alive and Well in California: Party Identification, Issue Positions and Voting Behavior." Paper prepared for annual meeting of American Political Science Association, 1972, pp. 13–14.

planation of those elections. Voters are classified as liberal, moderate, or conservative on the basis of a survey that asked them what they considered themselves to be. It is obvious from the table that Ronald Reagan was much more successful among conservative and moderate Republicans than among liberals and that he drew a substantial vote from conservative and even moderate Democrats. Moreover, the proportion of Republicans who called themselves conservatives was much greater than the proportion of Democrats who called themselves liberals. It is obvious that in California many voters perceive candidates in ideological terms and some of them cross party lines to vote for a candidate whose ideological orientation is close to theirs. It is worth noting that Reagan had a more liberal primary opponent in 1966, and the Democratic candidates in both elections had a more conservative primary opponent—in both cases Sam Yorty. These primary battles probably helped to heighten voter perceptions of the ideological leanings of these candidates. There have been long-standing ideological divisions within both of the California parties, often reflected in primary ballots. We do not want to argue that California gubernatorial elections are typical in their emphasis on ideology. We should also point out that factors other than ideology may lead a conservative Democrat to vote for Reagan or a liberal Republican to vote for Unruh. But these data do suggest that ideological factors may be salient enough to the voters in some campaigns to have a significant impact on the outcome of gubernatorial elections.

One variable affecting gubernatorial races is the ability of candidates to appeal to particular ethnic, racial, or religious groups. The Democratic party, in both national and state elections, has traditionally been able to attract certain ethnic minorities and Catholic voters, particularly in the most urban states of the Northeast and Midwest, although there is some evidence that voting along ethnic or religious lines has been declining. Since the early 1960s the Democratic party has won a huge majority of the black vote in most elections—both in the North and the South. When we talk about the voting appeal of a particular candidate, however, we mean that voters will change their normal voting patterns to choose a candidate of their own race, religion, or national origin.

For example, the Rhode Island Democratic party used to be dominated by Irish candidates. When John O. Pastore, of Italian background, first ran for governor and later senator in the 1940s and 1950s, he was more successful in Italian districts (and less in Irish districts) than Irish candidates had been. A Republican of Italian background, Christopher Del Sesto, had a similar experience in running for governor—eventually successfully (Lockard, 1959: 200–202). Litt (1965: 67) has concluded from a study of Massachusetts that "ethnic variations in gubernatorial elections have remained fairly constant for two generations, and ethnicity remains an important element in all aspects of Massachusetts public life. Yet, these ethnopolitical loyalties are no longer inflamed with the passions of old hatreds." His data show that in the late 1950s and early 1960s Italian voters in particular shifted from party to party depending on the ethnic heritage of the candidates. John Fenton (1966), in his study, *Midwest Politics,* repeatedly emphasizes the impact of ethnic factors on voting patterns in state elections. For example, in 1958 there were significantly different levels of support by ethnic and religious groups for the two major statewide Democratic candidates, one a Protestant and one a Catholic. Jack Holmes (1967) devotes a substantial part of his book, *Politics in New Mexico,* to the impact that Spanish-speaking citizens and Indians have had on the politics of that state. It is obvious that the ethnic backgrounds of candidates, and not just the party loyalties of these groups, have affected the outcome of state elections. There is evidence that in Utah a candidate's chances of winning state elections depends in part on whether he is a Mormon, because that religious group is so strong.

The impact of the black vote on politics has rapidly expanded in the last two decades with the removal of barriers to black voting in the Deep South and the mobilization of the black vote in both the North and the South. Although the black vote is usually heavily Democratic, both the percentage cast for Democratic candidates and the size of the black turnout vary substantially, depending on the candidate. Black candidates and white candidates sympathetic to black viewpoints have frequently owed their victory in state elections to black voters—particularly in the South. Black voters have also played a crucial role in some Democratic primaries. The refusal of black voters to support Democratic candidates unsympathetic to their views was illustrated in the 1966 gubernatorial election in Georgia. After Lester Maddox won the Democratic primary, black voters almost completely deserted the Democratic ticket and divided their support between a conservative Republican, Bo Callaway, and a liberal Democrat, Ellis Arnall, who was seeking a write-in vote (Bartley, 1970: 77). In 1964 only 16 percent of the black voters in Arkansas supported the Republican candidate, Winthrop Rockefeller, who was challenging Democratic Governor Orval Faubus. But 2 years later, after Rockefeller had made an intensive effort to gain black support, he won 71 percent of the black vote against Democratic candidate Jim Johnson, a strong segregationist—and the black vote provided Rockefeller's margin of victory (Bass and DeVries, 1976: 101).

## VOTING TURNOUT IN GUBERNATORIAL ELECTIONS

In chapter 4 we discussed and tried to explain the variations among the states in the level of voting turnout in gubernatorial primaries. It is equally interesting to find out if larger proportions of voters cast ballots in the general elections for governor in some states than in others, and speculate about why these differences exist. There are some difficulties, however, in making such comparisons among the states because some states elect governors in presidential election years, some in nonpresidential years, and some in both. Turnout is generally higher in presidential election years, and it is not surprising to find that in every state that has elected governors in both presidential and nonpresidential years, there has been higher average turnout in presidential years in voting for governor—a difference averaging 13 percentage points among the states. This means that it is misleading to compare turnout in states that elect governors in presidential and in nonpresidential years.

In Table 6–9 we have summarized the data on turnout in governors' races outside the South from the 1946–50 period through 1976 (the

**Table 6–9**
**Total gubernatorial general election turnout in nonsouthern states compared to other measures, 1946–1950 to 1976**

| | Turnout as percent of voting-age population | | | Two-party competition* | | Presidential turnout | |
|---|---|---|---|---|---|---|---|
| State | All election years | Presidential election years | Nonpresidential election years | 1946–58 | 1960–76 | Avg. percentage | Rank |
| S. Dak. ........... | 68.0 | 73.3 | 63.4 | R | R | 74.0 | 3 |
| Idaho ........... | | — | 60.0 | R | R | 75.7 | 2 |
| Wyo. ........... | | — | 59.0 | C | R | 70.2 | 15 |
| Utah ........... | | 71.9 | — | C | C | 76.5 | 1 |
| N. Dak. ........... | 65.5 | 70.0 | 57.6 | R | C | 72.4 | 7 |
| W.Va. ........... | | 69.8 | — | D | D | 73.3 | 4 |
| R.I. ........... | 64.4 | 69.8 | 58.9 | D | D | 71.8 | 10 |
| Mass. ........... | 63.3 | 74.0 | 57.2 | C | C | 71.4 | 12 |
| Minn. ........... | 61.8 | 74.0 | 56.6 | C | C | 72.2 | 8 |
| Ill. ........... | | 68.6 | — | C | C | 71.6 | 11 |
| Hawaii ........... | | — | 53.6 | — | D | 51.4 | 38 |
| N.H. ........... | 60.7 | 68.3 | 53.1 | R | C | 72.9 | 5 |
| Del. ........... | | 68.2 | — | C | C | 70.7 | 14 |
| Ind. ........... | | 68.1 | — | C | C | 71.1 | 13 |
| Conn. ........... | 60.0 | 61.8 | 59.7 | C | C | 72.8 | 6 |
| Pa. ........... | | — | 51.8 | C | C | 65.3 | 28 |
| Calif. ........... | | — | 50.7 | R | C | 63.5 | 31 |
| N.J. ........... | | — | 50.2 | C | C | 67.5 | 20 |
| Nev. ........... | | — | 49.7 | R | C | 59.5 | 34 |
| Iowa ........... | 59.0 | 69.9 | 49.6 | R | C | 72.0 | 9 |
| Wis. ........... | 57.9 | 70.7 | 48.8 | R | C | 68.6 | 18 |
| Nebr. ........... | 57.7 | 67.9 | 51.9 | R | C | 65.7 | 26 |
| Mont. ........... | | 67.8 | — | C | C | 69.9 | 16 |
| Kans. ........... | 57.2 | 64.8 | 50.7 | R | R | 66.3 | 25 |
| Colo. ........... | 56.9 | 69.4 | 53.3 | C | R | 67.6 | 19 |
| Mich. ........... | 56.6 | 68.4 | 49.9 | C | C | 66.6 | 23 |
| Wash. ........... | | 64.2 | — | C | C | 69.0 | 17 |
| Mo. ........... | | 64.0 | — | D | D | 66.5 | 24 |
| Vt. ........... | 56.6 | 63.3 | 49.9 | R | R | 66.7 | 22 |
| Oreg. ........... | 53.8 | 60.2 | 52.0 | R | C | 67.3 | 21 |
| Alaska ........... | | — | 48.7 | — | D | 46.3 | 39 |
| N. Mex. ........... | 53.8 | 61.4 | 48.3 | C | C | 60.9 | 33 |
| Ohio ........... | 53.1 | 64.9 | 49.7 | C | C | 65.3 | 27 |
| N.Y. ........... | | — | 48.1 | R | C | 63.6 | 30 |
| Maine ........... | 48.9 | 54.9 | 46.3 | R | C | 65.1 | 29 |
| Okla. ........... | | — | 43.8 | D | D | 63.2 | 32 |
| Ky. ........... | | — | 41.6 | D | D | 54.7 | 36 |
| Ariz. ........... | 45.5 | 53.0 | 40.1 | D | C | 52.1 | 37 |
| Md. ........... | | — | 40.0 | D | D | 54.7 | 35 |

* Party competition (based on maps in Chapter 2): R = Republican majority; D = Democratic majority; C = competitive.

same elections used in our study of primaries). The data show the vote for governor for the two major parties as a percentage of the voting-age population of the state in each election year.[3] Because of the effect of presidential elections, we show in separate columns the vote totals in presidential and nonpresidential years, as well as the average for all years for states having both types of elections. (During the period covered, many states shifted from two-year to four-year terms, usually scheduling these elections in nonpresidential years, and such states have fewer elections recorded in presidential than in nonpresidential years.) The rank-ordering of the states is an approximation. We first rank-ordered the three groups of states: those with elections of both types, those electing only in presidential years, and those electing only in nonpresidential years. We then combined the three lists as best we could. The ranking is approximate because states having both types of elections differ in the proportion of elections in each category and in the range of turnout between races in presidential and nonpresidential years.

Keeping in mind the imprecision of our ranking, we can look for explanations for the differences. The differences are substantial. Turnout in presidential years ranged from over 70 percent to less than 55 percent of voting-age population; in nonpresidential years it ranged from just over 60 percent to 40 percent. A comparison with turnout in primary elections (Table 4–3) shows that there is little similarity between the two rankings. In Table 6–9 we have included the information from Chapter 2 on levels of party competition in these states. Contrary to what we might expect, the states with highest gubernatorial voting are not those with strongest two-party competition. Several of those with highest turnout (including South Dakota, Idaho, North Dakota, West Virginia, and Rhode Island) are ones in which one party has held a majority position during all or much of the time period we are considering. It is true that most of the states with the lowest levels of turnout (including Maryland, Arizona, Kentucky, Oklahoma, and

---

[3] Turnout is based on the Census Bureau figures for voting-age population. In recent years the Census Bureau has begun to include members of the armed forces stationed in a state in this figure; previously its data were based on civilians. We have used the census figures including the armed forces beginning in 1970. Starting in 1972 the figures also include those in the 18- to 20-year–old group, who had become enfranchised in all states. These two changes increase the denominator of the fraction and have the effect of reducing the percentage of those voting in the most recent years. (Similar calculations are used in estimating voting-age population in other chapters.) Southern states are excluded from Table 6–9 because many states did not consistently have gubernatorial contests throughout the period.

Maine) have also had a single party in control. The consistently competitive states are among those in the middle.

There is a closer match between turnout in governor's races and that in presidential races. Table 6–9 shows the average turnout in six presidential races from 1952 through 1972, and also the rank order of the states on this dimension. Most of the states that rank high on gubernatorial turnout also rank high on presidential turnout, although there are some states where voting for governor is considerably higher or lower than one would expect. A comparison between levels of turnout for the two offices in presidential years shows that turnout for president is usually higher, as we would expect, though the differences are often small and average 2 percentage points for all states having some elections in presidential years. (This figure is somewhat misleading because many states had gubernatorial elections only in a few of the early presidential years, when turnout generally was higher; the actual gap between presidential and gubernatorial voting in presidential years is probably more than two points).

We can draw several conclusions about turnout in gubernatorial general elections:

1. The shift to gubernatorial elections in nonpresidential years has led to lower turnout for gubernatorial races.
2. Turnout generally is higher in those states with high turnout for presidential races, whether or not the governor's race is in presidential years, if we control for the timing of the election.
3. Although the states with lowest turnout have low party competition, there is no consistent relationship between turnout and two-party competition.
4. The factors leading to high turnout in gubernatorial general elections are different from those that we found to cause primary turnout.

## STATE LEGISLATIVE ELECTIONS

Every two years, when voters go to the polls, they find on the ballot the names of legislative candidates, often near the bottom of a long list. Every two years millions of voters cast a vote for these candidates (while other millions do not bother to), but we know very little about the reasons that affect this type of voting decision. Rarely, if ever, have pollsters asked voters any questions about their votes for state legislative candidates. We are entirely dependent for information on aggregate voting returns, and even these have seldom been scrutinized by political scientists.

There are several reasons for believing that party loyalty has an important influence on legislative voting. Surveys at other levels have shown that voters fall back on party loyalty when they know little about the candidates, and certainly many state legislative candidates are obscure, lacking the resources for the campaigning necessary to become known to voters. Many legislative districts are won year after year by the same party, a pattern that suggests the importance of party voting. In a multimember district, if all of the candidates of one party win approximately the same vote, this suggests that party loyalty is the dominant factor in voting.

Both national and state political trends have an influence on legislative voting. A particularly strong candidate for governor may sweep candidates for the state legislature into office with him. If a candidate from the usual minority party wins the governorship but fails to carry enough of his party's candidates into the legislature, the result may be divided government. A particularly strong national trend can also affect state legislative seats. Sometimes a governor loses his party majority in the legislature in the middle of a four-year term if there is a major national trend toward the other party. In those states where the voting laws make it particularly easy to cast a straight party vote (by checking one box on the ballot or pulling one lever on the machine), there is the greatest chance that national and/or state party trends will have an effect on state legislative elections. The stronger the influence of party affiliation on voting, however, the less likely it is that national or state trends will affect legislative races.

We know very little about how much of an asset incumbency is in legislative races. Where the rate of turnover is high, legislators do not become well enough known to benefit much from incumbency. On the other hand, if little is known about legislative candidates, the fact of incumbency may be more salient than anything else. Over a period of time, some legislators may be able to develop a political base, through doing favors, making speeches, and gaining visibility, as most congressmen do. It is difficult to generalize about legislators because they differ so much in their opportunities to gain visibility. A legislator who is only 1 out of 10 or 20 in a large metropolitan area has much more difficulty attracting attention in the media than one who is the only representative or senator in a more rural county.

It is equally difficult to generalize about candidate and issue characteristics of campaigns. It is probably true to say that issues seldom play an important part in campaigning at this level. The voters simply pay too little attention to become familiar with the stands taken on issues by several candidates. Moreover, the candidates often ignore the issues and concentrate on establishing name familiarity and an image. In multimember districts where more than a couple of legislators are elected at large, it may be very difficult for the candidates to achieve even a minimum name recognition from the voters. Most single-member districts are small enough, however, for the candidates to contact a large proportion of voters firsthand. It is perfectly feasible for legislative candidates to campaign door-to-door. Moreover, it is very likely that a candidate who has been active in community affairs over a number of years will be well known to many voters in his or her district. In short, many voters may be motivated by personal knowledge and impressions of candidates. In the absence of survey data, it is very difficult, of course, to estimate how important these motivations are or to pinpoint those elections in which candidate or issue characteristics are most important.

## DIVIDED GOVERNMENT

If we turn from speculation about the causes of legislative voting to its results, we are struck by frequency of divided government: control of one or both branches of the legislature by the party that does not control the governorship. Every state has had some experience with divided government in recent years, except for the handful of southern states in which the Democrats have never relinquished control of the governorship. Table 6–10 summarizes the frequency of partisan divisions between the governorship and the lower house (1947–78) and shows the conditions under which the divisions have occurred. It is worth noting that out of 35 nonsouthern states (excluding Alaska, Hawaii, and the nonpartisan states), there were 23 that had partisan divisions for at least 10 of the 32 years, and all of them were divided at least 6 years. (Five southern states with no divided government are omitted from the table.)

With very few exceptions, members of the lower house serve two-year terms. Almost all governors serve four-year terms. We might expect, therefore, that governors would be most vulnerable to opposition control of the lower house during the second half of four-year terms. Table 6–10 shows, however, that almost two thirds of the lower houses under opposition control were elected at the time of the gubernatorial election. Moreover, in less than half of those sessions

**Table 6–10**

**Divided partisan control of the governorship and the lower house in 43 states for 1947–1978 period (1946–1976 elections)**

| State | Total Years | Governor and legislative elections coincide | Midterm elections No shift in house control | Shift in house control | Partisanship Dem. gov., Repub. house | Rep. gov., Dem. house |
|---|---|---|---|---|---|---|
| N.H. | 6 | 6 | | | 6 | |
| N. Dak. | 14 | 8 | 4 | 2 | 14 | |
| S. Dak. | 8 | 6 | 2 | | 8 | |
| Vt. | 14 | 14 | | | 12 | 2 |
| Kans. | 14 | 12 | | 2 | 12 | 2 |
| Maine | 16 | 10 | 4 | 2 | 14 | 2 |
| Conn. | 14 | 8 | 4 | 2 | 12 | 2 |
| N.J. | 10 | 2 | 2 | 6 | 8 | 2 |
| Ohio | 14 | 10 | 2 | 2 | 10 | 4 |
| Ill. | 14 | 6 | 2 | 6 | 10 | 4 |
| Iowa | 12 | 10 | 2 | | 8 | 4 |
| Idaho | 10 | 6 | 4 | | 8 | 2 |
| Wyo. | 10 | 4 | 2 | 4 | 8 | 2 |
| Mass. | 14 | 10 | 4 | | | 14 |
| R.I. | 8 | 8 | | | | 8 |
| Md. | 10 | 10 | | | | 10 |
| W.Va. | 12 | 6 | 6 | | | 12 |
| Ky. | 6 | 2 | 4 | | | 6 |
| Okla. | 8 | 4 | 4 | | | 8 |
| N. Mex. | 10 | 10 | | | | 10 |
| Oreg. | 8 | 4 | 2 | 2 | | 8 |
| Calif. | 6 | 6 | | | | 6 |
| Alaska | 6 | 2 | 2 | 2 | | 6 |
| Hawaii | 4 | 4 | | | | 4 |
| Ariz. | 12 | 10 | | 2 | 2 | 10 |
| Nev. | 12 | 8 | 4 | | 2 | 10 |
| Wash. | 14 | 6 | 4 | 4 | 2 | 12 |
| Tenn. | 4 | 2 | 2 | | | 4 |
| N.C. | 4 | 2 | 2 | | | 4 |
| Va. | 6 | 4 | 2 | | | 6 |
| Fla. | 4 | 2 | 2 | | | 4 |
| Ark. | 4 | 4 | | | | 4 |
| S.C. | 4 | 2 | 2 | | | 4 |
| N.Y. | 8 | 4 | 2 | 2 | 4 | 4 |
| Del. | 16 | 8 | 4 | 4 | 8 | 8 |
| Pa. | 8 | | | 8 | 4 | 4 |
| Ind. | 12 | 2 | 2 | 8 | 8 | 4 |
| Mich. | 24 | 18 | 4 | 2 | 12 | 12 |
| Wis. | 6 | 6 | | | 4 | 2 |
| Mo. | 8 | 4 | 4 | | 4 | 4 |
| Mont. | 14 | 6 | 4 | 4 | 6 | 8 |
| Colo. | 8 | 4 | 2 | 2 | 6 | 2 |
| Utah | 16 | 10 | | 6 | 10 | 6 |
| Total | 432 | 270 | 90 | 72 | 202 | 230 |
| Percentage | | 62.5 | 20.8 | 16.7 | 46.8 | 53.2 |

under opposition control elected in the middle of a governor's term was there a shift of partisan control at midterm; in the remainder the opposition party had held control also during the first half of the term. Only in Pennsylvania and Indiana were losses of partisan majorities at midterm the only or the major cause of opposition control. A governor is most likely to lose partisan control of the legislature if the midterm election occurs in a year when there is a major national trend in favor of the opposition party. Of the 18 cases in which Democratic governors lost a majority of the lower house in midterm (in 1946–76 elections), 5 losses were in 1966, 3 each in 1950 and 1960, and 2 in 1946. Of the 18 cases of losses by Republican governors, 5 were in 1964, and 3 each in 1954, 1958, and 1968. It is also evident from the last two columns of the table that there were an almost equal number of cases when Democratic governors had a Republican house and when Republican governors had a Democratic house to contend with.

The circumstances of opposition control of state senates are more complicated. Senators in a large majority of states serve four-year terms, which are usually staggered so that only half are elected at one time. This means that, with a four-year governor's term, the election of only half of the senators can be affected by the coattails of a gubernatorial candidate. We are concentrating on lower houses in our analysis of divided government because the complicating factor of staggered terms is not present.

The election of a governor of one party and a lower house with a majority of the other party at the same time can be explained by one or more of three things: the behavior of voters, the action or inaction of parties and candidates, and the operation of the electoral and districting system. The most direct, simplest explanation for divided government is that a substantial number of voters have split their ticket. They have done so for a number of reasons. Party loyalty may not be strong enough to produce straight-party voting, and the strength of party loyalty presumably varies from state to state. A major cause of split-ticket voting occurs in states where one party usually has a majority. When the minority party produces a candidate for governor who is strong enough to win election, many voters who support him do not support his party's candidates for the legislature. The minority party often has difficulty finding strong candidates for legislative office. Voters who cross party lines in voting for governor or for another major office often support their own party's candidates for lesser office. In short, we may expect to find ticket-splitting in states where party loyalties are weak or where the minority party wins the governorship.

The second explanation for divided government is simply the failure of one or both parties to run candidates for every legislative seat. In such districts, of course, voters of one party do not have an opportunity to vote a straight ticket. In states where one party is usually in the majority, the minority party often fails to field a complete legislative slate, even in those years when its gubernatorial candidate is successful. It may even fail to run candidates in districts that its gubernatorial candidate wins.

Finally, the electoral and districting systems may distort the effects of voting so that a party whose legislative candidates win a majority of votes may fail to win a majority of legislative seats. These distortions can take several forms. The single-member district system of representation is an inaccurate way of translating votes into legislative seats because it wastes the votes of the losing party in each district. A simple example will show how that system can turn a voting majority into a legislative minority. Assume that a state has 10 single-member districts, with 10,000 votes cast in each. The Democrats win 4 districts, each by a margin of 8,000 to 2,000. The Republicans win 6 districts, each by a margin of 6,000 to 4,000. The Democrats, with 56 percent of the total vote, will have won only 4 of the 10 seats because their supporters were so heavily concentrated in 4 districts that they won those by lopsided margins, and wasted votes.

The distribution of Democrats and Republicans in a state may be such that one party almost inevitably wastes more votes than the other. The Democrats, for example, might have very heavy concentrations of voters in the large cities but have only a minority of voters scattered throughout the rural districts. It is also possible that gerrymandering will occur, that the party controlling the legislature will deliberately draw district lines in such a way as to waste as many votes as possible for the minority party. Before the courts in the 1960s forced state legislatures to adopt standards of population equality in apportionment, there were large variations in the size of districts. The rural parts of the state had smaller districts and were thus overrepresented. In many northern states, where the Democrats were predominantly urban and the Republicans rural, the Democrats were underrepresented, often so badly that they could not win a legislative majority when they won the governorship. Divided government no longer is caused by lack of population equality in apportionment, but it may be caused by differences in the wasting of votes and gerrymandering.

Some states use multimember districts without any form of proportional representation. In a four-member district, for example, each voter selects four legislators. If most voters cast a straight-party vote, the district is likely to elect either four Democrats or four Republicans. A party that wins numerous multimember districts by narrow margins would minimize the wasting of votes. A party that has a large minority in such a multimember district gets no seats, while it might win at least one seat if the large district were broken up into single-member districts.

In order to test these various explanations of divided government with data, we have examined voting patterns in a sample of non-southern states, most of which had opposition control of the lower house quite frequently. For each state we have collected statewide and district data on the percentage vote cast for governor and for the legislature, and on the number of legislative candidates running. The easiest factor to measure is the number of districts in which only one party ran a legislative candidate. We have also added up the total number of votes cast for all legislative candidates, in order to compare the partisan percentage of the legislative and gubernatorial vote. (This was not done for two states having many candidates who ran un-opposed.) In those states having multimember districts, we averaged the vote for all Democratic legislative candidates and that for all Republicans, to avoid counting more than one vote for each voter. Obviously the use of percentages is imprecise, but raw figures would be misleading because the total vote cast for legislators is less than for governor.

We have also attempted to compare the vote cast for gubernatorial and legislative candidates in each party in each district. Because gubernatorial voting data are usually available by county, this can be done in one-county and multi-county districts. (In cases where parts of two or more counties form a district, we assumed that the partisan percentages for governor in part of the county were the same as for the whole county.) In large counties containing a number of single-member districts, however, there was usually no breakdown available of the gubernatorial vote by district, and only a rough comparison of legislative and gubernatorial voting is possible. On the other hand, in states where the counties were not divided but elected members at large, an exact comparison of the legislative and gubernatorial votes was possible.

We have also examined evidence that one party was handicapped because the districting system wasted more of its votes than were wasted in the other party, and we have looked at the consequences of using multimember districts. This evidence is not measured precisely, but is evaluated as carefully as possible.

The summary of the data for these states is found in Table 6–11.

**Table 6–11**
**Comparison of votes cast for governor and lower house and house seats won in ten states**

| State | Year | Winning percentage of votes for governor | Winning percentage of votes for house seats | House seats won Majority party | House seats won Minority party | Won unopposed when gov. candidate: Won | Won unopposed when gov. candidate: Lost | Won opposed when gov. candidate: Won | Won opposed when gov. candidate: Lost |
|---|---|---|---|---|---|---|---|---|---|
| Okla. ...... | 1962 | R 55.4 | — | D 95 | R 25 | 47 | 24 | 7 | 17 |
| Kansas .... | 1970 | D 54.8 | — | R 84 | D 41 | 20 | 10 | 16 | 38 |
| Iowa ...... | 1966 | D 55.6 | R 54.9 | R 89 | D 35 | 1 | 2 | 29 | 57 |
| R.I. ........ | 1964 | R 61.1 | D 63.2 | D 76 | R 24 | 1 | 1 | 17 | 57 |
| W.Va. ..... | 1968 | R 50.9 | D 56.9 | D 63 | R 37 | 2 | 2 | 32 | 27 |
| Wash. ..... | 1964 | R 56.0 | D 52.4 | D 60 | R 39 | 0 | 0 | 10 | 50 |
| Oreg. ..... | 1962 | R 56.6 | D 52.2 | D 31 | R 29 | 3 | 1 | 2 | 25 |
| Mont. ..... | 1968 | D 56.4 | R 50.8 | R 58 | D 46 | 2 | 2 | 17 | 37 |
| Mich. ..... | 1964 | R 56.1 | D 58.5 | D 72 | R 38 | 4 | 0 | 33 | 35 |
| Ohio ...... | 1970 | D 55.5 | D 50.7 | R 54 | D 45 | 2 | 0 | 27 | 25 |

The first two columns show which party got the most votes for governor and for its legislative candidates and what that percentage was. The next two columns show the distribution of seats. The last four columns show, for the party that won a majority of house seats, how many of its seats were won against opposition and how many were won in districts carried for the govenorship.

A brief examination of voting patterns in each state will make the table more meaningful. In only two of the states, Oklahoma and Kansas, can divided government be explained by the failure of one party to contest a large number of legislative seats. In Oklahoma the Democratic party, traditionally in the majority, won 71 of its 95 house seats without opposition, including 24 districts carried by the Republican candidate for governor. In Kansas the Republican party, normally in the majority, won 30 of its 84 seats without opposition, including 10 in districts the Democratic governor won. (The Democrats, however, won 11 seats without Republican opponents.) In both states there was also considerable evidence of split-ticket voting. In 38 Kansas districts the voters voted Democratic in the governor's race and Republican in the house race. (Note, however, that in Kansas data are not available for the gubernatorial vote below the county level, and 25 of these 38 districts were Republican legislative districts in larger counties voting Democratic for governor.) In general we can conclude that the failure of the traditional minority party to run candidates and split-ticket voting both contributed to divided government in Oklahoma and Kansas.

The next three states, Iowa, Rhode Island, and West Virginia, are ones in which one party has frequently dominated the House while the other was electing a governor. Until 1974 Democratic governors in Iowa had regularly faced Republican legislators; in both Rhode Island and West Virginia, Republican governors consistently faced Democratic house majorities. In the 1966 election in Iowa there was a gap of more than 10 percentage points between the statewide Democratic vote for governor and that for House seats, and there were 57 districts won by Republican legislators and the Democratic candidate for governor. (Iowa used at-large elections in multimember counties, permitting exact comparisons of voting.) In Rhode Island the evidence of split-ticket voting was even more dramatic in the 1964 election. Despite the weakness of the Republican presidential candidate in Rhode Island, the party's candidate for governor won 61.1 percent of the vote, while Republican legislative candidates polled only 36.8 percent throughout the state. This suggests that no more than 60 percent of those voting for the Republican governor also voted for a Republican legislator. Democratic legislative candidates carried 57 of the 74 contested seats they won in districts that voted for a Republican for governor. (In Rhode Island the availability of district-level gubernatorial data makes such comparisons exact.)

In West Virginia the evidence of split-ticket voting is less dramatic, partly because in 1968 the Republican candidate won the governorship with only 50.9 percent of the vote, while his party was winning 37 of 100 seats. Most of the 27 seats won by Democrats in counties voting Republican for governor are in multimember counties with at-large elections where Democrats won some or all of the seats. One further explanation for split-ticket voting is party registration. In 1968 the Democrats had 64.9 percent of the registration among voters registered with a party, and they held a majority of the registered voters in all but one of the districts that voted Republican for governor and Democratic for the legislature. In short, West Virginia is a Democratic state, where the voters are much more likely to shift their allegiance in a governor's race than in a legislative race.

Washington, Oregon, and Montana are not only similar in their geographic location, but they are states where party organizations and party loyalties might be expected to be weak. (Washington, for example, is one of two states with the blanket open primary.) In Oregon and Washington all or most of the cases of divided government have occurred under Republican governors; in Montana there has been an almost even split between Democratic and Republican governors. In all three states included in our study there has been a gap of 7 to 9 percentage points in the statewide vote between the governor's race and legislative races. In each case the governor won with from 56 percent to 56.6 percent of the vote. In each state a large proportion of districts that contributed to the legislative majority for one party voted for the other party for governor. (Although all three states make some use of at-large, multimember districts that facilitate voting comparisons, both Washington and Oregon have some counties divided into districts, for which gubernatorial data are not available below the county level.) It is worth noting that in Oregon the Democrats got only a 31–29 legislative majority despite winning 52.2 percent of the statewide legislative vote, while in Washington the Democrats won a 60–39 majority of seats despite an almost identical statewide vote percentage. In other words, in Oregon divided government was not caused by the alignment of districts, and in fact that alignment almost prevented a Democratic majority in the House despite the split-ticket voting that occurred.

In Michigan divided government occurred under Democratic governors up until the courts ordered legislative reapportionment; beginning in 1964 Republican governors frequently faced a Democratic legislature. It is clear that reapportionment benefited the Democrats in the House (and even more in the Senate, which had been heavily rural), but it is not clear exactly how much other factors have contributed to divided government. Democratic voters are heavily concentrated in Wayne County (Detroit) and other metropolitan centers, and Republicans dominate most other areas. In 1960 the Republicans cast 33 percent of the legislative votes in Wayne County but elected only 1 of 38 House members there; in 1964 they cast 28 percent and elected 2 of 37. Many Democratic votes are similarly wasted in rural counties. The districting system and the distribution of Democratic and Republican voters could produce divided government even if every voter cast a straight-party vote. But, as Table 6–11 shows, there was a gap of almost 15 percentage points between the gubernatorial and legislative votes, a relatively large amount of ticket-splitting.

Ohio is unique among our examples because in the 1970 election the Democrats failed to win a majority of house seats despite casting a majority of legislative as well as gubernatorial votes. There was some ticket-splitting, and the Democratic legislative vote (50.7 percent) was almost 5 percentage points less than the gubernatorial vote. (If uncontested races are omitted, the Democratic percentage of the legislative vote falls just below 50 percent.) Almost half of the Republican seats were won in districts in which the district, or at least the whole county, was carried by the Democratic governor. Until 1966 Ohio had at-large elections of legislators in its urban counties, a system that wasted large numbers of votes for both parties and encouraged distortion in translating legislative votes into seats. Even a single-member district system can be costly to the minority party, of course. In the 1970 election the Republicans won 37 percent of the legislative seats in Cuyahoga County, but only 3 of 17 seats; in Hamilton County the Democrats won 41 percent of the vote but only 2 of 9 seats. In Ohio the operation of the districting system, the geographic distribution of partisan voters, and split-ticket voting all have contributed to divided government, even though malapportionment has ended.

Fewer than a dozen case studies do not provide a solid basis for conclusions about the causes of divided government, but they suggest several plausible explanations. Single-member districting systems are notoriously poor methods for translating party voting strength into legislative seats, and multimember districts (without proportional representation) are even worse. How the distortions in districting actually affect party balance depends on the geographic distribution of voters attached to each party and the intentions and skills of the majority of legislators who adopted the districting plan. To understand exactly how a districting plan affects legislative seat distribution would require detailed analyses of the state elections over a period of elections.

In almost all of the cases we have examined, however, split-ticket voting was a major explanation of divided government. In other words, voters cast a gubernatorial majority for one party and a legislative majority for the other party. There may be a number of reasons for such a voting pattern. It seems most likely to occur in states where one party has held a majority position for a prolonged period and consequently has the allegiance of a majority of voters as well as a larger supply of candidates capable of making serious legislative races. Voters are more likely to break away from their party allegiance to vote for a gubernatorial candidate than to vote for a legislative one, particularly if the dominant party has better-known and frequently incumbent legislative candidates running. Where one-party dominance is even stronger, particularly in the southern and border states, the minority party may fail to run legislative candidates in a large number of districts, including ones where its gubernatorial candidate wins. In such states it is not uncommon to find, as in the 1962 Oklahoma election, that the minority party fails to run enough candidates to get a legislative majority even if all of them won. The growing two-party competition in many such states may increase the number of contested legislative races. On the other hand, the general decline in the strength of party loyalties and the growth of split-ticket voting throughout the country may make divided government more likely in the years ahead.

# 7 ★ ★

# State parties and national politics ★ ★ ★

Throughout this book we have emphasized the interdependence of state and national political forces and parties. In the first chapter we noted a number of national factors that influence state politics: constitutional and legal factors, political trends, and the national political culture. In chapter 2 we described how the level of two-party competition in states is affected by national political alignments and realignments. In our studies of state elections, we have shown how the success of gubernatorial and legislative candidates—and the likelihood of divided government—are affected by national political trends during a presidential or even a congressional election year.

In this chapter we turn to the relationships between state political parties and the presidential nomination and election campaign, which is of course the keystone of the national political system. We also examine more briefly the relationships between state parties and congressional campaigns. Those who participate in national conventions and in presidential campaigns are usually persons who have played an active role in some aspects of state politics. Candidates for the presidential nomination go to state and local party leaders and activists in search of support. Presidential campaigns often coincide with, and may influence the outcome of, statewide campaigns for major offices such as senator or governor.

These obvious interrelationships suggest a number of questions that we ought to explore:

1.  What are the goals of state party leaders and activists who partici-
    pate in the presidential selection process?
2.  How does the presidential selection process, and particularly the
    nomination, affect state parties?
3.  How is the presidential selection process influenced by the goals
    and tactics of state leaders, the procedures and practices of state
    parties, and the variations in state laws—particularly regarding
    nominations?
4.  What trends are occurring that affect the answers to these ques-
    tions?

The most obvious characteristic of the presidential nominating process is that it is undergoing rapid changes that have eroded the influence of state parties and their traditional leadership. A generation ago, in states with relatively strong state and/or local party organizations, the leaders of these parties (often governors or mayors) were able to handpick the delegations to the national convention that were chosen in committees and conventions, and sometimes were able to handpick those elected in primaries. These leaders were in firm command of their delegations at the national conventions and were able to function as power brokers, with their power depending on the size of the delegation. In recent years a majority of the delegates have been selected in state primaries, which have usually been contested, while the rest have been chosen in state conventions that have usually been characterized by open competition. Most of the delegates no longer are loyal to state and local political leaders but to presidential candidates. Prominent state and local party leaders and office holders sometimes are lucky to be able to win a seat at the national convention.

## THE GOALS OF STATE PARTY LEADERS

Although state party leadership is neither as powerful nor as united as it used to be in most states, it is still important to recognize that state leaders often have goals substantially different from those of national candidates, goals that pertain to the success of the state party. First, they want to support a presidential winner, someone who can get nominated and elected, and they want that support to be recognized and rewarded by the winner. This goal has several implications for the strategy to be followed by state leaders. During the early stages of the nomination race they must be cautious; while it would help to be identified early with the eventual winner, it would hurt to get firmly committed to a loser. They want a nominee who can get elected, but they also want one who can carry their state so that the party will get some credit for the election of the president.

Second, and more important, the state party leaders want a presidential candidate who will help—or at least not hurt—the state and local candidates who are running in the same election. It is a fair assumption that most state party leaders are more interested in the election of state and local candidates than in the presidential election. In those states that choose a governor during presidential years, victory in the gubernatorial race is much more important to the state party than the outcome of a presidential campaign. If there is no gubernatorial election, presidential coattails may affect the congressional, legislative, and local races. This is why state party leaders are more concerned about whether a presidential candidate will do well in their state than whether he can win a majority of votes in the electoral college. One of the reasons why so many leaders of state parties were hostile to George McGovern's nomination in 1972 was that they believed he would run so poorly in their states that other candidates on the ticket would be defeated. In 1960, Democratic leaders in some of the more rural, heavily Protestant states were afraid that John Kennedy would not do well among Democratic voters in their states and that other candidates would be hurt by this weakness.

A third goal affecting the strategy of state party leaders is to maintain unity and avoid serious divisions in the state party, if possible, during the presidential nominating campaign. Two examples from the 1960 Democratic convention are pertinent. Governor David Lawrence of Pennsylvania, a powerful leader in the traditional sense, endorsed Kennedy and won almost unanimous support from the state delegation for him; but he took this step only after he became convinced that Kennedy's support among other party leaders, labor unions, and rank-and-file Democratic activists was strong enough so that the party could unite behind him and no one else (Wise, 1962). On the other hand, Governor Bert Combs of Kentucky endorsed Lyndon Johnson for the nomination, but carefully avoided putting pressure on the members of his delegation, some of whom voted for Kennedy or Stevenson. Combs had been elected the previous year after a divisive primary, and he did not want to create disunity within his faction of the Kentucky Democratic party by alienating those delegates who were allied with him but who supported other presidential candidates. It was a classic example of a party leader giving higher priority to state party unity than to presidential politics (Jewell, 1962).

A closely related goal of state party leaders is to maintain control over the process by which the state party makes its decision about supporting a presidential candidate. In the example mentioned above, it was not only important to Governor Lawrence that party unity be maintained, but that he be the agent of party unity. At the same convention, Governor Pat Brown of California gained a reputation of being ineffective because the state's delegation was split down the middle and he lacked the ability to create order out of the chaos. Those who challenge the established leaders are sometimes not only interested in advancing the cause of a presidential candidate but also eager to wrest power away from the party establishment. Sometimes the state convention that selects delegates to a national convention also chooses a state party committee or other party officials; in such cases state and national political conflicts may become entwined. In 1956, for example, the Kentucky Democratic party was deeply divided between Senator (and former Governor) Earl Clements and newly elected Governor "Happy" Chandler. There were bitter battles in many of the county caucuses and on the floor of the state convention. When the smoke had cleared away, Chandler had wrested control of the state party from Clements and, incidentally, had won control of the delegation to the national convention.

The final goal of state party leaders is to secure the nomination and election of a presidential candidate whose position on major issues is acceptable to them. Although this goal is often subservient to others, it sometimes assumes importance. Southern Democratic leaders opposed the nomination of John Kennedy and George McGovern not only because these candidates appeared likely to run poorly in southern states but also because they disagreed with their positions on a variety of domestic issues. Actually, a candidate's stand on issues is usually intertwined with other factors. State party leaders are familiar with the attitudes of state voters on major issues and they want a candidate whose views are acceptable to the voters so that the candidate can carry the state and help state and local candidates.

The other political activists who may challenge the established leadership for control of the party and for a role in the nomination process are likely to be more concerned about issues. They may represent the interests of a particular group (labor unions, blacks, other ethnic groups) who are supporting a particular presidential candidate. Many of the political activists in a state who become involved in presidential politics have less interest in state politics and do not share the concern of party leaders to enhance the prospects for success of state and local tickets. If they become embroiled in caucus and convention battles, which may affect the control of the state party machinery, it is a byproduct of their effort to influence the presidential nomination. These groups are sometimes criticized by party leaders because they become active in state politics only during presidential campaigns or perhaps in an occasional Senate race. Some of those who enlist in campaigns for a presidential candidate, however, maintain their interest in politics and subsequently play an active role in state political affairs.

The decision of state party leaders to support or oppose a candidate at the national convention is often based in part on their prediction as to whether or not the candidate will do well in their state, thereby helping state and local candidates; but this prediction is not always correct. Students of national conventions have developed a measuring technique to calculate the success of such predictions. First, they calculate the support a state's delegation gives to the winning nominee, using a winner-support ratio (the percentage of the nominee's total votes in the convention that were cast by that state delegation divided by the percentage of the total convention votes held by that delegation); obviously a state delegation giving all of its votes to candidates other than the nominee has a ratio of zero. Second, they calculate the amount of gain (or loss) for the party's presidential candidate in that state, compared to the preceding presidential election vote of the party. If the predictions of party leaders are correct, the greatest gains by a party's presidential candidate will occur in those states whose delegations support the winning nominee at the convention (David, Goldman, and Bain, 1964: 269–78).

Data on individual elections show wide differences in the accuracy of predictions. A classic example of a convention in which state party leaders made successful predictions was the 1928 Democratic convention that nominated Al Smith, the first Catholic presidential candidate of a major party. Smith increased the Democratic presidential vote by a huge margin in the northeastern industrial states that had supported him at the convention, but in the traditionally Democratic South, whose state delegations had opposed him, he did badly and even failed to carry five of them. A somewhat similar situation occurred the next time the Democrats nominated a Catholic presidential candidate; in

1960 John Kennedy's convention strength and his electoral strength were both high in the northeastern industrial states and low in the South. Harry Truman in 1948 was another Democratic candidate who ran strongest in the states that had provided him with the greatest support at the convention (David, Goldman, and Bain, 1964: 295–308).

There are several examples of conventions at which many of the state delegations guessed wrongly about the electoral strength of candidates. In 1952 Dwight Eisenhower's strength at the Republican convention was greatest in the northeast industrial states, while his major opponent, Robert Taft, had greater western and southern support. In the election, however, Eisenhower made relatively modest gains in the Northeast, but did well in the West and particularly in the South, where he carried several long-time Democratic states. The reason for this reversal was that Eisenhower campaigned more extensively in the South than his predecessors had and proved to have a broad national appeal as a campaigner (David, Goldman, and Bain, 1964: 295–308). In the 1964 Republican convention the delegates from southern states almost unanimously supported Goldwater, while there was some opposition to him from northeastern states. The northeastern Republican delegations were correct in predicting that Goldwater would do badly in their states, but southern delegations failed to foresee that Goldwater would do worse in most southern states (outside the Deep South) than other recent Republican candidates had done. Goldwater's success in several states of the Deep South, however, did contribute to the development of state Republican parties in that area.

## STATE PARTY ORGANIZATIONS AND PRESIDENTIAL NOMINATING CAMPAIGNS

We can distinguish three patterns used by state parties for the selection of delegations to national conventions. The first is one in which the leadership of the party selects delegates who can be counted on to vote as they are instructed to; the state convention or committee formally ratifies choices already made by the leadership. The second pattern is one in which the state convention becomes an arena for conflict between various factions or the supporters of particular candidates. The third selection pattern is the use of presidential primaries; the choice is made by the voters, although the party leadership may seek to control or at least influence that choice.

## Decline of strong party organizations

The best examples of strong party leadership control over delegations to national conventions were found in the past in the states that had strong, well-disciplined party organizations and that had not adopted a primary. The county, city, or precinct meetings that selected delegates to the state convention would be organized and run by local leaders loyal to the state organization. A large proportion of these delegates would be persons holding state or local patronage jobs or others who were clearly indebted to the party organization. Their function at the state convention was to applaud the speeches with enthusiasm and to vote for the slates of national convention delegates that were presented to them. This slate would consist of prominent party leaders and public officials and party workers being rewarded for long and faithful service. The leader of the delegation was likely to be the governor, a senator, or the mayor of a major city. The leader or leaders of the state delegation might be committed to a presidential candidate before the national convention met. If not, they would bargain at the convention (in "smoke-filled rooms" or elsewhere), secure in the knowledge that wherever they led, the delegation would follow.

Obviously strong party discipline depended on control of government. It was the leaders who were governors or mayors of major cities who controlled their delegations most firmly. Schlesinger (1972: 16) has provided a rough measure of gubernatorial influence by comparing the cohesion of Republican state party delegations when the state party controlled the governorship with delegations when the party did not control the governorship. He looked at those national conventions having significant contests. The state party delegations with a Republican governor were more cohesive than those without in the 1940, 1948, 1964, and 1968 conventions, and were less cohesive in the 1952 convention. In 1976 the small number of state delegations with Republican governors were less cohesive than other delegations at the Republican convention.

In those parties that did not hold power in a state, or even in a large metropolitan center, it was more difficult for leaders to exercise authority. However, a number of such parties were dominated by small groups of leaders, who exercised power in part because there was little incentive for other politicians to contest control of a minority party. Sometimes the power of these minority leaders rested in part on their control over federal patronage in the state, when their party held power in Washington. A good example is the Republican parties in southern states. Up until the 1950s, those parties were very weak and were often run by small cliques of men whose only source of patronage or influence was the national party and who bargained every four years with their party's presidential candidates. The weaker the minority party, the easier it was to maintain control, but the more vulnerable the leadership was to a challenge if the base of the party were expanded, as happened to the southern Republican parties in the 1950s and 1960s.

Several forces have eroded the control of governors, mayors, and other party leaders over the selection of national convention delegations. The first, and more gradual, has been the decline of party organizations throughout the country, the erosion of patronage as the major motivation for party workers, and the other political and socioeconomic factors that have made the disciplined state party organization virtually a relic of the past. Second, the traditional minority parties, Democrats in the North and, later, Republicans in the South, have been transformed into more competitive parties, and in the process the old-time leadership cliques have been displaced.

During the last 20 to 30 years presidential nominating campaigns have become more intensive and also more open, with the supporters of candidates challenging established party leaders to gain seats on delegations; this has been especially true in the Democratic party where the rules were changed in 1972 to give these challengers much greater opportunities. It is not unusual for a governor to be defeated in his bid for a position as a delegate because he is pledged to a candidate who gets beaten in the state primary. Such defeats account in part for the declining participation of governors in national conventions. In the 1968 convention more than 90 percent of the governors in both parties were delegates to their national conventions. In the 1972 and 1976 conventions this figure had dropped to about three fourths for Republicans and less than two thirds for Democrats (Huckshorn, 1976: 220).

In addition to these trends, the rapid increase in the number of states holding presidential primaries in 1972 and 1976 has fundamentally changed the presidential nominating process and its effects on state politics. It was not until after World War II that candidates for the presidential nomination began the practice of campaigning from state to state. Harold Stassen campaigned extensively though unsuccessfully in 1948. In 1952 General Eisenhower resigned from his NATO post in Europe after his first primary success and returned to campaign personally for the nomination, and Robert Taft, his major opponent, also carried out a personal campaign. On the Democratic side, Estes Kefauver carried out extensive state-by-state campaigns in 1952 and 1956, and Adlai Stevenson, who had been nominated in 1952 without any effort, found it necessary to campaign in order to win primaries in 1956 (Davis, 1967: 56–67). The pattern that was established in these elections was followed during the 1960s and 1970s by most candidates for the presidential nomination. Candidates not only campaigned in the states having primaries, or at least in those where their prospects for election justified the use of that tactic; they also developed state organizations and often made personal appearances in some of the states nominating by convention. It was not unusual for one or more of the presidential candidates to speak at a state convention.

## Divided state party organizations

We are interested in the effects of these campaigns for the presidential nomination on state politics and party organizations. Have campaigns created, or perhaps exacerbated, divisions within the state parties, and have such divisions had lasting effects on the party? Several patterns emerge from a review of state politics during divisive presidential nominating campaigns. Frequently a state party has been united in support of a single candidate, either because the party leadership has been strong enough to generate support for the candidate of its choice or because there has been genuine consensus among rank-and-file party workers in support of one candidate—perhaps one coming from the same region. An example might be the support among Democrats in New England states for John Kennedy in 1960 or in southern states for Lyndon Johnson that same year. Another pattern is one in which members of a state political party are divided in their support for presidential candidates, but they agree to disagree. The divisions over presidential politics do not result in bitter personal antagonism, and they are forgotten after the election is over. There may be a deliberate effort to prevent presidential campaigns from affecting party unity, as in the case of the Kentucky Democratic party in 1960, mentioned earlier.

Some state parties have factional divisions that may persist for many years. The factions may be based on regional, urban-rural, socioeconomic, or other divisions within the state, or they may be based largely on personalities. Each faction may be led by a prominent state leader, such as a governor or ex-governor, who commands a wide following among voters. In other cases, the scope of these personal factions may be limited to persons who are active in the party organization. It is possible that both factions in a state will line up behind the same presidential candidate, perhaps competing for seats in the state delegation. It is perhaps more likely that the state factionalism will be reflected in presidential politics. This means that a presidential candidate who seeks the support of leaders in one state faction must recognize that he will probably lose the support of the other faction.

We are most interested in examining another pattern of linkage between national and state politics: those cases in which divisions over presidential nominations lead to a split or a change in the power balance within a state party organization. The major leaders of a state party may be divided over the choice of a presidential candidate, and this division may not be easily healed after the campaign is over. If the party leadership supports one candidate, the supporters of another may succeed in winning control of the state convention, and the insurgents may win control of the state party committee and maintain their power after the presidential election is over. A number of recent presidential campaigns have attracted new groups of political activists into the state party, enlarging and fundamentally changing the political base of the party organization. Good examples are the Eisenhower campaign in 1952 (particularly in southern states), the Goldwater campaign in 1964, the Eugene McCarthy and Robert Kennedy campaigns in 1968, and the McGovern campaign in 1972. Of course it is true that some of those who campaign for presidential candidates take no interest in state parties and candidates, but others expand their range of political interests and activities to include campaigns at the state level and, in some cases, set their sights on positions within the state party organization.

Several examples can be used to illustrate state party factionalism and its relationship to presidential politics. In 1960 the Ohio Democratic party was divided into two factions: one led by Governor Michael DiSalle and another headed by the party leader in Cleveland, Ray Miller. DiSalle had hoped to establish his control by running in the state presidential primary as a favorite son, but the Miller faction threatened to run a slate against him committed to John Kennedy. DiSalle shifted tactics, under pressure from Kennedy, and won control of most of the delegation by running as a favorite son pledged to Kennedy. The Ohio delegation at the national convention remained divided into factions but united in support of Kennedy. Kennedy's tactics, and his popular support in the state, had affected both the tactics of factional leaders and the balance of power between them (Wildavsky, 1962).

In 1960 the skillful and aggressive tactics of the Kennedy campaign forced a badly divided and contentious New York-state Democratic delegation to support him. A state party that had once been under "boss" control was now uncontrollable, and vulnerable to raiding by the Kennedy organization. One observer described the party organization in these terms:

The large New York delegation, then, was headed by a number of leaders, each with a different set of objectives and power bases to gain the acquiescence of rank-and-file delegates. No leader had exclusive control of the application of sanctions or the reward system of New York politics. . . . The net result is a more responsive relationship within the party between the leader and the rank-and-file. This explains in large part the support of Kennedy not by dictatorial boss methods but as a result of a cautious "feeling out" process between leaders and other members of the delegation to determine which candidate would yield most toward victory on the local as well as the national level (Swanson, 1962: 213–14).

The Texas Democratic party has been split into factions, roughly along liberal-conservative lines, for a number of years. As far back as 1944, it sent two delegations to the national convention, which divided the votes of Texas between them. In 1948 the liberal wing of the party was in control, and many of the dissenters supported a states rights ticket. In 1952 a conservative Democrat, Governor Allan Shivers, was firmly in control of the party, but the liberal minority held their own state convention and sent a separate delegation to the national convention, where it failed to gain recognition. In September, after the national convention, the state Democratic convention met again, still under Shivers' control, and voted to support the Republican Eisenhower-Nixon ticket for the presidential election. During the 1960s, however, the Texas Democratic party came under the control of Lyndon Johnson and Governor John Connally, who were conservative in state politics but supported the national Democratic party and its candidates (although in the early 1970s Connally shifted to the Republican party).

The Texas Republican party after 1952 offers a classic example of the impact of a presidential nominating contest on a state political party. The party for a number of years had been under the control of a conservative faction, which had supported Robert Taft in the 1940 and 1948 conventions and was committed to him again in 1952. The Eisenhower supporters within the party were convinced that large numbers of dissatisfied Democrats could be attracted to the party by Eisenhower's candidacy, and they worked hard to attract these new recruits to the precinct meetings that would choose delegates to the county conventions that in turn would elect delegates to the state convention. The Eisenhower leaders had two objectives: first, to defeat the existing leadership and select a delegation committed to Eisenhower, and second, to expand the base of the Republican party so that it would become competitive in state and national elections. The Republican party organization had become accustomed to holding its precinct meetings in the homes of members, which were perfectly adequate for the handful of loyal workers who usually came. In 1952, however, in the large cities many of these meetings were swamped with new Republicans, most of them supporters of Eisenhower. The outnumbered Taft supporters frequently walked out and elected their own set of delegates. The state party chairman and leader of the Taft forces, Henry Zweifel, found his home invaded by 100 Eisenhower supporters, who took charge of the meeting and elected their own delegates to the county convention. Zweifel retreated to his front lawn along with a few Taft supporters to elect a rival set of delegates (David, Moos, and Goldman, 1954: vol. 3, chap. 14).

Rump conventions and dual sets of delegates were the norm for many of the Texas precinct meetings and county conventions, leading inevitably to two sets of state conventions that sent delegations to the national convention. The Taft forces insisted that the party must be saved from "mob rule" and that persons who had been Democrats only yesterday had no right today to participate in Republican precinct meetings. The Eisenhower leaders insisted that the party must expand its base and welcome dissident Democrats if it was going to win elections. At the national convention the Texas dispute became the focal point of the credentials fight between Eisenhower and Taft; the Eisenhower delegates were all seated and their votes proved crucial to Eisenhower's nomination. In the aftermath of the election, Eisenhower leaders moved into positions of power in the state party, continuing efforts were made to attract Democrats into the party, and the Republican party began its long and only partially successful effort to become competitive in state politics. The contest over the presidential election had been the catalyst for that effort, as it was in several of the other southern Republican parties.

Twelve years later the Goldwater movement had a significant impact on the Republican party in a number of states. Goldwater attracted a large and devoted following among conservative Republicans. Many of them were political activists who held positions of influence in state and local Republican organizations. Where they were in the majority, these organizations supported Goldwater's candidacy. Many of the Goldwater supporters had not been active in Republican party affairs in the past, but they were mobilized during the 1964 campaign. Like the Texas Eisenhower supporters 12 years earlier, they attended precinct and county meetings, frequently in large enough numbers to win control and elect delegates who were totally committed to Goldwater. The tactics followed by the Goldwater organization were bold and effective:

But the new Goldwater-style of preconvention politics did not waste time on winning over county and state organizations, but concentrated on actually taking over the county and state organizations by an inundation of the Goldwater volunteers. It was indeed a revolutionary doctrine. It meant that the Goldwater delegates sent to San Francisco would be not merely the run-of-the-mill party workers under the command and the bidding of regular party leaders. Here was a new breed of delegate, most of whom had never been to a national convention before. . . . They were going there for one purpose: to vote for Barry Goldwater. To woo them away to another candidate would be as difficult as proselytizing a religious zealot (Novak, 1965: 345–46).

Georgia, Oklahoma, Kansas, and Washington are four examples of states in which the Goldwater forces won enough votes in the state convention so that they were able to oust the established leadership or at least to force these leaders to hand over a large share of the state's convention votes to the Goldwater group. At the precinct and county levels, in these and other states, it did not require huge numbers of supporters to win victories. The established party organization, relying on the apathy of most partisans, had been able to maintain its control with a small number of loyalists. The Goldwater leaders found that they could often win control of precincts with 20 or 30 enthusiastic workers and, by concentrating their activities on areas of strength, could win control of enough county or district conventions to assure a majority in state conventions, even in states where Goldwater could not have won a majority or even a plurality if all Republican voters had been polled (Novak, 1965: 348–54).

Some of the Goldwater activists lost their enthusiasm for Republican politics after his defeat in the November election. But others turned their attention to state politics, and began to consolidate and expand the successes that they had gained in county and state conventions in 1964. In some state parties, the organization came under the control of strong conservatives who had been committed to Goldwater. In other state organizations, factional divisions were formed or grew deeper, based at least in part on the conflicts over presidential politics.

The Democratic workers who joined the presidential campaigns of Eugene McCarthy and Robert Kennedy in 1968 were at the opposite end of the ideological spectrum from the Goldwater volunteers, but in other respects they were very similar. Some, of course, were experienced members of state and local party organizations, but many others had little or no experience in politics or at least had not been a part of the regular party organizations. Included in their ranks were large numbers of college students and other young people. They were motivated by a variety of domestic issues, particularly civil rights, but above all they were driven by a determination to end U.S. military commitments in Vietnam.

The Kennedy and McCarthy supporters not only worked in primary elections, but also organized in an effort to capture control of state conventions from the established party orgnizations, most of which were committed to the candidacy of Hubert Humphrey. Neither Kennedy nor McCarthy could match the success of Goldwater in the 1964 state Republican conventions. A number of the state conventions, particularly in June after Kennedy's death, developed into angry confrontations between the party leadership, commanding a majority of delegates and committed to Humphrey, and the McCarthy forces. The McCarthy group demanded, but seldom got, a share of the delegates at the state level equal to the proportion of delegates that they had won in district conventions or primaries. Although the party leaders seldom insisted on a "winner-take-all" policy, they were seldom generous in allocating delegates to the minority group. After the 1968 election, many of those who had been drawn into the campaign by enthusiasm for Robert Kennedy or Eugene McCarthy continued their involvement in Democratic politics, campaigning for particular candidates or seeking to win a share of power in state and local party organizations, though they did not win power in state organizations on a scale comparable to the success achieved after 1964 by Goldwater Republicans.

The dissatisfaction within the Democratic party over procedures used for selecting delegates in the nonprimary states led to the formation of the McGovern Commission after the 1968 elections, and the recommendations of this commission opened the way to increased participation by political amateurs in the presidential selection process in 1972. Briefly, the McGovern Commission brought about three kinds of change in the selection process:

1.  All Democrats had to be given a full opportunity to participate in all steps in the delegate selection process, with the rules clearly defined, and meetings publicized, open to all, and scheduled for no earlier than the start of the presidential election year.
2.  Procedures were established (and strengthened in 1976) to avoid unit rules and winner-take-all rules and to assure that supporters of candidates getting a reasonable minority of the vote (such as 15 percent) at any stage in the selection process could elect their share of delegates.
3.  The state parties were required to take "affirmative action" steps designed to make sure that blacks, women, and younger members had a fair opportunity to get elected to delegations (a provision weakened in 1976 because of criticisms that it established a quota system).

The effect of these new rules was to make it impossible (or at least very difficult) for the established state and local party leadership to control the selection of national convention delegates by manipulating the timing and procedures of precinct and county meetings, by excluding previously underrepresented minorities, or by imposing the views of a majority of delegates on a minority who supported other candidates. The supporters of George McGovern, many of whom had first enlisted in the Robert Kennedy or McCarthy campaigns, were quick to take advantage of the rules. They were well organized and fully capable of utilizing the procedures that had been developed to protect the political amateur and outsider. McGovern's nomination in 1972 was due not only to his popularity with a plurality of voters in many primary states but also to his ability to mobilize large numbers of volunteers and their skill in winning a large share of delegates in the convention states under the new rules. The campaign for the Democratic nomination and in the election in 1972 not only gave new power to large numbers of political amateurs but it also caused deep divisions in a number of state parties between the established leaders, many of whom perceived McGovern as a sure loser who would hurt state and local tickets, and the amateurs who were eager to claim the victory at the national convention that had been denied to them four years earlier.

It is difficult to pinpoint exactly how particular state parties have been affected by recent presidential campaigns, but it is clear that state organizations are now seriously handicapped in their ability to influence the presidential nominating process. It is also clear that the base of volunteer Democratic workers is broader and more varied than it used to be, and that many of these workers are playing a role in state and local primaries and elections. The new breed of political activists often have a relatively weak sense of party loyalty. They pick and choose those candidates whom they are prepared to support. In some states these new activists may have no interest in trying to win control of the state organization because it has lost whatever influence it had over nominations. In other states the meetings of state party conventions and committees may be an arena for continuing conflict between the establishment and new political forces because control of the organization is still perceived to be a means to important political goals.

## State procedures for presidential nominations

The procedures for nominating presidential candidates are established by the legislatures of each state, but in recent years these legislatures have been responsive to the requirements imposed by the national parties, particularly the Democratic party. There has been an expansion in the number of states using primaries, with considerable variation in the types of primaries used. The stricter rules established by the national Democratic party has led some legislatures to pass laws flexible enough to permit state Democratic parties to follow these rules without imposing them on state Republican parties. As a result of these changing rules and conflicting pressures, there is tremendous variation in the procedures used by the state parties. There is no reason to try to remember all of the technical details of state procedures, particularly because they keep changing, but an understanding of the various procedures employed is necessary in order to see how each affects the ability of the state party organization to retain some influence over the nomination process.

Table 7–1 is a classification of nomination procedures designed to distinguish between those in which the state party is most able to control the process and those that are most open to outside control. Although some state parties may not continue to use the procedures used in 1976 and illustrated in the table, the classification should remain valid. In the table the state parties are classified along two dimensions. (Unless a *D* or *R* is listed beside the state, both state parties used the same procedures.) The categories across the top describe

**Patterns of presidential nominating processes in 1976 affecting permeability of state parties**

| National delegate selection procedure | Presidential preference primary | | | | | |
| --- | --- | --- | --- | --- | --- | --- |
| | Vote binding on delegates | | | Vote advisory | | No primary |
| | Run by state | | Run by party | | | |
| | Open | Closed | | Open | Closed | |
| **Selected in primary** | | | | | | |
| Can be pledged; state-run .............. | R.I. Tenn. | S. Dak. | | Ga.–D Ill. N.J. | N.H. Pa.–D Md.–D Nebr. | N.Y. Tex. Ala. Ohio |
| Pledged; party run ..................... | | | Ariz.–D Conn.–D Utah–D | | | |
| Unpledged only; state run .............. | | | | | Pa.–R W.Va. | La.–D |
| **Selected in caucuses and conventions** | | | | | | |
| Primary to choose members of convention that picks delegates .................. | Ind. Mich.–R Ark. Mont.–D | Oreg. | | Mont.–R | | Del. |
| Candidate organizations choose delegates as allocated ...................... | Wis. Idaho | Mass. N.C.–D Ky.–D Fla.–D Nev.–D Calif. | | | | |
| Party meetings choose members of convention that picks delegates ........... | Mich.–D Ga.–R | N.C.–R Ky.–R Fla.–R Nev.–R Md.–R | | Vt. | | Miss. N. Mex. Colo. Iowa N. Dak. Me. Mo. Hawaii Conn.–R Utah–R    S.C. Okla. Wash. Minn. Kans. Va. Wyo. Alaska La.–R Ariz.–R |

the method by which voters were able to express a presidential preference. The categories on the left side of the chart apply to the methods of choosing delegates to the national convention. As we move from left to right and from top to bottom on the chart, we move in the direction of increasing control of the party organization over the nominating process.

There are three major categories for the expression of presidential preference. First are states where the voters are able to state their choice for president and that choice is binding on the delegates. Second are the states with advisory votes or "beauty contests," which are not binding. Third are those states in which the voters do not have a chance to express a preference for presidential candidates. We have distinguished between open and closed primaries because the party has less control in states where the primary is open to all voters. We have also noted that in three states (Arizona, Connecticut, and Utah) there was no state primary but the Democratic party ran what amounted to a primary at polling places across the state, the results of which were binding on delegates.

The various procedures for selecting delegates are more complicated. The basic distinction is between states in which delegates are selected in the primary directly by voters and states with other methods of selection, but the subcategories deserve some explanation. In most cases where delegates are selected in primaries they can be pledged to a candidate, but there are a few exceptions (both West Virginia parties and the Pennsylvania Republicans). In most states where delegates are chosen in the primary, there either is no presidential preference vote or the vote is only advisory. Although delegates may be pledged, they are usually not required to be. In some of the larger states (such as New York, Pennsylvania, New Jersey, and Ohio) using this system, it used to be common for the party organization to try to retain control by running a slate of delegates who were either unpledged or were pledged to favorite sons. In the states where delegates are selected in a primary and there is also a binding presidential preference vote (Rhode Island, Tennessee, and South Dakota), the allocation of delegates to the various slates is based on the percentage of the preference vote, but generally the determination of which candidates on the slates become delegates depends on the votes won by each.

There are three general methods of selecting delegates, other than the primary. In the first, a convention selects the delegates, but delegates to that state convention are chosen in a primary; the table shows that this procedure usually accompanies a binding presidential preference primary. The second method, which has become increasingly common in the last few years, applies only to delegates who will be bound by a preference vote. Each presidential candidate, through agents that he picks in each state, chooses as many delegates as that candidate is entitled to on the basis of the preference vote. They may be chosen after the preference vote, or a list may be prepared before the vote. The choices may be ratified by a party convention, but the candidate's organization—not the party organization—controls the choice. The final method is to have party conventions at the state or district level (whose members are not chosen in primaries) elect the delegates. This is the most common method used in states with no presidential preference primary, but it is used in a few states having binding preference primaries—particularly by border and southern Republican parties.

The procedure for nominating presidential candidates largely determines whether the choice will be made by a large group of voters or a small group of political activists, a point we will document with statistics later in the chapter. The procedure also determines the potential for party organizational control of the process, but actual control depends on such other factors as the strength of the party organization and the ability of supporters of particular presidential candidates to create strong organizations. In all the state parties selecting delegates in primaries (those at the top part of table 7–1), it is possible for the organization to run a slate that is pledged to its preferred candidate, or to a favorite son, or unpledged. It is also possible for supporters of other candidates to run slates. Where the organization is strong, and there is no binding preference vote, it may be able to control the selection of delegates. But we have noted that in states like New York, Pennsylvania, Ohio, and New Jersey, the organization is no longer strong enough to prevent open competition among slates pledged to major candidates or to play a decisive role in such contests.

Among the state parties selecting delegates in conventions, it seems obvious that the party organization will have least influence in those few states where delegates are bound by a preference vote and delegates to the state convention are chosen in a primary, such as Indiana and Oregon. The party organization also has little or no opportunity for influence in the next bloc of states, those where the delegates are bound by a preference vote and are chosen in fact by candidate organizations. The party organization has more influence where delegates, although bound by a preference vote, are chosen by the party. Table 7–1 shows that in North Carolina, Kentucky, Florida and Nevada the Democrats let the candidate organization make the choice but the Republicans gave the choice of committed delegates to a party convention. In this latter situation, so-called trojan horse delegates were often elected—those who were bound to vote for one candidate but preferred another and who might vote their own preferences on other issues that arose at the national convention. Obviously the state party organization has its greatest influence in the large number of states in the lower right-hand corner of table 7–1—those in which the party convention chooses delegates and there is no preference primary of any kind. Keep in mind, however, that it is possible for the supporters of a candidate to win control of a state convention and deny the party organization any influence over the choice of delegates. Such contests usually begin at the precinct and county level, and the role of the party depends on the strength of its grass-roots organization and its decision about whether it is prudent and feasible to try to influence the nominating process.

If we wanted to make Table 7–1 more complicated, or if we had a three-dimensional chart, we could add another element to the classification: the level at which delegates are chosen or preference votes calculated. There are substantial differences between the practices of the two parties in some states, largely because the national Democratic party has developed precise requirements designed to assure proportionality among candidates. Some state parties (but not the Democrats in 1976) used a statewide winner-take-all system. The candidate who won a plurality of the statewide preference vote would win all of the delegates. Some states used the statewide vote to assign delegates to candidates on a proportional basis, perhaps with a minimum figure (such as 15 percent) being necessary to get any delegates. When the votes were tabulated by districts, usually congressional districts were used. Some state parties used a winner-take-all system in each district (the so-called loophole primary), but the Democrats will not use such a system beginning in 1980. Some state parties used a proportional system within each district, again with a minimum percentage necessary to win any delegates.

Obviously, the major result of a proportional system is to help presidential candidates not strong enough in a state to carry it, or not strong enough in a district to carry it. Any districting system rewards those candidates with localized strength. It is likely that candidates who are strong in some states will be weak in others, and so it is unlikely that any particular system is inherently favorable to a particular candidate. California used to have a winner-take-all system in both parties, and this used to make it an enormously important primary, as it was for Goldwater in 1964 and McGovern in 1972. In 1976 the Democrats had a proportional district system and the Republicans a winner-take-all system in California. Former Governor Reagan was so obviously ahead that President Ford made a minimal campaign effort there. On the other hand, it made sense for Jimmy Carter to campaign against Jerry Brown, the Democratic governor and obvious leader, because he could win some delegates in most districts. In fact Carter's defeat in several of the late primaries failed to slow him up because the proportional and district systems guaranteed that he would pick up some delegates in each state and thus carry his delegate total closer and closer to a majority.

The impact of differing winner-take-all, proportional, and district systems on presidential candidates is not hard to calculate. It is more difficult to determine whether any of these systems facilitates or obstructs party organizational control of the nomination process. In 1976 the Democratic parties in some of the larger urbanized states insisted on retaining the winner-take-all district system, the loophole primary. This permitted the organization greater influence in those congressional districts where it had strong local organizations. However, in districts where it was weaker, it created the possibility that the party organization might win no delegates at all. Obviously in some states, the party organization may gain a temporary advantage from elections being conducted at a particular level, with or without proportionality, but it seems unlikely that any of these systems of delegate-counting is inherently favorable or unfavorable to the party organization.

## PRESIDENTIAL PRIMARIES

### Growing importance of primaries

The presidential nominating process has been transformed in recent years by the growth in the number of states holding presidential primaries and by the growing intensity of campaigning by candidates in these states. The first presidential primaries were adopted during the first few years of the 20th century by a few states where the Progressive movement was strong. By 1912 there were 12 states in which some form of presidential primary was required. The movement was further spurred by the tempestuous Republican convention of 1912, in which William Howard Taft defeated Theodore Roosevelt with the help of delegates won in state conventions that were under Taft's control. By 1916, 26 states used primaries for presidential nominations. But from 1929 to 1948 the primary movement went into a decline; about half of the states that had used the presidential primary abandoned it and only one state adopted it. Equally important was the fact that presidential candidates downgraded the primaries. Some candidates permitted their names to be used in some primaries, but with rare exceptions they did not campaign in these states. There were few direct contests between major candidates, and the primaries did not seem to have much impact on the decisions made by national nominating conventions. Even those candidates who entered primaries and had some success did not win enough delegates, either directly or through the impact of their victories on delegates in convention states, to assure a victory at the national convention. In 1940, for example, the Republicans had a wide-open nominating race. Although Thomas E. Dewey won six of the seven state primaries in which he was on the ballot and won half of all primary votes cast, he was defeated at the convention after seven ballots by Wendell Wilkie, who had won less than 1 percent of the primary vote (Davis, 1967: 24–36, 43–57).

After World War II there was a gradual increase in the importance of presidential primaries. Table 7–2 shows that, except for a short-lived increase in 1956, there was not much increase in the number of states using primaries until 1972 and 1976. But the number of votes cast in primaries, which had never exceeded 8.5 million and had seldom been more than 5 million, increased to 12.7 million in 1952, and then leveled off for a period of 20 years. The most significant change was in the tactics of candidates and the impact that primaries had on their fortunes. In 1948 Harold Stassen campaigned vigorously in Republican primaries, and his defeat in Oregon by Dewey appeared to play an important part in Dewey's nomination. Four years later the close battle between Dwight Eisenhower and Robert Taft in a series of primaries foreshadowed an equally close battle between the two at the convention. That same year, however, Estes Kefauver's success in a series of primaries did not bring him the Democratic nomination, as party leaders and the Truman administration threw their support to Adlai Stevenson, who had not sought the nomination. Four years later, however, Stevenson campaigned actively in primaries, where he beat Kefauver and other candidates and won the nomination.

**Table 7–2**
**Growth in number of presidential primaries and vote cast in primaries**

| | Number of states holding primaries | | Votes cast in primaries (in thousands) | | | Total primary vote as percentage of total presidential |
| | | | | | | election vote |
| Year | Dem. | Rep. | Dem. | Rep. | Total | |
|------|------|------|------|------|-------|------|
| 1948 ........... | 14 | 12 | 2,151 | 2,653 | 4,804 | 10.4 |
| 1952 .......... | 15 | 13 | 4,909 | 7,801 | 12,710 | 20.8 |
| 1956 ........... | 19 | 19 | 5,833 | 5,828 | 11,661 | 18.9 |
| 1960 .......... | 16 | 15 | 5,687 | 5,538 | 11,224 | 16.4 |
| 1964 .......... | 16 | 16 | 6,247 | 5,935 | 12,182 | 17.3 |
| 1968 .......... | 17 (2) | 16 (1) | 7,535 | 4,474 | 12,009 | 16.5 |
| 1972 ........... | 23 (2) | 22 (2) | 15,994 | 6,188 | 22,182 | 29.1 |
| 1976 .......... | 30 (3) | 30 (3) | 15,925 | 10,260 | 26,185 | 32.8 |

Note: The numbers include the states and the District of Columbia. The numbers in parentheses in 1968, 1972, and 1976 are the subgroup of states (included in the total) for which no data are available on the vote cast, generally because voters voted for delegates who were unpledged, and candidate names were not on the ballot: New York and Alabama, and (in 1976) Texas. The total presidential vote used as a basis for percentages in the last column includes the two-party vote and in 1968 the Wallace vote.

Source: *Congressional Quarterly, Guide to U.S. Elections.* Washington, D.C., 1975, pp. 332–49, and *Congressional Quarterly Weekly Reports* for 1976.

In 1960 John Kennedy defeated Hubert Humphrey in Wisconsin and West Virginia and won most other primaries against minor opponents. His victories were crucial to his nomination because they overcame the doubts of party leaders that he could win. Nixon in 1960 romped through the Republican primaries without a defeat or any serious opposition. In 1964 Goldwater's nomination depended partly on his narrow victory over Rockefeller in California and on the failure of any Republican candidate to put together a string of Republican primary victories, but it depended more on his great success in convention states. In 1968 Richard Nixon defeated all opponents with ease in the large number of primaries where he campaigned actively, though he stayed out of California, where Reagan was unopposed. In the Democratic campaign Robert Kennedy and Eugene McCarthy dueled from one state to another, with Kennedy winning most primaries until he was killed on the night of his California victory. But the nomination went to Hubert Humphrey, who had avoided all the primaries, but who locked up state conventions with the aid of the Johnson administration.

In the campaigns from 1956 through 1968 every successful nominee (except for incumbent presidents and Humphrey in 1968) found it necessary to campaign very actively in the primaries. In most of these campaigns some measure of success in the primaries was essential to win the nomination. It is not clear whether Barry Goldwater, with his delegate strength in convention states, could have won in 1964 if he had lost California. Robert Kennedy's death denied us an opportunity to learn whether his primary victories in 1968 would have given him enough political strength to defeat Humphrey, whose delegates came from convention states. Despite the importance of primaries during this period, there is no candidate, except probably John Kennedy, who started the primary campaign as a complete underdog and won the nomination because he upset the front-runners in primaries.

The 1972 and 1976 primaries were different, in several respects. First, there was the sharp increase in the number of primaries, from 15 in 1968 to 23 in 1972 and 30 in 1976. This had the obvious consequence of making the primary campaign longer, more exhausting, more expensive, and more saturated by media coverage. It forced some change in the tactics of candidates because they were no longer able to devote long periods of time to campaigning in each of the states, but it did not lead them to reduce the proportion of states in which they chose to campaign. The increase in the number of primaries also meant that a much larger proportion of delegates was chosen in primary states. In the Democratic convention the proportion of delegates chosen in primary states increased from 40 percent in 1968 to two thirds in 1972 and three fourths in 1976. In the past, primaries had been important largely because of what they proved to party leaders around the country about who could win. Although this factor remained important, it now became possible for a candidate to capture the nomination directly by winning primaries.

In both 1972 and 1976 large numbers of Democratic candidates sought the nomination. The early primaries destroyed the hopes of many candidates, including Edmund Muskie, the front-runner in 1972, and Jackson, Bayh, and Wallace in 1976. Both times the nomination was won by a candidate who was almost unknown to the voters and ignored by the experts at the start of the primaries: George McGovern in 1972 and Jimmy Carter in 1976. Both men won pluralities in large numbers of primaries, developed momentum throughout the campaign, and worked skillfully in the convention states as well. McGovern's nomination divided the party so badly that he was swamped in the November election, but Carter's appeal to voters was much broader, and he emerged from the convention as the leader of a remarkably united party. In 1976 the primaries demonstrated President Ford's weakness, and Ronald Reagan's strength, as campaigners. In state after state the two men battled almost evenly for the support of primary

voters and state convention delegates. The advantages normally enjoyed by an incumbent president in convention states proved ineffective in the primaries. The result of this battle was a narrow victory
for Ford and a deeply divided party.

In 1972 and 1976 there were not only more primaries, but there was
much greater competition in those states where primaries had often
been empty arenas. Four large industrial states can serve as examples:
Pennsylvania, New Jersey, Illinois, and Ohio. In previous years the
political leaders had largely controlled the selection of delegates in
these states, with occasional exceptions. In the presidential preference
polls there was sometimes only one candidate running, or there were
no names on the ballot and only a few voters wrote in names, or—in
Ohio—the governor or another party leader headed an uncontested
slate as a favorite son. But all of these states had competition in the
1972 Democratic primary and in the primaries of both parties in
1976. No longer were the candidates and their local supporters willing
to give state and local party leaders a monopoly on the primaries that
restrained or eliminated competition. Almost every state primary in
1976 was an open battle between two or more of the leading candidates.[1]

A consequence of both the increasing number of primaries and the
more intensive level of competition was a sudden upsurge in the number of voters in state primaries where their presidential preference
could be clearly measured. After hovering around 11 or 12 million
for 5 elections, the total rose to 22 million in 1972 and 26 million in
1976. As a percentage of the general election presidential vote, the
primary vote had been gradually falling from over 20 percent to less
than 17 percent; it rose to 29 percent in 1972 and almost 33 percent in
1976.

## Voting turnout in presidential primaries

We discovered (in chap. 4) that the level of participation in gubernatorial primaries varies substantially from state to state. We would
expect variations also in presidential primary turnout, although the
reasons for such variations may not be entirely the same. The lower
the level of voting in presidential primaries, the greater the likelihood
that the state party organization can influence the outcome. On the
other hand, the higher the turnout, the more likely it is that the voters

---

[1] Descriptions and analysis of recent presidential primary campaigns can be
found in: Novak (1965), Hart (1973), Davis (1974), Stout (1970), White (1969, 1973),
and Hadley (1976).

are a representative sample of voters in the state and that the primary is actually a good measure of which candidate is most likely to carry the state if nominated.

The same difficulties that we encountered in measuring the gubernatorial turnout apply to presidential primaries; the major problem is to establish a base of comparison. Table 7–3 summarizes data on turnout in presidential primaries in given elections (1960–76) for nine states that have held presidential primaries in all or nearly all of these

**Table 7–3**
**Turnout in presidential primaries in states with closed primaries, 1960–1976**

| Year | Votes cast in presidential primaries (in thousands) and degree of contest* | | | Primary vote as percentage of registered vote | | Primary vote as percentage of presidential general election vote | | |
|---|---|---|---|---|---|---|---|---|
| | Dem. | Rep. | Total | Dem. | Rep. | Dem. | Rep. | Total |
| New Hampshire | | | | | | | | |
| 1960 .......... | 51 C | 73 C | 124 | | | 37 | 46 | 42 |
| 1964 .......... | 31 W | 94 C | 125 | 41 | 63 | 17 | 90 | 44 |
| 1968 .......... | 55 C | 104 C | 159 | 60 | 67 | 42 | 67 | 54 |
| 1972 .......... | 88 C | 117 C | 205 | 69 | 66 | 76 | 55 | 62 |
| 1976 .......... | 82 C | 112 C | 194 | 55 | 62 | 56 | 60 | 58 |
| Pennsylvania | | | | | | | | |
| 1960 .......... | 197 W | 987 U | 1,184 | 7 | 37 | 8 | 40 | 24 |
| 1964 .......... | 256 W | 451 C | 707 | 9 | 17 | 8 | 27 | 15 |
| 1968 .......... | 595 C | 287 C | 882 | 22 | 10 | 26 | 14 | 19 |
| 1972 .......... | 1,375 C | 184 W | 1,559 | 49 | 7 | 77 | 9 | 40 |
| 1976 .......... | 1,385 C | 797 U | 2,182 | 49 | 35 | 60 | 36 | 48 |
| West Virginia | | | | | | | | |
| 1960 .......... | 389 C | 123 U | 512 | 60 | 32 | 82 | 31 | 61 |
| 1964 .......... | 131 U | 115 U | 246 | 20 | 30 | 24 | 45 | 31 |
| 1968 .......... | 149 U | 81 U | 230 | 23 | 23 | 40 | 26 | 30 |
| 1972 .......... | 369 C | 96 U | 465 | 55 | 27 | 133 | 20 | 61 |
| 1976 .......... | 372 C | 156 C | 528 | 53 | 46 | 87 | 50 | 71 |
| Maryland | | | | | | | | |
| 1960 .......... | 287 C | — | 287 | 33 | — | 51 | — | — |
| 1964 .......... | 502 C | 98 | 600 | 53 | 27 | 69 | 25 | 54 |
| 1968 .......... | — | — | — | — | — | — | — | — |
| 1972 .......... | 570 C | 115 C | 685 | 45 | 24 | 113 | 14 | 51 |
| 1976 .......... | 592 C | 166 C | 758 | 44 | 35 | 81 | 25 | 55 |
| Florida | | | | | | | | |
| 1960 .......... | 322 U | 51 U | 373 | 19 | 15 | 43 | 6 | 24 |
| 1964 .......... | 393 U | 101 C | 494 | 20 | 22 | 41 | 11 | 27 |
| 1968 .......... | 512 C | 51 U | 563 | 24 | 8 | 76 | 6 | 26 |
| 1972 .......... | 1,265 C | 414 C | 1,679 | 53 | 42 | 176 | 22 | 65 |
| 1976 .......... | 1,300 C | 610 C | 1,910 | 47 | 54 | 83 | 44 | 65 |
| Nebraska | | | | | | | | |
| 1960 .......... | 90 U | 79 W | 169 | | | 39 | 21 | 28 |
| 1964 .......... | 61 W | 139 C | 200 | | | 20 | 50 | 34 |
| 1968 .......... | 163 C | 200 C | 363 | 56 | 61 | 95 | 62 | 68 |
| 1972 .......... | 193 C | 194 C | 387 | 60 | 53 | 114 | 48 | 67 |
| 1976 .......... | 175 C | 208 C | 383 | 49 | 55 | 76 | 59 | 66 |

**Table 7–3—(continued)**

| Year | Votes cast in presidential primaries (in thousands) and degree of contest* | | | Primary vote as percentage of registered vote | | Primary vote as percentage of presidential general election vote | | |
|---|---|---|---|---|---|---|---|---|
| | Dem. | Rep. | Total | Dem. | Rep. | Dem. | Rep. | Total |
| South Dakota | | | | | | | | |
| 1960 .......... | 25 U | 48 U | 73 | | | 20 | 27 | 24 |
| 1964 .......... | 28 U | 85 U | 113 | | | 17 | 65 | 39 |
| 1968 .......... | 64 C | 68 U | 132 | 53 | 39 | 54 | 45 | 47 |
| 1972 .......... | 28 U | 53 U | 81 | 18 | 27 | 20 | 32 | 26 |
| 1976 .......... | 59 C | 84 C | 143 | 33 | 44 | 40 | 56 | 48 |
| Oregon | | | | | | | | |
| 1960 .......... | 286 C | 227 U | 513 | 59 | 56 | 78 | 56 | 66 |
| 1964 .......... | 273 U | 284 C | 557 | 53 | 71 | 54 | 100 | 71 |
| 1968 .......... | 373 C | 312 C | 685 | 70 | 74 | 104 | 76 | 84 |
| 1972 .......... | 408 C | 282 C | 690 | 61 | 59 | 104 | 58 | 78 |
| 1976 .......... | 433 C | 299 C | 732 | 58 | 63 | 89 | 62 | 75 |
| California | | | | | | | | |
| 1960 .......... | 2,000 C | 1,518 U | 3,518 | 47 | 52 | 62 | 47 | 54 |
| 1964 .......... | 2,492 C | 2,172 C | 4,664 | 53 | 68 | 60 | 75 | 66 |
| 1968 .......... | 3,181 C | 1,525 C | 4,706 | 68 | 44 | 98 | 44 | 65 |
| 1972 .......... | 3,563 C | 2,284 C | 5,847 | 64 | 62 | 77 | 50 | 73 |
| 1976 .......... | 3,374 C | 2,336 C | 5,710 | 65 | 72 | 91 | 61 | 76 |

* C = Contested races, with two or more serious candidates or slates; U = uncontested races, with only one serious candidate or slate; W = write-in race, in which no candidates are listed on ballot but names are written in.

years and in which party registration is a prerequisite for voting in the primaries. In this table we have compared the vote cast in the Democratic and Republican presidential primaries with the registered vote for each party, where that figure is available. We have also compared it with the vote cast for that party's presidential candidate in the November election, and compared the combined vote in the two primaries with the total presidential vote. Table 7–4 provides the same data (except for the comparison with party registration) for eight other states. All except Massachusetts are ones where a voter does not need to be registered with a party to vote in the primary; in some states he may request a ballot of either party, and in others he can keep his party preference secret while voting. Massachusetts is included with this group because the large number of independents in that state can vote in either party's primary.[2] All but two of these states have held primaries in all five elections.

---

[2] New Hampshire, like Massachusetts, permits an independent to claim party membership on the day of a primary and vote in that party's primary. Perhaps arbitrarily, we have listed New Hampshire in the category of closed-primary states because there seems to be less evidence that there are many independents who do vote in a party primary. In both states, however, an independent must give up that independent status, at least temporarily, to vote in a party primary.

**Table 7–4**
**Turnout in presidential primaries in states with open primaries, 1960–1976**

| Year | Votes cast in presidential primaries (in thousands) and degree of contest* | | | Primary vote as percentage of presidential general election vote | | |
|---|---|---|---|---|---|---|
| | Dem. | Rep. | Total | Dem. | Rep. | Total |
| **Illinois** | | | | | | |
| 1960 ............. | 53 W | 783 U | 836 | 2 | 33 | 18 |
| 1964 ............. | 90 W | 828 C | 918 | 3 | 43 | 20 |
| 1968 ............. | 12 W | 22 W | 34 | 1 | 1 | 1 |
| 1972 ............. | 1,225 C | 34 W | 1,259 | 64 | 1 | 27 |
| 1976 ............. | 1,312 C | 776 C | 2,088 | 59 | 33 | 46 |
| **Wisconsin** | | | | | | |
| 1960 ............. | 843 C | 339 U | 1,182 | 101 | 38 | 68 |
| 1964 ............. | 789 C | 300 U | 1,089 | 75 | 47 | 65 |
| 1968 ............. | 734 C | 490 C | 1,224 | 98 | 60 | 73 |
| 1972 ............. | 1,130 C | 289 C | 1,419 | 140 | 29 | 79 |
| 1976 ............. | 740 C | 592 C | 1,332 | 71 | 59 | 65 |
| **Indiana** | | | | | | |
| 1960 ............. | 437 C | 428 U | 865 | 46 | 36 | 41 |
| 1964 ............. | 579 C | 400 C | 979 | 49 | 44 | 47 |
| 1968 ............. | 777 C | 508 U | 1,285 | 96 | 48 | 61 |
| 1972 ............. | 751 C | 417 U | 1,168 | 106 | 30 | 55 |
| 1976 ............. | 614 C | 632 C | 1,246 | 61 | 54 | 57 |
| **Ohio** | | | | | | |
| 1960 ............. | 315 U | 504 U | 819 | 16 | 23 | 20 |
| 1964 ............. | 494 U | 616 U | 1,110 | 20 | 42 | 28 |
| 1968 ............. | 549 U | 615 U | 1,164 | 32 | 34 | 29 |
| 1972 ............. | 1,212 C | 693 U | 1,905 | 78 | 28 | 48 |
| 1976 ............. | 1,118 C | 936 C | 2,054 | 56 | 47 | 51 |
| **New Jersey** | | | | | | |
| 1960 ............. | 218 U | 305 U | 523 | 16 | 22 | 19 |
| 1964 ............. | 6 W | 18 W | 24 | — | 2 | 1 |
| 1968 ............. | 28 W | 89 W | 117 | 2 | 7 | 4 |
| 1972 ............. | 76 C | 216 U | 292 | 7 | 12 | 10 |
| 1976 ............. | 361 C | 242 U | 603 | 25 | 16 | 21 |
| **Michigan** | | | | | | |
| 1972 ............. | 1,588 C | 337 C | 1,925 | 109 | 17 | 56 |
| 1976 ............. | 709 C | 1,063 C | 1,772 | 42 | 56 | 50 |
| **Tennessee** | | | | | | |
| 1972 ............. | 494 C | 115 C | 609 | 138 | 14 | 52 |
| 1976 ............. | 334 C | 243 C | 577 | 41 | 38 | 40 |
| **Massachusetts** | | | | | | |
| 1960 ............. | 100 W | 61 W | 161 | 7 | 6 | 7 |
| 1964 ............. | 83 W | 92 W | 175 | 5 | 17 | 7 |
| 1968 ............. | 249 C | 106 C | 355 | 17 | 14 | 15 |
| 1972 ............. | 619 C | 122 C | 741 | 46 | 11 | 30 |
| 1976 ............. | 736 C | 188 C | 924 | 52 | 18 | 38 |

Note: Massachusetts is included because, although it is generally a closed primary state, independents can vote in either primary, and the state has a large proportion of independents.

* C = Contested races, with two or more serious candidates or slates; U = uncontested races, with only one serious candidate or slate; W = write-in race, in which no candidates are listed on ballot but names are written in.

The first conclusion to be drawn from these tables is that turnout varies with the level of competition. We have noted three levels of competition in both tables: write-ins (W), uncontested (U), and contested (C). A write-in primary is one in which there are no candidates listed on a primary preference ballot, and the turnout figures are based on the numbers of voters who write in the names of candidates. Not surprisingly, in such primaries the turnout is usually very low. (If convention delegates are chosen simultaneously, turnout may be larger for these races, but statewide data on that voting are not usually available.) We define uncontested primaries as ones in which there is only a single candidate or slate on the ballot (or only one that can be considered seriously competitive). Occasionally other names are written in, but we have not classified such contests as competitive unless there is a major write-in campaign. Contested races are ones with two or more serious candidates or slates, whether or not the race is close.

Turnout tends to be lower when there is a single candidate running and higher when there is a contest, particularly a close race between major candidates. Occasionally uncontested races produce a high turnout. In 1960 almost a million Republicans voted for Richard Nixon in the uncontested Pennsylvania primary (40 percent of the total who voted for Nixon in November); the same year in California one and a half million voted for Nixon, running unopposed (47 percent of the November vote). But in most states primary turnout has been higher (measured in absolute figures or as a percentage of the general election vote) in those years when there were competitive races. A good example is Nebraska, where primary turnout (as a percentage of the party's general election vote) was about 20 percent in write-in races, 39 percent in one uncontested race, and averaged 74 percent in 5 contested races.

The data on primary turnout are summarized in Table 7–5, where the 15 states that have had primaries since at least 1960 are listed roughly in order of turnout. Several points are clear from the table. The states in which turnout is highest (compared to the general election vote) are ones in which the primaries are most often contested. Most of these states (such as Oregon, Wisconsin, California, and New Hampshire) are ones which in recent years have held several highly publicized primaries that have had an important impact on the presidential nomination. The states at the bottom of the list have had fewer contested primaries, sometimes because of efforts by party organizations to prevent competition and to control the outcome. They include states like Ohio, Pennsylvania, Illinois, and New Jersey, with relatively strong party organizations.

**Table 7–5**
**Summary of turnout in presidential primaries in 15 states, 1960–1976**

| State | Average turnout in both party primaries as percentage of general election vote | Number of competitive primaries, both parties (out of 10) | Average turnout in each party primary as percentage of its general election vote, only competitive primaries | Average turnout in each party primary as percentage of its gubernatorial primary vote, only when both are contested |
|---|---|---|---|---|
| Oreg. | 74.8 | 8 | 83.9 | 143.3 |
| Wis. | 70.0 | 8 | 79.1 | 265.8 |
| Calif. | 66.8 | 9 | 68.7 | 113.4 |
| Md. | 53.3 | 7 | 54.0 | 111.7 |
| Neb. | 52.6 | 7 | 72.0 | 123.5 |
| Ind. | 52.2 | 7 | 65.1 | — |
| N.H. | 52.0 | 9 | 58.7 | 137.6 |
| W.Va. | 50.8 | 4 | 88.0 | 101.3 |
| Fla. | 41.4 | 6 | 68.7 | 114.4 |
| S. Dak. | 36.8 | 4 | 53.8 | 92.0 |
| Ohio | 35.2 | 3 | 60.3 | 129.0 |
| Pa. | 29.2 | 5 | 40.8 | 92.6 |
| Ill. | 22.4 | 4 | 49.8 | 90.5 |
| Mass. | 19.4 | 6 | 34.2 | 78.5 |
| N.J. | 11.0 | 2 | 16.0 | 19.0 |

Table 7–5 also shows that, with a few exceptions, the states rank in the same order if turnout is measured only for the contested primaries. In those states where contests are less frequent, voters get out of the habit of voting and are less likely to go to the polls even when there is a closely contested primary. West Virginia and Ohio are exceptions; both had very heavy turnout on the few occasions when there were contests. Finally, the last column of Table 7–5 compares turnout in contested presidential and gubernatorial primaries. In states where presidential turnout is high, compared to the general election vote, it is also higher than turnout for contested gubernatorial primaries, sometimes much higher (in such states as Wisconsin, Oregon, and New Hampshire). Where presidential primary turnout is low, it is slightly lower than gubernatorial primary turnout. The states that rank high in presidential primary turnout do not, as a group, rank high in gubernatorial primary turnout (see Chapter 4).

In the nine states listed in Table 7–3, where participation is limited to voters registered with the party, it is possible to compare turnout to party registration. The much higher turnout in contested than in uncontested primaries remains evident when registration is the basis for comparison. In most of the states there are relatively small differences in the proportions of registered Democrats and of registered Republicans who vote in those presidential primaries that are contested. One exception is Maryland, where the turnout is much higher in Democratic primaries (even though registration is heavily Democratic). A similar contrast in Pennsylvania is probably caused by less closely contested primaries in the Republican party. In California there have been some sharp contrasts between parties in the proportion of registered members voting in these primaries, but they have not consistently favored one party.

A recent study by Morris and Davis (1975) examined the factors associated with high turnout in presidential primaries for these nine states in 1964, 1968, and 1972, using party registration as the basis of comparison. Their findings, based on careful statistical analysis of a smaller number of primaries, confirm our findings that competition is highest in contested primaries, less in uncontested ones, and least in those with only write-in voting. They also found that the larger the number of candidates on the ballot, the larger the turnout, and that this factor was more important than the number who actively campaigned. Democratic primaries with closer outcomes had higher turnout than one-sided contests in that party; and Democratic winner-take-all contests had higher turnout than other forms of primary, but that method was not permitted in Democratic primaries beginning in 1976. Turnout was not affected by differences in state law concerning whether delegates were bound by the outcomes of preference polls—perhaps because voters were not generally familiar with such technicalities.

One way of putting the turnout in presidential primaries into perspective is to compare it with the number of voters who participate in mass meetings at the precinct, county, or other levels to choose delegates for district and state conventions where this method is used for selecting delegates to national conventions. For obvious reasons, it is difficult to measure exactly how many persons do participate in such local meetings, but estimates have been compiled for Democratic meetings in a number of states in both 1972 and 1976, years in which the Democratic nomination was highly contested and party rules were designed to facilitate participation. The absolute numbers of participants were consistently low, often less than 20,000. There are a few states in which the turnout at caucuses in one or both years was from 10 percent to 16 percent of the Democratic presidential vote cast in November: Mississippi, South Carolina, Oklahoma, Washington, and Minnesota. In the remaining states the caucus turnout was less than 10 percent of presidential vote and often as low as 2 percent to 5 percent: Iowa, Maine, Hawaii, Wyoming, Missouri, New Mexico, Colorado, Nevada, North Dakota, and Virginia. In states with party registration data available, caucus turnout was usually only a few percent of that total.[3]

By contrast, Tables 7–3 and 7–5 show that turnout in contested primaries has usually been between 50 percent and 80 percent of the general election presidential vote and is usually between 40 percent and two thirds of the party registration. Another way of illustrating the difference is to look at states that adopted the primary for the first time in 1976. In Vermont, turnout in the 1972 Democratic meetings was estimated at 2,500; it rose to 38,700 in the 1976 Democratic primary. In Nevada the increase was from 4,000 to 75,200. In Georgia the increase was from 20,000 in 1972 to over 500,000 in 1976. Obviously in states without a presidential primary the nominating process can be controlled either by the party organization or by other groups that are able to mobilize relatively modest numbers of voters.

### Crossover voting in primaries

Earlier in this book (chapter 4), we discussed the problem of analyzing primary turnout in those states where the laws permit voters to participate in the primary of either party without any requirements for party registration. Voters in a number of states holding presidential primaries have a similar freedom of choice. In some states, such as Wisconsin, the voter need not disclose which primary he is voting in; in other states, including several in the South, he may ask for a ballot for either party, subject only to loosely enforced rules about affirming that he has voted or will vote for that party. The existence of laws permitting voters to shift from one presidential primary to the other every four years does not mean that voters are actually doing this in large numbers. Estimating how much crossover voting occurs is a difficult and imprecise business. The term *crossover voting,* although commonly used, is misleading because it suggests votes being cast in one party's primary by voters who are clearly identified with the other party and normally vote in its primaries. But open primaries also permit voters who are independent or have no strong identification

---

[3] Figures for turnout in the 1972 Democratic caucuses come from the Coalition for a Democratic Majority Task Force on Democratic Party Rules and Structure, which issued a report, "Toward Fairness and Unity for '76," Appendix C. The data for the 1976 Democratic caucuses were compiled by the *Congressional Quarterly,* which kindly made them available to us.

with a party to shift back and forth between primaries over a period of years.

In 1976 13 of the states holding presidential primaries permitted voting in them without requiring party registration, but in a very few of these it is possible to estimate the extent of crossover voting. In eight of these, one or more factors prevented an analysis: the lack of a direct vote measuring presidential preferences, low turnout limited to write-in votes, and the fact that 1976 was the first year in which some state presidential primaries were held, or the first year in which primaries were open. Massachusetts, which permits independents as well as those registered with a party to vote in a party's primary, had contested primaries only in 1968, 1972, and 1976, and in each year a very large proportion of the turnout was in the Democratic primary.

We will briefly examine Michigan and Tennessee, states with primaries only in 1972 and 1976, and Indiana, Ohio, and Wisconsin, states with longer records of primaries (see Table 7–4). If an examination of aggregate data shows that from one presidential primary to the next there is a large shift in turnout between the two parties (measured in absolute terms or as a percentage of total turnout or of the party's general election vote), we can reasonably conclude that some of this shift is caused by voters going from one primary to the other. This might be most likely to occur under one or both of two conditions: if one primary was more closely contested or was generally recognized as more crucial to the nominating campaign than the other, or if one of the candidates competing in one primary was unusually popular with a segment of voters in the other party. We must recognize, however, that presidential turnout may vary from one fourth to three fourths of the general election voters, depending very much on the level of competition. In other words, large variations from year to year in the proportion of voters choosing the Republican or Democratic primary could be largely or even entirely the result of voters' choosing whether or not to vote, rather than choosing between primaries.

The data regarding turnout in crossover primary states in recent years are shown in Table 7–4. Although Tennessee and Michigan held primaries only in 1972 and 1976, both states show great shifts in party turnout from one primary election to the next. Tennessee is a state in which Democratic party loyalties have been eroded in recent years to the benefit of the Republican party and in 1968 the Wallace candidacy. In 1972 the Democratic primary was more closely contested, and won by Wallace; turnout was concentrated in that primary. In 1976, with Wallace's strength shrunk, Carter dominating the Democratic primary, and a very close Republican contest between Ford and Reagan, Democratic turnout dropped and Republican primary turnout more than doubled. The contrast between 1972 and 1976 is even more dramatic in Michigan, where the two-party balance is quite close and turnout in the two parties' gubernatorial primaries has been fairly close over a period of years. In 1972 the Democratic presidential primary turnout was much higher than it had ever been in gubernatorial primaries, undoubtedly because George Wallace, who won the primary, attracted many Republican and independent voters. Four years later, with Wallace a minor factor and with a highly important battle occurring in the Republican party, Democratic turnout was less than half of the 1972 figure, while Republican turnout more than tripled. Independents and probably some Democrats had entered the Republican primary. A *New York Times* sample survey (May 19, 1976) in Michigan showed that in 1976 half of those who had voted in the Democratic primary for Wallace four years earlier and who were at the polls again stayed in the Democratic primary and half chose the Republican primary (two thirds of these voting for Reagan). About half of all those in the Republican primary identified themselves as Republicans, 15 percent as Democrats, and the rest as independents.

Indiana is a state in which voters can choose which presidential primary to vote in, but the data show a remarkable consistency in primary voting patterns, with the Democratic primary attracting from 49 percent to 64 percent of the voters in five elections, even though three of the Republican primaries were uncontested. This consistency may result in part from the fact that primaries are held at the same time for many important state and local offices, even though gubernatorial and senatorial candidates were not chosen in primaries until 1976. Ohio is another state in which the voters have a free choice, but there is little evidence of shifting between primaries. In the 1960, 1964, and 1968 primaries neither party had contests, and so there was no incentive for shifting. In 1972, when only the Democrats had a contest, the Democratic primary did attract an unusually large vote, probably some of it from Republicans.

Wisconsin is an interesting state in which to analyze crossover voting. The state had contested, and often very important, primaries from 1960 through 1972, with a turnout that was consistently higher in the Democratic than the Republican primary—where primaries were usually either uncontested or at least not very close. Democratic presidential primary turnout was also very much heavier than usually occurred in contested Democratic gubernatorial primaries. In 1972, with Wallace in the running, the Democratic primary attracted 80 percent of the total primary turnout, a record for recent years. In 1976, with the Republicans having a close contest for a change, Republican turnout more than doubled in absolute terms and rose to 45 percent of the total primary turnout.

The aggregate data analysis in Wisconsin can be supplemented by survey data, collected by the Research Laboratory of the University of Wisconsin at Madison (Adamany, 1976) for the 1964, 1968, and 1972 elections and collected by the *New York Times* for the 1976 election. In the elections from 1964 through 1972, about 10 percent of those voting in each primary described themselves as independents; from 16 percent to 22 percent of those in the Democratic primary identified as Republicans; and from 4 percent to 14 percent of those in the Republican primary identified as Democrats. Clearly more Republicans participated in Democratic primaries (which had more contests) than the reverse, but the data do not adequately explain or reflect the Democratic primary turnout surge in 1972. According to the *New York Times* survey in 1976 (April 8), a high proportion (58 percent) of those in the Democratic primary identified as independents, and another 8 percent were Republicans.

Although the data for all four elections confirm that a substantial proportion of those voting in each party's primaries do not identify with that party, they provide no clues to the amount of shifting that occurs, because respondents were not asked which primary they had voted in four years earlier. The surveys also confirm that those who identify with a party often vote differently from those otherwise identified who vote in that primary. In all three years he was on the Democratic primary ballot, 1964, 1972, and 1976, George Wallace did much better among Republicans than among other groups. Eugene McCarthy in 1968 also did better among Republicans in the Democratic primary. Interestingly, Jimmy Carter in 1976 did almost equally well among all three groups of voters in the Democratic primary (Adamany, 1976; *New York Times*, April 8, 1976).

In recent years there has been not only a rapid increase in the number of states holding presidential primaries, but an increase in the amount of competition and voter turnout in those states that have had primaries for a number of years. The consequence has been a decrease in the state party organization's ability to control the selection of delegates to national conventions. As the presidential nominating campaigns have grown both more intensive and more extensive, state party leaders have found it impossible to isolate their states from these campaigns by using favorite sons or uncommitted delegations as a way of avoiding primary competition. In several states the laws have been changed to permit the names of presidential candidates to appear directly on the ballot or to bind delegates to the choice made in a presidential preference poll. We have seen that contested primaries, particularly contests between major candidates, lead to substantial increases in voter turnout, a development that further undermines the influence of the party organization. The adoption of the presidential primary in states that do not require registration by party reduces the party organization's influence even further by allowing independents and voters loyal to the other party to vote in the primary and possibly to play a decisive role in determining its outcome. In short, all of the major trends in presidential primaries that have occurred in recent years have reduced the influence of state party organizations on the presidential nomination.

### Format and timing of primaries

We have been concerned with the effects of the procedures and turnout in presidential primaries on the influence of party organizations within the state. It is not often recognized that the format and timing of a state's primary help to determine how much impact that state has on the national nominating process. An analysis of the 1972 Democratic primaries by Lengle and Shafer (1976) examines the effect of three types of primary laws used by states that year: a statewide winner-take–all system, a proportional division of delegates based on the statewide vote, and a district plan under which the candidate with the most votes in each district wins all the delegates there. The authors point out that

as long as top state party officials could select and direct their delegations, a state's power at the Convention faithfully reflected the size and Democratic-vote criteria. The bigger the state, the more claim it could have on potential nominees. The more reliably Democratic the state, the more muscle it could throw behind its choice (Lengle and Shafer, 1976: 32).

The winner-take-all system is the only one that maintains the power of the large, urban, industrial states, because it allows their delegations to cast a large bloc vote for a single candidate. A proportional system breaks up that bloc vote and gives an advantage to states that may be relatively small but that give a large margin in the primary to one candidate. In somewhat similar fashion, a district system fragments the vote, at least in those states where a variety of candidates have enough local strength to win a plurality vote in one or more districts. On the basis of the 1972 primaries, the authors concluded that the increasing use of proportional and district plans would weaken the influence of northeastern parties, while strengthening those in the Midwest, West, Border, and South. There is no certainty, however, that primary competition would be greatest and the votes most fragmented in the same states in every election year.

In 1972, as in previous years, the states were free to choose the type of primary they wanted, but since then the national Democratic party has narrowed the range of choice for state Democratic parties. The statewide winner-take-all system was banned prior to the 1976 primaries, and at the 1976 convention the district winner-take-all system was eliminated for the future. Now the states are limited in choice to using the proportional system on a statewide basis or on a district basis. Under either system, the influence of the large states is reduced unless a single candidate captures a large proportion of the primary vote. The national Republican party has continued to permit winner-take-all systems, and consequently some state legislatures—as we have mentioned—have flexible laws permitting the two state parties to choose their delegates on different bases.

The influence of state parties on the nomination is also affected by the timing of the primaries. Because timing has a psychological effect on the nominating campaign, rather than a mathematic effect on convention delegations, its effect is hard to measure. Some of the states that traditionally hold their primaries early, notably New Hampshire and Wisconsin, have played major roles in the rise and fall of prospective candidates. The momentum that is generated by early victories can be of critical importance for candidacies like those of McGovern in 1972 and Carter in 1976. A candidate who does poorly in the early primaries, like Muskie or Lindsay in 1972 or Bayh or Shriver in 1976, may find that his candidacy has come to a halt without having ever gotten off the ground. Voters in the early primaries usually have a larger number of candidates to choose from; those in the later primaries may be restricted to a few whose candidacies are still viable.

From the viewpoint of state party leaders, there are costs and benefits associated with both early and late primaries. In a state with an early primary the state leaders have the maximum opportunity to influence the nomination and to become allied with a winner early in his campaign; they run the risk of becoming committed to someone whose candidacy has expired by the time the convention meets. Party leaders in late-primary states have fewer opportunities to influence outcomes (unless the contest is very close), but they also have a better chance of picking a winner. Whether state leaders prefer an early or late primary may well depend on whether they want to be king-makers or just supporters of the right king.

In recent years there has been something of a scramble among states to launch the primary season. For many years the New Hampshire primary was held in early March, and no others were scheduled until early April. In 1976 five other states established primaries in March, including Illinois and Massachusetts, which moved up their April primaries, and Florida, which in 1972 moved ahead its late May primary. New Hampshire responded by scheduling its 1976 primary on February 24 and passing a law that the New Hampshire primary would be held one week ahead of the earliest date set by any other state. But many of the states establishing primaries for the first time in 1972 or 1976 scheduled them for May or June. Legislative decisions about scheduling presidential primaries are not necessarily based on the desire to maximize influence on the nomination. In the case of a state like New Hampshire, the goal seems to be to attract public attention. In many states presidential primaries coincide with primaries for other offices, very few of which are held before May.

## The national nominating process

Up until now we have been concentrating on the effects that changes in the presidential nominating process have had on state political parties and on the power of party leaders. Now we want to turn that question around and ask how the presidential nominating process is affected by the variety of laws, procedures, and practices that are followed by the states and state parties. In the past the control exercised by party leaders over most state delegations meant that, if there was no obvious presidential candidate—such as an incumbent —national convention decisions were often made by these leaders, the power brokers who bargained among themselves and with candidates. The winner-take-all system used in most states enhanced the power of large states and forced the candidates to appeal to those interests that were dominant in the large states.

Congress has never exercised its authority over presidential nominations by adopting a national primary or by imposing any restrictions on state primary laws, although it has had an impact on the nominating campaign by authorizing matching federal funds to help

pay for it. In the absence of federal legislation, the states have determined whether and when to hold primaries, what kinds of primaries
to establish, and what restrictions, if any, to impose on the selection
of delegates in conventions. Most of the recent changes in the rules
and procedures for primaries have resulted from requirements of the
national Democratic party, specifying that delegates be selected in
proportion to votes cast rather than on a winner-take-all basis. Moreover, the increasingly complicated rules established by the national
Democratic party for selecting delegates by conventions and caucuses
may have contributed to the shift of many states to presidential primaries. Some states have amended their primary laws to make both
state parties conform to the Democratic rules; other have permitted
the two parties to follow different rules, each in conformity to their
national party requirements.

Despite the nationalizing effect of national Democratic party rules,
much variation remains in state primary rules and practices. This
variety, and the tactics used by candidates to adjust to it, have a number of important consequences for the nominating process. The long
time span of the primary season results, of course, from state legislative decisions. Because there is little geographic concentration of primaries held at one time, candidates must expend time and resources
flying back and forth across the country. (One proposal for national
legislation would be to set up a series of regional primaries, so that
a state that wanted to hold a primary would have to schedule it on the
day set aside for primaries in that region.)

During the 1950s and 1960s Florida was the only southern state
holding a presidential primary, and consequently the primary system
was biased against not only southerners but also other candidates
who might appeal particularly to southern voters. Ronald Reagan's
campaign in 1976 was seriously damaged by the fact that he lost eight
of the first nine primaries (from February 24 to April 27). Except for
Florida and North Carolina, all of these were in the Northeast or Midwest. Most of the southern and all of the western primaries were held
in May and June, and Reagan won most of them. But he was under
intensive pressure to drop out of the race in March and April because
only his areas of weakness and not his areas of strength had held primary elections during this period. Had he succumbed to this pressure,
the history of the 1976 Republican nomination contest would have been
quite different.

Probably the legal aspect of state primary laws that has the greatest
potential for affecting presidential nominations concerns the eligi-

bility of voters. Any state that does not require voters to be registered
with a party makes it possible for the outcome of a presidential primary to be determined by voters from outside that party—either independents or those identified with the other party. We indicated earlier
that it is difficult to measure the extent of so-called crossover voting,
but there are a few examples of primaries in which it appears to have
had a significant effect on the outcome. In 1972 it seems clear that
George Wallace picked up a substantial vote from Republican and
independent voters in the Democratic primaries in Wisconsin and
Michigan at least. In 1976 Ronald Reagan benefited most from Wallace's weakness and apparently picked up votes from many persons
who had previously voted in Democratic presidential primaries in such
states as Wisconsin, Michigan, Tennessee, and perhaps other southern
states. The national Democratic party tried to pressure state parties
into seeking state legislation to ban crossover voting under the threat
of not recognizing delegates chosen in such primaries, but the effort
was unsuccessful. One of the obstacles to adoption of a national primary is presumably the necessity of imposing uniform eligibility requirements for participation.

One of the less obvious consequences of the present system under
which the focus of the nominating campaign shifts each week from
one set of two or three states to another concers state and local issues.
If an important primary is being held in a state where a particular
issue is salient, the outcome of the primary may depend heavily on
the stand taken by candidates on that issue. Thus, busing dominated
the Florida and Michigan primaries in 1972 and influenced the Massachusetts primary four years later. It is possible that some of the candidates will become committed to a stand on a particular issue early in
the campaign because of its importance in a few states, perhaps to
the detriment of their subsequent campaigns. On the other hand, as
the number of states holding primaries increases, it becomes less
likely that an issue dominant in just one or two states will make much
impact on the campaign. There is another related point that deserves
mention. It appears that some voters use the presidential primaries
not so much to affect the choice of a nominee but, in the words of
George Wallace, "to send them a message." In other words, some
voters cast a protest vote, to show the strength of sentiment against
busing or abortion, for example. The votes cast in several state primaries in 1976 for Ellen McCormick, the anti-abortion candidate, are
a good example. Whether such protest voting would be less frequent
if a national primary were held is difficult to predict. But it is clear

that delegates chosen in primaries are more likely to reflect a protest vote than are those selected by party leaders.

No two presidential nominating campaigns are alike, but some of the more familiar patterns in recent years illustrate how the candidates have adjusted to the complex, varied system of independent state primaries. The candidates have a great deal of flexibility in determining which primaries to enter and in which to campaign actively. In some states the candidates must take the initiative to get on the ballot; in others active candidates are put on the ballot by state officials but can withdraw. In any event, the candidate may campaign vigorously in the state, or may avoid a campaign and thus claim that he should not be judged by the results in that state. As a result, of course, not every state primary is a test among all of the significant candidates. The candidates also have the opportunity to predict in advance what their prospects are, to discount anticipated losses, and—like a football coach making dire predictions before the big game—to claim a moral or psychological victory in the face of defeat. Because the press and other expert observers play the same game of predictions, it sometimes does not matter so much who wins the primary as who does better or worse than expected. As the primary season goes on, however, such psychological victories assume less importance and the actual delegate count assumes more importance. In 1976 Jimmy Carter suffered defeats in several primaries late in the campaign that might have been fatal to the front-runner at an earlier stage, but—under the proportional and districting systems used for distributing delegates—each defeat brought his delegate count closer to the needed majority.

Perhaps the most significant difference between a national presidential primary and a state-by-state season of primaries is that victory under the latter systems depends very heavily on momentum. The candidate who, like McGovern in 1972 or Carter 1976, starts out as an underdog, wins more than expected in the earily primaries, and begins to accumulate pluralities and occasional majorities as the primary campaign continues—this is the candidate who can win the nomination. The underdog who fails to generate substantial support in one of the early primaries fades into oblivion very quickly. The candidate who is perceived as a front-runner at the start carries a very heavy burden because he is expected to win and his failure to do so in early primaries can put his candidacy into a very fast tailspin.

Recent primary campaigns have demonstrated that, unless he is very well known (like an incumbent President), a candidate must devote enormous amounts of time campaigning in individual states—

particularly those with early primaries. Jimmy Carter demonstrated in 1976 the advantages of holding no public office, because a candidate could devote full time to a campaign without being accused of neglecting his official duties. As the number of primary states has increased, it would seem logical that the importance of campaigning in individual states would decline—simply because it would become impossible to organize every precinct and shake hands with every voter in every primary state. But the candidates have dealt with that problem by starting sooner. It has become common for serious candidates, and some not so serious, to start intensive campaigning a year and a half or more before the national conventions. Some of those who fell by the wayside in the 1976 Democratic campaign, such as Birch Bayh, were ones whose active campaigns were too little and too late, who failed to devote enough time and resources to the early primaries where they had to do well to survive. But even Jimmy Carter, who started early and campaigned exhaustively in almost every primary state, discovered late in the primary campaign that his resources were spread too thin and he was vulnerable to strong opponents who concentrated in a few states.

The primaries are vulnerable to criticism on a number of grounds, some of which would remain valid in a national primary and some of which are a product of the present system. In all states the primary ballot provides voters with only an opportunity to indicate their first choice, and not a rank ordering of choices. Two of the strongest vote getters in the 1972 Democratic primary, McGovern and Wallace, aroused the intense opposition of large proportions of Democrats; McGovern was, and Wallace would have been, a weak candidate in the November election. Although the nomination campaign is long and growing longer, and is publicized by the media, it does not acquaint most voters very quickly with the policy positions of the candidates. When a new candidate like McGovern or Carter appears on the scene, the voters begin to develop an image of him that is dominated by personality, while the media devote more attention to his electoral prospects than to his program. Survey data support the impression that Eugene McCarthy in 1968 and George McGovern in 1972 won votes in early primaries from persons who knew little about their policies. As their issue positions became better known, both (but particularly McGovern) began to lose popular support.

It has frequently been argued that the present primary system forces candidates to recruit large numbers of volunteer workers and attract millions of voters by building a constituency that is relatively narrow but intensely loyal. McGovern, it was said, recruited his workers and many of his voters from the young, the disaffected, the opponents of the Vietnam War, the radicals; but it was these followers who helped create an image of him as a radical—too radical for large numbers of Democratic voters to accept. A similar analysis has been applied to Goldwater's success in winning the 1964 Republican nomination, though his victory was based much more heavily on state conventions than on primaries.

In the last analysis, the primary-dominated nomination process must be judged, not by its popularity with the media or even the breadth of its participation, but by its success in selecting the strongest candidate available to the party—the one most likely to win. McGovern was a creature of the primaries; without his string of ever more impressive victories he would never have become a serious candidate. His disastrous defeat in the November election led many observers to conclude that the new emphasis on primaries was destroying the effectiveness of the nominating process. In 1976 there were more primaries than ever, and Jimmy Carter owed his nomination very largely to his success in them. But his primary successes were built on much broader foundations, and he led a remarkably united party into the November election. Meanwhile, Republicans were learning in 1976 how damaging a bitterly divisive primary campaign can be to a party.

## CONGRESSIONAL ELECTIONS

The offices of U.S. Representative and Senator are unique. They bridge the gaps of federalism in the American political system. They are national offices, but are elected from inside states. The House is even elected from essentially local areas—districts of about a half-million population—while at least the Senate is elected from a state-wide constituency. Their dual placement as a national office with a state or local constituency, makes them critical points at which the national and local party systems intersect.

The relationship of the two congressional offices, however, to the political party structure within the states is quite different. The senatorial electorate is the whole state. Thus, the party organization which matches that electorate is the state-level party itself. The House, however, is elected from districts inside the state (except for the five smallest states entitled to only one House member each—Alaska, Delaware, North Dakota, Vermont, and Wyoming) which must be apportioned equally by population. Prior to the enforcement of that requirement, House district boundaries frequently matched county boundaries. Even the boundaries of multiple-county districts included whole counties and their corresponding party units. Since the mid-1960s, however, district boundaries have divided and crossed county boundaries, so that the district does not correspond to any preexisting party structure. Most states provide that a congressional district party committee shall exist to match the jurisdiction of that office, but in very few instances is that party unit anything other than inactive.

The result for the two federal offices, however, is about the same, regardless of the difference in their congruence with preexisting party structures. Neither office is of much concern to party leaders. The state party is more concerned with the in-state offices, while the county party concentrates more on offices cognate to it. Senators can be more important to their home parties on occasion (Huckshorn, 1976: 204). Most frequently, they are regarded as important when their party does not hold the governorship or other major state offices; by default, the senator can, if he wishes, exercise some leadership within the state party. We do have examples of senators leading factional fights within their state parties, even though their party held numerous other state offices, but this type of involvement is quite rare. (Republican Senators Capehart and Jenner of Indiana were examples; see Munger, 1960; Fenton, 1966: chap. 7. Nebraska's Senator Hruska was another; see Huckshorn, 1976: 208.)

Something of the sense of isolation by congressmen from the local party and it from congressmen may be indicated by two comments. One, from a defeated candidate for the House: "In our state, a congressional candidate is a step-child and must act for himself" (quoted in Huckshorn and Spencer, 1971: 96). The other, from a local political leader who, in referring to the previous leader of the county party who also became a House member, insisted: "But he was the leader regardless" (personal interview). Congressional candidates of both parties in California agreed that the state party leaders "were so oriented toward the state campaigns that they had little time" for them (Leuthold, 1968: 42).

Congressmen and senators—especially senators—are, nevertheless, the most important national-level contacts available to state party chairmen. When state party chairmen were asked to rank officials in order of their importance to the state party, 37 percent ranked the governor first, but following next were the senior U.S. senator (19 percent) and the junior U.S. senator (13 percent). Although the senators ranked as less important than the governor, they outranked all others including the state party's own national committeeman and the congressmen, who were tied at 2.6 percent each (Huckshorn, 1976: 204).

Senators and congressmen were listed by the state chairmen (54 percent and 32 percent, respectively) as their principal contacts with the national and public party officials (Huckshorn, 1976: 206). They far outranked the party's own national committeeman (20 percent) or any other official or institution, including the national chairmen and the White House staff. The matters on which the state chairmen interacted with national-level officials were narrow but pragmatic: patronage and election campaigns. The association of county party leaders with the congressman from the particular congressional district, however, is much closer (though equally variable), as is the relationship between the state party chairmen and the senators.

Although we lack systematic evidence concerning elections to the U.S. Senate, we do have nationwide data for House elections. Since all 435 districts hold elections every two years, this office provides our best opportunity for a nationwide view of how parties function in elections. We will look at House elections, beginning with candidate recruitment and ending with the general election, to trace the activities of political parties at both local and state levels.

The critical step of candidate recruitment takes place at the beginning of a candidate's effort to seek a particular office. Since most House members are incumbents, that step has taken place at some point prior to any one election. A survey of nonincumbent losing candidates in 1962, however, examined recruitment occurring immediately prior to that election. Some 65 percent of them reported that party leaders were "major sources of influence" in their decision to run for the House (Huckshorn and Spencer, 1971: 49). By level of party organization, more candidates reported they had received "encouragement" from local party leaders than from either state or national party leaders. Among Republicans, 74 percent received encouragement from local leaders, 54 percent from state leaders, and 15 percent from members or staff of the national committee. The relative standings of the three party levels among Democratic candidates was similar (Huckshorn and Spencer, 1971: 61–64).

A national sample of congressional incumbents (interviewed in 1966) also reported an active involvement of party leaders in their decisions to run for office. Since they were incumbents, the time of that decision ranged back into the 1930s for the most senior members. Pointing to the major source of their decision to run for the

House, 45 percent were recruited by party leaders, while the proportions by other types of recruitment actors were faction (14 percent), friends and associates (7 percent), and self (79 percent). Taking factional and party leaders together, almost 60 percent of this set of incumbent congressmen were recruited by party activists, which closely matches the figure reported in the prior study. But in no instance did either the incumbents, or the local party leaders who were also interviewed, point to any role by the state-level party. For them, "party" was entirely local, which largely meant "county" (Olson, 1976).

Although both studies point to an active involvement of party leaders—at varying levels—in candidate recruitment in House elections, they also indicate the rather low involvement of parties in the election campaigns themselves. For example, only about 15 percent of the campaign managers for the nonincumbent losers in 1962 had much prior party experience or were holding party positions (Huckshorn and Spencer, 1971: 99). Instead, friends or business associates accounted for the largest proportion of the campaign managers.

Congressional candidates in 1964 were asked to rate the amount of campaign help they received from various levels of their political parties. Almost none indicated they had received assistance from the state party. Over half, however, rated both the national and local party units as providing either "considerable" or "some" help in their election campaigns (Fishel, 1973: 106).

These findings are not entirely dissimilar from the 1962 study of losers. Their closest agreement is in the candidates' evaluations of the inadequacies of their national parties: 43 percent of the 1962 losers rated the lack of national party support as an important factor in their election loss, while 43 percent of the 1964 candidates also rated the national party as supplying "not much" or no campaign help. There was general agreement between the two studies on the local party: 60 percent of the 1962 losers thought the lack of support from the local party was important in their election loss, while 50 percent of the 1964 candidates rated the local party as providing "not much" or no campaign assistance.

Their greatest disagreement was with respect to the state level of the party. While almost none of the 1964 candidates received campaign assistance from the state party, that party level was ranked intermediate in importance between the local- and national-party level by the 1962 losing candidates.

A set of congressional campaigns in California illustrate the diversity of relationships between state party leaders and congressional candidates. The leaders of the state party, including the gubernatorial candidates, "gave little assistance beyond endorsements." Beyond this rather routine act, further involvement depended upon the personal initiatives of the congressional candidates and their evaluations of their specific districts. Some promoted party rallies and invited the state candidates to attend, while other congressional candidates avoided them. Although Democrats were more active in these respects than Republicans, even the former stressed their association with President Kennedy more than with Governor Pat Brown (Leuthold, 1968: 42).

Most of the above studies depend upon the estimates and ratings by congressional candidates themselves. An alternative method, used in the 1966 study, was to interview both congressmen and the party leaders in the home districts. Their accounts largely agreed, indicating that the extent to which congressmen "relied" upon their party in elections varied from very much to very little. The diversity of the electoral relationship between congressman and party could be placed in five categories:

1. Reliance upon party in both nominations and general elections— 22 percent.
2. Reliance upon factions in both nominations and general elections —8 percent.
3. Party reliance in general elections but self-reliance in nominations —19 percent.
4. Party reliance in nominations, with self-reliance in general elections—14 percent.
5. Self-reliance in both nominations and general elections—36 percent.

These varying electoral relationships are compounded of the cohesion and capacity of the district party, the party and the congressman's own competitive status, and the factional alliances between the congressman and the party leaders in his district (Olson, 1976).

The several studies of congressional campaigns agree that competitive status does have an impact upon them, at least in some ways and to some extent. For example, the 1964 winners and losers differed in their evaluation of the utility of their local parties (though they agreed in their evaluation of the national and state parties). Losers, more than winners, estimated their local party was of "not much" or no help in their congressional campaigns (Fishel, 1973: 106). The losers in the 1962 election substantially agreed in their evaluation of the local party, but the near-winners gave the state, and especially the national, party better ratings than did the losers (Huckshorn and Spencer, 1971: 134). Thus, while both studies find that competitive status has an impact on how candidates evaluate the electoral utility of political parties, they disagree on what that impact is.

The broader measure of the party-candidate relationship of electoral reliance also varies by competitive status of the party, but only in one respect. Some congressmen are elected from districts in which their party is a minority; that is, most candidates of their party lose, so that they are among the only elected officials of their party within their respective districts. In those instances of minority-party status (though they themselves are winners and usually have personally safe seats), congressmen do rely upon their party to protect their nomination, but must rely upon their own efforts in the general election.

Aside from this circumstance, however, the differences in competitive status of the parties, as distinguished between safe and competitive, do not make any difference in the distribution of congressmen among the other four categories of electoral reliance. The internal condition of the district's party makes the critical difference. If the parties in the district are themselves well-organized (similar to the cohesive type identified in Chapter 3), congressmen will ordinarily rely upon their party in both nominations and general elections; this type of party, however, is usually safe within its own district, so general elections are not usually critical matters to either the party or the congressman. If the district parties are bifactional in their internal organization, congressmen will rely upon a faction if they are friendly with one of them, or will resort to self-reliance if they reject both of the major factions of the district parties. Congressmen who rely upon the party in general elections but depend upon their own campaign organization to protect their nomination are usually from safe parties. But the congressmen had experienced contests in the primaries, or had previously defeated party favorites in their own initial nomination, and thus kept their personal supporters in readiness to guard against the potential eruption of opposition from within their own party.

The self-reliant congressmen are distributed between both safe and competitive parties. What leads to the lack of their dependence upon the party in elections is that there is little of a party to depend on. It is similar to the multifactional state party discussed in Chapter 3. These district parties are understaffed, not very active, and are usually divided into numerous hostile segments. Congressmen could not safely rely on this type of party even if they wished to. But there is one other circumstance in which congressmen have resorted to self-reliance—when the party has been either cohesive or bifactional, but they and its leaders have been hostile to one another. In that case, congressmen avoid their district party as much as possible (Olson, 1976).

Several congressional campaigns in California tend to illustrate the self-reliance electoral relationship with the party. Most of the parties would be characterized as multifactional and were not sufficiently organized to offer substantial campaign resources. Nevertheless, the competitive candidates did receive more party-related assistance than did either the sure winners (incumbents) or the sure losers. Incumbents had the resources of their office and the personal resources of name recognition, issue familiarity, and financing, so that they had little need for the political party. On the other hand, the sure losers—though various party participants had been involved in their decision to become candidates—were denied most of the assistance they requested from the party. Rather, party leaders concentrated what few resources they had into the more competitive districts (Leuthold, 1968: 79).

The several studies of congressional elections give more of a nationwide view of political parties and elections than is presently available from studies of elections for any other office. Although the congressional office is ordinarily peripheral to the main concerns of the party (either state or county), elections to that office reflect the prevailing practices of their respective states. If party leaders recruit candidates to the state legislature and county commission, they are likely to also recruit for the congressional office. If county leaders ordinarily confer among themselves on endorsements on state offices, they will ordinarily use the same procedures to make a congressional nomination. If the party is bifactional in county politics, each faction will ordinarily support rival candidates to the U.S. House. If a party is multifactional in county and state politics, few congressional candidates would be able to wield it for their own purposes into any more of a competent or cohesive entity during the short campaign. Thus, the congressional office presents us with a view of the diversity of election practices and party organization found among the counties and states of the Union.

# 8 ★ ★ ★

# The future of state politics ★ ★ ★

Most of those who have gazed into the crystal ball of American politics in recent years have found it to be cloudy. There is no reason to expect our perceptions of the future of state politics to be any clearer. Rather than trying to make firm predictions that may prove to be faulty, we think it is more useful to call attention to some of the trends—often contradictory in their implications—that we find in American state politics.

We start with several assumptions. The most obvious point is that the future of state politics is closely tied to that of national politics. The states cannot escape the effects of changing levels of national party identification or changes in control of national government, for example. A second assumption is that the American states will continue to be important, independent centers of decision-making, despite the influence of the federal government and the growing importance of metropolitan areas. In other words, state government remains important, and therefore the study of state parties and elections remains a subject of interest. We will begin by looking at some of the forces that seem to be eroding or at least altering state political parties, and then turn to trends that are more supportive of party institutions.

## SIGNS OF EROSION OF STATE PARTIES

If state parties are declining in importance, it is largely a consequence of, or at least coincides with, a similar trend at the national level. A number of commentators have raised questions about whether the party system still serves the needs that it once did in the political system. Among the more articulate of these is Walter Dean Burnham (1970: 132–33): "It is clear that the significance of the party as an intermediary link between voters and rulers has again come into serious question. Bathed in the warm glow of diffused affluence, vexed in spirit but enriched economically by our imperial military and space commitments, confronted by the gradually unfolding consequences of social change as vast as it is unplanned, what need have Americans of political parties? More precisely, what need have they of parties whose structures, processes, and leadership cadres find their origins in a past as remote as it is irrelevant?"

### Public attitudes toward parties

There is evidence that the attachment of American voters to parties, as well as their confidence in partisan institutions, is declining. As we noted in chapter 6, the proportion of voters identifying with a party has declined from approximately three fourths to two thirds in the period since the early 1960s. Surveys of voter opinion in a number of states have shown similar increases in the proportion who are independent. Some of the explanation for this trend is demographic, such as the increased geographic mobility in the country and the increasing proportion of younger persons (18 to 30), who have weaker party loyalties than older persons. It is also evident that these younger voters are much more likely to be independent than were similar age groups a generation ago. It is unclear what are the attitudes of independents toward the party system. How many have simply broken away from the local environment and family ties that would reinforce party loyalty? How many have no interest in parties or see no purpose in identifying with them? How many are actually disillusioned with parties and clearly hostile to the party system? (Asher, 1976: chap. 3; Miller and Levitin, 1976: chap. 7).

Dennis (1975) has summarized much of the survey data that is available on trends in public support for parties in this country. He finds that in some respects support for parties remains high or at least has not declined in recent years; but he also finds some evidence of change. For example, voters in Wisconsin are much more willing to agree with the proposition that party labels should not appear on the ballot. (But polls in Minnesota showed voter support for a recent decision to put the party label on the ballot for legislative candidates, ending the long established nonpartisan character of the legislature.) Dennis cites national survey data showing that from 1964 to 1972 there has been a decline in the proportion of voters who believe that elections and parties contribute substantially to making government pay attention to what the people want. He also notes that data from the 1972 and 1974 period shows that parties are generally regarded less favorably by citizens than are other political institutions. Such data provide us with some clues about citizen attitudes, but they do not offer much depth of understanding about how voters perceive parties, what they expect of them, and in what ways they are disappointed. Nor is it obvious what kinds of behavior disillusioned voters may engage in. Will they refuse to become identified with a party, stay out of party caucuses and even primaries, or refuse to vote in general elections?

## Independent voting

We have more evidence about the behavior of voters and those who work in politics than we do about attitudes and perceptions, and so we will concentrate on this behavior in an effort to understand what trends are occurring in the party systems of the states. First, it is evident that there is a decline in voting along party lines for state offices. We described this trend in some detail for gubernatorial voting in Chapter 6. The immediate consequence of this trend has been to strengthen two-party competition in some states—those that used to be dominated by a single party. The fact that a majority of voters in such states are no longer totally loyal to one party has enabled the minority party to capture the governorship and win more legislative seats, to establish a foothold as a competitive party. But in the long run the decline of voting along party lines may weaken both parties in the states, depriving them of dependable bases of voting strength and creating occasional landslides in support of popular candidates.

If party loyalty is less frequently the determinant of voting in state elections, what is taking its place? Voters may be more impressed by the fact of incumbency than they used to be in state elections, but governors do not usually gain the same advantages from incumbency that congressmen do. We have described some of the kinds of issues, taxation for example, that sometimes play a large role in state elections. Issues are likely to remain important in gubernatorial elections. but there is no way to predict what kinds of issues will be salient in state elections of the future. The clearest trend probably is the increasing importance of the candidates' characteristics. The highly successful gubernatorial candidate of the future is likely to be one who is capable of appealing across party lines, who knows how to make effective use of the media, who has attractive personal qualities —rather than one who has climbed the ladder of political office by winning the support of party leaders and workers. It is not necessarily true that anyone who can afford an expensive television advertising campaign and who hires a good PR firm can win elections, but it is true that use of television and other media are frequently crucial to the success of campaigns. If the voters are relying less on party loyalty than on their perception of candidates, the care and feeding of the candidate's image become highly important. One has only to look at the two most recent governors of California, Ronald Reagan and Jerry Brown, to understand the importance of gubernatorial image.

## Party organizations and primaries

It has become a truism that party organizations are declining in importance, and there is no reason to anticipate a reversal of that trend. The traditional party organizations of the eastern and midwestern cities no longer have a supply of new immigrants to provide votes in return for jobs and services. One by one, the old bosses are dying—most recently Mayor Daley of Chicago—and no one of comparable skill and power is replacing them. This does not mean that the organizational tasks performed by traditional party machines have become irrelevant. Despite the increasing role of the mass media, those who manage political campaigns still find it necessary to conduct registration drives, poll the precincts, and get out the vote. They still need workers to stuff the envelopes, man the banks of telephones, and sometimes campaign door-to-door. But increasingly these jobs are performed, not by a stable group of precinct leaders and party faithful but by the volunteers who are mobilized by particular candidates. There is some continuity of party workers from election to election and candidate to candidate, but there is also considerable turnover. The new breed of political workers is motivated not by promises of jobs and other favors but by their interest in particular policies and their enthusiasm for particular candidates.

The formal machinery of the party has grown rusty in some states and localities, but in others it still serves important purposes, and there may be contests between the supporters of particular candidates for control of that machinery. But the party organization has lost most of the sanctions that it once had to maintain discipline over party workers. A precinct worker who is rewarded with a job can be punished by taking away the job, though even this type of discipline seems to have grown lax in many party organizations. But a worker who wins a precinct office as a byproduct of his efforts to elect a particular candidate cannot be effectively punished if he refuses to work for some other candidate nominated by the party. While the traditional party organizations and workers have been most interested in contests for state and local offices, the new political amateurs are often drawn into politics by their interest in presidential candidates, and their participation in other levels of political races may be spasmodic. State and local party organizations in the near future are not likely to wither away, but they are likely to be less disciplined, more fluid in membership, and less capable of influencing the decisions of voters than used to be the case a few years ago. They will often become empty shells, filled from time to time by the supporters of particular state or national candidates.

What is the future of the primary election in this period of change? We have noted that primaries were established in a period of one-party domination in many states, and we have reported the argument of V. O. Key and others that the establishment of the primary—by depriving the party or its nominating function—contributed significantly to the atrophy of party organizations. The primary was designed by reformers who distrusted party bosses and machines, but it is a partisan institution. The primary laws transferred control over nominations from the organizations to the broad mass of voters who identified with the party and (in most states) were willing to register with that party or at least publicly indicate their desire to participate in that party's primary. But if the trend toward independence from party identification should continue, extending to half or two thirds of the voters, who would be left to vote in the primaries? If voters lose interest in the parties or become disillusioned with them, will they continue to vote in the primaries?

The answers to these questions remain obscure, but there are some trends involving state primaries that we can recognize. First, there does not seem to be any consistent trend in rates of participation in primaries. In those states where the pattern of party competition has changed, there have been changes in the two-party share of the primary vote, though we have noted that these changes have lagged behind the general election vote. Some states have gained or lost in primary participation, perhaps related to levels of competition in the primaries, but there is no national trend clear enough to be meaningful. Party loyalties may be weakening, but this trend has not produced a decline in primary voting, possibly because there has been some easing of the restrictions on voting in primaries.

There are several states that have shifted from closed to open primaries. Several of the states without party registration have abandoned the requirement that voters who may be challenged swear allegiance in some form to a party's candidates before voting in the primary. Several of the states have abandoned the rigid deadlines on shifting registration from one party to the other—in some states under the pressure of court rulings. The effect of these changes has been to make it easier for a voter to vote in either primary he or she wishes, and to shift back and forth from one party's primary to the other. We do not know what the consequences of these trends are or are likely to be. Do voters know that in many states it is easy to shift from one primary to another? How many do it? How many want to do it? The almost total absence of pertinent survey data precludes even a tentative answer to these questions.

It is possible to foresee a trend that would make the primary system compatible with, and perhaps more attractive to, an electorate whose party loyalties were weak, voters who wanted to "vote for the man, not the party" in primaries as well as general elections. We may see more states adopting open primaries or modifying closed primaries so that it becomes very easy to shift registration and so that the distinction between the two forms is almost meaningless. More states might adopt the blanket primary to permit voting in each party's primary for different offices at one time, the ultimate convenience for voters without party loyalties. Several states now permit registered independents to vote in either party primary, and if the number of independents increases, there may be pressure on other state legislatures to adopt such rules. These changes would all have the effect of permitting the voters to enter whichever primary appeared to be more interesting or more competitive, or included the candidate who was most appealing or best known to the voter. Perhaps the ultimate effect of such changes would be the creation de facto of a nonpartisan primary. This is what Louisiana has already done by holding one primary in which all voters and all candidates can participate, with a runoff between the two top candidates serving as the general election.

There are signs, which we described in Chapter 3, that the influence of party organizations over primaries is declining. Several of the states that have experimented with legal preprimary endorsements by party organizations have abandoned them—notably Massachusetts, where the endorsements had little impact on Democratic primaries but simply contributed to party fractionalization. In New York the parties abandoned state conventions for preprimary endorsements in primaries and soon discovered that the organization's endorsement often resembled an albatross hung around the neck of the endorsee. We need to get some opinion survey data on voter attitudes toward party endorsements in primaries, but in several states there is circumstantial evidence that the voters either don't care about such endorsements or react negatively to them when they vote in primaries. We have also noted, in chapter 7, the sharp decline in the influence of party organizations over the process of choosing state delegates to national presidential nominating conventions. At a time when party organizations were cohesive, disciplined groups, it was possible for the organization to make endorsements with a minimum of controversy and depend on the party faithful to vote for the endorsee and persuade others to vote for him in the primary. Now it is increasingly likely that the state party convention will be an arena in which the supporters of contending candidates fight for the votes necessary for endorsement, with the battle continuing throughout the primary campaign and with the endorsement itself having a minimum effect on either the party activists or the average voters in the primary.

If primaries become open to more voters, including those having little or no commitment to the party, and if the impact of the party organization on primaries continues to fade away, what difference will it make? The influence of party organizations will be further eroded and their activities will diminish. Party leaders will devote less effort to recruiting candidates if they are unable to give the recruit any effective help against self-starting candidates in a primary. If voters can wander back and forth between party primaries, there is less likelihood that the party's nominee will represent the views and interests traditionally associated with that party, and the organization may be reluctant to work for candidates who are clearly mavericks. Candidates may shift parties more often in their search for tactical advantage. Party cohesion in the legislature, which remains strong in some states, may be eroded if legislators become dependent on voters in both parties for victory not only in the general election but also in the primary. If in fact the parties simplify the voters' task by helping them to judge the records of officials and hold them responsible, this function may lose its effectiveness if candidates are nominated in primaries that are almost nonpartisan in substance if not in form.

There is another side to the coin, another aspect of more open primaries and other recent and projected trends that we should recognize. There are broader opportunities for citizens to participate in government and less need for them to defer to the judgment of party leaders or anyone else. The franchise has been fully opened up with the removal of obstacles to black voting in the Deep South, extension of the franchise to those 18 and older, and the end of state residence requirements. Not only are primaries open to more voters, but the Democratic party has adopted procedures to open up party caucuses to the voters—particularly those that play a role in the presidential nominations. The end of one-party domination in many states gives voters two parties, an alternative route for political activity if one of the parties is under tight local control. But, despite all of these trends, there are no clear signs that voters in large numbers are taking advantage of these opportunities. Voting participation at many levels is declining, partly because newly enfranchised voters, particularly the youngest, are turning out in low numbers. It is true that many students, housewives, and other amateurs are participating in party caucuses and meetings for the first time and are getting elected to state and national conventions. But as we noted in chapter 7, the percentage of persons taking part in caucuses as part of the presidential nominating process is still very low. Whether voters believe that they can not have any real impact on decisions or whether relatively few are interested enough to play more than a minimal role is not clear.

## Party competition

We have described in some detail in chapter 2 the evidence that party competition has been growing in almost all of the states—first in the North as a delayed consequence of the New Deal and later in the South after national Republican candidates in the 1950s began making a serious effort to win votes there. The much more competitive character of state party politics is perhaps the most important difference between the states today and the nature of state politics before World War II. There are many reasons for believing that competitive state politics is here to stay, despite occasional slumps that minority parties may experience in particular states. The decline and fall of regionalism, the spread of urbanization and industry, the greater mobility of population, the decline of ethnic factors in party loyalty—all these developments contribute in one way or another to two-party competition at the state level.

Yet there remains a nagging feeling that in some states, at least, two-party competition may be eroding because of the weakness of the Republican party. Predicting political trends is a risky business, and predictions that endure on the printed page are particularly vulnerable to ridicule by those with the advantage of hindsight. After the Democratic debacle in 1928, when presidential candidate Al Smith could not even carry all of the Solid South, it would have taken great skill and courage to predict that in 4 years a realignment would be under way that would raise the Democratic party to majority status for at least 45 years. After President Nixon carried every state but Massachusetts and the District of Columbia in the 1972 election, it would have been foolhardy to argue that the Republican party was in deep trouble.

Of course the Republican party has done reasonably well in presidential elections since 1952; it has been decisively beaten only in 1964. Kennedy's popular margin in 1960 and Carter's electoral vote margin in 1976 were razor-thin. But the Republican party has not controlled Congress since the 1953–54 session. At the state level the Republican position is even worse. The party lost 11 governorships in 1970, and a few more in the next three elections. In the 1974 and 1976 elections the Republican party lost control of many state legislatures, including some where it had long records of comfortable majorities. After the 1976 election, New Hampshire was the only state that had both a Republican governor and a Republican majority in both houses of the legislature, a record that may not have been equalled in a hundred years.

The Republican weakness is particular striking in two areas. The first is in traditionally Republican states. Not long ago, for example, North Dakota was assumed to be a solidly Republican state. But the Democrats won every gubernatorial election in that state from 1960 through 1976—six elections in a row. Iowa lost its status as a secure Republican state in the late 1950s and 1960s, but it is still surprising to discover that even the presence of a Republican governor could not keep that state legislature from going Democratic in both houses in the 1974 and 1976 elections. In Kansas the 1976 election brought a Democratic majority in the lower house (and almost in the senate), the first such victory in either house in modern times. These examples presumably do not mean that the Republican party is soon to become a minority party in the plains states, but they do suggest that there is virtually no territory left that may be described as safely Republican in state elections.

The more serious problem for the Republican party is in the South. The trend toward the Republican party, and thus toward two-party competition, that spread in varying degrees to every southern state in the late 1950s and early 1960s seems to have come to a stop, and begun to recede. In no southern state (except Arkansas with its two-year term) has the Republican party been able to win consecutive gubernatorial elections; in none except Virginia has it elected two governors in the postwar period; in none has it held gubernatorial power for more than four years in a row. In no state (except Tennessee) has the Republican party come close to winning a majority in either legislative house. Only in four southern states has the Republican party been able to gain as many as one fourth of the seats in one legislative house, which might be considered the minimum necessary to be taken seriously as a legislative party. These are Tennessee, where the party has usually held one third to one half of the seats in both houses since 1966; Florida, with both houses having roughly one third of the seats Republican since 1966; Virginia; and North Carolina, where the modest Republican legislative minority was eroded by the 1974 and 1976 elections. In parts of the Deep South the few Republican legislators are just about as lonely as they were a decade ago. Gubernatorial and senatorial elections can be won by weak parties having popular candidates. Legislative elections are a much sterner and more reliable measure of a state party's real strength, and in many southern states the Republican party is obviously failing the test.

Obviously in the era of Watergate, the 1974 Democratic landslide, and the 1976 Carter election, it is a difficult time for the Republican party to make progress in southern states. But the rebuilding of the Democratic party in many northern states occurred in large part during the early 1950s, that is the early years of the Eisenhower administration. During that period, and again during the Nixon administration, the Democratic party was stronger than its presidential record indicated, because of its growing base of power in the states outside the South. At present, we must conclude that in state politics the Republican party is weaker than its record in the 1968, 1972, and 1976 presidential races would suggest, because in the North it has lost the competitive advantage it once held in many states and has slipped into minority status in some of them, while in the South it has very largely failed to capitalize on the frequent success of its presidential candidates and the occasional victories of its candidates for state-wide and congressional office.

## SIGNS OF STRENGTHENING OF STATE PARTIES

As usual in American politics, there are a number of developments which contradict the trends we have just discussed. In a variety of ways, political parties are showing signs of continued importance in state politics and of even increased significance.

We have never been settled in our thinking or in our practices about the proper place of political parties in our government. However strong and important parties may have been in our past, they have coexisted with strong antiparty sentiments. Our present confusion about parties is not new, but is a continuation of that very strong ambivalence toward parties (Ranney and Kendall, 1956; chap. 6; Gelb and Palley, 1975: 7–20; Ranney, 1975).

The same forces and unrest and dissatisfaction which have greatly increased the number of presidential primaries have worked inside political parties and have had, perhaps paradoxically, the effect of strengthening their internal organization. Consider our situation in 1948 and 1952. Democrats were faced with dissension from Southern Democratic parties over the two main issues of civil rights and petroleum. Southern party delegations walked out of the 1948 Democratic National Convention and formed the core of the Dixiecrat third party candidacy of then-Governor Strom Thurmond. In 1952 and 1956 Democrats struggled over the "loyalty oath" requirement that Southern Democratic delegations at least pledge that they would place the party's nominee on their state ballots under the label of the Democratic party. Twenty years later, however, a Southerner gained the Democratic nomination, and all of the southern Democratic parties worked hard for the party ticket.

The Democratic party has defined a number of criteria which its state parties must meet as a condition of being admitted to the national convention. These national guidelines were forged initially in the crucible of the fight over civil rights, initiated by Southern dissension. The unrest among Northern Democrats over Vietnam and over race relations in northern cities were also powerful stimulants to internal reform.

The main point to be stressed, however, is that national centralization of the Democratic party is one important result of unrest and unhappiness about politics. The very dissatisfactions with "the system" have resulted in an organizational strengthening of the political party. Never before has either major national party defined criteria by which state parties shall be judged, much less attempted to enforce such criteria upon them.

The criteria concern the right to participation. All categories of persons are to be admitted, even encouraged, to participate in the internal affairs of the party. While this requirement is stated in terms of the presidential selection process, the effect extends to in-state activities as well. More persons, not fewer, are now participating in their political party, and a wider diversity of persons are participating than previously.

Republicans have experienced the winds of internal reform much less than have Democrats. They have imposed fewer criteria and requirements upon their state parties, although their committees have endorsed the same general goals of open participation as have Democrats.

Republicans have been beset by rapid changes in the characteristics of their adherents and participants. The rapid growth of southern Republicans has brought a diverse set of people into the party. Urban conservatives of the Eisenhower period, and race-oriented conservatives of rural areas of the Goldwater period have added to and displaced the traditional mountain support for Republicans. This growth, coupled with national Democratic policies, has largely driven southern blacks out of the Republican party. Simultaneously, Republicans have been losing support and elites in northern cities and suburbs. While a Strom Thurmond, for example, has entered the Republican party, a John Lindsay has left.

To the extent that persons, especially political activists, have changed parties, those changes have increased the ideological consistency of each party. While such party switches have been expressed in terms of national politics, the switchers also change parties at state and local levels as well. The result has been to reduce factional conflict within the former party and to increase the leadership core of the new party.

There is another national source of party coherence—Congress. At the height of Southern Democratic defection from the national party, in the 1964 Goldwater-Johnson election, which resulted in a national Democratic landslide (though also in a reverse Republican surge in the South), Democrats in Congress threatened to discipline any of their members who supported the Republican nominee for President. Two Southern Democratic congressmen did support Goldwater—in the same election in which Thurmond became a Republican—but remained in Congress as Democrats. Early in 1965, the Democratic Caucus disciplined the two members by demoting them to the bottom of the seniority lists of their respective committees. One member, Albert Watson of South Carolina, promptly resigned his seat, and ran again in the special election as a Republican, while the other, John Williams of Mississippi, left the House two years later. Since that time, no congressman has overtly supported an opposition presidential candidate. This congressional pressure has had an important effect on state parties, especially in the South. One-party dominance locally, and the seniority system nationally, have protected Southern Democratic power in congressional committees. With the protection of automatic seniority gone, congressmen and their local supporters have had less reason to remain Democrats if their genuine policy preferences led them to support Republican candidates. But on the other hand, if their agreement with Republicans was not quite that strong, then they had renewed reason to remain within the Democratic fold.

Another source of change in the party system, again mainly impacting the South, has been the voter rights acts which have admitted large numbers of blacks as active participants in Southern politics. Republicans have made some efforts to attract black support; governors and senators alike have appointed blacks to their staffs in positions active with and visible to the black electorate.

But the impact of an expanded and diversified southern electorate has been felt mainly among Democrats. In every southern Democratic party, blacks now participate in conventions, on committees, as officers, and as candidates for elective office. The sight of Dr. Martin Luther King, Sr., and Governor George Wallace on the same platform as the same time at the 1976 Democratic National Convention symbolized the merger of forces occurring in each state Democratic party throughout the South.

The result has been an extensive realignment of political forces within the nation's most distinctive region—the South. Southern Democrats are now more like national Democrats than at any other time in the past century. We expect these trends to continue, in part because of the continuing urbanization and industrialization of the South, and in part because of the spread of civil rights and poverty issues in the remaining 75 percent of the country.

## A common party system among states

Why does each state have two political parties? Further, why does each state have the *same* two political parties as all the others? Given the size of our nation, and the diversity among the 50 states, we might expect a variety of state parties to form in response to the circumstances of their respective states and to gain control of state governments. We might expect three- and four-party systems in at least some states, and in those with two parties, those parties might be different from the main one nationally.

The thrust of the preceding argument is that these developments are less likely now than at any time in our past. We have a greater degree of national uniformity of conditions now than previously. We have more centralized parties nationally than previously. The conditions promoting a consistency of party formation and alignments are greater now than ever before.

We created a nation from largely independent states before political parties had developed. Politics and elections centered upon the individual states. Creation of a new nation created a new political arena—a common set of national offices. For the first time, politically ambitious persons in states could aspire to occupy national offices (especially in Congress). For the first time, political elites, previously restricted to their states, could aspire to and compete for a common set of offices. Once in office, they interacted over common policies. No state, by itself, had a majority of votes in Congress to adopt the policies its elites preferred. They were forced to form alliances across state lines. Leaders of national policies, in turn, were forced to look to state leaders for support. Indeed, national leaders traveled through the states seeking allies and attempting to build local bases of support. Political parties, as we know them today, grew out of these developments in the early years of the new nation (Lipset, 1963: 29–51; Goodman, 1967; McCormick, 1967). The amazing development was that the same parties quickly formed in most of the states. It was in this early period that a wide variety of parties could most easily have formed in the states, and when each state could have developed distinctive party systems.

The presidential election has been a powerful catalyst in the formation of a common party system throughout the country. The device of selecting the electoral college separately within each state helped link in-state political elites to like-minded peers among all the states. Likewise, those seeking national office had a powerful inducement to attempt to organize and influence the course of intrastate politics as the means of influencing national politics.

But perhaps—we can only speculate—the selection of the U.S. Senate by state legislatures was an equally key ingredient in the development of a common party system throughout the states. For over a century, U.S. senators were elected by the state legislatures. Those persons elected in local districts to fill a state office were directly involved in the selection of national officials. Likewise, those elites attempting to shape national politics, had to reach into the states to influence the selection of senators whom they preferred. The famous Lincoln-Douglas debates were not part of a presidential contest, but rather, were part of a senatorial contest. They were seeking to be selected by the Illinois legislature as a U.S. Senator from that state. This debate illustrates the concentration on national policy even in an intrastate contest, and also illustrates the often public means by which the state legislators' choices were shaped. The same incident illustrates also the extent to which the in-state electorate was involved, by contesting elites, in the issues and choices of national politics.

We have had distinctive state parties in our past. They have been formed in times of economic crisis in the Midwest and of racial turmoil in the South. Perhaps the surprising development is that we have not had more. Invariably, however, they have either died out or have merged with one of the two major parties. It is only in New York State that minor parties have continued to exist over a span of decades and to actively participate in their state's politics. We would guess that the conditions now are less favorable to the growth of distinctive state parties than at any time in our nation's past.

## Party in government

Governors and state legislators propose and vote on state policy consistently with their political party. They rarely attain a complete consistency of party alignment, and the rate of party voting varies among the states. But given the diversity among our states, officials tend to react to public policy questions more consistently by political party than perhaps we expect (LeBlanc, 1969; Flinn, 1964; Jewell and Patterson, 1977: chap. 16).

Party discipline and party voting in Congress are less than in European democracies—in part, at least, because of the separation of powers system. This system is duplicated in each state, and provides one reason why party discipline is not absolute.

Population diversity is an important factor diluting party consistency on issues. As state legislators respond to their respective and different districts, they vote differently on legislation. But the political party remains a generalized statement of preferences on questions of public policy. Over a wide variety of issues and over a long period of time, the political party provides a frame within which public officials tend to think and act. We would guess that this policy coherence between parties in each of the states will tend to persist. We would guess that the parties across the states will tend generally to support consistent points of view simply because of the greater degree of national uniformity of party composition and socioeconomic conditions.

But political parties, perhaps especially in the United States, are not so much a means of making policy choices as they are a means of selecting public officials and of organizing government (Lowi, 1967). Here, again, the possibilities for evolving factions and combinations outside of and to displace the standard national parties have been almost endless. While one-party legislatures have formed factions, and while some two-party legislatures have formed bipartisan factions in selecting their speakers and committee chairmen, yet all of these permutations have occurred within the two main parties. We suspect that the conditions are less propitious now than in our past for the emergence of third-party formations among the officials of state government.

## Nominations

Our wide-open primaries are the greatest single source of weakness in our state parties, for all of the reasons expressed previously. Yet at least some state parties have attempted to at least place a filter between all those who wish to be candidates and those who actually run in the party primary. We noted in chapter 3 that over 25 percent of the state parties play some role as organizations in their nomination process. In some states, of which Massachusetts Democrats and both of California's parties are the best examples, the effort has failed, and others (New York, Indiana) have recently abandoned the convention method of nominating candidates. In the other states, however, party conventions either endorse candidates or impose conditions (such as a minimum proportion of the convention vote) upon those seeking to enter the primary. These steps are intermediate between a convention nomination, on the one hand, and a completely unrestrained election on the other. These intermediate steps seem to be working in the state parties using them.

The distinction between "open" and "closed" primaries in voter registration does not seem to have much impact on state parties and their nominations. The various endorsement and convention procedures discussed above seem to have a greater impact on nominations. The open appeals in the 1976 presidential primaries by candidates of both parties to other-party voters to "crossover" into the candidates' primaries has a potentially great disruptive effect on state parties. The timing of most state elections to occur in the nonpresidential years might help insulate state parties from this effect.

## Campaign finance

The future of state political parties can be greatly affected by new regulations concerning campaign finance. Public financing, particularly, will be important. The key question is: Who will receive public funds? To the extent that public financing is allocated to individual candidates, they will tend to wage individual campaigns. To the extent that public funds are allocated to, or through, political parties, candidates will have reason to cooperate with one another through their political party. In the 1976 presidential campaign, the presidential candidates devoted some of their time to fund raising for their parties, because their own funds were supplied and limited by the government. The same regulations permitted state and local parties to raise their own funds and to blend their campaigns, to a certain extent and in certain ways, with that of the presidential nominee.

As states begin to consider either more stringent campaign finance regulations and/or public financing, they will have a potentially great impact on their political parties. Indeed, the extent to which the party should, or should not, be involved at all in the receipt and disbursement of public campaign funds may be a critical question in the debates. But whether the issue is faced overtly or not, whatever is done on this matter can have an important impact on the future of our political parties.

## State party revitalization

Many state political parties have, in the past 15 years, opened permanent headquarters. They have raised funds and employed professional staff. A number of them have attempted to provide support to their legislators in the state capitol, and most attempt to be involved and helpful in elections.

Some of the state parties have also attempted to become involved in the new technologies of public opinion polling, of mass media production, and of professional campaign management. To the extent that parties are able to master (and finance) these skills, candidates will be encouraged to cooperate with their state party.

An important ingredient in the revival of state party organizations, apparently, has been the discovery by state chairmen of one another. In both parties, but especially in the Republican, the state chairmen have formed regional associations through which they have met and helped one another. They have apparently learned of new activities and support available to them, and have improved their own morale as a group. They have formed a distinctive subgroup within their national party and have lobbied for and obtained membership on their national committee. Here is yet another way in which state and national politics will be linked. One result, especially among Republicans, will be an increased flow of services and aids from the national party to their state party organizations (Huckshorn, 1976: Chapter 7).

## SUMMARY

The trends in the future of state parties and politics are quite contradictory. In that respect, we continue an ancient tradition in American politics.

In sum, adherence to political party seems to be deteriorating in the electorate, but increasing among political elites. While party identification is decreasing in the electorate, and split-ticket voting increasing, state parties are being strengthened and party cohesion maintained in the state legislatures.

The key actors in this process are the political elites. They, in effect, make the decisions to which the electorate responds. But political elites look to the electorate; they seek to tailor their campaigns, their appeals, and their voting to the electorate. An election campaign is a short-run event. A candidate seeks to win the immediate election, rather than to contribute to a party victory at some later date. In their search for short-run advantage, candidates are tempted to run individual campaigns and to ignore (we have seen examples of sabotage, even) their party colleagues in the same election. Once elected, however, the same political elites more interact in office by political party than we might expect, given the individualist circumstances of their campaigns.

None of the trends we have discussed here are inevitable. Our fate is not sealed by unseen forces. Rather, the fate of state politics is in our own hands and will develop out of the ways in which we as citizens and participants interact with one another in the political arena of our respective states.

# Appendix ★ ★ ★

Figures 2–1 through 2–4 (in Chapter 2) showing the levels of state party competition for various time periods, are based on data concerning party control over and strength in both the governorship and the legislature. These calculations include both the percentage of time controlled and the percentage of vote for governor and the proportion of seats held in the legislature by each party. Data for the governorship are reported in Tables A–1 and A–2; those for the legislature are given in A–3. The tables show, for each state, the number of years of control (Y lines). The second line for each state (M) shows the average percentage vote for each party in the years when the party won and, for the legislature the average percentage of seats held when that party had a legislative majority. The data for southern states (Table A–2) also show the percentage of elections that were contested by both major parties; the winning margin includes only contested races; and legislative control is omitted because the Democrats regularly controlled the legislature, usually by huge margins.

The maps of Figures 2–1 through 2–4 indicate levels of competition, based on the data in the tables in this Appendix and using the criteria that follows below for the three categories. (Figure 2–1 is based only on competition for the governorship.)

## One-party dominant

*Governorship*—The minority party may not always run a candidate. The majority party usually wins by 60 percent to 65 percent or more. The minority party rarely if ever elects a governor; exceptions may occur if the majority party is deeply split. *Legislature*—The minority party does not contest many of the legislative seats and usually has less than 15 percent of the seats.

## Majority party

*Governorship*—Both parties normally contest. The majority party usually wins by less than 60 percent. The minority party wins at least once during the period. The party controlling the legislature for a majority of the period also controls the governorship a majority of the time (but in many cases less than it controls the legislature). *Legislature* —One party controls both houses either all of the time or a very large proportion of the time (more than three quarters). With a few exceptions, however, the minority party usually has at least one fourth of the legislative seats.

## Two highly competitive parties

The remaining states are classified as competitive. There is considerable turnover in control of the legislature and the governorship; often the same party does not control the governorship and both legislative branches. Any state where one party dominates the legislature and the other dominates the governorship also fits into this category.

**Table A–1**
**Party control of governorship by years and average winning margin in nonsouthern states by major time periods**

| States | Years and margins | Time periods of control | | | | | | | |
|---|---|---|---|---|---|---|---|---|---|
| | | 1901–32 | | 1933–46 | | 1947–60 | | 1961–78 | |
| | | Election years | | | | | | | |
| | | 1900–30 | | 1932–44 | | 1946–58 | | 1960–76 | |
| | | D | R | D | R | D | R | D | R |
| Maine | Y, | 4 | 28 | 4 | 10 | 6 | 8 | 8 | 6 |
| | M | 47.9 | 57.2 | 52.2 | 62.0 | 55.2 | 59.9 | 51.6 | 51.4 |
| N.H. | Y, | 4 | 28 | 0 | 14 | 0 | 14 | 6 | 12 |
| | M | 47.2 | 55.4 | — | 53.5 | — | 56.7 | 59.9 | 52.4 |
| Vt. | Y, | 0 | 32 | 0 | 14 | 0 | 14 | 8 | 10 |
| | M | — | 66.0 | — | 64.9 | — | 62.7 | 58.8 | 54.3 |
| Mass. | Y, | 8 | 24 | 8 | 6 | 8 | 6 | 6 | 12 |
| | M | 45.3 | 54.4 | 50.9 | 52.4 | 56.1 | 51.9 | 52.9 | 55.5 |
| R.I. | Y, | 6 | 26 | 12 | 2 | 12 | 2 | 12 | 6 |
| | M | 49.3 | 53.8 | 56.7 | 53.6 | 55.8 | 50.9 | 57.3 | 58.2 |
| Conn. | Y, | 8 | 24 | 9 | 5 | 8 | 6 | 14 | 4 |
| | M | 45.8 | 55.3 | 47.3 | 49.7 | 53.7 | 52.1 | 56.3 | 53.8 |
| N.Y. | Y, | 16 | 16 | 10 | 4 | 4 | 10 | 4 | 14 |
| | M | 49.9 | 49.5 | 53.4 | 52.1 | 49.6 | 54.9 | 58.6 | 50.1 |
| N.J. | Y, | 16 | 16 | 8 | 6 | 7 | 7 | 13 | 4 |
| | M | 50.7 | 52.8 | 53.3 | 52.6 | 53.9 | 54.3 | 58.1 | 59.7 |
| Del. | Y, | 0 | 32 | 4 | 10 | 4 | 10 | 12 | 6 |
| | M | — | 54.0 | 51.6 | 52.4 | 53.7 | 52.1 | 51.6 | 54.3 |
| Pa. | Y, | 0 | 28 | 4 | 10 | 6 | 8 | 10 | 8 |
| | M | — | 56.0 | 50.0 | 53.6 | 52.3 | 54.6 | 54.9 | 53.8 |
| Md. | Y, | 28 | 4 | 10 | 4 | 6 | 8 | 16 | 2 |
| | M | 52.8 | 49.3 | 53.6 | 49.5 | 59.2 | 55.9 | 61.6 | 49.5 |
| W.Va. | Y, | 4 | 28 | 14 | 0 | 10 | 4 | 10 | 8 |
| | M | 49.5 | 51.0 | 56.0 | — | 54.3 | 53.9 | 58.3 | 52.8 |
| Ohio | Y, | 18 | 14 | 8 | 6 | 10 | 4 | 6 | 12 |
| | M | 50.1 | 51.1 | 51.9 | 56.1 | 54.6 | 53.3 | 54.2 | 57.1 |
| Ind. | Y, | 8 | 24 | 12 | 2 | 4 | 10 | 8 | 10 |
| | M | 45.9 | 51.8 | 53.4 | 51.0 | 53.6 | 55.7 | 53.3 | 55.7 |
| Ill. | Y, | 4 | 28 | 8 | 6 | 4 | 10 | 12 | 6 |
| | M | 38.1 | 54.8 | 55.4 | 51.9 | 57.1 | 51.4 | 52.7 | 58.1 |
| Mich. | Y, | 4 | 28 | 6 | 8 | 12 | 2 | 2 | 16 |
| | M | 41.7 | 59.2 | 53.0 | 53.1 | 52.8 | 60.3 | 50.5 | 54.0 |
| Wis. | Y, | 0 | 32 | 2 | 6 | 2 | 12 | 12 | 6 |
| | M | — | 54.9 | 52.5 | 49.6 | 53.6 | 55.5 | 53.0 | 52.3 |
| Minn. | Y, | 4 | 26 | 0 | 8 | 6 | 8 | 12 | 6 |
| | M | 51.8 | 51.7 | — | 56.2 | 53.6 | 59.5 | 56.1 | 51.6 |
| Iowa | Y, | 0 | 32 | 6 | 8 | 4 | 10 | 6 | 12 |
| | M | — | 58.0 | 51.9 | 56.0 | 52.7 | 55.1 | 58.6 | 55.0 |
| Kans. | Y, | 6 | 26 | 2 | 12 | 4 | 10 | 10 | 8 |
| | M | 44.2 | 55.3 | 51.1 | 52.1 | 56.0 | 54.7 | 54.8 | 53.2 |
| Nebr. | Y, | 12 | 20 | 8 | 6 | 2 | 12 | 14 | 4 |
| | M | 50.7 | 50.4 | 50.8 | 70.6 | 50.2 | 59.4 | 55.5 | 61.5 |
| N. Dak | Y, | 6 | 24 | 6 | 6 | 0 | 14 | 18 | 0 |
| | M | 51.4 | 61.9 | 56.6 | 53.4 | — | 64.4 | 52.1 | — |
| S. Dak. | Y, | 4 | 28 | 4 | 10 | 2 | 12 | 8 | 10 |
| | M | 50.0 | 56.1 | 57.1 | 57.5 | 51.4 | 61.8 | 56.1 | 54.8 |
| Ky. | Y, | 20 | 12 | 11 | 3 | 13 | 1 | 14 | 4 |
| | M | 52.5 | 52.4 | 55.5 | 50.5 | 57.6 | — | 55.1 | 51.2 |

# 334 American state political parties and elections

## Table A–1 (continued)

| States | Years and margins | Time periods of control | | | | | | |
|---|---|---|---|---|---|---|---|---|
| | | 1901–32 | | 1933–46 | | 1947–60 | | 1961–78 |
| | | Election years | | | | | | |
| | | 1900–30 | | 1932–44 | | 1946–58 | | 1960–76 |
| | | D | R | D | R | D | R | D | R |
| Mo. | Y, | 16 | 16 | 10 | 4 | 14 | 0 | 14 | 5 |
| | M | 49.7 | 51.3 | 56.1 | 50.1 | 53.9 | — | 57.7 | 55.2 |
| Okla. | Y, | 24 | 0 | 14 | 0 | 14 | 0 | 10 | 8 |
| | M | 51.9 | — | 60.0 | — | 59.1 | — | 56.1 | 55.5 |
| Mont. | Y, | 24 | 4 | 8 | 6 | 4 | 10 | 10 | 8 |
| | M | 51.6 | 59.7 | 49.8 | 53.6 | 55.7 | 51.2 | 54.1 | 53.2 |
| Idaho | Y, | 10 | 20 | 10 | 4 | 0 | 14 | 8 | 10 |
| | M | 49.4 | 51.9 | 55.3 | 53.8 | — | 53.6 | 62.6 | 51.2 |
| Wyo. | Y, | 12 | 20 | 10 | 4 | 6 | 8 | 6 | 12 |
| | M | 53.2 | 55.5 | 53.4 | 59.8 | 50.9 | 53.3 | 55.8 | 57.2 |
| Colo. | Y, | 20 | 12 | 6 | 8 | 10 | 4 | 6 | 12 |
| | M | 53.6 | 50.6 | 56.6 | 55.2 | 56.3 | 54.8 | 53.8 | 54.4 |
| Utah | Y, | 12 | 20 | 14 | 0 | 2 | 12 | 14 | 4 |
| | M | 55.5 | 49.1 | 52.4 | — | — | 49.4 | 62.1 | 52.7 |
| Nev. | Y, | 20 | 10 | 12 | 2 | 6 | 8 | 14 | 4 |
| | M | 53.4 | 52.3 | 58.7 | — | 58.7 | 55.4 | 65.1 | 52.2 |
| N. Mex. | Y, | 12 | 8 | 14 | 0 | 8 | 6 | 12 | 6 |
| | M | 51.6 | 52.3 | 54.0 | — | 53.8 | 53.2 | 53.8 | 50.8 |
| Ariz. | Y, | 12 | 8 | 14 | 0 | 8 | 6 | 6 | 12 |
| | M | 51.4 | 50.9 | 68.3 | — | 57.8 | 55.4 | 51.8 | 55.3 |
| Wash. | Y, | 8 | 20 | 10 | 4 | 6 | 8 | 6 | 12 |
| | M | 48.5 | 55.8 | 59.4 | 50.2 | 54.6 | 51.6 | 52.1 | 54.6 |
| Oreg. | Y, | 16 | 14 | 4 | 8 | 2 | 12 | 4 | 14 |
| | M | 59.2 | 51.6 | 38.6 | 67.7 | 50.5 | 60.1 | 58.5 | 55.0 |
| Calif. | Y, | 0 | 30 | 4 | 10 | 2 | 12 | 10 | 8 |
| | M | — | 56.3 | 52.5 | 53.0 | 59.7 | 71.1 | 51.7 | 55.2 |
| Alaska | Y, | | | | | 2 | 0 | 10 | 8 |
| | M | | | | | 59.6 | — | 52.4 | 48.9 |
| Hawaii | Y, | | | | | 0 | 2 | 16 | 2 |
| | M | | | | | — | 51.1 | 55.4 | — |

Note: Because some four-year terms overlap time periods, an election victory occurring in one time period may result in control that extends into the next time period. The odd-year elections in Kentucky and New Jersey are included within the appropriate years. Data for third-party and independent candidates are not included. When the years of Democratic and Republican control add up to less than the total years in the time period, it means that other parties won one or more elections.

**Table A–2**

**Party control of governorship by years and average winning margin and number of two-party contests in southern states by major time periods**

| States | Years and margins | Time periods of control | | | | | | | | |
|---|---|---|---|---|---|---|---|---|---|---|

| | | 1901–46 | | | 1947–60 | | | 1961–78 | | |
|---|---|---|---|---|---|---|---|---|---|---|
| | | Election years | | | | | | | | |
| | | 1900–44 | | | 1946–58 | | | 1960–76 | | |
| | | D | R | Con-tests | D | R | Con-tests | D | R | Con-tests |
| Tenn. .......... | Y, | 40 | 6 | 23/23 | 14 | 0 | 6/6 | 14 | 4 | 3/4 |
| | M | 60.8 | 52.3 | | 72.4 | — | | 62.6 | 52.0 | |
| N.C. .......... | Y, | 46 | 0 | 12/12 | 14 | 0 | 3/3 | 14 | 4 | 5/5 |
| | M | 62.9 | — | | 69.2 | — | | 57.2 | 51.4 | |
| Va. ........... | Y, | 46 | 0 | 8/12 | 14 | 0 | 3/3 | 19 | 8 | 4/4 |
| | M | 69.4 | — | | 62.8 | — | | 55.8 | 51.6 | |
| Fla. ........... | Y, | 46 | 0 | 10/12 | 14 | 0 | 4/4 | 14 | 4 | 5/5 |
| | M | 77.5 | — | | 78.1 | — | | 58.5 | 55.1 | |
| Tex. .......... | Y, | 46 | 0 | 20/23 | 14 | 0 | 7/7 | 18 | 0 | 8/8 |
| | M | 80.7 | — | | 85.2 | — | | 62.2 | — | |
| Ark. .......... | Y, | 46 | 0 | 20/23 | 14 | 0 | 7/7 | 14 | 4 | 9/9 |
| | M | 76.2 | — | | 84.3 | — | | 69.4 | 53.4 | |
| La. ........... | Y, | 46 | 0 | 4/12 | 14 | 0 | 0/3 | 18 | 0 | 3/5 |
| | M | 88.9 | — | | 96.0 | — | | 66.1 | — | |
| S.C. .......... | Y, | 46 | 0 | 0/18 | 14 | 0 | 0/14 | 14 | 4 | 3/4 |
| | M | 98.9 | — | | — | — | | 55.0 | 52.0 | |
| Ga. ........... | Y, | 46 | 0 | 0/22 | 14 | 0 | 0/5 | 18 | 0 | 3/4 |
| | M | 86.9 | — | | 98.1 | — | | 58.6 | — | |
| Ala. .......... | Y, | 46 | 0 | 10/12 | 14 | 0 | 4/4 | 18 | 0 | 2/4 |
| | M | 79.3 | — | | 85.4 | — | | 79.8 | — | |
| Miss. .......... | Y, | 46 | 0 | 0/12 | 14 | 0 | 0/3 | 18 | 0 | 3/4 |
| | M | 93.0 | — | | 97.5 | — | | 61.3 | — | |

Note: The proportion of contests includes only those in which there was a Republican as well as a Democratic candidate; third-party and independent candidates are excluded. The winning margin is calculated in, and averaged for, only elections in which there was some opposition candidate (not just a Republican one).

**Table A–3**
**Party control of state legislatures by years and average percentage of seats held by majority party by major time periods**

| | | Time periods of control | | | | | | | | | | | |
|---|---|---|---|---|---|---|---|---|---|---|---|---|---|
| | | 1933–46 | | | | 1947–60 | | | | 1961–78 | | | |
| | Years and | Senate | | House | | Senate | | House | | Senate | | House | |
| States | percent | D | R | D | R | D | R | D | R | D | R | D | R |
| Maine | Y, | | 14 | | 14 | | 14 | | 14 | 2 | 16 | 6 | 12 |
| | % | | 87 | | 80 | | 85 | | 77 | 85 | 70 | 58 | 63 |
| N.H. | Y, | | 14 | | 14 | | 14 | | 14 | | 14 | | 18 |
| | % | | 69 | | 59 | | 75 | | 66 | | 66 | | 61 |
| Vt. | Y, | | 14 | | 14 | | 14 | | 14 | 18 | | 2 | 16 |
| | % | | 80 | | 83 | | 82 | | 88 | 73 | | 52 | 67 |
| Mass. | Y, | | 14 | | 14 | 2 | 10 | 10 | 4 | 18 | | 18 | |
| | % | | 62 | | 58 | 60 | 57 | 54 | 56 | 73 | | 73 | |
| R.I. | Y, | 2 | 12 | 10 | 4 | 2 | 6 | 14 | | 18 | | 18 | |
| | % | 52 | 62 | 60 | 56 | 52 | 59 | 64 | | 75 | | 77 | |
| Conn. | Y, | 12 | 2 | | 14 | 8 | 6 | 2 | 12 | 16 | 2 | 10 | 8 |
| | % | 58 | 58 | | 70 | 64 | 74 | 51 | 76 | 65 | 64 | 65 | 62 |
| N.Y. | Y, | 6 | 8 | 2 | 12 | | 14 | | 14 | 2 | 16 | 8 | 10 |
| | % | 56 | 59 | 51 | 57 | | 62 | | 63 | 57 | 58 | 57 | 54 |
| N.J. | Y, | | 14 | 2 | 12 | | 14 | 2 | 12 | 6 | 12 | 12 | 6 |
| | % | | 72 | 61 | 68 | | 73 | 70 | 70 | 71 | 65 | 64 | 67 |
| Del. | Y, | | 14 | 4 | 10 | 8 | 6 | 6 | 8 | 10 | 6 | 10 | 8 |
| | % | | 61 | 62 | 64 | 66 | 59 | 68 | 56 | 64 | 63 | 67 | 61 |
| Pa. | Y, | 2 | 12 | 6 | 8 | | 14 | 4 | 10 | 8 | 8 | 12 | 6 |
| | % | 68 | 66 | 64 | 61 | | 61 | 52 | 62 | 57 | 55 | 55 | 52 |
| Md. | Y, | 14 | | 14 | | 14 | | 14 | | 18 | | 18 | |
| | % | 71 | | 83 | | 69 | | 77 | | 80 | | 85 | |
| W.Va. | Y, | 14 | | 14 | | 14 | | 14 | | 18 | | 18 | |
| | % | 77 | | 75 | | 68 | | 71 | | 74 | | 76 | |
| Ohio | Y, | 4 | 8 | 4 | 10 | 4 | 10 | 4 | 10 | 4 | 12 | 6 | 12 |
| | % | 73 | 69 | 69 | 66 | 60 | 73 | 54 | 74 | 63 | 60 | 61 | 60 |
| Ind. | Y, | 8 | 6 | 6 | 8 | | 14 | 4 | 10 | 8 | 10 | 4 | 14 |
| | % | 75 | 70 | 78 | 67 | | 67 | 70 | 75 | 59 | 58 | 67 | 63 |
| Ill. | Y, | 8 | 6 | 6 | 8 | | 14 | 4 | 10 | 4 | 12 | 6 | 12 |
| | % | 65 | 59 | 54 | 53 | | 66 | 52 | 55 | 58 | 58 | 59 | 53 |
| Mich. | Y, | 2 | 10 | 4 | 10 | | 14 | | 12 | 6 | 8 | 12 | 4 |
| | % | 53 | 72 | 58 | 66 | | 73 | | 66 | 62 | 60 | 59 | 52 |
| Wis. | Y, | 2 | 8 | 2 | 8 | | 14 | 2 | 12 | 4 | 14 | 10 | 8 |
| | % | 42 | 65 | 60 | 66 | | 78 | 55 | 74 | 64 | 63 | 63 | 53 |
| Iowa | Y, | 4 | 8 | 4 | 8 | | 14 | | 14 | 8 | 10 | 6 | 12 |
| | % | 56 | 87 | 62 | 85 | | 83 | | 79 | 55 | 70 | 67 | 67 |
| Kans. | Y, | | 14 | | 14 | | 14 | | 14 | | 18 | 2 | 16 |
| | % | | 75 | | 74 | | 86 | | 75 | | 72 | 52 | 65 |
| N. Dak. | Y, | | 14 | | 14 | | 14 | | 14 | | 18 | 4 | 14 |
| | % | | 86 | | 88 | | 90 | | 90 | | 73 | 56 | 70 |
| S. Dak. | Y, | 6 | 8 | 4 | 10 | 2 | 12 | | 14 | 4 | 14 | | 16 |
| | % | 61 | 91 | 60 | 84 | 57 | 82 | | 80 | 53 | 70 | | 70 |
| Ky. | Y, | 14 | | 14 | | 14 | | 14 | | 18 | | 18 | |
| | % | 70 | | 70 | | 73 | | 74 | | 70 | | 71 | |
| Mo. | Y, | 10 | 2 | 10 | 4 | 12 | 2 | 10 | 4 | 18 | | 18 | |
| | % | 87 | 56 | 71 | 59 | 60 | 56 | 62 | 59 | 70 | | 67 | |
| Okla. | Y, | 14 | | 14 | | 14 | | 14 | | 18 | | 18 | |
| | % | 94 | | 90 | | 89 | | 85 | | 83 | | 78 | |
| Mont. | Y, | 6 | 8 | 10 | 4 | 4 | 10 | 8 | 6 | 16 | | 8 | 10 |
| | % | 52 | 65 | 66 | 58 | 62 | 60 | 60 | 62 | 58 | | 62 | 58 |

**Table A–3 (continued)**

| States | Years and percent | Time periods of control | | | | | | | | | | | |
| --- | --- | --- | --- | --- | --- | --- | --- | --- | --- | --- | --- | --- | --- |
|  |  | 1933–46 | | | | 1947–60 | | | | 1961–78 | | | |
|  |  | Senate | | House | | Senate | | House | | Senate | | House | |
|  |  | D | R | D | R | D | R | D | R | D | R | D | R |
| Idaho | Y, | 8 | 6 | 8 | 6 | 6 | 8 | 2 | 12 |  | 18 |  | 18 |
|  | % | 72 | 62 | 81 | 58 | 58 | 66 | 61 | 63 |  | 58 |  | 59 |
| Wyo. | Y, | 4 | 10 | 6 | 6 |  | 14 | 2 | 10 |  | 16 | 2 | 16 |
|  | % | 56 | 63 | 68 | 66 |  | 67 | 52 | 67 |  | 60 | 56 | 62 |
| Colo. | Y, | 10 | 4 | 6 | 8 | 4 | 10 | 6 | 8 | 2 | 16 | 6 | 12 |
|  | % | 71 | 73 | 79 | 68 | 62 | 64 | 63 | 67 | 54 | 59 | 59 | 58 |
| Utah | Y, | 14 |  | 14 |  | 6 | 8 | 4 | 8 | 8 | 10 | 8 | 10 |
|  | % | 80 |  | 81 |  | 56 | 62 | 75 | 62 | 55 | 62 | 55 | 64 |
| Nev. | Y, | 4 | 8 | 14 |  |  | 14 | 14 |  | 12 | 4 | 14 | 4 |
|  | % | 62 | 56 | 67 |  |  | 65 | 60 |  | 70 | 56 | 69 | 54 |
| N. Mex. | Y, | 14 |  | 14 |  | 14 |  | 12 | 2 | 18 |  | 18 |  |
|  | % | 86 |  | 78 |  | 75 |  | 81 | 51 | 75 |  | 73 |  |
| Ariz. | Y, | 14 |  | 14 |  | 14 |  | 14 |  | 10 | 8 | 8 | 10 |
|  | % | 99 |  | 98 |  | 94 |  | 78 |  | 75 | 58 | 59 | 59 |
| Wash. | Y, | 12 |  | 12 |  | 6 | 6 | 10 | 4 | 18 |  | 12 | 6 |
|  | % | 78 |  | 75 |  | 66 | 55 | 60 | 66 | 63 |  | 60 | 55 |
| Oreg. | Y, |  | 14 | 4 | 10 | 2 | 10 | 4 | 10 | 18 |  | 10 | 8 |
|  | % |  | 74 | 63 | 76 | 63 | 77 | 58 | 81 | 65 |  | 57 | 59 |
| Calif. | Y, |  | 14 | 6 | 8 | 2 | 10 | 2 | 12 | 16 |  | 16 | 2 |
|  | % |  | 67 | 56 | 58 | 68 | 67 | 60 | 59 | 62 |  | 61 | 51 |
| Alaska | Y, |  |  |  |  | 2 |  | 2 |  | 10 | 6 | 14 | 2 |
|  | % |  |  |  |  | 90 |  | 83 |  | 70 | 60 | 64 | 63 |
| Hawaii | Y, |  |  |  |  |  | 2 |  | 2 | 16 | 2 | 18 |  |
|  | % |  |  |  |  |  | 56 |  | 65 | 66 | 56 | 72 |  |
| Tenn. | Y, | 14 |  | 14 |  | 14 |  | 14 |  | 18 |  | 16 |  |
|  | % | 88 |  | 81 |  | 86 |  | 81 |  | 69 |  | 67 |  |
| N.C. | Y, | 14 |  | 14 |  | 14 |  | 14 |  | 18 |  | 18 |  |
|  | % | 96 |  | 91 |  | 96 |  | 91 |  | 88 |  | 83 |  |
| Va. | Y, | 14 |  | 14 |  | 14 |  | 14 |  | 18 |  | 18 |  |
|  | % | 95 |  | 95 |  | 94 |  | 93 |  | 89 |  | 84 |  |
| Fla. | Y, | 14 |  | 14 |  | 14 |  | 14 |  | 18 |  | 18 |  |
|  | % | 100 |  | 100 |  | 98 |  | 97 |  | 77 |  | 78 |  |
| Texas | Y, | 14 |  | 14 |  | 14 |  | 14 |  | 18 |  | 18 |  |
|  | % | 100 |  | 100 |  | 100 |  | 100 |  | 95 |  | 93 |  |
| Ark. | Y, | 14 |  | 14 |  | 14 |  | 14 |  | 18 |  | 18 |  |
|  | % | 100 |  | 98 |  | 100 |  | 98 |  | 99 |  | 98 |  |
| La. | Y, | 14 |  | 14 |  | 14 |  | 14 |  | 18 |  | 18 |  |
|  | % | 100 |  | 100 |  | 100 |  | 100 |  | 99 |  | 98 |  |
| S.C. | Y, | 14 |  | 14 |  | 14 |  | 14 |  | 18 |  | 18 |  |
|  | % | 100 |  | 100 |  | 100 |  | 100 |  | 96 |  | 93 |  |
| Ga. | Y, | 14 |  | 14 |  | 14 |  | 14 |  | 18 |  | 18 |  |
|  | % | 99 |  | 99 |  | 99 |  | 99 |  | 89 |  | 91 |  |
| Ala. | Y, | 14 |  | 14 |  | 14 |  | 14 |  | 18 |  | 18 |  |
|  | % | 100 |  | 97 |  | 100 |  | 99 |  | 99 |  | 99 |  |
| Miss. | Y, | 14 |  | 14 |  | 14 |  | 14 |  | 18 |  | 18 |  |
|  | % | 100 |  | 100 |  | 100 |  | 100 |  | 98 |  | 99 |  |

Note: When the years of Democratic and Republican control add up to less than the total years in the time period, it means that control of a legislative chamber was evenly divided for one or more sessions.

# References ★ ★ ★

Adamany, David (1976). "Cross-over Voting and the Democratic Party's Reform Rules." *American Political Science Review* 70 (June): 536–41.

Agranoff, Robert (1972) *The New Style in Election Campaigns.* Boston: Holbrook Press.

Alexander, Herbert (ed.) (1976a). *Campaign Money: Reform and Reality in the States.* New York: The Free Press.

———— (1976b). *Financing Politics.* Washington: Congressional Quarterly Press.

Althoff, Phillip, and Samuel C. Patterson (1966). "Political Activism in a Rural County." *Midwest Journal of Political Sciences* 10 (February): 39–51.

Anderson, Totton J. (1959). "The 1958 Election in California." *Western Political Quarterly* 12 (March): 276–300.

Asher, Herbert (1976). *Presidential Elections and American Politics.* Homewood, Ill.: Dorsey Press.

Banfield, Edward C., and James Q. Wilson (1963). *City Politics.* New York: Alfred A. Knopf.

Barbrook, Alec (1973). *God Save the Commonwealth: An Electoral History of Massachusetts.* Amherst: University of Massachusetts Press.

Bartley, Numan V. (1970). *From Thurmond to Wallace: Political Tendencies in Georgia, 1948–1968.* Baltimore: Johns Hopkins University Press.

Bartley, Numan V., and H. D. Graham (1975). *Southern Politics and the Second Reconstruction.* Baltimore: Johns Hopkins University Press.

Bass, Jack, and W. DeVries (1976). *The Transformation of Southern Politics.* New York: Basic Books.

Beck, Paul A. (1974). "Environment and Party: The Impact of Political and Demographic County Characteristics on Party Behavior." *American Political Science Review* 68 (September): 1229–44.

Bicker, William E. (1972). "Ideology is Alive and Well in California: Party Identification, Issue Positions and Voting Behavior." Paper prepared for annual meeting of American Political Science Association.

Black, Merle, and E. Black (1973). "Party Institutionalization in the American South: The Growth of Contested Republican Primaries." Paper prepared for annual meeting of Southern Political Science Association.

Black, Merle, D. M. Kovenock, and W. C. Reynolds (1974). *Political Attitudes in the Nation and the States.* Chapel Hill: Institute for Research in Social Science, University of North Carolina at Chapel Hill.

Blank, Robert H. (1973). "State Electoral Structure." *Journal of Politics* 35 (November): 938–44.

Bone, Hugh (1946). "Political Partes in New York City," *American Political Science Review* 40 (April): 272–82.

———— (1951). "New Party Associations in the West." *American Political Science Review* 45 (December): 1115–25.

*Book of the States,* 1974–75 (1974). Lexington, Ky.: Council of State Governments.

Bowman, Lewis, and Robert Boynton (1966). "Activities and Role Definitions of Grass Roots Party Officials." *Journal of Politics* 28 (February): 121–43.

Burnham, Walter Dean (1970). *Critical Elections and the Mainsprings of American Politics.* New York: Norton.

Campbell, Angus, and Warren E. Miller (1957). "The Motivational Basis of Straight and Split Ticket Voting." *American Political Science Review* 60 (June): 293–312.

Carney, Francis (1958). *The Rise of the Democratic Clubs in California.* New York: Holt, Eagleton Institute Cases in Politics.

Childs, Richard S. (1967). "State Party Structures and Procedures: A State-by-State Compendium." New York: National Municipal League, mimeo.

Clotfelter, James, and W. R. Hamilton (1972). "Electing a Governor in the Seventies," in Thad Beyle and J. Oliver Williams (eds.). *The American Governor in Behavioral Perspective.* New York: Harper and Row.

Converse, Philip E. (1966). "Information Flow and the Stability of Partisan Attitudes," in Angus Campbell et al., *Elections and the Political Order.* New York: Wiley.

Congressional Quarterly (1975). *Guide to U.S. Elections*. Washington, D.C.

—— (1976). *Weekly Reports*. Washington, D.C.

Conway, M. Margaret, and Frank B. Feigert (1968). "Motivation, Incentive Systems, and the Political Party Organization." *American Political Science Review* 62 (December): 1159–73.

Costikyan, Edward N. (1966). *Behind Closed Doors*. New York: Harcourt, Brace & World.

Cowart, Andrew (1973). "Electoral Choice in the American States." *American Political Science Review* 67 (September): 835–53.

Crotty, William J. (1968). "The Party Organization and its Activities," in William J. Crotty (ed.), *Approaches to the Study of Party Organization*. Boston: Allyn and Bacon.

—— (1971). "Party Effort and its Impact on the Vote." *American Political Science Review* 65 (June): 439–50.

—— (1977). *Political Reform and the American Experiment*. New York: Crowell.

Cummings, Milton C., Jr. (1966). *Congressmen and the Electorate*. New York: Free Press.

Cutright, Phillips (1963). "Measuring the Impact of Local Party Activity on the General Election Vote." *Public Opinion Quarterly* 27 (Fall) 372–86.

—— (1964). "Activities of Precinct Committeemen in Partisan and Nonpartisan Communities." *Western Political Quarterly* 17 (March): 93–108.

Dauer, Manning J. (1972). "Florida: The Different State," in William C. Havard (ed.), *The Changing Politics of the South*. Baton Rouge: Louisiana State University Press.

David, Paul T. (1972). *Party Strength in the United States, 1872–1970*. Charlottesville: University Press of Virginia.

David, Paul T., R. M. Goldman, and R. C. Bain (1964). *The Politics of National Party Conventions*. Washington: Brookings.

David, Paul T., M. Moos, and R. M. Goldman (1954). *Presidential Nominating Politics in 1952*. Baltimore: Johns Hopkins Press.

Davis, James W. (1967). *Presidential Primaries: Road to the White House*. New York: Crowell.

Davis, Lanny J. (1974). *The Emerging Democratic Majority*. New York: Stein and Day.

Dennis, Jack (1975). "Trends in Public Support for the American Party System." *British Journal of Political Science* 5 (April): 187–230.

DeVries, Walter, and V. L. Tarrance (1972). *The Ticket-Splitter*. Grand Rapids, Mich.: Eerdmans.

Dunn, Delmer D. (1969). *Public Officials and the Press*. Reading, Mass.: Addison-Wesley.

Dunn, Richard E., and Martin D. Glista (1973). "Illinois Legislative Races: Separating the Winners from the Losers." *Public Affairs Bulletin* 6 (Jan.–Feb.) Carbondale, Ill.: Public Affairs Research Bureau, Southern Illinois University.

Eisenberg, Ralph (1972). "Virginia: The Emergence of Two-Party Politics," in William C. Havard (ed.), *The Changing Politics of the South.* Baton Rouge: Louisiana State University Press.

Elazar, Daniel (1972). *American Federalism: A View from the States,* 2nd ed. New York: Crowell.

Eldersveld, Samuel J. (1964). *Political Parties: A Behavioral Analysis.* Chicago: Rand McNally.

Epstein, Leon (1958). *Politics in Wisconsin.* Madison: University of Wisconsin Press.

Eulau, Heinz, et al. (1961). "Career Perspectives of American State Legislators," in Dwaine Marvick (ed.), *Political Decision-makers.* Glencoe, Ill.: Free Press.

Eyre, R. John, and Curtis Martin (1967). *The Colorado Preprimary System.* Boulder: University of Colorado.

Fair, Daryl R. (1964). "Party Strength and Political Patronage." *Social Science Quarterly* 45 (December) 264–71.

Fenton, John H. (1957). *Politics in the Border States.* New Orleans: Hauser Press.

———— (1966). *Midwest Politics.* New York: Holt, Rinehart and Winston.

Fishel, Jeff (1973). *Party and Opposition: Congressional Challengers in American Politics.* New York: David McKay.

Flinn, Thomas A. (1964). "Party Responsibility in the States: Some Causal Factors." *American Political Science Review* 58 (March): 60–71.

Gelb, Joyce, and Marian L. Palley (1975). *Tradition and Change in American Party Politics.* New York: Crowell.

Gilbert, Charles E. (1967). *Governing the Suburbs.* Bloomington: Indiana University Press.

Glantz, Stanton A., et al. (1976). "Election Outcomes: Whose Money Matters?" *Journal of Politics* 38 (November) 1033–38.

Goodman, Paul (1967). "The First American Party System," in William N. Chambers and W. D. Burnham (eds.), *The American Party System.* New York: Oxford University Press.

Graber, Doris A. (1972). "Personal Qualities in Presidential Images: The Contribution of the Press." *Midwest Journal of Political Science* 16 (February): 46–76.

Gump, W. Robert (1971). "The Functions of Patronage in American Party Politics: An Empirical Reappraisal." *Midwest Journal of Political Science* 15 (February): 97–107.

Hacker, Andrew (1962). "Pressure Politics in Pennsylvania: The Truckers vs. the Railroads," in Alan F. Westin (ed.). *The Uses of Power.* New York: Harcourt, Brace and World.

———— (1965). "Does a 'Divisive' Primary Harm a Candidate's Election Chances?" *American Political Science Review* 59 (March): 105–10.

Hadley, Arthur T. (1976). *The Invisible Primary.* Englewood Cliffs, N.J.: Prentice-Hall.

Hahn, Harlan (1967). "Turnover in Iowa State Party Conventions." *Midwest Journal of Political Science* 11 (February): 98–105.

Harder, Marvin, and Thomas Ungs (1966). "Midwest County Party Chairmen." Wichita State University, unpublished manuscript.

Hart, Gary W. (1973). *Right from the Start: A Chronicle of the McGovern Campaign.* New York: Quadrangle.

Havard, William C. (ed.) (1972). *The Changing Politics of the South.* Baton Rouge: Louisiana State University Press.

Hecock, Donald S., and Henry M. Bain (1957). *Ballot Position and Voter's Choice.* Detroit: Wayne State University Press.

Hofstetter, C. Richard (1971). "The Amateur Politician: A Problem in Construct Validation." *Midwest Journal of Political Science* 15 (February): 31–56.

Holmes, Jack E. (1967). *Politics in New Mexico.* Albuquerque: University of New Mexico Press.

Howard, Perry H. (1972). "Louisiana: Resistance and Change," in William C. Havard (ed.), *The Changing Politics of the South.* Baton Rouge: Louisiana State University Press.

Huckshorn, Robert J. (1976). *Party Leadership in the States.* Amherst: University of Massachusetts Press.

Huckshorn, Robert J., and Robert C. Spencer (1971). *The Politics of Defeat: Campaigning for Congress.* Amherst: University of Massachusetts Press.

Ippolito, Dennis, and L. Bowman (1969). "Goals and Activities of Party Officials in a Suburban Community." *Western Political Quarterly* 22 (September): 572–80.

Jacobson, Gary (1975). "The Impact of Broadcast Campaigning on Electoral Outcomes." *Journal of Politics* 37 (August): 769–93.

Jewell, Malcolm E. (1962). "Leadership and Party Unity: The Kentucky Democratic Delegation," in Paul Tillett (ed.), *Inside Politics: The National Conventions, 1960.* Dobbs Ferry, N.Y.: Oceana.

———— (1967). *Legislative Representation in the Contemporary South.* Durham, N.C.: Duke University Press.

———— (1969). *Metropolitan Representation: State Legislative Districting in Urban Counties.* New York: National Municipal League.

Jewell, Malcolm E., and S. C. Patterson (1977). *The Legislative Process in the United States*, 3rd ed. New York: Random House.

Johnson, Donald, and J. Gibson (1974). "The Divisive Primary Revisited." *American Political Science Review* 68 (March): 67–77.

Keech, William R., and D. R. Matthews (1976). *The Party's Choice.* Washington: Brookings.

Key, V. O., Jr. (1949). *Southern Politics.* New York: Alfred A. Knopf.

———— (1956). *American State Politics: An Introduction.* New York: Alfred A. Knopf.

———— (1964). *Politics, Parties, and Pressure Groups,* 5th ed. New York: Crowell.

Kim, Chong Lim (1970). "Political Attitudes of Defeated Candidates in an American State Election." *American Political Science Review* 64 (September): 879–87.

———— (1974). "The Nature of Elite Support for Elections." *American Political Quarterly* 2 (April) 205–19.

Kim, Jae-On, J. R. Petrocik, and S. N. Enokson (1975). "Voter Turnout Among the American States: Systematic and Individual Components." *American Political Science Review* 69 (March): 107–23.

Kingdon, John W. (1966). *Candidates for Office: Beliefs and Strategies.* New York: Random House.

Klain, Maurice (1955). "A New Look at the Constituencies." *American Political Science Review* 49 (December): 1005–19.

Kostroski, Warren L. (1973). "Party and Incumbency in Postwar Senate Elections: Trends, Patterns, and Models." *American Political Science Review* 67 (December): 1213–34.

Kovenock, David M., and J. W. Protho et al. (1973). *Explaining the Vote.* Chapel Hill: Institute for Research in Social Science, University of North Carolina at Chapel Hill.

Lebedoff, David (1972). *Ward Number Six.* New York: Scribners.

LeBlanc, Hugh L. (1969). "Voting in State Senates: Party and Constituency Influences." *Midwest Journal of Political Science* 13 (February): 33–57.

Lee, Eugene (1960). *The Politics of Acquaintance.* Berkeley: The University of California Press.

Leege, David C. (1970). "Control in the Party Nominating System: The Case of Indiana," in James B. Kessler (ed.), *Empirical Studies of Indiana Politics.* Bloomington: Indiana University Press.

Lengle, James I., and B. Shafer (1976). "Primary Rules, Political Power, and Social Change." *American Political Science Review* 70 (March): 25–40.

Leuthold, David (1968). *Electioneering in a Democracy: Campaigns for Congress.* New York: John Wiley.

Levin, Murray B. (1962). *The Compleat Politician.* Indianapolis: Bobbs-Merrill.

Lipset, Seymour M. (1963). *The First New Nation.* New York: Doubleday.

Litt, Edgar (1965). *The Political Cultures of Massachusetts.* Cambridge, Mass.: M.I.T. Press.

Lockard, Duane (1959). *New England State Politics:* Princeton: Princeton University Press.

───── (1963). *The Politics of State and Local Government.* New York: Macmillan.

Lowi, Theodore J. (1967). "Party, Policy and Constitution in America," in William N. Chambers and W. D. Burnham (eds.), *The American Party System.* New York: Oxford University Press.

Lubell, Samuel (1951). *The Future of American Politics.* New York: Harper.

Lyford, Joseph P. (1959). *Candidate.* New York: Holt. Eagleton Institute Cases in Practical Politics.

McCleskey, Clifton, E. L. Dickens, and A. K. Butcher (1975). *The Government and Politics of Texas,* 5th ed. Boston: Little, Brown.

McCormick, Richard P. (1967). "Political Development and the Second Party System," in William N. Chambers and W. D. Burnham (eds.), *The American Party System.* New York: Oxford University Press.

McKean, Dayton D. (1967). "Patterns of Politics," in James W. Fesler (ed.), *The 50 States and Their Local Governments.* New York: Alfred A. Knopf.

McNitt, Andrew D. (1976). "Gubernatorial and Senatorial Nominations: An Empirical Analysis of the Influence of Party Organization." Paper prepared for the annual meeting of Southern Political Science Association.

Markham, James (1961). "Press Treatment of the 1958 State Elections in Pennsylvania." *Western Political Quarterly* 14 (December): 912–24.

Mileur, Jerome, and George Sulzner (1974). *Campaigning for the Massachusetts Senate.* Amherst: University of Massachusetts Press.

Miller, Warren E., and T. E. Levitin (1976). *Leadership and Change: The New Politics and the American Electorate.* Cambridge, Mass.: Winthrop.

Mitau, G. Theodore (1960). *Politics in Minnesota.* Minneapolis: University of Minnesota Press.

Mitchell, Stephen A. (1959). *Elm St. Politics.* New York: Oceana.

Morris, William D., and O. A. Davis (1975). "The Sport of Kings: Turnout in Presidential Preference Primaries." Paper prepared for annual meeting of American Political Science Association.

Munger, Frank (1960). *The Struggle for Republican Leadership in Indiana, 1954.* New Brunswick, N.J.: Rugers. Eagleton Institute Cases in Practical Politics.

Niemi, Richard, and M. Kent Jennings (1969). "Intraparty Communications and the Selection of Delegates to a National Convention." *Western Political Quarterly* 22 (March): 29–46.

Nimmo, Dan (1972). "The Amateur Democrat Revisited." *Polity* 5 (Winter): 268–76.

Nimmo, Dan and Robert L. Savage (1972). "The Amateur Democrat Revisited," *Polity* 5 (Winter): 268–76.

Novak, Robert D. (1965). *The Agony of the G.O.P. 1964.* New York: Macmillan.

Olson, David M. (1963). *Legislative Primary Elections in Austin, Texas, 1962.* Austin: Institute of Public Affairs, University of Texas.

——— (1971). "Attributes of State Political Parties: An Exploration of Theory and Data," in James A. Riedel (ed.), *New Perspectives in State and Local Politics.* Waltham, Mass.: Xerox.

——— (1976). *Congressmen and Their Congressional District Parties.* Greensboro, N.C.: University of North Carolina at Greensboro, unpublished manuscript.

———. (1977). "The Electoral Relationship between Congressmen and Their District Parties." Paper presented at the annual meeting of the American Political Science Association.

Owens, John R., E. Constantini, and L. F. Weschler (1970). *California Politics and Parties.* New York: Macmillan.

Parker, John D. (1970). "Candidate Recruitment: A Model and a Multi-Office Study." Unpublished dissertation, University of Georgia.

Patterson, Samuel C. (1963). "Characteristics of Party Leaders." *Western Political Quarterly* 16 (June): 332–52.

——— (1968). "The Political Cultures of the American States." *Journal of Politics* 30 (February): 187–209.

——— (1976). "American State Legislatures and Public Policy," in Herbert Jacob and Kenneth Vines (eds.), *Politics in the American States,* 3rd ed. Boston: Little, Brown.

Patterson, Samuel C., and G. R. Boynton (1969). "Legislative Recruitment in a Civic Culture." *Social Science Quarterly* 50 (September): 243–63.

Peel, Roy V. (1935). *The Political Clubs of New York City.* New York: Putnam.

Piereson, James E. (1974). "Determinants of Candidate Success in Gubernatorial Elections, 1910–1970." Unpublished paper.

——— (1975). "Presidential Popularity and Midterm Voting at Different Electoral Levels." *American Journal of Political Science* 19 (November): 683–94.

Piereson, James E., and T. Smith (1975). "Primary Divisiveness and General Election Success: A Re-examination." *Journal of Politics* 37 (May): 555–62.

Rakove, Milton (1975). *Don't Make No Waves . . . Don't Back No Losers: An Insider's Analysis of the Daley Machine.* Bloomington, Indiana University Press.

Ranney, Austin (1968). "The Representativeness of Primary Electorates." *Midwest Journal of Political Science* 12 (May): 224–38.

——— (1975). *Curing the Mischiefs of Faction: Party Reform in America.* Berkeley: University of California Press.

——— (1976). "Parties in State Politics," in Herbert Jacob and Kenneth N. Vines (eds.), *Politics in the American States,* 3rd ed. Boston: Little, Brown.

Ranney, Austin, and L. D. Epstein (1966). "The Two Electorates: Voters and Non-Voters in a Wisconsin Primary." *Journal of Politics* 28 (August): 598–616.

Ranney, Austin, and Wilmoore Kendall (1956). *Democracy and the American Party System.* New York: Harcourt, Brace.

Riggs, Robert E. (1963). "The District Five Primary—A Case Study in Practical Politics." *Arizona Review of Business and Public Administration* 12 (March): 1–14.

Roback, Thomas H. (1975). "Amateurs and Professionals: Delegates to the 1972 Republican National Convention." *Journal of Politics* 37 (May): 436–68.

Salisbury, Robert H. (1965–66). "The Urban Party Organization Member." *Public Opinion Quarterly* 29 (Winter): 550–64.

Scheele, Raymond H. (1972). "Voting in Primary Elections." Unpublished dissertation, University of Missouri.

Schlesinger, Joseph A. (1965). "Political Party Organization," in James G. March (ed.), *Handbook of Organizations.* Chicago: Rand McNally.

——— (1966). *Ambition and Politics: Political Careers in the United States.* Chicago: Rand McNally.

——— (1971). "The Politics of the Executive," in Herbert Jacob and Kenneth N. Vines (eds.), *Politics in the American States,* 2nd ed. Boston: Little, Brown.

——— (1972). "The Governor's Place in American Politics," in Thad Beyle and J. Oliver Williams (eds.), *The American Governor in Behavioral Perspective.* New York: Harper and Row.

Seagull, Louis M. (1975). *Southern Republicanism.* New York: John Wiley.

Seligman, Lester G., et al. (1974). *Patterns of Recruitment.* Chicago: Rand McNally.

Sindler, Allan P. (1955). "Bifactional Rivalry as an Alternative to Two-Party Competition in Louisiana." *American Political Science Review* 49 (Sept.): 641–62.

——— (1956). *Huey Long's Louisiana*. Baltimore: Johns Hopkins Press.

Sittig, Robert F. (1962). "Party Slatemaking and the Direct Primary in Illinois and Other States." Unpublished dissertation, Southern Illinois University.

Smith, Rhoten A., and Clarence J. Hein (1958). *Republican Primary Fight: A Study in Factionalism*. New York: Holt. Eagleton Institute Cases in Practical Politics.

Smith, Terry B. (1973). "Primary Election Structure and Political Behavior." Unpublished dissertation, Michigan State University.

Snowiss, Leo M. (1966). "Congressional Recruitment and Representation." *American Political Science Review* 60 (September): 627–39.

Sorauf, Frank J. (1954). "Extra-legal Political Parties in Wisconsin." *American Political Science Review* 48 (September): 692–704.

——— (1956). "State Patronage in a Rural County." *American Political Science Review* 50 (December): 1046–56.

——— (1963). *Party and Representation*. New York: Atherton Press.

——— (1976). *Party Politics in America,* 3rd ed. Boston: Little, Brown.

Soule, John W., and J. W. Clarke (1970). "Amateurs and Professionals: A Study of Delegates to the 1968 Democratic National Convention." *American Political Science Review* 64 (September): 888–98.

Soule, John W., and Wilma E. McGrath (1975). "A Comparative Study of Presidential Nominating Conventions: The Democrats 1968 and 1972." *American Journal of Political Science* 19 (August): 501–517.

Stout, Richard T. (1970). *People*. New York: Harper and Row.

Sundquist, James L. (1973). *Dynamics of the Party System*. Washington: Brookings.

Swanson, Bert E. (1962). "The Presidential Convention as a Stage in the Struggle for Political Leadership: The New York Democratic Delegation," in Paul Tillett (ed.), *Inside Politics: The National Conventions, 1960*. Dobbs Ferry, N.J.: Oceana.

Tipton, Leonard, et al. (1975). "Media Agenda-setting in City and State Election Campaigns." *Journalism Quarterly* 52 (Spring): 15–22.

Tobin, Richard J., and Edward Keynes (1975). "Institutional Differences in the Recruitment Process: A Four-State Study." *American Journal of Political Science* 19 (November): 667–92.

Tolchin, Martin, and Susan Tolchin (1971). *To the Victor: Political Patronage from the Clubhouse to the White House*. New York: Random House Vintage Books.

Truman, David (1951). *The Governmental Process.* New York: Alfred A. Knopf.

Turrett, J. Stephen (1971). "The Vulnerability of American Governors, 1900–1969." *Midwest Journal of Political Science* 15 (February): 108–32.

Verba, Sidney (1965). "Comparative Political Culture," in Lucian W. Pye and Sidney Verba (eds.), *Political Culture and Political Development.* Princeton, N.J.: Princeton University Press.

Walker, Jack L. (1966). "Ballot Forms and Voter Fatigue: An Analysis of the Office Block and Party Column Ballots." *Midwest Journal of Political Science* 10 (November): 448–63.

———— (1969). "Diffusion of Innovation Among the American States." *American Political Science Review* 63 (September): 880–99.

Weber, Ronald E. (1969). "Competitive and Organizational Dimensions of American State Party Systems." Paper prepared for annual meeting of Northeastern Political Science Associations.

Weeks, O. Douglas (1972). "Texas: Land of Conservative Expansiveness," in William C. Havard (ed.), *The Changing Politics of the South.* Baton Rouge: Louisiana State University Press.

White, Theodore H. (1965). *The Making of the President, 1964.* New York: Atheneum.

———— (1969). *The Making of the President, 1968.* New York: Atheneum.

———— (1973). *The Making of the President, 1972.* New York: Atheneum.

Wiggins, Charles W. (1973). "Are Southern Party Leaders Really Different?" *Journal of Politics* 35 (May): 487–92.

Wiggins, Charles W., and William L. Turk (1970). "State Party Chairmen: A Profile." *Western Political Quarterly* 23 (June): 321–33.

Wildavsky, Aaron B. (1962). " 'What Can I Do?': Ohio Delegates View the Democratic Convention," in Paul Tillett (ed.), *Inside Politics: The National Conventions, 1960.* Dobbs Ferry, N.Y.: Oceana.

Wilson, James Q. (1959). "A Report on Politics in Los Angeles." Joint Center for Urban Studies, City Politics Reports, Edward Banfield (ed.).

———— (1962). *The Amateur Democrat: Club Politics in Three Cities.* Chicago: University of Chicago Press.

———— (1973). *Political Organizations.* New York: Basic Books.

Wise, Sidney (1962). "The Decision-Making Process in the Pennsylvania Democratic Delegation," in Paul Tillett (ed.), *Inside Politics: The National Conventions, 1960.* Dobbs Ferry, N.Y.: Oceana.

Wolfinger, Raymond E. (1972). "Why Political Machines Have Not Withered Away and Other Revisionist Thoughts." *Journal of Politics* 34 (May): 365–98.

Wright, Gerald C., Jr. (1974). *Electoral Choice in America.* Chapel Hill: Institute for Research in Social Science, University of North Carolina at Chapel Hill.

Wright, William E. (1971). *A Comparative Study of Party Organization.* Columbus, Ohio: Charles E. Merrill.

Young, Roy (1965). *The Place System in Texas Elections.* Austin: Institute of Public Affairs, University of Texas.

# Index of names

## A

Adamany, David, 297
Agnew, Spiro, 43, 111, 210
Agranoff, Robert, 183, 192, 199–200, 204, 214
Alexander, Herbert, 205–12
Althoff, Phillip, 79, 90
Anderson, Totton, 197
Asher, Herbert, 225, 314

## B

Bain, R. C., 181, 267–68
Banfield, Edward C., 198
Barbrook, Alec, 102
Bartley, Numan V., 170, 248
Bass, Jack, 248
Beck, Paul, 72, 75–76, 189–90
Bell, Charles, 80
Bicker, William E., 166, 231, 246–47
Black, Earl, 137, 161–62
Black, Merle, 9, 137, 161–62
Bone, Hugh, 84
Bowman, Lewis, 89, 189
Boynton, G. Robert, 89, 189
Bridges, Styles, 107
Brooke, Edward, 100
Brown, Edmund, Jr. (Jerry), 104, 208
Brown, Pat, 166, 218, 266
Bryan, William J., 26
Buckley, James, 110
Burnham, Walter Dean, 314

Busby, George, 207
Byrd, Harry F., Jr., 94, 111, 172
Byrd, Harry F., Sr., 43, 107, 115–16, 119, 152, 169

## C

Calloway, "Bo," 179, 248
Campbell, Angus, 181
Carney, Francis, 84
Carter, Jimmy, 30, 49, 63, 213, 283, 286, 297, 303–4, 322
Cary, Hugh, 103, 205–6, 217, 219
Chafee, John, 220
Chandler, A. B. "Happy," 266
Childs, Richard S., 61
Clarke, J. W., 78
Clements, Earle, 266
Clotfelter, James, 213
Combs, Bert, 265–66
Connally, John, 109, 173, 273
Constantini, E., 46, 237
Converse, Philip, 201
Conway, M. Margaret, 78–79
Costikyan, Edward N., 95
Cowart, Andrew, 230–31, 241
Creager, R. B., 41
Crotty, William J., 72–75, 189, 192, 205–6, 212
Crump, "Boss," 171
Cummings, Milton C., Jr., 227
Cutright, Phillips, 75, 189

# Subject index

*This book has been set in 10 and 9 point
Melior, leaded 3 points. Chapter numbers are
36 point Melior Semibold and chapter titles
are 24 point (small) Melior Semibold. The
size of the type page is 27 by 46 picas.*